This Is What You'll Get

This Is What You'll Get

by

Bobbie Collings

Copyright © 2021-2023 by Bobbie Collings

All rights reserved. No part of this book may be reproduced or used in any manner without written permission of the copyright owner except for the use of quotations in a book review. For more information, address: bobbie.collings.author@gmail.com

SECOND EDITION

Print ISBN : 978-1-80227-193-5
eBook ISBN : 978-1-80227-211-6

This novel is dedicated to my cousin, Catherine Kidd, whose encouragement and guidance helped me through some difficult times.

Whilst the places visited by the characters in this novel exist, the characters themselves don't and are purely figments of the author's imagination. Any resemblance to real life people would be entirely coincidental.

Contents

Book One: Demons   1

Book Two: The Idiot   31

Book Three: The Adolescent   121

Book Four: Crime & Punishment   239

Book One

Demons

Chapter 1

Katerina was in trouble, and she knew it.

Since her eighteenth birthday, a mere five months previously, she had been blissfully happy. And now she wasn't. She was in trouble and, as she lay supine in her bed, she tried to concentrate on potential solutions to her plight rather than the churn in her stomach or the bile in her throat. She couldn't come up with any. Instead, she felt sure that only one course of action was available to her, and that it would destroy her. She wasn't one for drama, exaggeration, or hyperbole so she didn't come to this conclusion emotionally. She believed that if she acted, the inevitable outcome would destroy her, and if she didn't, she'd continue to feel as she had for the past fortnight, miserable and anchorless.

She slid out of bed and slipped her dressing gown over her pyjamas. Despite her care, Scott stirred. "Can't you sleep?"

"Afraid not. Sorry to have woken you. I'll have a quick read in the lounge then come back when I feel sleepy".

She picked up her Kindle and quietly left the bedroom. As she glanced to her right, she saw that Ilya's bedroom door was open, from which she deduced that he had chosen to spend the night at Katie's. The lounge was cold, so she flicked the boiler switch to 'on' before boiling the kettle to make herself a mug of tea.

As she sat at the table, sipping the drink, her thoughts turned to Scott. Not for the first time, she asked herself what on earth she was doing sharing her bed with him. Yes, he was ridiculously good looking, and the sex had been a welcome outlet, but his vanity radiated from him, and she knew that she was unable to behave naturally when with him, purposely using her wit and intelligence to put him off his stride, as a weapon to counter his air of superiority. Ten days into a new relationship and already yearning for solitude. Thankfully, he'd be leaving in the morning. He was bound to ask when they would next be seeing each other, and they would agree to something within the following few days.

Despite her opinion of him, she was happy enough for their relationship to continue for a while. She felt she would benefit from a distraction from the cause of her current distress.

This wasn't the first time in her life that she had been in trouble, but previous difficulties had been caused by circumstance, and, because they had occurred during the early years of her life, she had needed other people, adults, to overcome them on her behalf as best they could.

She had been born in a small town in the environs of St Petersburg. Her father had never been known to her, and she had come to understand that even her mother hadn't been too sure which of her lovers had impregnated her. There was no shortage of affection, but that was all her mother could provide for her. The two of them lived with Katerina's grandparents, sharing a bedroom with another couple and their infant son. The identity of the three people with whom she shared an intimate space for the first few years of her life had remained unknown. Katerina's grandparents had little time for their daughter or granddaughter, clearly resenting them for further crowding their already-cramped apartment.

Katerina and her mother spent most of their daylight hours walking streets and making the best of a rusty swing and a creaky roundabout in the local park. Katerina always carried with her an unclothed and hairless doll which had been spotted in a bin alongside the only bench in the park which had not been vandalised. The doll was Katerina's comfort; a bottle of vodka was her mother's.

It was Ivan who provided the means of progressing from a life of near destitution to one of moderate comfort. He was the manager of a store frequented by Katerina's mother and, because he had taken a liking to her, the vodka had been sold at a significant discount. Katerina's mother had initially felt suspicious of the offer, expecting to be asked to provide an alternative form of payment, but there had been no need for concern: Ivan turned out to be a decent man. He was also a loving father to his son, Ilya, two years older than Katerina. Ivan's wife had died in childbirth, his parents had taken pity and the decision was taken that Ivan would manage one of the stores owned by his father, would live with Ilya in the apartment above the store and that one of Ivan's sisters, who had two children of her own, would care for Ilya while Ivan was at work.

These domestic arrangements continued until Ivan suggested that Katerina and her mother should move into his apartment. The offer was gratefully accepted, and Katerina began to live a normal childhood. She and Ilya were close enough in age for them to enjoy playing with each other, yet distant enough for Ilya to engage in some mild mental bullying and to be independent enough to leave the apartment to play football with his friends. As the two children got older, Katerina found herself increasingly required to entertain herself. It was Ivan's collection of books which provided salvation.

Tolstoy, Pushkin, Turgenev, Chekhov, Dostoevsky—she read them all. Novels or short stories, it didn't matter. She digressed at times to non-fiction, learning about the overthrow of the Russian monarchy, the influence of Stalin after the Second World War, Gorbachev's perestroika. She felt great pride in her country, in the achievements of Russian nationals—the greatest novelists and composers, the first man in space, the first woman in space.

She branched out from the mainstream and immersed herself in the works of Anna Akhmatova and Aleksandr Solzhenitsyn, feeling less patriotic with each book she read. She used her pocket money to buy a second-hand CD player and a selection of CDs recorded by American and British musicians. Her taste in music began to develop, as did her knowledge of the English language. Before long, she stretched herself by reading western novels, initially children's books but, before long, some of the classics—Bronte, Austin, Steinbeck, Hardy, P. G. Wodehouse. And then Dickens—oh, the joy of sharing her leisure-time with David Copperfield and Mr Micawber, Nicholas and Kate Nickleby, Esther Summerson and Richard Carstone, Pip and Magwitch. Inevitably, lifestyle in the Western Hemisphere appeared increasingly appealing.

This was her life—school, reading, listening to music, watching as many English language television programmes and films as possible, swimming in the freezing waters at the lido located on the outskirts of her hometown—until it appeared clear to her, and those around her, that her mother had become an alcoholic and needed to be saved. Too little, too late: she died of liver cancer. Katerina was an orphan, being raised by a man who had become her mother's lover and then husband and living with a boy two years older than she, who at times was her best friend and at others her tormentor. Ivan had lost a second wife and he gave up, deciding that he no longer wanted to live in the town, or indeed the country, in which he had suffered such distress. He decided to try his luck in England and arranged for the three of them to have a crash course in basic English. They moved at the earliest opportunity: Ivan, with two children in tow.

Whilst it wasn't easy for any of them, not once did they regret the decision. Katerina adapted quickly to her new environment, Ilya less so. Ivan's work ethic paid dividends and, in time, the three of them began to thrive. Once Ilya had become proficient in the English language, a clear path lay ahead of him. A good looking, cheeky, sporty boy, with an interesting upbringing, he easily made and retained friends and endeared himself to sports coaches.

Katerina's introspection created more challenging terrain. She was different to the other girls in her peer group, and she found out that schoolgirls aren't sure how to deal with someone who seems content to remain on the outside. Here was an attractive, vibrant, and interesting girl who appeared to have no interest at all in the subject matter of their chatter. Occasionally their uncertainty created tension, relieved by a spiteful comment or a hurtful tease. Katerina didn't appear to be at all concerned, and the clarity of her self-esteem seemed to both alienate her and cause a desire for her friendship. Whatever the feelings of her year-group, her teachers loved her. Quick to learn, attentive, interested in new topics, confident without a hint of brashness, Katerina became the star pupil in most subjects, and if any of her classmates needed help, she readily provided it. Over time, and throughout time, she was envied and pitied, admired and vilified, looked up to and down upon. She was an alien, yet everyone secretly wished they could be like her.

Katerina's relationship with Ilya was similarly complex. They were brother and sister yet unrelated; his father was her carer; they were opposites in personality yet similar in character; people wanted Ilya to like them because he was popular whereas people wanted Katerina to like them because popularity didn't concern her.

The main thing they had in common was their nationality. They conversed only in Russian. Even when Ivan was engaging with them in English, when Katerina and Ilya spoke to each other they reverted to Russian. "Come on guys, English," Ivan would plead, "we're in England now. All things English, eh?" To no avail.

They led settled lives, even after Ivan formed a relationship with a lady-friend named Chrissy. They met at a charity event, and it suited them both to speed through the getting-to-know-about-you period to quickly arrive at the wanting-to-know-about-your-body period. Ivan was teased mercilessly by Ilya and Katerina, yet they were delighted that he was finding happiness once again with a female. The three of them spent an increasing amount of time with Chrissy and they eventually moved out of the house Ivan had been renting in Brighton to move in with Chrissy. On several occasions they met Chrissy's wealthy sister Anna and her husband Charlie, and Anna, especially, appeared to be delighted that Chrissy had, out of the blue, become a member of a family. Ilya and Katerina were required to move schools, a minor challenge after emigrating from Russia to England, and within a few months Ilya was just as popular with his new peers and Katerina just as mysterious to hers.

Ivan dropped the bombshell one weekend, just after the four of them had finished eating their Sunday roast dinner. He was required to return to Russia. His father had died suddenly, and somebody had to run his business enterprise; if it failed, Ivan's mother and sisters would suffer dramatically. Katerina remained silent while Chrissy bawled her eyes out and Ilya argued with his father. None of them saw or heard Katerina leave the room, nor were they aware when she left the house to catch the bus into Chichester. She sat for over two hours on a bench in the Cathedral grounds before catching a bus home. Where she would live, and with whom, was yet to be decided. All she knew for certain was that, although she was an orphan and younger than the age of independence, nobody would be forcing her to return to Russia. She may be a Russian girl, and she may still think in Russian much of the time, but England was her home, it was where she wanted to develop into adulthood. No way would she go back there.

The house was quiet when she returned. She went immediately to her bedroom and picked up her paperback copy of Anna Karenina. She'd read no more than a paragraph when there was a knock on the door. "Come in".

"Hi," said Chrissy. "Would you mind coming downstairs so we can have a quick chat?"

Katerina followed Chrissy down the stairs and into the lounge. Ivan and Ilya were there, stony-faced, and silent. Chrissy sat next to Ivan, and Katerina next to Ilya. Chrissy addressed Katerina. "I guess that was a bit of a shock. Have you had a chance to think things over?"

"Yes".

"Any conclusions?"

"Yes. I'm staying here, in England. Whatever Ivan and Ilya decide is up to them, but I'm not going to return to Russia".

"You're thirteen, for Christ's sake!" bellowed Ivan.

Chrissy ignored him. "Are you sure that's the right decision for you?"

"I have absolutely no doubt. I'm staying in England".

"Where would you live?"

"I haven't sorted that yet. But I will. By the time Ivan leaves I will have come up with something".

"Won't you miss Ivan and Ilya if you stay, and they leave?"

"Of course. But not as much as I'd miss living here if I went back with them".

"Would you consider living with me? How would you feel about that?"

"What do you mean?"

"Exactly what I say. How would you feel if Ivan went back to Russia to look after the family business and you and Ilya remained here, living with me?"

Katerina stared at her. She then looked at Ivan and Ilya. Ivan was impassive; Ilya appeared to be trying to keep his emotions in check. She looked back at Chrissy. "That would be awesome".

She heard Ilya sigh and saw Ivan's head slump forward.

"That's what we'll do then," confirmed Chrissy, as if it had been decided that they'd have treacle tart for pudding rather than lemon meringue pie.

Ivan disappeared through the Departure Gate at Heathrow Airport, and that was the last Chrissy, Ilya and Katerina saw of him. The three then lived together, no blood-tie between any of them, and the household was as calm as any traditional household could hope for.

Circumstances were improved further when Anna and Charlie spent some of their savings on a four-bedroom house in Chichester city centre for Chrissy and her wards to live in.

It was Ilya who upset the equilibrium. It was the day after Katerina's fourteenth birthday and she had returned from school, dumped her bags, called out to Chrissy before remembering that Chrissy had said she would be doing a big-shop after work, and entered her bedroom to change. As she was unzipping the skirt of her uniform, Ilya walked in without knocking. "I've another present for you," he announced.

"But you've already given me a present. Those books. They're brilliant".

"I've another one".

"What is it?" she asked, excitedly.

"I'm going to let you hold my prick".

She stared at him in horror. "I don't want to".

"Why not? Jessica has and she loved it".

"Well, get her to hold it again then cos I'm not going to".

"Go on. You know you want to".

"I don't and I won't. Now leave me alone so I can get changed".

He huffed out of the room. She closed the door behind him and stared at her reflection in the full-length mirror attached to the wall. She then left her bedroom, walked along the landing, and knocked at Ilya's bedroom door. "Come in," he said. She opened the door and stepped in. Ilya was lying on his bed flicking through a magazine. "What?"

"Never, ever come into my bedroom again without knocking and hearing me telling you it's OK".

He didn't respond.

"Do you understand what I've just said?"

"Yes".

She returned to her room, closed the door and, once again, studied herself in the mirror. The skirt zip was still undone, and the waistband had begun to slip over her right hip bone. She removed the skirt, then her tie and shirt, and tried to assess herself dispassionately. It was obvious she had entered the next stage in her life. She removed her bra and pants, took another long look at herself, then put on her dressing gown before sitting at her desk. She randomly picked up one of the many paperbacks littering the surface of the desk; it was Tess of the d'Urbervilles. She put it down and moved across the room to lie on her bed. She fully considered Ilya's proposition and revisited some of the many comments she had heard uttered by boys at her school. She knew that she now had to do the best she could to become, at best, invisible or, at least, undesirable.

Nobody needed to explain to her that her female classmates were wary of her. This didn't concern her in the slightest, and she felt no shame in having remained true to herself. She was included to the extent that she didn't experience the loneliness of an outcast, yet she was in a position whereby spending time in the way she wished didn't create uncomfortable confrontations.

She knew it would now be more difficult with boys, who were clearly becoming more interested in her body, and in their need for female affirmation. So be it. She would find ways to negotiate the rest of her school days under their radar. She made another decision; she undid the tie around her dressing gown, parted the garment, opened her legs and, for the first time in her life, discovered another feature associated with the stage of life she had just entered.

During the next four years, she excelled academically, became county-standard in competitive swimming, accepted invitations which suited her and politely declined those which didn't, and widened and deepened her knowledge of, and love for, literature and music. Regarding everything she could control, she was content. Boys' desires were a greater challenge and, for two years, until he left school after completing his final exams, she was wary of Ilya, and for four she was not included on any of the 'fit-lists' doing the rounds.

As she progressed to upper school, preparing for her A Level exams, she found her own desires were beginning to reveal themselves to her. She began to suffer an internal battle: she wanted to experience more than self-pleasure yet couldn't contemplate yielding to infantile male cravings. Her lack of wisdom became a major concern. Her high level of intelligence was innate, her knowledge was clearly beyond the level normally attained by someone of her age, but her lack of wisdom, she felt, needed to be addressed before she could truly become the person she aspired to be.

Finally, two conversations resolved this period of anguish: the first was during a telephone call she made to Anna on her eighteenth birthday; the second after saying to Anna, "Unless you say no". From anguish to five months of bliss to knowing that she was in trouble.

She rinsed her mug, returned to her bedroom, removed her dressing gown, and got back into bed. She still felt wide awake.

Chapter 2

Lene sat alone in her treatment room, head in her hands. She was aware that she needed to pull herself together, for the good of her husband, her daughters, and her Business, but that demanded too much of her at present. Self-pity was by far the easier option.

Almost twenty years previously, it had been Anna who had taken the initiative. Again, just last summer, it had been Anna who had made a suggestion, and Anna who had dismissed Lene's words of caution. She should have said no to Anna, but she hadn't.

Their relationship had begun at university. Three weeks into her Law Degree course, Anna formed the conclusion that she had made a dreadful mistake. Her fellow students were as dull as the cousin she had avoided since he had said to her, when they were both thirteen years old, "I shall never marry. Girls don't really serve a useful purpose, do they? And I can't understand why so many of my friends are into sport. What a waste of time that is. And as for music and reading, well, you might as well study the contents of your fridge". "What are you interested in, then?" "Beetles and bugs. Most people think they're the same, but clearly beetles chew and bugs suck". Beetles and bugs! What the fuck? Thankfully, Anna soon discovered that her cousin was in the minority regarding what turns boys on.

During week four, she noticed her. Initially, she concluded that a young daughter of a professor had arrived to deliver a forgotten lunchbox, but, as she studied her more attentively, she realised that this was a fellow student. Tiny, no taller than five feet, no larger than size 6, a face which was extraordinarily pretty, almost painful to look at, high, prominent cheek bones and hair so blonde that the bearer had to have been born in one of the Nordic countries.

Anna followed her down a long passage. The girl was carrying a stack of books, and Anna felt she should intervene and say, "Hey, let me take those for you". Before leaving the building, the girl stopped at a notice board and Anna saw her add her name to one of the extra curricula group lists.

Once Anna had watched her leave, she approached the board. 'Muscles and Joints'. *Lene Mattsson.* Anna added her name below Lene's. *Anna Swift.*

The following Thursday afternoon, Anna was behaving like a private detective attempting to spot her client's partner meeting up with her lover. It worked—she followed the blonde into the room and successfully sat alongside her. "Hi," she said, which was the most she had said to anyone that week. The girl turned to face her. "Hi," she replied. "I saw your name on the list. L E N E. How on earth do you pronounce that?" "Like it's spelled L A Y N E R". "Layner?" "That's right," she said, smiling. "Well, Hi again Lene. It's lovely to meet you. I'm Anna". "Hello Anna".

So, it was as easy as that. Over a drink following the session, Anna admitted that she had absolutely no interest in muscles or joints ("unless you can smoke them").

"Why did you enrol, then?"

"Because I wanted to meet you".

"Why did you want to meet me?"

"Oh, I don't know. Because I'm looking for a friend and you looked nice, I suppose".

"Nice?"

Anna laughed, nervously. "Well, you can see someone and immediately say to yourself, 'I don't like the look of him,' can't you? The opposite of that".

"What's nice about me?"

"Er, your hair for a start. The way you're all in proportion. And your face. Bloody hell, Lene, you're just so pretty. I've only just clocked your eyes. I've never seen eyes that colour".

"That's kind of you to say, but I'd be considered fairly plain back home, and my eye colour isn't at all unusual for a Swede. Most of us have blue eyes".

"They're not blue, Lene, they're the colour of ice under a cloudless winter sky".

"Hey, who's the poet? Well, how about this—your eyes are like conkers freshly released from their shell, and your face is like something you see on billboards advertising make-up or hair products".

"Am I in proportion too?"

Now Lene was laughing. "Stand up and let me see". Anna stood. "Take off your jumper". Anna did so. "Pretty much, although maybe your knockers are the size you'd expect to see on a girl with a bigger waist and hips".

"That's a bad thing?"

"Maybe, if you were constructing the perfect body shape. I don't suppose any of the male students would see it that way, though. Or the professors, probably".

"You've made me feel self-conscious now," said Anna, peering down at her chest and doing up another button of her blouse.

Lene giggled and suggested that the only reason Anna felt that she was 'all in proportion' was that she had a flat chest, a skinny waist and a non-existent bum.

Anna thought it best to change the subject. "So, why muscles and joints for you?"

"I intend to become a beautician after I've finished my studies".

"Will you be returning to Sweden?"

"Oh no, I've been based in England for a while. My parents moved over here when I was a kid".

"What's your subject here?"

"Political Science".

Anna burst out laughing. Lene looked at her, nonplussed. "Sorry, sorry," said Anna as she dabbed at her eyes. "Just saw the funny side of it, that's all".

"Do you fancy another drink?"

"Are you staying for another?"

"Are you kidding? This is the most fun I've had since Bjorn Borg won Wimbledon when I was like one year old!"

Throughout their three-year University stint, they had been almost inseparable. Boyfriends came and went, hair was held away from the other's face while the evening's mixture of alcohol and curry was ejected into the toilet basin, manuscripts were swapped to be proofread, and opinions were shared and criticised. They each swore lifetime allegiance to the other as if they were Knights of the Round Table.

The only time they risked their friendship was the evening that Lene's boyfriend was spotted by Anna with his hand inside the bra of a girl who had befriended the two of them in Year Two.

"I'm sorry, Lene. I didn't know whether or not I should tell you".

A reply lost in a passage of sobs.

"I thought I should because I'd have wanted you to tell me if it had been Toby".

A hand taken away from the face and waved in inexplicit acknowledgement.

"Can I get you anything?"

"Bccrd".

"What?"

Lene gathered herself. "Bacardi".

"Coke?"

A nod.

"Ice?"

"For fuck's sake, just get me a fucking Bacardi will you?"

Anna sloped off and returned with a full tumbler of Bacardi, coke, ice and, just to be on the safe side, a slice of lemon.

"Did I ask for lemon?"

Anna stuttered an apology and stumbled towards the tumbler to remove the errant fruit.

Lene laughed. Anna laughed too: the relieved sort.

"What are you going to do?"

"Make him jealous and regretful".

"Juicy! Anyone in mind? How about Carlos? He more or less masturbates every time he sees you".

"Urrggh".

"So, no-one springs to mind?"

"Not at the moment. Pity, because I'm in the need for some therapy".

Anna stepped towards her friend and pulled her into an embrace. "I'll provide it for you," she whispered.

"You don't have a penis, Anna. You know how partial we both are to a penis being available to us".

"Maybe, but I'm fairly sure I can make you feel loved tonight". Anna kissed Lene then took her by the hand to guide her into the bedroom, where they made love. They slept an exhausted sleep and, when they both woke up and began the day, it was as if none of the events of the previous evening had happened. Lene's boyfriend no longer existed to her and Anna and Lene continued their relationship without embarrassment or any reference to their night of revelation and pleasure, both on the look-out for the next male lover.

After graduation, whereas Anna joined a local firm of solicitors and met Charlie on a beach in France, Lene began a CIDESCO study programme and gained a Diploma in Beauty and Spa Management. Whilst working at a salon, she added a Beauty Therapy Diploma. Her diligent studying didn't prevent her from leading an active social life, and she participated in a number of unwise relationships with men who were totally unsuitable, but entertaining, nevertheless. Finally, she met and took a liking to a man she was happy to introduce to her parents: Greg. Kind, thoughtful, caring—everything her previous boyfriends hadn't been. He asked her father if it would be acceptable to propose to his daughter, and then did just that. Lene gave birth to twin girls before their first wedding anniversary.

Lene and Anna remained firm friends yet met socially no more than two or three times a year. When they did meet, they drank, giggled and sparked off each other as if they were still on campus. Wherever she worked, Lene was Anna's beautician, and it was Anna and Charlie who provided the finance required for Lene to establish her own salon.

In her business life, Lene was forthright, adventurous, and optimistic. As a wife and mother, she was cautious, steady, and traditional. Both styles were appropriate for the outcomes she desired, and she became increasingly happy and fulfilled as the years went by.

Until now. Once these memories had flooded through her, Lene focussed once more on her misery. Whichever way she looked at it, she couldn't avoid the fact that she had never expected to be in the state in which she found herself. She didn't quite know how on earth she was going to get out of it in one piece.

BOOK ONE: *Demons*

CHAPTER 3

Charlie had every reason to feel happy and self-satisfied: villa in the south of France, cottage in the South Downs, health, wealth, sports car, racehorse, gorgeous wife. What on earth was the matter with him?

He should have said no to Anna, there was absolutely no doubt about that. What on earth had he been thinking? What on earth had *she* been thinking, suggesting it? He'd agreed to it for sound reasons, he told himself, with the best of intentions, persuaded by Anna's reasoning. Not at all for his own benefit or pleasure.

If only he'd convinced her that it was madness.

Until two weeks previously, just about everything in Charlie's life had worked out well. He had enjoyed a happy, settled childhood, being the only child of loving parents, and, since the age of sixteen, had visualised a clear path for himself. On the way to achieving his objectives, decision making had come naturally to him, and he was motivated to take risks once he had weighed them up against potential benefits. His actions demonstrated that ambitions can be fulfilled without injustices being committed. He respected people's opinions yet didn't shirk opportunities to expound his own.

Charlie was popular among his peers but felt more comfortable in the company of a few close friends than he did in a large social gathering. He had always been in good physical shape but hadn't considered himself a sportsman, apart from a stint at rugby in his younger days, until he had been living with Anna for a while and decided to have a go at fencing. As Anna spent an increasing amount of time horse riding, Charlie's interest in the art of fencing developed and he had reached a competitive standard.

He'd never had trouble attracting girls, partly because of his pleasant facial features, but mainly because he treated them with respect and as equals. However, none of his girlfriends motivated in him a desire for a long-term relationship. Not until he met Anna, nearly twelve years previously, when Charlie was 26 and Anna 25.

He had been on his own, sitting outside a café on La Croisette, sipping a 1664. For one reason or another, she hadn't been in a relationship for a while and he had finished his just prior to leaving England, taking the decision while making the final travel arrangements. It had become increasingly apparent to him that he did not want to return to his girlfriend after his three-week-drive in France, during which he would be visiting his favourite parts of the country.

Anna had been with a group of friends, and they were crossing the Promenade de la Croisette which runs parallel to the beach. He had heard them chatting, in English, and they clearly intended to spend a lazy couple of hours sunbathing. 'She's lovely,' he thought to himself. Auburn hair, which was swept back off her face to reveal a high forehead and impeccable eyebrows, straight nose, and full lips. Slight dimples and barely any makeup. Charlie had finished his beer and had followed the group of girls, finding the four of them laying out their towels and stripping down to their swimwear. Three were wearing bikinis, but the girl he had expressly followed was in a swimsuit: black, halter neck, high cut, low back. Charlie judged her to be four inches or so shorter than he, so around 5' 5" and, if he were required to buy clothes for her, at that minute, without studying her further, he'd go for a size ten.

He couldn't take his eyes off her as he cautiously approached the group. Cautiously, because this was not his style of behaviour. He hated to make a female feel uncomfortable. Couldn't stand brashness, lechery, or dominant male behaviour. But still, he couldn't take his eyes off her. She had the loveliest face, and the deepest, softest, hazel eyes. If anyone had told him she was there as the star of a film that was to be launched at the Cannes Film Festival, he would have shrugged and said, "I'm not surprised. I'll have to look out for it once it's released in England".

As he neared the girls, he contemplated his appearance, not so much through vanity but because he wanted to assess himself through her eyes. Thankfully, he had shaved and washed his hair before leaving his holiday apartment that morning, was wearing chino shorts, a polo shirt and deck shoes. He saw her turn her face to look at him, and he wanted to say something as quickly as he could, as he appreciated that attractive females are often discomforted by being ogled at by men of all ages. Charlie hated that about his sex. "Cor, I could give her one". "Hey, love...." and then some crappy, corny joke, or innuendo. "Excuse me, I'm very sorry to interrupt you. I've no wish to intrude or be a nuisance, but I felt I just had to introduce myself. My name is Charlie, and I'm here on holiday from England. This is horribly forward of me, and I'd hate to cause offence, but if I don't take this opportunity to introduce myself to you (he was looking specifically at Anna when he said this) I have a feeling I will regret it forever". The girls must have felt reasonably secure from being in a group, on a public beach, because they invited him to join them.

By the time they had their first swim together in the Med, they had arranged to meet for dinner, just the two of them. Within two years, they were working together, then living together, and then married to each other. Neither of them wanted children, they both loved France, so were happy to spend their holiday time there, and their love for each other did not wane through familiarity. Friends of theirs formed and terminated relationships, but their bond remained resolute throughout. As an added bonus for Charlie, for the first time ever, he found himself in a relationship where his partner happily initiated intimacy. If Anna fancied it, she made it happen, sometimes suggesting something a little quirky or risky.

Their unforeseen good fortune came in the form of a windfall. They had been married for a little over four years, during which time Charlie's financial services firm went from strength to strength, when a large insurance brokerage offered a takeover. No money changed hands but, instead, Charlie exchanged 100% of the shares in his company for a handful of shares in the insurance brokerage. These shares he was able to sell for £13.65 million when the brokerage joined the Alternative Investment Market. Understandably, life had been comfortable for Charlie and Anna since then. They had both decided that they had no wish to work again. £9 million went into safe investments, with the aim that it would generate an income sufficient to provide a wonderful lifestyle, without any risk to the capital. It was also important to them both to give financial assistance to Anna's sister, Chrissy, who had committed to bringing up two children unrelated to her or each other, and to Anna's friend Lene, who was establishing herself in business.

Charlie and Anna chose not to move to a different part of England, instead buying a secluded cottage in the South Downs, a couple of miles from where they had previously lived. They also bought a villa in France, on the Mediterranean coast, at the foot of the Pyrenees. They had known that they would be spending a considerable amount of time in France, so the location of the property they had decided to buy had to be perfect. They discussed this at length, and finally agreed upon a list of necessities: the South for the weather; the coast; not a main tourist area, but somewhere more traditional, with a relaxed feel; a reasonable distance from an airport which had good connections to Gatwick; ideally, somewhere from which they could easily drive to Barcelona, their favourite city, other than London; accessible to hills or mountains, so that they could walk to escape the fiercest summer heat. The location became obvious. Whilst it was perhaps not their favourite place in France, it was the only one which ticked all the boxes: the Cote Catalan.

After a couple of sorties in the region, they found what they were looking for. It was a villa in Le Racou, a small seaside village to the south of Argeles sur Mer. They didn't negotiate on price, simply agreeing to pay the amount requested by the vendor. The entire process was executed without too much stress or delay.

Anna and Charlie split their time between their two homes. Nothing formal or pre-arranged, but simply going from one house to the other as dictated by their whims and social preferences. If Anna didn't have any unmissable horse-riding events in her diary, and Charlie was keen for a change and didn't mind falling behind with his development as a proficient fencer, they simply arranged flights to Perpignan, locked up their cottage, and away they went, returning whenever it suited them. Rarely would they be in separate countries to each other. They preferred to travel, and be, together.

Charlie made himself a coffee and sat in the Snug to contemplate.

It was cold, so he stacked and lit the log burner. He opened the Apple Music app on his phone and switched on the Bluetooth speaker. By the time The King of Limbs had progressed to track six, he was immersed in his thoughts. On conclusion of track eight, he understood clearly that his decision-making skills, and his talent at balancing risk and reward, could be put to the test before too long. He admitted to himself, though, as track one of Hail to the Thief tripped into track two that, as things stood, he had no idea whether he felt this anxiety, a stranger to him, unnecessarily or if it had also paid an unwelcome visit to others close to him. He also accepted that, for the first time in twelve years, doubt had seeped into his consciousness.

He pressed 'pause' on the music app, abandoned all thought of visiting the Fencing Club, reached for his tatty hardback copy of Bleak House, and started to read, yet again, Dickens' mesmeric description of fog enveloping London.

Chapter 4

While Charlie was reading his book, Anna was sitting upright in the saddle, soaking in the vista. It was a typical English January morning: various shades of silver and grey, even the stretch of beach separating her from the undulating plain of muddy sand and, beyond that, the English Channel.

She didn't kid herself; she was fully aware that she was to blame for the way she was feeling—sick to the depth of her stomach. There was a small degree of comfort in the knowledge that the suggestions she had made, and the actions she had taken, were mainly for the benefit of others, not herself: she had wanted to treat her husband and had felt committed to aid a young person who was clearly struggling. But that had been at the outset. The implications of her actions revealed themselves over time, almost imploring her to stop the process. But she hadn't. She hadn't because she had been enjoying herself, and now everything was at risk: her marriage, her friendship with someone who had been dear to her for twenty years, her relationship with her sister, her lifestyle, her happiness, her future.

She loosened her grip of the reins, leaned back, and allowed Garibaldi to select his footing down the dune. A slow walk across the sand and then a canter towards the sea. On reaching the gently lapping waves, she turned Garibaldi's head to the left, squeezed with her thighs, and then thrilled as they galloped towards East Wittering, her doubts, fears and concerns shedding themselves like an animal's coat in Spring, giving her respite for a while, only to return once she had eased her mount into a canter and then a walk.

Anna's sunny, cheerful, uncomplicated disposition gave strangers the impression that she was a little ditzy. In fact, she had an upper second law degree and possessed an abundance of that rarest of traits, common sense. From when they were toddlers, Chrissy, three years older than her sister, had been aware that Anna was the prettier, brighter, livelier, more popular. Rather than being resentful, Chrissy had always been a committed member of Anna's fan club.

Through their teenage years, almost inevitably it was Anna who was the first to reach the milestones they had discussed numerous times: the first to have a boyfriend, to be kissed, to be fondled, to see a boy's thingy (and to touch it! Anna, you didn't! What was it like?), to lose her virginity. Still no envy from Chrissy. Anna didn't wallow in these achievements, preferring to relate her experiences in their shared bedroom. Many a time their parents heard shrieks, giggles, and uncontrolled laughter from the siblings.

Anna went to university, Chrissy to work as an Administrator at a local Building Society branch. Then Anna met Charlie on a beach in the south of France, and Chrissy hooked up with one loser after another. Her disappointments caused her to become more caustic, for her temper to shorten and her language to become colourful.

Yet still no resentment towards Anna. In fact, the sisters became even closer, and Chrissy had no hesitation in asking Anna to give a presentation at her Book Club when encouraged to do so by other members.

"A what?"

"A presentation. On relationships. How to make them work".

"Why on earth would Book Club members be interested in hearing my views on making a relationship work?"

"Because 'relationships' has been the theme of the recent fiction we've been reviewing, and those who know you accept that you and Charlie are the only people who seem to be making a success of their partnership. Everyone's intrigued. Jealous too. Go on, you know how you like to gloat about Mr Fucking Perfect. Share the secrets".

"I don't gloat!"

"OK, maybe not. But anyone looking at you is given the impression of spying a rhino wallowing in mud".

"Well, thanks very much. Very complimentary".

After a little more persuasion, Anna had agreed.

"Well ladies. Thank you for inviting me to your Book Club. Unfortunately, I can't thank you for asking me to provide this presentation as I've been dreading it since Chrissy persuaded me to do it and am now wishing I was anywhere but here. I haven't done anything like this since I was at university, and, I have to admit, I'm pretty nervous".

Anna received some welcoming and supportive responses to her opening remarks, and she found herself relaxing and able to communicate without too much anxiety. She rarely needed to refer to her notes.

"This is certainly anything but a 'this is how you do it' instruction. I shall purely tell you as best I can how my husband, Charlie, and I go about our day-to-day intercourses. And, yes, I will get to the meaningful interpretation of that word too".

She received a welcome titter from her audience of twelve ladies, whose ages ranged from mid-20s to late-60s.

"It is accepted that there are four levels of development: unconsciously incompetent; consciously incompetent; consciously competent; and, finally, the Holy Grail, unconsciously competent. In terms of my day-to-day relationship with Charlie, that is, how we behave with each other and how we treat each other, we are safely moored in the unconsciously competent stage of our relationship. What I mean by this is that we behave with our partner in a way which is natural and true to ourselves, but which is also in a way which makes our partner feel comfortable. We do this without thinking. It is our natural behaviour, hence unconsciously competent. It helps, of course, that we each chose a compatible partner to start with, but we've gone through the four stages of development within our partnership, as many couples do, without straying from what made us compatible to start with, as many couples don't!

"With regard to our sexual relationship, it's more a case of being consciously competent. By that I mean we both make moves, or say words, which we know will result in intimacy. It's not just when we feel horny, or if we realise that we've gone a while without making love. It can be any time, for any reason.

"For example, I don't know about you, but my shopping lists are random; I just keep a notepad handy in the kitchen, and, when I realise we are running short of something, I add the item to the list. I try to maintain a bit of logic, using different parts of the page so that stuff needed from the supermarket isn't mixed up with what's going to be bought at the butcher's. This means there's gaps on the page. Last week, after I'd been to the supermarket and then dumped the bags in the car, I moved on to the butcher's. Looking down the list while waiting to be served I saw that Charlie had written, 'I adore your breasts' under where I'd written, 'pork chops'. It made me smile in the shop, and it also made me feel warm and loved. That was an example of my husband being consciously competent. By the way, he always refers to them as breasts. He reveres them and would never demean them by referring to them as tits.

"What is it that causes people to stray, and thereby become incompatible with their partner? Which actions often lead to separation and divorce? In my opinion, the main drivers are monetary concerns, child-rearing pressure, health worries and lack of sex. Let me make it clear, Charlie and I don't have any money concerns, we don't have children and, thankfully, we've both remained healthy. Hearing this may make some of you feel that I don't have a lot in common with you, so there's little validity in what I have to say this morning. May I ask you to please stick with me because it is the fourth driver, lack of sex, which, I believe, is something we can all take ownership of, even when it's more difficult than usual because one or more of the other three drivers are also in play.

"I recall once seeing Philip Larkin, the Poet Laureate, being interviewed shortly before his death. I can't remember the exact words but, when asked by the interviewer if he had any regrets, Larkin said something like, "I wish I'd had more sex". That was an unexpected reply, for both the interviewer and the viewer, because it's not the sort of thing we expect to hear from an old man who is considered to be part of the Establishment, and a fairly staid one at that.

"A second recollection which I'd like to highlight comes from Frasier Crane, the star of the sitcom series. For those of you who are not familiar with the TV series or the character, Frasier is a psychiatrist who has a radio show. In the episode I am referring to, he is having an off-air conversation with his friend, and radio show Producer, Roz, and Frasier is complaining about women who use sex to get what they want. Roz's defence is that many men, too, use sex as a form of bribery. Frasier's response is immediate and spiky. He says, "How can men use sex to get what they want. Sex *is* what they want"".

Anna's audience tittered and nodded.

"Somehow, those two comments, from Philip Larkin and Frasier Crane, are ingrained in me. I don't want to spend time during my final years ruing lack of sex. And I don't want my husband to either. Nor do I consider it fair to ignore what I, and perhaps you, know, which is that sex *is* what men want.

"In those heady early days of a relationship, sex is boundless. Any time, perhaps even anywhere. But even for the self-conscious or unadventurous, sex is a very important part of their relationship with their partner. And, in nearly every case, enjoyment is not one-way. Both parties get pleasure from the physical part of the relationship. And yet, over time, it fizzles out. Why? It shouldn't. I believe that normally it is us women who are to blame. We just can't be bothered. We don't have the energy. We've lost that desire and enthusiasm. We become consciously incompetent, and then, often fatally in terms of the relationship, unconsciously incompetent. And then we rant, rave, cry, seek vengeance when we find out our partner is having an affair. He's getting what he wants elsewhere. That's because he's not been getting it with *us*, because we've not been providing it. Even though we know it gives our partner pleasure. Even though it gives *us* pleasure. Even though we know that sex *is* what our partner wants.

"Ladies, I believe men are simple creatures; it's us females who are complicated. Men think about sex. A lot. They want to have sex. Often. They don't need to feel warm and loved before they'll even consider getting intimate. Let's face it, if the woman comes in from gardening just as the man has finished clearing out the loft, and the woman says, "would you like me to take you in my mouth?" he'll drop his trousers there and then and look at you impatiently. Also, there is that ridiculous male pride. They often have to go to the limits of their endurance before they'll succumb and ask if they can make love to us, or for us to give them some pleasure. We know this is true of them. We also know that, in the main, we're not like that. So, it certainly takes a conscious effort on our behalf in order to make a physical effort. But if we don't make that conscious physical effort, can we, should we, blame them for seeking their comforts elsewhere? Are we more at fault in creating the problem than they are for doing something to solve it?

"Has there been an item of clothing of yours which brings him to the boil when you wear it? Have you done something intimate with him which has caused you to wonder at the effect it has had on him? If so, have you worn that item of clothing again, and used it to entice him to bed? Have you re-enacted that form of intimacy? No? Why not?

"My advice is to be on the front foot, to maintain your part of the bargain. To provide your partner with sexual enjoyment and release. You never know, you may continue to enjoy it too. And if you don't, it's not a great hardship, is it? For the sake of maintaining your relationship? A quick, unrequested, once a week wank, and your husband will stay faithful, and be thankful he's got you.

"And by the way, if you *are* in the mood for it yourself, make sure you get him to do first whatever it is you want him to do. You won't need me to tell you how totally useless they are once they've had their pleasure.

"Thanks again for the invite. I'm happy to share with you some further thoughts if you'd like to voice any concerns or opinions".

After a short period of silence ('maybe it was my use of the word 'wank'' was Anna's immediate concern), there had been applause followed by an open discussion, during which even the most frumpy-looking ladies appeared to be at ease and, at times, somewhat saucy.

The first question she had been asked was, "If there's one thing that guarantees success, what would it be?"

"Role play," was her immediate response. "Charlie and I role play a lot. It's great fun. It gives you the chance to dress up and be experimental. It can go messy without impacting on your out-of-role play relationship. It's fantastic escapism and, in my experience, ends with great sex".

One of the older members of the Book Club, who had been silent throughout Anna's presentation and hadn't voiced any comments during the immediate post-presentation discussion, had brought the house down by saying, "Many, many years ago, after we got married and before we had kids, my husband and I had a day trip to the coast. Hastings, I think it was. Or it could have been Worthing. Anyway, we had a lovely day. You know, a walk on the front, penny arcade, fish and chips out of paper sitting on a bench overlooking the beach. When we walked back to the car for our journey home, I remember putting my arm through his, and I felt like a girl on her first date with a new boyfriend. I don't know why but maybe it was just because we were doing something different. Anyway, Clive drove us home and I looked out of the window thinking about all the nice, ordinary but nice, things we had done. And then I just leant towards Clive and undid his trousers. He was still driving so it was a bit awkward. He helped me as best he could but didn't say anything to me. I didn't say anything to him either. I finally arranged him so that his penis was out of his underwear. I then gave him a blowjob. Ridiculously dangerous, but I remember how thrilling it was. You know what, I'm going to sort another day out with him in the next few weeks, and I'm going to give him a blowjob on the way home again. I wonder if he'll remember that first time".

This had opened the flood gates, and, after a sharing of reminiscences and some howls of laughter, Chrissy brought the Book Club session to a close. 'Maybe their husbands are in for a shag tonight' had been Anna's final thought as she left the meeting to drive home. 'Hope the shock doesn't kill them!'

The following morning, Chrissy had telephoned Anna to thank her. "And how about Salty! How funny was that?"

"Who's Salty?"

"The lady who talked about her drive home with her husband".

"God, that was hilarious. So was she. Why's she named Salty?"

"Her maiden name was Sally Theresa Young. As I understand it, when she was at school she got lumbered with 'Salty'. Strangely enough, her husband's surname is Yorke so it still fits. She's a lovely lady. Owns a bookshop in Arundel. If you haven't been, you should. Charlie would love it. Mostly old books, but some specialist new ones. Loads of first editions and signed copies. People who know it spend hours in there".

"I can't believe we've never been. I'll make sure we do".

As Anna secured Garibaldi's hay net and brushed the sweat from his flanks as he munched contentedly, she recalled how she had felt on her drive home from the presentation. She had been on a high, exhilarated by adrenaline and inflated by the status which appeared to have been bestowed upon her. Yet her words now appeared ironic, her confidence foolhardy and her encouragements unsound.

She tidied everything away then climbed into her Land Rover Defender to drive home. Ridiculously, she felt nervous at the thought of going home to Charlie.

Book Two

The Idiot

Chapter 5

Nine months previously, Anna's only concern, as she entered Lene's salon, was what colour nail varnish she should go for.

Dani was her usual breezy and welcoming self. "Anna, how lovely to see you. I love it when you've got an appointment as Lene is always so excited".

"Great to see you, too, Dani. Yes, it seems ages since I saw Lene so we've a fair bit of catching up to do. How's life in your world?"

"Pretty good, thanks".

"Still going out with that guy you were telling me about? Jonathan, wasn't it?"

"Well remembered. No, I finished with him. He got a bit needy. Currently considering my options".

"Well, I'm sure you've plenty". Anna wasn't saying this to be kind. Dani was an attractive girl: quite stocky, but she carried it well, taller than Anna by at least two or three inches and a well-defined face with strong features.

"Anna!" exclaimed Lene as she entered the waiting area. They hugged. "I've been so looking forward to seeing you. Come on through".

Once in the treatment room they embraced again. "So, what have you been up to? You chat and I'll paint. By the way, I love your hair. The new style really suits you. As I've said before, you're a Jenna Coleman look-alike, but there's a hint of Kate Mara about you now".

"I've no idea who Kate Mara is, but I'm pleased you like the style. Before I get into my side of the chat, tell me, how have you been? How are Greg and the girls?"

"Everyone's really well, thanks. Business is good, too, so I've everything to feel grateful for".

"I'm so pleased. Now, Charlie and I are off to France shortly. Pick a nail colour for me and think wicked thoughts".

Lene laughed as she opened a drawer. "Right. Let's see what we can conjure up".

As soon as Anna returned to her car, she called Chrissy to suggest she drive to Chrissy's house so that they could have a catch-up before Anna and Charlie flew to France. As Chrissy poured the tea, Anna asked, "How are Ilya and Katerina?"

"Good, I think. Ilya's changed jobs, again. He's now working at a surf shop in East Wittering".

"The one called Shore in Shore Road?"

"Yes, I think that's the one".

"Cool shop".

"He seems to be enjoying it. As for Katerina, I hardly see her. Studying for her A' levels of course, but I get the feeling she'd prefer to stay in her room, even if she didn't have to work. If she's not studying, she's reading or listening to music. And that doesn't help. Her desk is stacked with Dostoyevsky paperbacks, and Radiohead dirges create an even more funereal atmosphere".

"Mmm, you have my sympathy and understanding. No boyfriend in sight?"

"No particular friend of any sort, as far as I can work out. You've got to know her reasonably well, and we've talked about this before. You have to agree, she's been in her own world for three or four years. Bit worrying, really".

"God, when you think what you and I were like in our mid-teens!"

"Let's not go there. How you didn't get pregnant, I'll never know".

"Wise beyond my years".

"Definitely when it comes to what goes on between boys and girls".

"You weren't exactly pure".

"That's true. Well, none of it has rubbed off on Katerina. Probably a good thing, I suppose".

"Strange really because she always comes across as socially aware. She's mentioned friends and parties several times over the years".

"Oh, she's popular enough, but I'm never sure whether she's simply acting a part, knowing she is expected to behave a certain way. She's a seventeen-year-old girl with a thirty-seven-year-old spinster's mindset, in many ways".

"That makes her sound a bit dowdy, which she's not. Maybe more like an old soul in a young body. Anyway, she'll sort it out. She's an extremely astute young lady. It'll be her eighteenth soon. Any thoughts for a present?"

"Difficult. You and Charlie were very generous when Ilya hit eighteen. There's no need to spend that much".

"Do you know what you're buying her?"

"Well, it's not like me to be this organised, but I've already got it. Well, not got it exactly, but paid for it. I'm buying her a car that a friend of mine is selling. Nothing fancy. She's kindly agreed to keep it on her drive until Katerina and I go and pick it up on her birthday".

"Oh, Chrissy, that's brilliant. What a wonderful present. That should get her out of her bedroom. That settles it, Charlie and I will pay for her driving lessons until she passes".

"Perfect".

"And how about you, how's work going? Any men keeping you company?"

"Work's fine. I'm thinking of upping my hours again once Katerina has finished her exams. As for men, well, I can't face being duped by another tosser. Why can't we all meet Mr Fucking Perfect on a beach in the south of France?"

"Someone will turn up when you least expect it".

They arrived at Perpignan Airport, cleared passport control, bypassed the baggage carousels, walked purposefully through the Arrivals and small airport lounge areas, crossed the road into the long stay car park and located their BMW convertible, which they had parked when flying back from their previous trip. They placed their backpacks in the boot and then Charlie began the short drive to Le Racou, using the season ticket code number to exit the car park. They had bought the car, a new one, in Perpignan shortly after finalising the purchase on the villa and found it ideal for their purposes: soft top, air conditioning, fun to drive yet practical, having four seats should they have invited guests to join them at the villa.

"Camille has been as brilliant as ever. Fridge fully stocked, packed freezer, drinks cabinet re-filled, windows open, everything clean and tidy. We say it every time, but she's a gem".

"And I noticed as we arrived that Thierry has the garden looking lovely".

"Christ, they're priceless. We can't have them deciding that they no longer want to look after the place for us. We are paying them enough, aren't we?"

"Anna," laughed Charlie, "they're the best paid house-minders in the whole of France. Relax, they love it".

"Yeah, I know. But still, we mustn't take them for granted. I'll buy them something nice when we're next in Barcelona".

With very little to unpack, as they kept as many clothes there as they did in England, and with no shopping to buy, they simply shed their light travel backpacks, poured two glasses of chilled fortified wine, opened a large packet of Salt & Vinegar crisps, walked through the French doors into the garden and over to their favourite reclining garden chairs, which Thierry has set up for them in the shade of the plane trees. Charlie carried them onto the patio in the sun.

"Shall I prepare a light meal this evening? I see that Camille has bought some prawns and salad. We could have that with baguette".

"Perfect. Do you want to wander down to the beach before we eat, or are you happy to stay here and just use the pool?"

"Stay here, I think. We'll beach tomorrow, shall we?"

"Fine with me".

Charlie finished his wine, took off his clothes, leaving them on the recliner, and strolled over to the pool. He wasn't a great swimmer, but managed a dive of sorts, and a couple of lengths, before joining Anna in the April sun. Neither of them wore swimwear in the garden unless they had visitors. They thought nothing of it now although, in the early days, they had both considered nude swimming and sunbathing to be thrilling and decadent. Initially, they had both been cautious regarding sun exposure, and applied liberal amounts of high factor sunscreen but, after several visits, application of factor 15 was all they both needed.

"Swimming, Anna?" asked Charlie as he fully reclined his chair.

"In a bit. I'll just finish this glass and have a think about what we may do over the next few days. You have a doze and by the time I've downed my wine I will have made a mental list of the must-dos over the next week or so".

"Fine with me. Want a top up?"

"No, I'm fine thanks".

After a while, with Charlie drifting off, Anna took the opportunity to study her husband's body. She knew it so well, but something about seeing him naked in the open air always prompted her to study him in a way she didn't in their bedrooms in England and France: dark hair, cut quite short, not a traditionally handsome face but a very pleasant one. People were always surprised to learn his age, and Anna felt certain that his boyish looks would stay with him over time. Great chest, shoulders, and upper arms. Slim waist and flat stomach (fencing is good for the core, apparently), 15 and a half inch shirts, 38-inch jackets, 32-inch waist trousers. Nice combo. She didn't allow her eyes to dwell too long on his groin area, which she knew intimately. Her gaze lingered on his strong thighs and defined calf muscles. 'A great body,' she thought. 'And the things it can do to me'. During each of their France trips, Anna conjured a bit of mischief. Their lovemaking in England was wonderful, but she aimed for something a little spicier when they were away, even if it was on only one occasion per trip. She spent a bit of time considering some options.

The following morning, Charlie strolled down to the boulangerie for pastries. Anna had still been asleep when he left the villa, so he bought 2 croissants as well as a pain au chocolat each to be on the safe side. He couldn't resist adding a pain au raisin, a pre-breakfast treat for himself. Plus, of course, a baguette.

He strolled across the road, sat on the wall which separates the car park from the beach and ate his pain au raisin. To his left he could see the buildings which were passed when driving from Le Racou to Argeles sur Mer—mostly villas, but also some low-rise apartments. In front of him the beach and, beyond that, the Med. To his right, the Pyrenees mountains plunging dramatically into the sea. These slopes are ideal for growing the Grenache grape which gives Collioure wine its depth and flavour. This was the wine they tended to drink while living at the villa, or perhaps Rivesaltes, which is a fortified wine produced from grapes grown in vineyards surrounding Perpignan Airport. Neither of them was a heavy drinker, but they tended to imbibe every evening during their French trips. They rarely drank alcohol with lunch, preferring water so that they felt they had the energy to do whatever they chose in the afternoon; it was so easy to be idle.

"Ah, you're awake. And up! Blimey, we off somewhere?"

"Don't be cheeky. I don't want to waste a minute of our first day here. What have you got me?"

"Baguette for later. Croissant, pain au chocolat, or both, for breakfast".

"Actually, a pain au raisin would have been my preference this morning".

"Er…"

"Only joking. Put the pastries on the table. The jam is already out. And the orange juice. I'll get the coffees".

It wasn't long before Anna was exclaiming, "God, they were lovely. How do the French do it? May I suggest a couple of hours on the beach, sea food lunch then back here for a laze by the pool. Baguette and cheeses, with some red wine, for supper, and then an early night".

"Deal. Will tonight be when you intend to serve up your French treat for me?"

"Not tonight, but I have something in mind. Haven't let you down yet, have I?"

There were three reasons why they often went to the beach, rather than stay by the pool in their lovely garden, with its shade and seclusion, while living in France: change of scenery; people watching; to swim in the sea. Anna and Charlie were rarely at the beach after 9am should they be visiting their villa in high season. They would go for an early, quick dip before strolling back to the villa, via the boulangerie, for a late breakfast. However, during Spring and late Summer, their favourite times for French stays, they tended to spend 4 or 5 mornings a week on the beach. Although there were alternative resorts to the north and south of them, they tended remain at Le Racou as the beach was just a four-minute walk from their villa. They would take towels, water, Kindles, and headrests—nothing more—with Charlie wearing swimming shorts, a t-shirt and flip-flops and with Anna in a bikini or swimsuit, a beach dress and Birkenstocks. They always applied their Piz Buin All Day Long Factor 15 before leaving the villa: all over application, assisting each other where necessary.

Le Racou is an old-fashioned seaside resort. There are small villas adjacent to one end of the beach, and a car park, behind a wall, at the other end. Beyond the villas and car park is the main, narrow, street with its bars, cafes, and beach-goods shops. To get to the beach from their villa, Charlie and Anna simply had to walk out of the gate, down the short, unmade road leading to the street, along the street, go across the road and turn right to go through a passageway linking the street to the beach. 4 minutes (4 minutes and 23 seconds to be exact: they'd timed it the first time they walked to the beach after buying the villa). Le Racou is situated to the south of the much larger resort of Argeles sur Mer. Further south again is Collioure, which is famous for its anchovies and for being a favourite haunt of Matisse and other famous Artists, who found the light so conducive to their style of painting. Beyond that is Banyuls sur Mer and then the border with Spain.

All in all, a terrific part of the world—great climate, not too crowded, missing the fussiness of the Cote d'Azur, with a backdrop of the Pyrenees, wonderful local wines, and sea food. Anna and Charlie loved it there. But then they also loved it in West Sussex, their home in England. Even a couple not madly in love with each other would find little to complain about.

They completed their swimming, sunbathing, people watching and vista gazing, rolled up their towels, donned their clothes and strolled to their favourite seafood restaurant, which was situated on the main street through Le Racou, en route to their villa.

By mid-afternoon, serotonin was seeping out of Charlie's ears and nostrils. For the twenty minutes before he had decided to do something about it, he had tortured himself by gazing at Anna, who was stretched out on her lounger, on her back, naked. She was probably dozing, he decided, but the straw hat she had placed over her face meant that Charlie could take in the wonders of his wife's body without her being conscious of his visual attention.

He was familiar with every inch of her, but never failed to be thrilled by looking at her and touching her. She had changed very little over the time he had known her, and what turned him on in the early days continued to arouse him now.

She was just 5' 5" tall but her thighs gave her the appearance of being taller. He loved her thighs: the slight crescent shape on the inside; the line down the outside defining her muscles, which were toned from hour upon hour of horse riding. He couldn't see her bum or back, of course, but he was fully aware that she had a tight bum and a V-shaped back, again due to horse riding developing her upper back and shoulder muscles, helping to accentuate her slim waist. Hairless, thanks to Lene, flat stomach, and then her breasts. He adored her breasts.

He walked over to where Anna lay, squatted beside her, and proceeded to use his hands to communicate his appreciation of her.

After four days of enjoying themselves at Le Racou, Anna suggested a mini break to either Barcelona or Llafranc.

"I'll see if the Barca hotel has a suite for us. If they're fully booked, I'll try the Llafranc hotel". He got lucky with their first choice.

It is a comfortable two-and-a-half-hour drive to the centre of Barcelona. They parked, then walked into their favourite hotel in the city, Hotel 1898, very close to the Plaza Catalunya. They were familiar to the staff, having frequented the hotel on several occasions since purchasing their villa in France. They tipped generously, not to be ostentatious but because they had always been well looked after. That, and the fact that they were a young, attractive, always well dressed, wealthy, foreign couple, meant they were memorable to the staff on the front desk and in the bar and restaurant. They wore shorts and t-shirts for the journey, knowing that they were likely to dress up for their evening in the hotel restaurant. Charlie had no idea what Anna had selected to pack in their overnight bag but was certain that he would be comfortable with the choice she had made for him and delighted with what Anna had packed for herself.

After checking in and dumping their bags in their suite, they enjoyed an hour in the hotel's Wellness Spa before taking the lift to the top of the building so they could have a quick read whilst relaxing on the loungers placed around the rooftop pool on La Isabella Terrace, with its panoramic view of the capital of Catalonia.

On returning to their suite, Charlie used the main bathroom to shave, shower, and dress while Anna used the shower in the en-suite bathroom. Charlie settled himself in the lounge area while he waited. Unlike most females Charlie had been associated with, Anna tended to be on time and, sure enough, at 8.20, ten minutes before their table reservation, she came out of the bedroom and smiled at him.

"All set? I'm hungry. Can't wait to eat that lobster dish I had last time. What do you fancy?"

"You. I know that's corny, but you look absolutely gorgeous," he replied, as he looked admiringly at his wife. She was wearing a white tennis-style dress: square neck showing very little cleavage; tightly fitted across her ample bust, back and waist; full, box-pleated skirt, the hem of which finished about three inches above the knee. Beautifully styled to accentuate her figure, demure, but as sexy as hell.

"Thank you. You look rather ravishing yourself".

"Thanks," he replied, casually looking down at his black leather moccasins, dark grey linen trousers and light grey, short sleeved Armani shirt. "That dress is stunning. Is it new?"

"Yes, I saw it in the Sunday Times Style magazine a couple of months ago and made sure I got hold of it before this trip. I knew we'd be tanning up, and this dress needs a tan. Come on, let's go and eat".

The Maitre d', who was expecting them, escorted them to their favourite table with its stunning view of the buzzing city. Within two minutes, a handsome young waiter presented them with menus. "Good evening, Senor Charlie and Senora Anna. Welcome back".

"Good evening Guillem, it's lovely to be back," replied Anna, with a smile. "How have you been?"

"I have been very sad. Now I can be happy again". Charlie noticed that, as with all their previous visits to this restaurant, Guillem paid attention solely to Anna.

"We don't need to see the menus thank you Guillem. We'd both like the smoked salmon to start, and then fillet steak, rare, with salad for me, and my wife will have your special lobster dish with clams. A glass of local Cava each with the smoked salmon, then a bottle of the 2010 Bodega Numanthia".

"Certainly, Senor," said Guillem, while smiling at Anna.

"My wife," repeated Anna with a giggle once Guillem had left them to take their order to the kitchen. "Listen to you!"

"Well, I mean, could he make it more obvious?"

"What?"

"Don't give me that mock innocence. Guillem was practically making love to you with his eyes and mind".

"Really? I hadn't noticed".

"Yeah, right. And you also thought I hadn't noticed about you too, didn't you?"

"What, that I'm not wearing a bra," replied Anna coyly, "and that, if you look closely, it's possible to discern my nipples under this white fabric?"

"Exactly that!"

"There's something you haven't clocked though".

"Oh? What's that?"

"I'm not wearing any knickers either".

"Really? So, all you have on is that beautiful white dress and your sandals?"

"Yep".

"Prove it".

"Don't you believe me?"

"It's not in my interest to believe you".

Anna paused and considered. "OK, wait until our starters have been served, then drop your serviette. Don't for Christ's sake do it while a waiter is nearby. You know what they're like. Especially Guillem. I'm happy to prove it, but to you, not to one of the restaurant staff. Not this trip, anyway".

Charlie looked into Anna's eyes, but she simply feigned innocence.

"Can I drop it yet?"

"No, I told you, after our starters have been served and the waiters have buggered off".

As they sat in silence, waiting for the first course to be served, it was clear to Charlie that Anna was gradually hoisting her skirt, bit by bit, up her thighs. As she did so, she looked at him and smiled.

They were served their smoked salmon and Cava. Before starting to eat or drink, Charlie dropped his serviette, a little too obviously for Anna's liking, onto the floor. He pulled his chair away slightly so that he could more easily bend down as if looking for a serviette hiding itself under the table. During the short time Charlie was on one knee, grappling about, Anna parted her legs, and he could just make out, he was sure that he could just make out, Anna's nakedness above her thighs.

Charlie resumed his place at the table.

"Now do you believe me?"

"Anna, if you've ever looked better than you do this evening, if you've ever turned me on more than you have today, well, I just don't remember it. If you choose to have pudding or coffee, I'm simply going to grab you by the hair and drag you back to the room".

"Well, I hope you're not thinking that we'll be returning to our room as soon as we've finished our meal. Oh no, young man, the night will still be young. We're going down La Rambla for a nightcap first".

"Ratbag".

Anna's cackle made a few heads turn.

As they ate their meal, they chatted about several routine subjects— when they might return to England; horse riding and fencing events in their diaries; the rest of their French stay; Chrissy, Ilya, and Katerina— before signing for their meal and leaving the hotel.

They spent an hour or so in a couple of bars off La Rambla. In the second, the only seating available was a stool each at the bar. Charlie bought their drinks, and they turned their seats to look at the bar interior, and its patrons. After a while Anna guided Charlie's focus with a nod of her head so that he could see a couple of men who were sitting at a table for four, facing them. The men were with their partners, who had their backs to Charlie and Anna. Anna uncrossed her legs and slid her bum to the very front edge of the bar stool. As she did so, she leaned back so her elbows were resting on the bar. "Listen," she said, "we must go. My imagination is running away with me, and I'm so turned on I'm worried that I'm going to stain the skirt of this dress".

"I'm right behind you". They left what remained of their drinks and walked rapidly back to the hotel, only just making it through the bedroom door before they fell on each other and, finally, released the sexual tension that had built up in their minds and bodies since they had left their suite earlier in the evening.

As Charlie had insisted that Anna did not remove her dress for their love making, she realised afterwards that there was a stain on the box pleat skirt after all.

CHAPTER 6

Their France trip lasted a little over three weeks, and, on the plane back from Perpignan, they committed to a return trip before the end of June.

"So," said Anna, "we'll be celebrating our wedding anniversary in England. Any idea what you'd like to do?"

"How about dinner and overnight at The Spread Eagle? We always enjoy it there".

"Great idea. I'll book it when we get home".

The day after their return, Charlie had a wander around their private back garden and noticed that three panels of fencing had been blown down. "Must have had some strong winds while we were away," he announced to Anna. "I'd best give Steve a call to ask if he's got time to pop round to sort it".

"OK. It'd be good to see him, anyway. It's been ages".

"Shall I ask him if he wants to eat with us after he's finished the fence? He may like to have a few drinks and stay over, too".

"Yes, nice idea. Give him a call, and I'll phone The Spread Eagle".

Charlie and Steve went way back. They had played in the same rugby team and formed a friendship outside of the sport. Whereas Charlie chose not to continue playing after he had become self-employed, Steve continued into his 30s. Steve was capable at all the things Charlie wasn't, which encompassed just about every form of manual work, and was the first person to be contacted if Charlie or Anna needed something to be done around the house or in the garden. Steve always insisted he would not take any payment, and the couple had to be increasingly imaginative to find ways to settle what they considered to be a debt: crates of beer; vouchers; event days such as a flight above the Downs in a Spitfire or a hair-raising spin around Goodwood racetrack alongside a rally driver; fishing tackle.

Steve was not the sort of man for whom you could buy anything that he would consider 'girly', so no clothing, after-shave, restaurant meals, spa treatments. Steve was what Charlie's mother had referred to as a 'proper man': huge chest, bulging muscles and thick thighs. "You need to get yourself into the gym, young man," she would say to her son. "Look at Steve. Now there's a proper man. What I wouldn't give to be twenty years younger". "Leave off, Mum, you're embarrassing yourself. And Steve". "She's not embarrassed me," Steve would say. "Come on Mrs Knightley, have a feel of these biceps".

"How did you get on?" asked Anna, once she had completed the dinner/bed/breakfast reservation at The Spread Eagle.

"Yep, Steve's going to sort the fence on Saturday. I've sent him a photo of the panels and he said he'll get them on Saturday afternoon and should be with us around 3".

"Eating and staying?"

"He said he'd love to".

By 7pm the following Saturday, the fence panels were up, a lasagne was in the oven, Steve was in the shower and Charlie was pouring the drinks: red wine for himself and Anna, Badgers Ale for Steve.

Steve joined them in the kitchen, picked up his glass, downed over half of the beer then said, "Cheers mate".

"Cheers Steve," replied Charlie as he sipped his wine. "Thanks again for sorting that so quickly. Please let me know how much we owe you and I'll get the cash from upstairs".

"You can reimburse me for the materials but I'm not taking no money from you two for the work so you can cut the crap".

Anna had been leaning against a worktop while this dialogue played out. She had to smile. It was almost word for word the same every time. As she watched Steve speak, she marvelled again, as she did every time she saw him, at his sheer bulk. He was massive. Not her type at all but she felt certain that he would be a great partner for someone. Chrissy, maybe, or one of the divorced ladies at the Yard? Although rough and ready, Steve was a lovely guy, good natured, considerate and gentle, despite his size. Not for the first time, Anna tried to work out what it was about him which caused him to split with so many girlfriends early in his relationship with them.

BOOK TWO: *THE IDIOT*

They finished the meal, with Steve eating the equivalent of Anna and Charlie's servings combined, and Charlie poured Steve's sixth beer and opened a third bottle of red. Anna stacked the dishwasher while Charlie and Steve settled in the Snug. Whilst in the kitchen, Anna poured herself a large glass of water. She was feeling tipsy already and it was not yet 10pm.

On entering the Snug, both men stopped talking and looked at her until she had sat on the sofa next to Charlie. "Don't let me interrupt you," she said. "Or was it some man-talk too polluting for my delicate ears?"

Steve laughed. "Not at all, Anna. We were just talking about our rugby days".

"You don't play anymore, then?"

"No. Knees are buggered".

"Do you miss it?"

"Not the game, no. I miss the post-match banter and beers, though".

Charlie interjected with, "Some of that banter may well have been too polluting for your delicate ears, Anna".

"Like what?"

"Not sure I can recall anything specific. Help me out here, Steve. What sorts of things did we talk about?"

"Lady parts?"

Anna snorted. "Lady parts? Why would hearing about lady parts corrupt me? I've got lady parts myself, so I already know all about them".

Steve chuckled. "And very fetching they are too, Anna".

"Are you flirting with me, Steve?"

"Wouldn't dream of it".

"Good, cos I'm a happily married woman, you know. Anyway, while we're on the subject of lady parts, why don't you ever stick with a partner? I've met some of them and they were very nice".

She clocked Steve and Charlie exchanging a look.

"What? Come on, what do you two know that I don't?" She took a long sip of her wine, so did Charlie, and Steve finished what remained in his glass.

"Come on," she repeated. "There's a story here, I know there is".

"You're too much of a lady to hear about it, Anna," claimed Steve.

"Bollocks. Come on, tell me why you never stick with a girlfriend".

47

"It's summed up by his rugby club nickname," answered Charlie.

"Did you all have a nickname? How boyish of you. Before you disclose yours, Steve, I need to know Charlie's".

"It was Snoops," replied Steve, with a smile.

Anna roared with laughter and turned to face Charlie. "Because you love the Peanuts strips? Oh my god that's so funny. Snoops! Jesus, it's no wonder you stopped playing so early. Any opponent finding out you loved Snoopy would take you for a right soft touch!"

Steve chuckled along with her. "The worst one was Cherub".

"Cherub? How on earth did a rugby player get stuck with Cherub?"

"Because during one post-match session this guy saw one of our teammates looking glum after we'd got hammered and instead of saying, "Cheer up," it come out as, "Cherub". Unfortunately for him, it stuck, and he had to live with it for five years or more".

Anna's giggles returned and she took another sip of wine.

"Right. Come on. I'm ready for it. What was yours, Steve?"

"It was The Exocet".

"And why were you known as The Exocet?"

Steve looked at Charlie, who answered for him. "I said earlier his nickname sums up why girlfriends can't stay with him for long".

Anna went quiet and tried to think logically through the alcohol haze. Finally, she suggested, "You've a very big penis".

"He has," confirmed Charlie. "Well deduced".

"I want to see it".

"Whoa, hold on," exclaimed Steve.

"No, seriously, I want to see it. You won't mind, Charlie, will you?"

"No, I don't mind. It's up to Steve".

Steve looked from one to the other. "Are you two serious?"

"I'm deadly serious. I'm intrigued that a male member can be of such a size that women can't cope. Come on, you never know, I may be able to provide some advice, you know, from a female point of view. As a potential recipient, so to speak".

"Charlie?"

"Go for it, mate".

Steve stood and removed first his trousers and then his boxers. Nothing was revealed because his shirt tails hid the area under discussion.

"Shirt off too," demanded Anna.

Steve removed his shirt and stood in front of Anna. She was silent for quite a while, and then said, "That, indeed, is a very large penis. I'll embarrass myself by saying I've seen a few in my time, but I've never come across anything like that".

Steve bent down in order to pick up his boxers.

"Hang on, what are you doing?"

"You've seen what my teammates saw in the shower, so you can now perhaps appreciate how I got lumbered with my nickname".

"Yes, that's true, but I haven't seen what your girlfriends have seen, which has caused them to cover their eyes in horror and run home to mummy".

"What are you suggesting?"

"Well, obviously I need to see it erect. Are you going to do it or is it best if I help?"

"Charlie, help me out here, mate".

"She has a point, Steve. A female viewpoint on why it's causing you a problem with your lady friends may be useful".

Anna stood up and stood next to Steve. "I'll give you a hand," she said and in no time at all, Steve's problem was clear for all to see. Anna wanted to comment but was speechless, capable only of staring at it. Unfortunately, Anna's touch and gaze tipped Steve over the edge and, for the next twenty seconds, he proceeded to ruin their rug. "Jesus," gasped Anna.

"Sorry about that," said Steve, rather sheepishly as he and Anna cleaned themselves up. Steve put his clothes back on and Anna did her best to try to salvage the rug with strategically placed reams of kitchen roll. She took a sip of water, her hand trembling as she held the glass. "I'm afraid I can't offer any advice, Steve. There's no way that's getting inside anything that doesn't live on a farmyard".

Whatever tensions the three of them were feeling were dissolved in their howls of laughter.

Chapter 7

Two days later, on Monday morning, Anna was bursting to tell someone about the events of Saturday evening, and there was only one person with whom she could share it. Thankfully, Lene's salon was closed on Mondays.

"Am I interrupting anything," asked Anna on the phone.

"I'm just about to vacuum the stairs".

"Well, how about you get that done while I drive over. I'll take you to lunch and let you in on a bit of gossip. Can it be gossip if it's about me? Probably not. Anyway, see you in a bit".

As Anna described the events in question, in full detail, Lene's facial expressions revealed a series of emotions: shock, horror, amusement, envy. By the time Anna was trying to explain the bit about how she was going to have to replace a ruined rug, neither of them could speak for laughing. Fellow patrons of the café became sucked in by the shrieks and guffaws emanating from the two attractive ladies in the corner and found themselves chuckling in unison.

Lene managed to take control of herself and asked, "And Charlie didn't mind?"

"Apparently not. To be honest with you, when we got to bed, we giggled like ten-year-olds then fucked like eighteen-year-olds. It was a great night".

Lene started laughing again then began to hiccup. That set them both off again and before long they were both crying.

"We need to change the subject," Lene spluttered between hics and cups.

"Here, sip this. Right, different subject. Let me think. OK, anniversary. I need to come up with a present for Charlie".

"You're useless with presents".

"I know. My mind always goes blank".

"And Charlie's brilliant with presents".

"Yes, I know that too. So, help me out here. What can I get him?"

Lene presented a number of suggestions, all rejected by Anna.

"It'll have to be sex, then," was Lene's final offering.

"Well yes of course, that goes without saying. But there must be a present too, surely".

Lene remained silent, her idea bank spent.

They sipped their drinks and pondered. Finally, Anna smiled broadly.

"You've come up with something".

"I have".

"And you're very pleased with it".

"I am".

"What is it?"

Anna shared her idea. "What do you think?"

It was fully two minutes before Lene responded. "Right, let me tell you all the reasons why this is a bad idea".

Anna parried them in turn. "So, it's decision time. Unless you say no, we're going for it".

Lene pondered. "OK, I'm in".

"Great. Keep the afternoon of 4th June free. I'll get back to you before then with the Plan".

They drank their orange juice and coffee and opened their cards before Anna ripped the wrapping from her present, a large box containing a pair of top-of-the-range Ariat riding boots.

"How did you know these are the ones I wanted?"

"You mentioned them a few months ago".

"Your care and consideration sickens me".

Charlie laughed. "Sorry to disappoint you".

"Now, you may have noticed that there isn't a second present on this bed".

"Not to worry".

"I'm giving you yours later".

"That'll do for me".

"No, not that. Well yes that, but something else too".

"Sounds intriguing. Any clues?"

She shook her head.

"Fair enough. So, what do you fancy for breakfast?"

As they drove towards The Spread Eagle in Charlie's Alfa Romeo 4C, Charlie said, "So, from now on we're not Charlie and Anna but Grant and Charlotte. Is that right?"

"Yes. Until we get back in the car to drive home tomorrow. Just take my lead".

"And we're having a light lunch, a lazy afternoon, and then dinner?"

"Yep".

"I hope Charlotte's good company".

"I believe that Charlotte will be such good company that Grant will be proposing before breakfast".

The female entered the restaurant wearing a floral summer dress, short sleeved, fitted at the waist and a flared skirt finishing four inches above the knee. Her partner was also attired in summer gear: grey cotton trousers and a charcoal polo shirt.

Ten minutes after they were seated at a table for four, another very attractive female entered. This lady was wearing a close-fitting red linen dress, the skirt of which was very short. The waiter enquired whether she was dining alone before seating her at a table for two.

"Isn't that…" the man began to ask his partner. "Shhh. Go with it," was the response.

After drinks had been ordered and served at both tables, and the 3 diners were contemplating the menu, the female with a partner walked over to the solo female and said, "Excuse me. I don't wish to disturb you but if you're dining alone, my boyfriend and I would welcome you to join us".

"That's very kind. If you're sure, that would be lovely".

By the time the waiter arrived to take their meal order, the three were sitting together, and agreeing with each other's complimentary comments about the hotel.

"So, are you here for business or pleasure?"

"Pleasure. I flew over from Stockholm on Friday. My brother got married here in Midhurst on Saturday".

"Oh, how lovely. Did it go well?"

"Yes, it was great thanks".

"So, how long are you staying in England?"

"My plane home is this evening. I'm just killing time really".

"Well then, kill it with us if you like. We're staying here tonight so we'll have plenty of time tomorrow to do the things we wanted to do".

"That would be great. Thank you".

"Pleasure. So, what do you do in Stockholm?"

"I work for a British IT company. How about you two? Are you staying at this lovely hotel for any particular reason?"

The male answered this. "We were given a voucher at Christmas. One night and one meal. We live hectic lives in Wimbledon, and this is the first chance we've had to use it".

"Yes," added his partner, "to be honest, we're going to approach the night away as a chance to resurrect our sex life. It's been disappointingly dormant recently for one reason or another".

"Charlotte, if you're going to mention our sex life to a total stranger, we should at least know her name first!"

The Swedish girl laughed. "I'm Hanne".

"Well, it's lovely to meet you, Hanne. I'm Grant, and my very forward partner is Charlotte".

"I'm pleased to meet you both. And thanks again for inviting me to join you. No female particularly likes to sit alone in a bar or restaurant".

"Why are you alone, may I ask?"

"I said she was forward, didn't I?"

"I don't mind at all. I split from my boyfriend a month ago. Bad timing really as it would have been nice to have someone with me for the trip and the wedding".

"That's a shame. And does your brother live over here?"

"Yes, in Portsmouth. His fiancée, well, his wife now, lives in Midhurst and after their honeymoon she'll be moving into Anders' flat".

"And you're flying back tonight?"

"Yes, a taxi is booked for 7pm to take me to Gatwick. Late home, I'm afraid".

"Oh well, we've got a few hours together. Let's make the most of it. Another glass of wine?"

By the time they had finished their meal, they were behaving together as if old friends: chatting, laughing, flirting.

"Shall we ask for our coffees to be served in the conservatory?" asked the lady in the floral summer dress.

They strolled through and the blonde sat down first, selecting a comfortable settee laden with cushions. The male took the chair opposite, and his partner sat on the settee. The couple's attention was drawn to their new friend's thighs: her dress, being short and tight, rode up considerably as she sat. By comparison, the floral dress appeared modest.

They sipped their coffee and continued to talk before a slight pause in the conversation prompted the girl in the floral dress to rest her right hand on the blonde girl's left thigh. The man's attention was immediately drawn. He said, "I hear Stockholm's expensive, and that no shops, bars or restaurants accept cash these days. Is that right?" As the question was answered, he watched the hand taking advantage of the length of skin revealed.

The hand's owner asked, "I mentioned that part of the reason for us taking time out is to attempt to rekindle our sex life. Is that something you may wish to help us with, while you're killing time before returning home?"

"If your hand gets any higher up my thigh, I think you will have already answered your own question. Yes, I don't see why not".

"Excellent. It's after 3 so we can now get the key to our room. We've already checked in. Grant, if you could collect the key from reception, Hanne and I will meet you outside the room. In fact, I know I said we'd role play the whole time we're here, Charlie, but shall we be our own selves now?"

"Suits me," responded Lene. "I have to say I found Charlotte and Grant somewhat pretentious".

Charlie closed the door behind him and the three stood in a triangle, facing each other.

Anna broke the somewhat awkward silence. "Charlie, would you like to undress both of us. Then please make yourself comfortable on that chair facing the bed. This is a view-only production, so don't even think about joining us".

Charlie stood behind Lene and lowered the zip of her dress, from neck to waist. She let it slip from her shoulders and down her body before stepping out of it, to reveal pretty, duck-egg blue bra and knickers. "Could you unclasp me please?" asked Lene. He undid her bra and lay it on a chair. She then proceeded to slowly remove her knickers to reveal a neatly trimmed, narrow, vertical line of blonde pubic hair.

"My turn please Charlie". Charlie helped Anna to shed her dress and bra, which he lay beside Lene's. Anna removed her knickers before taking Lene's hands and gently drawing towards her. With Lene being considerably shorter than Anna, as well as having a waif-like body, she appeared several years younger, despite having given birth to two daughters. Their figures were very different to each other's yet there was outstanding beauty in them both.

Anna bent down and kissed Lene on the lips. She then took Lene's face in her hands and kissed her again, passionately this time. Charlie could see that they were interlocking tongues, and that this appeared to be arousing them more than he could recall a girl being turned on by one of his kisses.

After separating, they walked towards the bed, hand in hand. Anna leaned back against the headboard and Lene knelt on the bed facing her. Charlie sat down on a chair, as instructed.

Anna studied Lene. 'She's even slighter than I remember her to be,' she thought. 'Narrow shoulders beneath her lovely face, thin arms, small breasts'. Anna never considered herself to be 'big' in any way, yet she felt over-endowed in Lene's company. Flat chested, but extremely prominent nipples, the sight of which caused Anna to inhale deeply, as she had the first time she had viewed them. They protruded from dark brown areolas like charred corks. "Lie back," demanded Anna. "Let me start with these".

Nearly three hours later, Lene was ready to leave.

"I'll walk you to your car," offered Charlie.

"Thank you. Bye Anna. I hope I see you very soon".

Anna was still naked in bed, with the quilt pulled up to the top of her chest. "I'll phone you tomorrow".

Lene nodded, produced a strained smile and opened the door.

"And Lene?"

"Yes?"

"Thank you".

"It was my pleasure, Anna. Truly it was".

Charlie returned to the room and sat on the side of the bed.

"Charlie, would you mind cancelling our table and ordering room service?"

"What would you like?"

"See if they can do some sort of seafood pasta. Plus a bottle of Champagne and some mineral water".

After Charlie had placed the order, Anna said, "Get in".

"What about room service?"

"They can leave it outside".

Charlie undressed and got into bed alongside Anna.

"Did you enjoy your anniversary gift?"

"The best present I've had since my parents gave me an Action Man. Ouch, that hurt".

"I'm knackered".

"Can't say I'm surprised. I counted four orgasms for you and three for Lene".

"Was it four? Seemed like one very long one".

"How did that all come about?"

"I haven't told you this before, but Lene and I had a one-night stand during our last year at Uni. I simply asked her if she'd like to do it again. I was a bit desperate to come up with an acceptable present for you, to be totally honest".

"Some present".

"You're not cross with me?"

Charlie looked genuinely puzzled. "Why would I be cross with you?"

"Receiving that much pleasure from somebody else. Being that intimate".

"No, not cross at all. It was beautiful".

"Was it beautiful? Is that how you'd describe it?"

"Yes, absolutely. It was insanely sexy, of course, but it was also beautiful. Thank you again".

"What would you like me to do? You have a free choice".

Chapter 8

The following afternoon, Anna telephoned the salon.

"Hi Dani, it's Anna. Is Lene free?"

"Hi Anna. She's just settling up with a client. If you could hold on for a minute or two, I'll let her know you're on the phone".

Two minutes later, Lene said, "Hello Anna".

"Lene, are you OK?"

"Yes, I'm fine".

"Oh god, you regret it don't you? I'm so sorry".

"Hang on a minute. Dani, could you transfer this into my room?" A minute later, Lene was speaking to Anna again. "What makes you think I regret it?"

"You sound so flat. Really down. I've fucked up, haven't I?"

"No, you haven't fucked up. I'm not down and I don't regret it, not for one second. I loved everything about yesterday afternoon".

"Really? You're not just saying that so I'll get off the phone and leave you alone?"

"It was special. If I sound flat, it's because, even though I was tired last night, I wasn't able to sleep much. Please don't worry about anything Anna. Like I said, I loved everything about it".

"Thank god for that. And Greg was OK when you got home?"

"Yes, he was absolutely fine. Don't worry, everything's good. Look, I must go as I've a client booked in. Speak soon, eh?"

"Yes, we'll have a good chat before we leave for France".

"Good. Bye Anna".

"Bye Lene".

The heat hit them as they exited the plane at Perpignan. Looking to their left, as they descended the steps, they could see Canigou standing proud. No snow on the peaks this time. Standard arrival procedure until, less than an hour later, they drove through the gates at the entrance to their property, parked in the shade, removed their backpacks from the boot and let themselves in.

Camille had re-stocked so all that they needed was a fresh baguette. They decided that they would immediately walk to their favourite restaurant for a late lunch and pick up a baguette on their way back. After returning, relaxed and replete, they removed their clothes and settled on their loungers in the shade.

"So, anything particular on the agenda this trip, Charlie?"

"Will you be up for a mountain walk?"

"Most definitely, but let's do very little during the next few days. We can drive up to Prats early one morning when we fancy it and get a hike in before the afternoon heat makes it uncomfortable".

"Good idea".

"And I definitely want to spend a few days in Barcelona again".

"Me too. How about a couple of nights at Hotel 1898 after we've been here a few weeks? Perhaps we could drive down to Llafranc next week and have two or three nights at the BlauMar?"

"Perfect".

"OK, I think I'll make a phone call now to get it arranged".

Twenty minutes later he re-joined Anna in the garden. "Right, Llafranc all booked but we'll arrange Barca after we get back".

The following morning, refreshed after a good night's sleep, morning orange juice and coffee, they chose to walk together to buy their morning pastries, which they ate while sitting on the car park wall, overlooking the beach. After a while, Anna broke the peace, saying, "I know I say it every time we're here, but I'll never get tired of this. Such a simple pleasure, but I can't think of anything I'd prefer to be doing right now".

"I agree. No place I'd rather be, and no-one I'd rather be with".

Anna turned her head to look at him. "I love you so much Charlie. I know we have a privileged life, but it would be nothing without you".

"How lovely. Anna, I adore you".

They visited Prats de Mollo a few days later and enjoyed a wonderful morning walk in the mountains, a relaxing afternoon at the town's lido and, to end the day, dinner, and a sound night's sleep at The Belle Vue Hotel.

It was shortly after they had arrived back at the villa, and Anna was in the kitchen preparing lunch, that Anna's phone rang. It was rare for either of them to be contacted while they were in France and Anna didn't recognise the number.

"Hello. Oh, hi Katerina. Happy 18th Birthday! I was going to phone later, but thought I'd give you a chance to open all your presents. No, not at all, it's a pleasure. Tell me, what else did you get?"

As Anna continued to chat, Charlie joined her in the kitchen, having anticipated being needed to carry something out into the garden.

"Just a minute Katerina, Charlie's just walked in. Charlie, it's Katerina phoning to thank us for the driving lessons".

Charlie took the phone from Anna. "Happy birthday Katerina. Having a good day? Excellent. Hey, don't mention it, it's a pleasure. What have you planned for this evening? Great, sounds fun. Enjoy the rest of your day. I'll pass you back to Anna".

"Hi again. Look, you're probably keen to get on with other things but, before you go, Charlie and I were wondering if you wanted to join us here in France for a holiday". Anna glanced at Charlie as she said this, inviting a response. Charlie shrugged, then nodded. "Long or short as you like. We'll sort out the flight, pick you up from the airport, and book your flight home whenever you feel you've had enough of us. No, really, we'd love you to. You could probably do with a break after all those exams. Have a think about it and check with Chrissy. We're free from Thursday of next week, so any time to suit you should you decide you'd like to come. OK, great. Speak to you again later. Enjoy your day".

Anna finished the call and immediately said, "Is that OK? As I was talking to her, I just thought it would be a nice thing to offer. It would give Chrissy a break, too".

"No, that's absolutely fine. Nice idea".

"Great, thanks. She's going to have a word with Chrissy and phone me back. I'm pretty sure she's going to say yes".

Katerina phoned back within half an hour to tell Anna that she would love to fly out for a holiday. Anna suggested she email her passport details so they could book her flight plus a taxi to take her to the airport. All the arrangements were made, and Anna emailed Katerina to confirm the taxi and flight details, reassuring her that either she or Charlie would be at Perpignan Airport to collect her.

On Monday, after several restful days, they packed their requirements for a three-night sojourn at Llafranc in the Costa Brava. They had been fortunate that a suite had been available at The BlauMar as it is a popular hotel overlooking the Mediterranean in the beautiful resort of Llafranc. On Wednesday, they travelled around the region in the BMW, roof down, exploring villages and coves.

"Where did you say we're eating tonight?" asked Anna, as she sipped her coke at the beach café they had spotted from the coast road.

"I've reserved at table at eight o'clock at the Terraplata".

"Have we eaten there before? I can't remember".

"No, we haven't, but it was recommended to us by that couple we met the last time we stayed here. Do you remember? He seemed a decent bloke, but she was a right pain in the arse".

"Oh yeah, I remember. She had the hots for you and kept trying to get you to join her in the pool".

"Spoiled my day. Anyway, they'd eaten at the Terraplata and, I have to say, it did sound rather good".

"Great. Looking forward to that then. Shall we have a quick dip while we're here? Then we can mosey back to the hotel, get changed, and stop off for a drink somewhere on our walk to the restaurant".

"Perfect".

By 6.30pm Charlie had showered and was standing in the bathroom while Anna was in the shower. "Are we dressing up tonight, or going casual?" he shouted, so that Anna could hear him over the hissing of the steaming water.

"I'm wearing that white dress I wore in Barcelona. It's too nice not to wear again. Is that OK?"

"Lovely. Are you intending to wear anything underneath it this time?"

"Pardon. Can't hear you over this shower". Anna turned the water off and her head appeared as she slid back the shower door.

"I was asking if you'd be wearing any underwear".

"I will, but I've another little surprise for you".

"What's that then?"

"Not telling you now. Get dressed, then go and have a seat on the balcony while I get ready. I won't be long".

They walked in the general direction of the restaurant. Charlie was wearing loafers, thin cotton trousers and a short-sleeved shirt. Anna told him that he was looking particularly handsome. "Thank you. Scrubbed up well yourself. You're wearing bra and knickers, I can tell, so what's the surprise? Is the lingerie new and particularly enticing?"

"It is new, as a matter of fact. I think you'll like it. It's very pretty. But no, that's not the surprise".

"When are you going to tell me?"

"This looks a nice little bar. Let's pop in here. I'll tell you over a glass of fizz".

They settled into a quiet corner of the dark, low-ceilinged bar and the waiter delivered their glasses of cava.

"Right, this is yours". Anna took from her handbag a small item of technology and passed it to Charlie.

"What is it?"

"A remote control".

"For what?"

"My 'Alive Love Egg'. The perfect way to spice up our time away, I think you'll agree".

"What on earth is an 'Alive Love Egg'?"

"If you can work out how to turn it on, you'll see".

Charlie looked at the remote and easily configured its operation. He turned it on and moved the dial. Anna immediately grabbed hold of the table in front of her with both hands.

"Jesus," she said, quietly.

A quizzical look from Charlie.

"Turn it down".

Charlie made the adjustment and asked, "Anna?"

Anna had now regained her equilibrium, but her eyes still appeared a little out of focus. "It's inside me. The Love Egg".

Charlie looked back at the remote. "Oh. I see. How thrilling". He changed the setting.

Anna once again held on to the table-top and lowered her head, trying to control her body. "You'll need to turn it down again". Charlie complied. "This will take a bit of getting used to. Please don't overdo it. I'm happy to keep it in and for you to decide when to turn it on, and how much power to use, but you'll have to bear in mind my welfare. And it would be mortifying if I had an orgasm in the middle of a crowded restaurant".

"Oh, I don't know".

"I mean it. If you don't behave, I'll take it out".

"OK, OK," he smirked. "Do you really think it could make you come?"

"No question. It's intense".

"I'll be good. Now, another quick glass before we go?"

"That'd be lovely thanks".

Charlie walked to the bar, taking the remote with him. Once he had ordered two glasses of cava, he turned the remote back on, keeping the setting at 'low', and turned to look at Anna. There she was, sitting on her own, trying to appear calm. 'I love these French treats Anna conjures up for us,' thought Charlie, as he returned, carrying the glasses.

"Is everything all right?"

"Just about. Would you know by looking at me?"

"You do look a bit on edge, I must admit. But I don't think anyone would clock you're on the verge of climaxing".

"That's reassuring. If you want a conversation, you'll have to turn it off for a while".

"Sorry. Forgot it was still on," teased Charlie.

They were seated in the restaurant and had ordered their starter and main courses before Charlie surreptitiously changed the dial on the remote control from 'off' to 'low'. Anna sat back and placed the palms of her hands on her thighs. Initially, she looked at Charlie while taking account of the sensations, but, before long, her gaze began to drift as she tried to think of something boring. Charlie watched as Anna's lower lip was held between her teeth.

The waiter arrived and, as he placed Anna's starter in front of her, Charlie increased the setting. He watched Anna roll her eyes while trying to say, "Gracias".

"Thanks," she said after the waiter had frowned at her before walking away. "Off now. I want to enjoy this".

Charlie didn't touch the remote again until after their dinner plates had been cleared and they were awaiting the arrival of their cognacs. Once the drinks were served, he moved the dial to 'low'. Anna hadn't noticed, so the vibrations inside her took her by surprise. She sat back and lowered her head as she thrilled to the sensation. She took up her glass and noticed with surprise that her hand was shaking. She sensed the rumble of the beginnings of an orgasm. She took a sip and returned the glass to the table. Anna realised she had lost some of her self-control: she kept fiddling with her hair; she was holding her face in her hands; she even found herself resting her forehead on the table. Other diners were too engrossed in their meals and conversations to notice that Anna's body was behaving in a similar way to that of a six-year-old desperate for the toilet. The orgasm was building. 'Oh god, not in here,' she thought.

Charlie wavered the intensity so that Anna experienced alternating sensations inside her.

"Turn it off, finish your drink, pay the bill and let's go".

Anna took Charlie by the hand and led him into the backstreets of the town. When they reached an alleyway, she dragged Charlie into it behind her. She opened her bag and placed it on the ground. Then she hoisted her skirt, removed her knickers and placed them in the bag. Next, she took hold of the short lead and pulled the Egg out of her body, placing it in the bag. Whilst she was doing this, Charlie had undone his trousers and dropped them, and his boxer shorts, to his ankles. Anna leaned back against the wall and held up her skirt. Charlie grasped and raised her right leg, then entered her. Within a minute, Anna enjoyed blessed relief and, ten seconds later, so did her husband.

Chapter 9

Two days after Charlie's birthday, which was celebrated at a vineyard near to Collioure, Anna and Charlie were sitting at a table at the little café within the terminal building at Perpignan Airport, waiting for Katerina's arrival on the 2pm flight from Gatwick. As usual, the easyJet plane was running late so they had some time to kill. Although lunch would be available for Katerina once they had driven back to the villa, they bought a drink and baguette for her. Finally, a little after 2.30, Katerina exited through the sliding doors and looked at the faces of the people waiting behind the barrier. Anna spotted her and gave a wave. Katerina smiled and walked over to the couple. Anna's first thought on seeing her was, 'She doesn't look much like a holidaymaker'. Katerina was wearing white Converse trainers, black jeans and a dark green V-neck t-shirt.

"Hi Katerina, lovely to see you. Good flight?"

"Hi Anna. It's lovely to be here. Yes, the flight was fine thanks. Hello Charlie".

"Welcome Katerina. It's great you could come over to spend some time with us".

"It is very kind of you both to invite me. I've been really looking forward to it".

"Is this all you've got?" asked Charlie, as he attempted to slip a backpack off Katerina's shoulders.

"It's fine Charlie, thanks. I can manage it. Yes, this is all I need, I'm sure".

"Fair enough. Let's get you to the car and we can catch up on the drive home".

Anna walked ahead with Katerina while Charlie followed behind. He was surprised by how little she must have brought with her bearing in mind she was aware that she could stay as long as she liked. Maybe she planned to return to England sooner than they had anticipated?

Once they were in the car, backpack in the boot, hood down, Katerina in the back eating the baguette and sipping the bottle of water, and

Anna asking Katerina random questions about how she'd got on with her A' levels, Chrissy, Ilya, and potential job opportunities Katerina may be considering, Charlie concentrated on driving while listening to the way Katerina was conversing with Anna.

He drew a few immediate conclusions: she liked and respected Chrissy, appearing to consider her an older, mature friend; she was exasperated with Ilya, believing him to be a nuisance to her and an irritant rather than an older male with whom she had a close relationship and from whom she could learn; she was confident without being brash, had high self-esteem without being arrogant, and worldly, despite her limited experiences. He'd obviously spent some time with her since she'd moved in with Chrissy, but he couldn't claim to know her well.

As they drove through the gates, Katerina spotted the sign. "L'Aubaine. Did I pronounce that correctly? What does it mean?"

"Yes, good pronunciation. It's French for The Windfall. We named it that because we could buy it only because of the money Charlie made through selling his Business".

"Cool. Hey, it's lovely," Katerina added as she looked around the garden and then the front of the property.

"Thank you. Come on in. Let me show you around so that you know where everything is. Before I forget, the water from the tap is fine to drink, but there's plenty of mineral water in the smaller fridge if you prefer. And the wifi code is on your bedside table".

Once the tour was finished and they were on the upstairs landing, Anna said, "You can dump your bag in your bedroom. That's your own bathroom. Get changed, have a shower if you wish, and then we can have a relax in the garden or a swim in the pool while we have a chat about what you may like to do while you're here".

"Thanks. I'll have a shower later if that's OK. I'll just get into my costume for now. A dip in the pool would be perfect".

"Great. See you outside when you're ready. Anything I can get you? Food, drink, suntan lotion?"

"Nothing to eat thanks. Suntan lotion would be good though please".

"No problem. I'll take some into the garden with me and you can keep hold of it. Factor 15 or 30?"

"30 please. My Russian skin needs to be treated with care. I don't think I could ever get as brown as you two, however long I stayed here". Anna smiled at her and said over her shoulder as she started down the stairs, "See you in a bit".

Charlie was waiting for her, on a sun lounger in the shade. He had placed a jug of lime cordial with tons of ice and three glass beakers on a small table between two vacant loungers.

"Katerina's just getting changed and will join us in a minute. She fancies a swim in the pool. She seemed in good form in the car". Anna placed the Piz Buin on the table and sat down. "From what Chrissy was recently telling me, I was expecting her to be surly and non-communicative. I think she'll be fine here. If she gets too much, just say. I'll have no problem with you deciding to go off on your own for a while if you wish".

"OK, thanks. We'll see how it goes".

Katerina came out of the villa and walked towards them. They stopped talking and watched her approach. She was wearing a dark blue, featureless, swimsuit and had a pale blue sarong tied around her waist.

"Cold drink Katerina?" asked Charlie as Katerina sat next to Anna.

"Thank you," and she poured a glass of juice for herself. "Shall I pour yours too?"

"Lovely, thanks," replied Charlie, and Anna added, "Yes please Katerina".

"I know I've been here only five minutes, but could I ask a favour?"

"Of course," said Anna, reassuringly.

"Could you call me Katya?"

"No problem. Do you prefer that to Katerina?"

"Increasingly so".

She didn't provide an explanation and the three of them settled back, all surprisingly comfortable in the silence that followed.

"Oh, I nearly forgot," said Anna, getting up hurriedly, "I told Chrissy I'd phone her as soon as you arrived. Anything you want me to say, or would you like to speak to her yourself?"

"No, I'm fine thanks. Just tell her I'll give her a call in a few days". Anna went into the villa to make the call.

"So," said Charlie, "I'm sure Anna's already said, but please treat this place as your own while you're here. If you fancy anything to eat or drink, and we have it, just help yourself. Don't ask, there's no need. And if we haven't got what you were after, just say and we'll get it. I mean it Katerina, sorry, Katya, just relax, come and go as you please and, as I said, help yourself".

Katerina had been looking directly at him while he spoke. He couldn't help remarking to himself that it was unusual for people to look you in the eye, especially youngsters.

Katerina replied, "Thank you, that's very kind of you. Is it OK if I have a swim now?"

"Well, that didn't last long, did it?" responded Charlie, laughing. "What did I say about doing as you please?"

Katerina laughed with him. "Oh yeah. Sorry," and she stood, unwrapped the sarong, walked over to the pool and completed a perfect dive into the deep end. Anna re-joined Charlie and watched Katerina in the pool. "I wouldn't challenge her to a race. You know how much you hate losing".

"Impressive, isn't she? Reckon she'd give you a run for your money too".

"I think you're right," she replied, having watched Katerina complete another two lengths of crawl.

A while later, Anna rose and said, "She'll need her towel. I left the towels for her on her bed, but it looks as though she hasn't brought the beach towel down".

Whilst in Katerina's bedroom, Anna noticed that the backpack had been emptied and the contents laid out on the bed ready to be put away. In addition to her Kindle and mobile phone, plus the clothes that Katerina had worn for the journey, and the swimming costume and sarong that she was currently wearing, she had: a pair of flip flops; three pairs of black ankle socks; three pairs of knickers; two bras; 2 pairs of shorts; three t-shirts; one fleece top; one bikini; two nighties; toiletries. Very little, and none of it feminine. Anna picked up a beach towel and the Kindle, leaving the two bath towels and hand towel on the bed, and took them downstairs and into the garden. She placed the towel near the top of the steps of the pool, ready for Katerina once she had decided to take a rest from her swimming activity and put the Kindle on the table next to Katerina's lounger.

Katerina rinsed off in the poolside shower and walked across the garden. "Thanks for the towel. Oh, and my Kindle".

"No problem. You're an excellent swimmer, Katya".

"Thank you. I was fortunate that our school had a fantastic pool, and they encouraged us to use it. I joined the swimming team early and stuck with it. We were Regional Champions at one point".

"You must try to keep it going now you've left," encouraged Anna. "It's so good for you, and brilliant for fitness".

"Yes, I intend to. We've all got membership at a local Club, and I use the pool whenever I can, although Chrissy and Ilya seem to be going there less and less. It will be a lot easier for me once I can drive".

"I gather Chrissy bought you a car for your 18th".

"She did. A six-year-old Mini. Only got thirty thousand on the clock. I was very lucky. You were all so generous".

"Now," said Anna as Katerina settled on her lounger having finished drying herself off, "what we were thinking was strolling down to the village in a bit. We'll show you where everything is and how to get to the beach. We can stop off for a drink on the way back, then Charlie is going to do a barbecue. We'll eat on the terrace. Then you can start your holiday for real tomorrow knowing what's available here and within walking distance. We can do some day trips once you've settled in".

"That sounds perfect, thank you".

"What about likes and dislikes?" asked Charlie. "You eat meat? What about shellfish?"

"Yes, I eat meat. I haven't had a lot of shellfish, but I've tried crab, and that was nice. I've never eaten lobster or oysters. I'd be happy to give them a go. Not so sure about frogs' legs or snails".

"We've rarely seen frogs' legs on the menu all the occasions we've been here, but snails are very popular in this area".

"Yes," added Anna, "although neither of us bother with them because they just swamp them with garlic".

"OK. Really, the only things I know I dislike are peanut butter and apricots".

"Snap. Especially together," responded Charlie, grimacing.
"Yes, that would be my worst culinary nightmare".

They returned to the villa two hours later, following Katerina's guided tour of Le Racou. She had pleased Charlie and Anna with her enthusiasm for the beach, and its proximity to their villa. She had also expressed appreciation of the shops, bars and restaurants available within walking distance. They had pointed out the best restaurants, highlighted where she would be able to buy the nicest snack foods and had bought her a cold beer in their favoured bar.

"Right," said Anna as Charlie was preparing their barbecued meal, "come and go as you please while you're here. The beach, a drink in a bar, a meal. Whatever you want to do, just do it. Just let us know you're off so that we don't worry about you".

"Thank you, Anna. Same goes for you two too. Please don't feel that you must entertain me all the time. If you want to go off somewhere yourselves, or have people or places to see, don't worry about leaving me. I'm used to entertaining myself. I'd be fine".

"OK, thanks. You don't spend a lot of time with friends then, at home?"

"Not really. There's a couple of girls that I've got on well with, but we don't seem to have a great deal in common. It's fine if we're out together at a bar or cinema or something but I'm not great at small-talk and I tend to prefer to do what I like, and it's not normally what others want to do".

"Like swimming, you mean?"

"Yes. That, and reading, listening to music, walking. God, I sound dull!"

"No you don't," said Charlie, who had heard what Katerina had been saying as he approached the dining table under the trees, carrying a large plate of food. "Help yourselves".

"Yes, and to bread and salad. Tuck in Katya".

"Looks lovely. What are these?"

"Scallops," answered Charlie. "Give them a try. These are langoustines, large prawns really. See what you think. Don't try to be polite. If you don't like anything, just leave it and let me know so that I try something else next time. So, you said you enjoy reading. What authors in particular?" asked Charlie.

"Well, Tolstoy, of course. I'm obsessed with Anna Karenina. I'm currently reading Dostoevsky".

"Crime and Punishment or The Brothers Karamazov?"

"Have you read them? Don't you think The Brothers Karamazov reflects human behaviour better than any other novel ever written? Actually, I'm re-reading his early novellas at the moment. I'd like to try to identify how his writing style changed over the years. He had a wretched life, and that was surely reflected in his novels".

"Just Russian authors?"

"No, not at all. There's plenty of British and Irish authors I enjoy reading, and I occasionally find myself getting interested in some topic so get stuck into non-fiction books on the subject. I'm at home with Russian literature though, and I'm determined that, at least in my head, Russian remains my first language".

Anna interjected with, "I love hearing you and Ilya speak Russian," then added, "All that stuff you mentioned doesn't seem like holiday reading to me, but there again, Charlie's idea of a light read would be Dickens or Hardy".

"For me, reading is entertainment, and a good book, which makes me think, is more entertaining than one I skip through because it's such an easy read. Sorry, I sound a bit pompous, don't I? I'm not pompous at all, really I'm not".

Charlie responded with, "Nothing wrong with being passionate about books. Look, while you're here, let me suggest you try Don Winslow's Cartel trilogy, if you haven't already read it. Plenty of thought-provoking stuff about the drug trade, and a great read too".

"OK, thanks, I will. I'll download the first one later. How about you, Anna? Do you read much?"

"Not really. I love my horsey magazines, although I normally manage to get through a novel whenever we're in France. Mostly light stuff".

There was a period of relative silence as they ate. Charlie had poured two glasses of Collioure wine, Katerina expressing a preference to stick to beer.

"You also mentioned music. Who in particular?"

"Loads. Nick Drake if I'm feeling contemplative. Nick Cave when I want to lose myself. African music to be uplifted. But then, every time I listen to Radiohead, I wonder why I bother with anyone else".

"Which is your favourite Radiohead album?"

"OK Computer. Not just their best but the best album ever released, in my opinion. Karma Police is awesome".

Anna looked at Charlie in mock panic. "Is she your clone? Have you infiltrated her mind? Used hypnotherapy or something more sinister?"

"What?" asked Katerina, slightly alarmed.

"Well, for a start, Charlie's always listening to Radiohead when I'm not around. And when he owned hundreds of CD's, before it was all streamed, he categorised them by colour. I thought he was bonkers, but he'd say, "I'm in a green mood," and something lively would be played. Or, "Purple, I think," and I'd have to find something to do in another room".

Charlie starting to sing, badly, "For a minute there I lost myself, I lost myself".

Katerina joined in with the next line of lyrics, "Phew, for a minute there I lost myself, I lost myself". She saw him smiling at her and asked, "What's your favourite Radiohead track?"

"Street Spirit, from The Bends album, although Karma Police is right up there. Anna, there's always a decent sprinkling of green and yellow music on, it's not always blue, purple, or black. REM get played often".

Anna scoffed. "Oooh, let's get this party going. Somebody put on Everybody Hurts!"

Katerina laughed. "Perhaps Bad Day or Orange Crush would be better choices for a party?"

"You and I are going to get on famously," said Charlie to Katerina, smugly. "Your taste in music and literature is impeccable".

Anna sat back, amused and at ease, and watched the two of them converse.

As they were preparing for bed, after Katerina had insisted on clearing the table and stacking the dishwasher, Anna said to her, "Charlie and I are creatures of habit. In the summer, during the season when it's hot and crowded, we normally get up around 7, maybe have a quick coffee and juice before strolling down to the beach for a swim. We buy pastries and baguettes on the way back, then eat our breakfast here. You are more than welcome to join us any morning, but if you prefer to have a lie in, we won't disturb you before we leave".

"I would love to do that. It sounds perfect if you don't mind me dragging along with you".

"Well, that's great. We'll all go off together in the morning".

"Excellent," added Charlie. "I get the coffee and juice sorted before we go. Shall I get something for you too?"

"I'd love a coffee thanks. And a juice too if it's not too much trouble".

"Orange, apple or grapefruit?"

"Grapefruit, please".

Anna finished off by saying, "If you change your mind any morning, there's a 'Do Not Disturb' notice hanging up in your room. Just put it on the door handle".

"OK, but I don't think that will be necessary. Good night. Thank you for making me feel so welcome".

"Good night, Katya," Anna and Charlie replied, in unison.

Charlie tapped lightly on Katerina's bedroom door at 7.10 the following morning.

"Come in".

Charlie entered, carrying a small tray. "Good morning. Sleep well? I forgot to ask last night if you have cream or sugar with your coffee, so I've brought them both," he said as he put the tray on a coffee table which was placed in a corner of the room.

"A spot of cream, but I don't take sugar". Katerina was already dressed, wearing a t-shirt, shorts and flip flops. "I've got my bikini on under these, so I'm ready to go whenever you are". She added cream from the jug to her coffee then picked up and sipped her glass of grapefruit juice.

"OK, good. We'll give you a shout".

"I'll be in the garden. Want to make the most of this weather".

"Very wise. See you in a bit," and Charlie left her to it so that he could take Anna's coffee to her before it got cold.

They all entered the sea together, and Charlie sloshed around a while whereas Anna and Katerina swam away from the beach, both using strong breast stokes. He watched as they eventually stopped swimming, trod water, and chatted, before swimming back to join him.

"I've explained to Katya that you're brilliant at just about everything you do Charlie, except for swimming".

"Actually, to be truthful, I'm poor at one or two other things too, but thank you for reassuring her that I'm not a total numpty".

The girls laughed, and the three strolled across the beach to collect their towels for a quick dry-off before they walked to the boulangerie.

"That was absolutely gorgeous," exclaimed Katerina. "What a way to start a day".

"You hungry?"

"Starving".

"Good. Let's go and get breakfast sorted. Shall I buy them while you two stroll back, or would you like to choose what you'd like Katya?"

"No, I'm happy to leave it to you, Charlie. Anna and I could go straight back, and perhaps Anna could show me how the coffee machine works so I can sort drinks for us for when you get back".

"Good idea," said Anna. "I'll have a croissant please Charlie".

By the time Charlie returned to the villa, carrying two baguettes and a large bag of assorted pastries, the large table on the patio was laid with plates and cutlery, a jug of water and glasses, a small jug of cream, a pot of strawberry jam and another of butter. Anna was sitting at the table flicking through a magazine. Charlie placed the food on the table and heard Katerina shout from the kitchen window, "Coffee Charlie? I'm making us one".

"Yes please".

"Have you two planned anything for the day?" Charlie asked Anna.

"We've chatted about it and Katya seems to be content to spend the next few days here. I think she just wants to use the pool and relax with her Kindle. I've an idea she'd quite like to get a bit of a tan too".

"She's rather white, isn't she? She'll need to be careful".

"I've said that to her. She's promised she'll keep topping up her factor 30".

Katerina joined them, carrying a tray holding three mugs of coffee. "Let me know if I haven't got the strength right".

"Thanks Katya," said Charlie, taking a sip from the mug Katerina had placed in front of him. "No, that's perfect. Tuck in. Croissants, pains au chocolat, pains au raisin, baguette. Please, whatever you want. I've bought too many, so take whatever you want".

After they'd eaten, Katerina insisted once again on clearing the table. "Shall I put the dishwasher on? It'll be nearly full, with this lot and the dinner things from last night".

"That'll be great, thanks," replied Anna. "Should be straightforward but give me a shout if you can't get it to work. Dishwasher tablets are in the cupboard under the sink".

Twenty minutes later, Anna was lying on her back on a sunbed on the patio outside the French doors, Charlie was on a lounger in the shade of the trees, reading his Kindle, and Katerina was circumnavigating the pool, dragging a net through the water to collect bugs and leaves. Charlie stopped reading to watch her. 'What a sweet girl,' he thought. 'She couldn't have been more polite or thoughtful. Very mature to chat with, especially when we're on her favoured topics. Yes, I really like talking to her. Still hasn't developed a woman's body, though. Yes, her body is much younger than her mind'. However much he tried, he couldn't recall at what stage a girl's form finishes being shaped.

As he thought these thoughts while assessing Katerina, he hadn't realised that Anna had raised herself on the sunbed and had been contemplating her husband. She moved her gaze from Charlie to Katerina. It was the first chance she'd really had to fully consider the girl's appearance. 'She can definitely make more of herself. She's got a lovely face. Eastern European bone structure. Almost boy-ish. Small features, prominent cheek bones, a sort of concerned expression, but also a ready, open, smile'. Anna considered this further. 'Yes, that face needs a shorter hair style. She has lovely dark hair, almost black, but it's too thick and long for her delicate features. Her eyes are very dark too, and short hair would make them stand out. She'll develop a lovely figure. That bikini doesn't fit her terribly well, but she has a decent bust already and goes in nicely at the waist. Her hips are narrow, but her legs are her best feature. Very shapely thighs and slim calves. What must she be, 5' 3 or 4"? Yes, a bit shorter than I am. No doubt about it, she could make more of herself. Maybe if she did, she'd get that boyfriend Chrissy keeps banging on about'. Anna looked away from Katerina and back at Charlie. He had reclined his lounger and appeared to be snoozing. She looked back at Katerina, who was now sitting on the edge of the pool, with her legs dangling in the water.

Anna raised herself from the sunbed and walked over to Charlie, who looked up on hearing her approach. "Sorry to disturb you, Charlie, but would you mind taking one of the parasols, the big one is best, and making sure that Katya is in the shade. I don't think she should have too much sun until she's been here a while".

"Yes, good point". Charlie walked over to Katerina and positioned a parasol by the side of the pool. She watched him and said, "Thanks Charlie. I was feeling my shoulders start to burn a bit but couldn't be bothered to move. This is so lovely".

"No problem. Anna thinks it best if you limit your time in the sun for your first few days. Once your skin is used to it there'll be less of a risk. Keep topping up with lotion though".

"Yes, I will. Promise".

Charlie decided to have a quick dip while he was up. Katya watched him from the side.

"It's a lovely pool," she said.

"Thanks. We were very lucky. The previous owners had only recently had it installed when they needed to sell the villa for some reason. It had hardly been used".

"Mind if I join you for a quick one before I go and have a sit under the trees?"

"Not at all".

That was how they spent the rest of the day: in and out of the pool, alternating sun and shade. It was also how they spent the following day after their early morning swim in the sea.

BOOK TWO: *THE IDIOT*

It was during Katerina's third full day that Anna decided that she would ask Katerina if she would like to join her in a shopping and pampering trip to Perpignan. She wanted to choose her moment and words carefully as her intention was to help Katerina maximise her assets without making her feel any shame about her current appearance.

Katerina was sitting on the edge of the pool, under the parasol, with her legs in the water, reading her Kindle, and Anna was swimming slow, methodical lengths. After a while she swam over to Katerina and placed her forearms on the side of the pool to hold herself up.

"I'm going to book myself a trip to a hair salon I use in Perpignan when we're on one of our long stays. They also do manicures and pedicures, that sort of thing. Do you fancy keeping me company? We could have our hair and nails done together".

"It's lovely of you to ask me Anna but I haven't really got any money for that sort of thing. I feel bad enough as it is with you paying for my flights and providing everything here for me".

"Don't be silly. What girl of eighteen has money when they've only just finished school? Look, you're sensible enough to take this the right way: Charlie and I are anything but short of money. To be honest, we can't spend the income that's coming in, let alone the money we've got put by. I can't tell you how much pleasure it would give me to treat you to a day out in Perpignan. Hair and beauty salon, shopping, and lunch. We could buy you a few clothes so that you've got more choice of things to wear while you're here. On me. How about it?"

Katerina looked intently at her, and hesitated. "Oh, I don't know".

"Let me tell you what Charlie once said to me, many years ago. Most of the times when we appear to be undecided, we've already made the decision. It's instantaneous. We then spend ages justifying that decision to ourselves before finally voicing it. I mean it, Katya. It would honestly give me great pleasure. In fact, it would sadden me if you felt greedy or selfish or anything like that. Come on, let's have our hair done, get pampered, stock up our wardrobes and have a chatty lunch".

"OK, I'd love to. But so long as I buy the lunch".

"Deal. I'll go and book the appointments". Anna hauled herself out of the pool, grabbed her towel and walked towards the villa.

"Anna," shouted Katerina. Anna turned. "Thank you". Anna smiled, waved, and continued into the building.

When Anna returned to the garden, Charlie was on a lounger in the shade, and Katerina was lying next to him, on a sun bed, which Charlie had carried over from the patio.

"You'll be spending most of the day on your own tomorrow, Charlie".

"Oh, why's that?"

"Katya and I will be in Perpignan. We're shopping in the morning then Katya's buying me lunch. In the afternoon we'll be at the salon. Katya's having a manicure, pedicure, and leg wax while I'm having my hair done, then we're swapping over. We'll be back some time in the afternoon. Maybe we could eat out tomorrow evening".

"Have you booked it already, Anna?" asked Katerina.

"Yes. Got lucky. You're in the beauty salon at 2 and I'll be in the hair salon next door. We change places at 3. Back home about 4.30. Shower, change, pre-dinner drinks in the garden then out to a restaurant in the village".

"Sounds good," said Charlie.

"That's great Anna. How exciting!" Anna smiled at her, feeling very pleased with herself.

The following morning, with Anna driving her to Perpignan, Katerina asked, "Would you mind guiding me a bit when we're in the clothes shops?"

"Sure. What trend are you going for?"

"Yours".

"In what way?"

"Every time I've seen you since we first met you've been classy, feminine, and sexy. You always look terrific. I don't have your looks, but I'd like to try emulating your style as best I can".

"That's a nice thing to say. Yes, let's keep classy, feminine, and sexy in mind while we're checking through the racks".

"I guess you haven't thought feminine and sexy would be my thing, bearing in mind what you've seen me wearing".

"I wouldn't say that, Katya. I realise you wouldn't have had a lot of money to spare, and, for many people, new clothes aren't on their priority list".

"That's part of it. But there's more to it than that".

"Do you want to tell me?"

"I'll tell you more some other time. Let's just leave it for the moment that I haven't particularly wanted to be attractive to boys".

"Girls?"

"No, not girls".

"And you feel differently now?"

Katerina laughed. "Thankfully, the boys I'm referring to are all hundreds of miles away!"

Anna turned to face her and smiled. "Let's go for it, girl. We're going to have fun today".

It took over three hours of dedicated shopping before Anna would agree that they were done and that they should carry the bags back to the car before going to lunch. She had made a mental list of Katerina's requirements, and she was finally satisfied that it was mission accomplished: cream sandals; white trainers; linen trousers; two pairs of shorts; three skirts—one short A-line, one knee length pleated, one short straight; two summer dresses—one floral with a close-fitted bodice and a mid-thigh length flared skirt, one block coloured figure-hugging with a skirt which finished just above the knee; one cream blouse; one white, short-sleeved shirt with a light blue pin stripe; two polo shirts; one navy-blue linen jacket; three bra and knicker sets; two bikinis; one sheer beach dress; a pair of Rayban sunglasses; a straw trilby; a travel bag, bearing in mind the backpack would not be large enough to convey Katerina's possessions home.

Anna selected three tapas plates for the two of them to share, choosing the less expensive meals bearing in mind Katerina's insistence that she would pay for lunch.

"I just can't thank you enough, Anna. I've had the most wonderful morning and I absolutely love the clothes you helped me to select. Thank you so, so much".

"Please Katya, it really is my pleasure. I can't wait to see you in them all. We must make sure that you don't go home before you've tried them all out".

"Definitely. And you must wear that new dress you bought too. It's fantastic. You look absolutely gorgeous in it".

"Thanks. Yes, I'm really pleased with it. Charlie will love it too".

"I'm sure he will. By the way, how do you think I should have my hair done?"

"Yes, it's important we get that right. I've been thinking about it, and I have a style in mind which I think you should go for. We can ask the stylist her opinion before deciding. She speaks perfect English so it will be fine".

"What's the style?"

"Well, we recently watched a TV documentary called 'My Generation'. Twiggy was in it. She was a famous model way back before Kate Moss. Her facial features were like yours, and she had very short hair, which was probably radical at the time, but it was perfect for her. I think you should be bold and go for that".

"I don't know whether I'm that brave".

"Well, have a think about it, but don't decide until we've spoken to the stylist and looked at some photos. By the way, when you see the beautician, she'll be giving you a bikini wax, as well as waxing your legs and doing your nails. You OK with that?"

"Yes, that's good. I want to feel comfortable wearing my new bikinis".

It was nearly 6pm when they returned to the villa. Just before they pulled into the drive Anna said, "How about eating here tonight rather than going out. I'm still stuffed from lunch, and it may be nice to just chill out after a hot and busy day in the city. We could eat out tomorrow night instead".

"I was hoping you'd suggest that. I agree".

Charlie slipped on a pair of shorts and t-shirt as Anna switched off the engine. As the girls hauled the various bags out of the boot, Charlie said, "Well, there's no point in me asking if you've had a good day". He turned to look at Katerina. "Wow, Katya, you look terrific. I love your hair".

Katerina gave him an embarrassed smile and self-consciously ruffed up her fringe. "Thank you. I love it, but it's going to take a bit of getting used to".

"Well, I mean it. It really suits you. You've a lovely face, and that short style sets it off perfectly".

"I'm pleased you think so, Charlie. Katya took a bit of a risk and was very trusting. But I agree, it's perfect for her. By the way, we've decided to eat here, if that's OK. Katya bought us a lovely lunch, and just a light supper will suit us. Plus, we're a bit knackered. I realise you won't have eaten much but I can easily knock something up for you".

"No need for that. I'm happy with cheese and meats. There are prawns in the fridge still, and there's plenty of baguette left. I'll be fine".

"Great. We'll eat out tomorrow, and Katya can show off a new outfit".

"What did you get, Katya?"

"No, don't tell him. You can give us a fashion display later".

"OK," replied Katerina. "I'll take the bags up to my room and have a shower. Shall I come down in one of the outfits and join you in the garden?"

"Good idea. I'll pop up for a shower too. Charlie, could you sort the drinks out? A long G&T for me please. Ice and lime".

"No problem. What would you like Katya?"

"I'd like a gin and tonic too please. Not too strong. Ice and lime for me as well".

"They'll be on the table for when you both come down. Hey, is that something new for you too Anna?" he asked, pointing to the bag Anna was carrying into the villa.

"Yes, a new dress. Couldn't resist it".

"She had to get it Charlie. It's perfect for her. You'll love the neckline".

The two girls mounted the stairs and Charlie went into the kitchen. Twenty minutes later the three were sitting at the table under the trees sipping their drinks. Charlie had admired Katerina's new shorts and polo shirt, and she had agreed to model her other new purchases after she'd relaxed a while.

After they'd finished eating, and Katerina felt mellow from the gin, she agreed to participate in a fashion show. Initially, she showed off the other shorts and polo shirt worn with the trainers, then the trousers with the pinstripe shirt, sandals, and linen jacket.

"Now the A-line skirt with the blouse," insisted Anna. "I think they go really well together".

Once that combination had been admired by Charlie, Anna said, "Keep the blouse on and pair it with the pleated skirt". Charlie said that he thought that looked even nicer, although secretly he preferred the short A-line skirt.

"What does that leave?" asked Anna. "The dresses, of course, and that lovely straight skirt. Tell you what, put one of the bikinis on and wear the skirt too. That'll look great with the bikini top, then you can take the skirt off to show off the bikini".

Katerina was beginning to warm to showing off her new clothes and rather enjoyed a dramatic removal of the skirt.

"Love it," said Anna. "That's a really flattering bikini. Really shows off your figure. Right, now the other one and the beach dress. Wear the hat and Raybans too".

Katerina complied, and Charlie agreed that this bikini was even nicer than the previous one. "Very sexy with the hat," he risked saying.

"Tell you what," said Anna, "hold back the dresses until we go out somewhere. What does that leave? Just the lingerie, I think. To save embarrassing my husband perhaps it's best you don't model those. Katya, your new hairstyle, those fabulous clothes, your lovely face and terrific figure. You should feel very good about yourself".

"I do, Anna. And it's all thanks to you".

"OK, go get your comfortable clothes back on and we'll finish the evening off with a nightcap if you like".

"Actually, I think I'm ready for bed after the day's excitement. I'll just clear this lot away then I'll go up".

"No, leave it Katya, I'll do it, thanks," said Charlie.

"You sure? Thank you. Good night. See you in the morning".

They watched her walk back to the villa, then Charlie said, "Did you come home with the same girl?"

"Lovely to see, isn't it? Something's being going on. She's like one of those Russian doll sets: she looks good from the outside but there's several layers of her. The real Katerina is inside what she's been prepared to reveal. I'm fairly confident that she's starting to emerge".

BOOK TWO: *THE IDIOT*

CHAPTER 10

They enjoyed several languid days, with their routine maintained: coffee and juice; dip in the sea; breakfast in the garden; sunbathe; swim in the pool; lunch; sunbathe; another swim in the pool; drinks, either in the garden or at a local bar; meal, either in the garden or at a local restaurant. Katerina became increasingly relaxed, and her mood was further brightened by a phone call she received from Chrissy.

"Yes, it's fine. Go ahead and open it". A delay as she listened, and then, "OK that's great. Thanks". More listening before, "Thank you. Yes, I'm very pleased. I'll tell Anna and Charlie now. And I'm having a lovely holiday, thank you. I'll let you know as soon as we've sorted when I'm flying back".

Once she'd finished the call she said to Anna and Charlie, "That was Chrissy, phoning about my A' Level results. A-star in both French and English Lit and A in Philosophy".

"Katya, that's wonderful," responded Anna, excitedly. "You must be thrilled".

"I am, yes. Thanks".

"Delighted for you, Katya. We'll have Champagne with our lunch," added Charlie.

"What are your plans, Katya?" enquired Anna.

"I've one or two thoughts. Certainly not Uni. I'll let you know as soon as I've firmed something up. Listen, I'm probably outstaying my welcome. Do you think we should get my flight home sorted?"

"We won't hear of it, will we Charlie? Not unless you want to go. You're certainly not outstaying your welcome, and we've still loads to do while you're here".

"Absolutely," confirmed Charlie. "You don't want to go back yet, do you?"

"No, not at all. But you guys must want some time on your own".

"We have plenty of time together, don't you worry about that. No, stay for as long as you like. If you've something to get back for, then fine. Otherwise, forget about flights for the time being".

"Well, that's great, thank you. I'm loving it here".

One morning, as Charlie rose to sort the morning drinks, Anna said, "I'm thinking of a change of scene today. Would you mind if Katya and I spent the morning at the beach together? We could just have cereals and toast for breakfast, then I could pick up some lunch on the way back from the beach. It would be nice for the three of us to eat out this evening too".

"Nice idea. Do you want me to tell Katya when I take in her coffee and juice?"

"Yes please".

They were on the beach before 9am, planted their beach chairs and parasol, and laid out their towels. After a long swim they lay on the towels to allow the sun to dry them off. After a while, Anna sat up and said, "Shall we spend a bit of time in the shade. Maybe you could tell me what was on your mind last week. About why you haven't wanted to be attractive to boys".

Katerina hesitated, then agreed. Once settled, Anna took from the cool bag a bottle of mineral water for them to share.

"Ilya was the first to give me cause to feel the way I do. There's been plenty of others since".

"Oh dear, I was hoping that Ilya hadn't been involved in this. What did he do?"

"It's a combination of things. He propositioned me when I was fourteen. I made it clear he'd have to look elsewhere. Since then, apart from one occasion, he's not tried anything with me other than make suggestive remarks, but, over the past few years, I've hated his attitude to girls. He's had girlfriends who I think he treated badly. In fairness, he's been much better recently but, when his mates have been round, I've heard them bragging about what they've done, or what they're going to do with girlfriends. Not that long ago, one of them said to him, "Do you reckon your sister would toss me off if I asked her nicely?" I was there when he said it. Ilya just replied, "She's not my sister, but yeah, I reckon she'd enjoy it"".

"Katya, that's horrible".

"It is, isn't it? What made it worse was that I knew why Ilya said that. That I'd enjoy it I mean. It was hurtful of him not to blank his mate, but I knew why he said it".

"Why?"

"That was the other occasion I was referring to. I got home from school one day, a day Chrissy was at work, and Ilya was home. I called out to say hello and that I was making a cup of tea if he'd like one too. I assumed he was in his room, studying. When I took his tea in, he was lying on his bed, naked. He had his laptop open by his side and he was masturbating".

"What, knowing you'd be going in there? What happened?"

"I just stopped in my tracks, still holding his mug. I think I just said, "Ilya!" He carried on looking at his laptop while he rubbed himself. Didn't even look up at me. I put the mug on his bedside table and turned to go back out. He said, "Katerina, stay". I turned to look at him. I should have just carried on walking, but I didn't. I could see the screen of his computer. It was some porn site. That's what Ilya was watching while he masturbated. For some reason I was transfixed. I'd never seen a boy's penis before. You know, in real life, erect. Part of me wanted to watch to see what happened. Ilya realised I wasn't leaving, and he carried on. After a short while, I left him to it before he had finished".

"And how did you feel afterwards".

"Dirty. Dirty, but sexually aroused".

"Dirty because you stayed to watch?"

"Yes. I shouldn't have done that. Look, I know boys masturbate. I know they can't help it. But they should keep it to themselves, shouldn't they?"

"Most definitely".

"He has, though, behaved much better since he left school. But while Ilya has been much nicer to me and stopped tormenting me, the boys at school are just as annoying. I've noticed the way they look at me and other girls. It's not appreciative. It's leering. Like they want to just do to us whatever it is that turns them on. No thought about what we may want or not want. Some of the things they say to me are shameful, and degrading".

"Yes, I can see why you're put off and want to stay out of the limelight. So, you've not had a boyfriend at all?"

"No. It's only recently that it's started to bother me. I haven't wanted to put myself through all that. But I know seeing Ilya like that aroused me at the time, and I've thought about it more as I've got older. I'm ashamed to admit it, but that's the way it is. But I can't see how I'm ever going to have the confidence to be with a boy when I know how they think and what they want to do with me, like they've seen on their porn sites. And what they say to their friends".

"Oh Katya".

"I've never touched or been touched. I've seen one penis but that was on show, for his gratification, not mine. I've not even been properly kissed for Christ's sake!" Katerina was nearly in tears.

"Do you know what it's like to have an orgasm?"

"Yes, masturbation is lovely, but surely it can't be the same as when you're with somebody else, can it? I reckon I'll be a virgin for years, until I'm old enough to attract a man who doesn't think the way boys do".

"I understand you, Katya, if that's any help. It can't be easy for girls of your age in this internet porn generation. When I was your age, yes, boys masturbated, and probably looked at us girls with longing. But their imaginations weren't filled by visions of gangbangs, girlfriend abuse or whatever else they ogle now. Of course, there were porn films, but it wasn't easy for a boy to go into a shop and buy one, and then play it on the family TV. I was groped and propositioned, which was unacceptable, of course, but it was all reasonably harmless compared to what you're describing".

"So, you agree then? Succumb to it or stay the way I am for a few more years?" Katerina's bottom lip trembled with her ardour. "Unless".

"Unless what?"

"Unless you say no".

Anna smiled. "Come on Katya, unless I say no to what?"

She hesitated, then, "Oh, nothing. I shouldn't have said anything".

Anna let it be. "Let's go and have a swim to cool down a bit. We'll then come back and talk about it some more".

They thrashed and larked about in the Med as if they hadn't a care in the world and were a couple of friends on an annual holiday. When they returned to their spot on the beach Anna said, "Stay here, I'll go and buy a couple of cold beers to drink while we're addressing this problem of yours. As Charlie says when I'm down, "There's always a solution. Use your energy to find it". Back in a mo'".

A quarter of an hour later, Anna resumed, this time with them both sitting in the shade, sipping a beer. "Katya, you do know, don't you, that you are not alone in finding a solution to this? I'm here for you at any time. That's while you're with us on holiday, and when we're all back in England. Charlie too. Please trust me when I tell you that, although you feel desperate now, you'll find a way through it. *We'll* find a way through it".

"That's kind of you to say, but it seems that only time will get me through this. Time and finding a decent boy. If only there was a young Charlie available. I can't imagine that he was ever like Ilya or his friends, even at their age".

"No, you're probably right. He has been respectful of me from the day I met him. And he's always been mindful of the vulnerabilities of females and the less endearing traits of males. Despite what you've told me, I do believe that, in the main, Ilya is a lovely lad. He's polite, good company, honest. It just seems to be the sex thing that's been letting him down. To give him some benefit of the doubt, it's probably quite difficult for a lad of his age, these days. I'm not excusing him, not for a moment, but I'm simply suggesting that he will probably become a decent partner before too long".

"I've thought about this a lot. It seems clear that it will only be when I've met someone older, someone who's gone through the stage Ilya was grappling with, that I'm likely to be treated the way I want to be and deserve to be. The trouble is, I don't want to wait. I'm ready now. I'm eighteen and I don't want to be in my twenties before I experience what you and Charlie enjoy together".

"Don't you think that, once you've started work and are mixing with adults rather than students, you're likely to find who you're looking for?"

"Maybe. I hope you're right". Katerina paused, then added, "Anna, sex is all it's cracked up to be, isn't it? I'm not going to be disappointed, even when I've got lucky with a partner, am I?"

Anna laughed. "Oh, Katya, you are in a state, aren't you?! Look, you may have noticed that Charlie and I are very close, but Charlie wasn't my first boyfriend, and I'd had sex with previous guys. I found out quickly that I loved what the boys did to me, and I also loved doing things to them. Don't worry Katya, sex is fantastic. It's extra special with Charlie, though".

"That's been obvious to me this holiday".

"Have you heard that Billy Connolly observation: 'they say that women can't have sex unless they feel loved. And men can't feel loved unless they have sex. We're screwed'. Like so much of his humour, it's based on truth. Where Charlie and I succeed is that I feel loved by him all the time, so having sex with him is easy, and as we have sex a lot, he feels loved by me, in the way that men need the reassurance which only having sex provides for them.

"There are not many men who are as considerate with their partner as Charlie is with me, but not all boys or men behave the way Ilya, his mates and your male school friends have. As I said, I had some very enjoyable sex with the boyfriends I was with before Charlie.

"It's that old conundrum: all of this will be so much easier for you after you've had some experience, but it's too difficult for you at present to get that experience. Life's a bastard, in other words".

Katerina laughed in acknowledgement, then asked, "What age were you when you first had sex?"

"I think I was fourteen, when I allowed a boyfriend to put his hand inside my bra and pants. It wasn't anything more than that, just a bit of experimental fondling. I found that I enjoyed it, so was quite happy to go further. I remember acting a bit coy and shocked when he finally plucked up the courage to ask me to touch his prick".

"Were you fourteen then?"

"Yeah, I think I must have been. I don't think all girls are the same, but I loved the fact that my boyfriend got an erection through looking at me or touching me. Some of my friends seemed to be grossed out by it, but I've always thought it's flattering. Anyway, I had fun, even though I remember thinking what a bloody mess it was, the first time I made my boyfriend come".

"And what about when you first had sex? Made love, I mean".

"That would have been a bit later, with another boyfriend. I really liked him. I would have been sixteen, I guess. It was his first time too. A bit of a shambles, really, but I still enjoyed it. Couldn't wait to do it again".

Katerina didn't respond; she immersed herself in thought. It was clear to Anna that Katerina was digesting what Anna had been saying to her, so she allowed her some time before she asked, "Unless I say no to what?"

"Pardon?"

"That's what you said earlier, then stopped yourself". Katerina turned to face Anna, and it was clear that she was embarrassed and had been battling with deciding whether to share her thoughts.

"Anna, please don't be cross with me".

"Why on earth should I be cross?"

"Because I'm going to ask you something. I'm asking not because I feel desperate, or because you've offered to help me, but because I feel strongly about something. But you mustn't be cross. I'd hate it if you thought badly of me".

"Katya, for goodness' sake, relax. Say whatever it is you want to say. I'm far too fond of you for us to fall out over anything you might say to me or ask. Come on, take a deep breath, relax, and tell me what's on your mind".

"OK. Well, I'm going to come straight out with it. I want to ask if Charlie would help me".

"I've said that we will both do what we can to get you through this".

"Yes, but this is more than that. What I mean is I'd like Charlie to educate me".

Anna digested this, then asked, "Do you mean sexually?"

"Yes, but not just him, of course. I'd like him to educate me physically and you to guide me".

"Let me just check to make sure I've got this right. Are you saying that you'd like you and Charlie to be intimate, sexually?"

"Oh god, I shouldn't have asked. I'm so sorry. Please don't be cross with me".

"Katya, calm down. I'm not cross, I'm simply making sure we're both on the same wavelength before I respond. Is that what you're asking, to have sexual experiences with Charlie? Talk to me, Katya. This is too important for you not to say exactly what's on your mind".

"Well, the way I see it is this, and believe me Anna, this has been going through my mind for a while, not just this morning, while we've been talking. What I want to say is the three of us are together, here in this ideal environment. It's warm, comfortable, and non-threatening. You and Charlie have a cast iron relationship. He's kind and caring. You say he's a wonderful lover. I'm asking if Charlie can be the person who helps me to understand a man's body and who shows me what pleasures a man can give me. I know it's a selfish thing to ask, but I honestly feel that it would make a massive difference to my life if I knew what it was all about".

After a period of complete silence, Katerina put her head in her hands, fearing Anna's reaction and response. A minute later she said, "Say something, please, even if it's that you're going to book the first flight home for me".

"Katya, my first thought is to be pleased that you feel you can share that with me. My second is that most girls with those thoughts would choose to flirt with the man, which isn't difficult for an attractive young girl on a beach or around a swimming pool in a private garden".

"I wouldn't do that".

"I know, that's what I'm saying". She paused again. "Let me have a think about it".

"OK. And you're not cross with me?"

"I'm not cross with you, I promise". Anna rose and said, "I think it's time to go back. Charlie will be wanting his lunch, and I don't know about you but I'm starting to feel a bit peckish".

"Yes, I'm ready".

"And Katya, I'm not cross. Surprised, definitely, but not in a bad way I don't think. I'll give it some thought and will either let you know if I believe it to be a bad idea or talk to Charlie about it to find out what he thinks".

"Could you promise not to say anything to Charlie if you decide it's not a good idea? Only talk to him if you're seriously considering it?"

"Yes, I promise. Come on," and she took Katerina's hand as they started the short walk back to the villa.

Katerina offered to clear away after lunch, but Charlie insisted she should enjoy the afternoon in the garden and pool. Once she was engrossed in the novel she was reading, Anna left her and joined Charlie in the villa. "Charlie, I need to run something past you. About Katya".

"Sure. Is she OK?"

"Yes and no". Anna assured him that Katerina was greatly enjoying her holiday with them, then proceeded to relay details of Katerina's issues with boys.

"Poor girl. I recall very clearly what lads of her age think and say".

"It's really damaging her enjoyment of life, and her prospects too, I think".

"It's not an easy one for a girl like her. It'll get better, though, now she's left school".

"It will, although that hasn't stopped her from asking for help from us".

"I'm sure you've been talking to her about it all. That must have reassured her a bit. I'm happy to chat to her too if you think it would help".

"Look, I'll tell you straight what she's asked. She'd like you to provide some hands-on experience, under my guidance".

"How do you mean?"

"She's asked if you can demonstrate how a male can give a female pleasure in a respectful way. Educate her physically, are her words".

Charlie looked puzzled. "How could I do that?"

"Bloody hell, Charlie, I'm trying to tell you what she believes would greatly help her, without sounding too blunt about it. She wants you to educate her, sexually".

"You're kidding. Well, that's awkward".

"In what way?"

"Her holiday, with us. Won't you feel awkward knowing what she's been thinking about?"

"I think we should agree to it".

Charlie no longer looked puzzled, but amazed. "You think we should agree to me being sexual with Katya?"

"Yes, but not in that way".

"What do you mean, not in that way?"

"Charlie, she's been desperately unhappy. We don't want her to feel like that, do we? She's ready to fly. This is the one thing holding her back. She's eighteen, an adult. Let's face it, she's more mature than most of my friends my age. She wants to be an attractive, outgoing, young lady, but is terrified of how that is going to be interpreted. She's convinced that if she knew how to deal with the opposite sex, she'd be in control of the situations she's bound to find herself in. You know her well enough to understand that".

"But this is what we've all had to face. It's not easy for anyone who feels ready to be sexual. She'll just have to go through trial and error once she gets a boyfriend".

"Some crappy lad who thinks it's fine to shove his cock down her throat and half-strangle her as he bends her double over a table!"

"Anna!"

"No, I mean it. I'd hate to go through it all now. I feel very sorry for her".

"Not every boy would behave like that".

"No, of course not. You and I know that, but Katya has good reason to believe that's the sort of thing she'd have to put up with. And she'd expect the little shit to brag about it to his mates, too".

Charlie pondered. "You seriously believe this is a good idea, don't you?"

"Yes, I do. Just consider it as you would if you didn't know the person involved. You're aware there's a young adult who dresses in jeans and shapeless T-shirts, hiding behind her hair, trying to conceal the fact that she's shapely and attractive, who gives herself orgasms but wants more, and sees nothing but fog in front of her. What would you say is the ideal process to help her to clear the fog and start being confident about herself and in control of her life?"

He thought hard before responding. "Yes, OK, I take your point".

"If you were the one to provide her first experiences, she'd appreciate how enjoyable it is and worth the effort. She'd also understand how everything looks and feels, which would give her so much confidence, and, just as important, she'd have a standard, something against which she can measure the way boyfriends behave. If they don't treat her properly, which they probably won't, she'd recognise it and be able to deal with it".

"And what role would you play in all this?"

"Instruction, reassurance, being on hand if she wishes to bale out. Just making sure she's OK throughout it all".

"What sort of things would I be doing?"

"Well, making her comfortable with being an attractive female would be a good starting point. Getting her to realise that attractive females don't need to be thought of as whores or vassals".

"So, I'd be appreciative and respectful".

"Well, of course. You couldn't be anything but. And once she understands that is how you behave, even when she is naked and available to you, she'll begin to realise it's an advantage being desirable, not a reason to feel vulnerable".

"I'd see her naked, then? Available in what way?"

"Jesus, Charlie, you're not making this easy. I would expect you to give her pleasure. I want her to know a girl gets pleasure from it. That it's not simply a case that a girl is there to provide an opportunity for a guy to get his rocks off".

"You're telling me I should have sex with her?"

"No, not sex, but sexual pleasure".

"Well, if not sex, what? I'm not being dumb or difficult, but I do need you to spell it out, Anna, because I couldn't risk getting this horribly wrong".

"How do you get me to feel desired and appreciated? How do you get me to feel great that I look the way I do? What do you do to get me to experience the wonders of arousal and where it leads?"

"You know how".

"So do you". She watched him process all that they had discussed, then followed up with, "Well then, yes, or no?"

He poured himself a glass of water and drank half of it before announcing his decision. "Although I'm finding this somewhat surreal, OK, but stage by stage. We'll start slowly and see how she and I feel about it. You too. You must make it clear to her that if she feels threatened or uncomfortable, she tells you immediately. And to be frank with you, I'm attracted to her. What man wouldn't be? It won't be easy to keep natural desires at bay. If they start taking control, I'm out, before it gets dangerous. And don't underestimate how difficult it may be for you, watching me doing what you've suggested".

"Yes, fair enough. I agree with all that. I'll deal with all the arrangements and make sure each of us remains comfortable. It's the right thing,

Charlie, I'm convinced of it. That girl can be a superstar. A couple of weeks, that's all it will take, and then she can launch herself".

Katerina was the first to go in for a shower and to get changed into the clothes that she had decided to wear to the restaurant. Anna was waiting for her as she exited her bedroom. "Oh, hi Anna, am I making you late?"

"No, not at all. I just wanted a quiet word with you before we go. Look, you were emotional this morning on the beach, and I want you to have another think about what you asked. This is very important".

"I don't have to think about it anymore than I have. I know it's far too much for me to expect of you, and I'm fully prepared for you to say it's completely out of the question. But if you're asking me if I've thought better of it, the answer's no. I'm not a silly little schoolgirl acting on a crush. In fact, I think I'm rational, even compared to people much older. I'm asking because I truly believe it would help me. But Anna, I mean it, I don't expect you to agree to it, and that's fine".

"OK. Right, let's go and eat".

Before long, they were walking through the gates onto the lane to the village. "That dress is gorgeous, Katya. You look fantastic in it".

"Thank you, Charlie. Anna insisted on it in the shop". It was the tight-fitting scarlet one with the longer length skirt. She hadn't worn either dress up until then and had decided when in the shower to save the short one for another time.

It was still reasonably early when they left the restaurant, and, as they approached the villa, Anna said, "Charlie and I have spoken about it, Katya, and we're both prepared to help you, if you still want to do what we were talking about on the beach".

"Erm, yes, I haven't changed my mind. Are you sure you both think it's a good idea?"

"We wouldn't be agreeing to it unless it was clear to us that it is what you want, and that, even although it's rather an extreme thing to be doing, it makes sense".

"Makes sense because...?"

"Makes sense because we agree that it's the best way for you to overcome the problems which have been making you unhappy, and for you to return to England with the confidence to take control of situations you're going to be faced with. With the opposite sex, I mean".

Katerina stopped walking and waited until Anna and Charlie had turned to look at her. "Thank you for understanding me".

"Some caveats though, which Charlie and I both agree on. No intercourse. Charlie won't be making love to you, and we do it exactly as I say. Plus, if you want to stop at any time, we stop. That goes for Charlie and me too. No debate. No embarrassment. No apologies. We just stop and carry on enjoying the holiday together".

"Yes, of course. I agree". She paused, then added, "I'm happy, but nervous".

"We understand that. But once we get going, the nervousness will disappear. But if doubts creep in, tell us immediately. We'll start when we get back".

"What, tonight? Now?"

"Would you rather leave it?"

"No, not at all. I'd only get more nervous by delaying it. No, I'd love to start this evening. Is that OK with you, Charlie?"

"Katya, I promise you'll be fine. I won't do anything you don't want me to do. I'll stop if ever you want me to stop. And Anna won't leave us alone, so you can talk to her if you find it too awkward to say something to me. I won't hurt you, I promise".

"I know you won't. Oh my god this is so crazy!"

Chapter 11

The following morning, while they were taking their early morning dip, the three of them were standing in a triangle, the girls with their backs against the waves, Charlie facing them.

"Katya," said Anna, "what most girls get wrong is they don't tell their partner what they like, and, more importantly, what they don't. You may already know this, but men are suckers for praise, especially when it comes to their sexual prowess. I urge you to tell your man when he's done something which you particularly enjoyed. He'll fluff up his own feathers, and you're more likely to get the attention you want next time. If he's done something that you didn't like or which turned you off, tell him. How will he know otherwise? If you don't say, he'll probably keep doing it, then you'll resent him and he's in the doghouse and has no idea why".

"Makes sense".

"So, tell Charlie what you particularly liked about what he did last night, plus if there was anything you didn't".

Katerina turned to face Charlie. "There wasn't anything I wouldn't want you to do again. What I especially liked was the way you turned me on before you even started with your fingers. I felt aroused and I wanted more. And then when you gave me more, well, you know the response. Thank you for making me feel special and desired".

Charlie responded with, "You *are* special, Katya. You are also more desirable than you seem to realise. Thank you for giving me so much pleasure too".

They returned to their towels, dried off then set out for home. Before they reached the shops, Charlie said, "Shall I tell you what I fancy? A bacon baguette instead of our usual pastries. What about you girls?"

"Yes, for me," was an immediate reply from Anna.

"And me please".

"Great. I'll pop into the supermarket to get the bacon, and you two buy the baguette. Anything else we need Anna?"

"More juice and another pack of coffee would be useful to have in the fridge. Oh, and some fruit. That's all I can think of".

"OK, see you back there".

That evening, Charlie was on his own in the garden, setting up the barbecue. Anna and Katerina were in the kitchen, Anna preparing the salad and Katerina arranging the meats on a plate to take out to Charlie. "Did you marinade this pork?" asked Katerina. "Yes, I did it this morning. Would have been better to have done it last night really, but we were all somewhat busy!"

She watched Katerina flush a little, clearly engrossed in thought. "Do you want to leave it at that, Katya? Not go any further? You must decide at every stage".

"Anna, are you still comfortable with this? Am I being wanton?"

"I'm still comfortable, and I'll double-check that Charlie is too. As for you being wanton, no, I wouldn't think that for a second. As long as you're engaging in this for the reasons we've spoken about, then I feel none of us need to be concerned. I'd worry, though, if either you or Charlie were simply being active together purely for the enjoyment of it".

"I can totally understand that. I'm keen to learn more, become more confident, but you, too, must say if you want this to stop".

"You're very sweet. All good so far".

"I can't imagine how you felt, watching us last night. Would this be way outside the sort of thing you two would normally get up to?"

Anna gave this considerable thought before replying, "Actually, no, not so much. I won't tell you about it now but after all these years of being with Charlie, I seem to have experienced a few things myself lately which haven't been the norm. I'm increasingly of the opinion that if something is enjoyable and not hurting anyone, why not give it a go? I reckon most of us have some desires which we don't have the confidence to try out. Bit daft if we'd get more pleasure from it, and if we don't, at least we've found out and a lesson has been learned without damage being done. Anyway, enough of this for a while. I see that Charlie is ready to start cooking. Would you like to take the meat out?"

"Yes, of course". Katerina picked up the plate and started towards the door.

"Katya?"

Katerina stopped and turned to look at Anna.

"Do you want to stop, would you like us to continue tonight, or do you want to wait a while before deciding whether you want to try the next thing?"

"Tonight please".

Anna was amused by the instant response, without a hint of hesitation. "OK".

Katerina left the kitchen, carrying the barbecue meats to Charlie, and Anna finished off the salad, which she placed on a tray, ready for Katerina to take out once she had returned empty handed.

He lay beside her, kissing her lightly on the lips before resting his head on the pillow. Her breathing was still heavy, and her mouth was open, trying to intake oxygen. He held her hand.

Anna knelt by the side of the bed and held Katerina's other hand. She looked at Charlie and blew him a silent kiss. It took Katerina a while before she felt that she would be able to communicate. All she could articulate was, "Oh my fucking god".

Anna helped her out. "Are you OK, Katya? Was that enjoyable?"

"I didn't know anything like that was possible".

"That's what girls deserve to experience. Rest a while Katya. Charlie and I will go back down to have a drink. Come down too, if you like, but if you'd prefer to go to bed now, that's fine, we'll see you in the morning". Anna and Charlie silently left the room.

Katerina hadn't appeared downstairs by the time they decided to call it a night; neither of them were surprised, nor were they offended. Just as they began to climb the stairs, Anna said to Charlie, "Your restraint is admirable. You must feel the need for some release. First though, it's my turn".

Before too long, Charlie was asleep and Anna lay on her back, ruminating. She felt that she was not yet ready for sleep, so she took the opportunity to consider again what Charlie and Katerina had been doing together. She recalled the period immediately after Katerina's arrival. From her conversations with Chrissy, she had expected to receive a moody, non-communicative teenager, and that she and Charlie would have to compromise their normal behaviours to cajole her into being an acceptable house guest. As it was, Katerina had been engaging company from the minute they greeted her at the airport. Anna knew now that the contrast in behaviour was due to Katerina being able to be herself, away from Ilya, his friends, and her immature schoolmates. She was certainly different. It seemed to Anna that most young adults of Katerina's age were constantly checking their phone; she knew that Katerina kept hers in her bedroom and assumed that she looked at it only when she was on her own, getting changed or preparing to go to bed.

Also, what other teenager read Goethe? Not only read but would be able to critique him should she happen upon another person who knew the author's work. Katerina had admitted that she had read Crime and Punishment "at least five times" and each of Dostoevsky's other novels at least once. "I could recite Anna Karenina almost word for word," she'd said, with a self-conscious laugh. 'Yes,' thought Anna, 'she's a bit of a one-off. And I really like her. Charlie does too. Of course, he likes her in that she's an attractive eighteen-year-old girl, but there's no doubt he likes her as a person. She thinks the same way as he does. He has conversations with her which he probably wouldn't have with me. Strangely enough, he's probably more compatible with her than he is with me'. These thoughts didn't cause any feeling of guilt, jealousy, or resentment. On the contrary, they reassured Anna that what the three of them had been doing over the past few days was a reasonable consequence of the bond that had grown between the three of them. 'Yes,' her inner dialogue continued, 'I really like her, and her story about how boys made her feel, and what damage she felt that may do to her development into adulthood, saddened and worried me. She deserves to be happy. She has so much to offer. She can become a brilliant achiever. She needed help, and Charlie and I are providing it. I'm convinced that Katya will return home with a fresh outlook, and an inner strength to understand and control people and situations. She'll enjoy life more, there's no doubt in my mind'.

There was a knock at their door in the morning, a little earlier than Charlie normally rose to prepare their coffees and juice. Charlie was the first of them to say, "Come in".

Katerina opened the door and picked up a tray she had placed on the floor. On it were two mugs of steaming coffee, two glasses of orange juice, a plate on which she'd laid out a selection of pastries, two side plates and a small glass vase containing a selection of flowers picked from their garden.

Anna raised herself and said, "Wow, what service".

Katerina placed the tray on the bed, in between where they two of them lay. "I woke up early and couldn't get back to sleep. I was thinking about last night, and the night before. After a while I decided to go out and buy the breakfast. I picked the flowers on the way back in. I hope you don't mind".

"Of course not," replied Anna, reassuringly. "That's very thoughtful. Where's your breakfast? Have you had it already?"

"No, it's downstairs. I'll leave you to it. See you in a bit," and she left the bedroom, closing the door behind her.

"How sweet," said Charlie. Anna nodded in agreement and picked up a pain au raisin. As she chomped through it, Charlie sipped cautiously at his acidic juice and hot coffee; the inside of his top lip was very tender from colliding with Katerina's pelvic bone the previous evening.

"What are you two discussing so passionately?" asked Anna, breezily, as she joined Charlie and Katerina in the garden.

"Dickens," replied Charlie. "I'm saying A Tale of Two Cities, or maybe David Copperfield, but Katya disagrees. She insists that Bleak House is his greatest work".

"Come on, Charlie," teased Katerina, "surely you must accept that, the opening paragraph of The Tale of Two Cities excepted, even Great Expectations is a better novel, let alone Bleak House".

"Oh well, enough of that. Argue about it later. Do you both fancy a day out?"

"Good idea," replied Charlie. "What do you have in mind?"

"We haven't yet taken Katya to Collioure. Let's spend a couple of hours there, then we can drive down to Banyuls and have a late lunch.

Save us cooking anything tonight". Charlie and Katerina were both up for it so, half an hour later, they were in the BMW, the hood was down, Anna was driving, and Katerina was beside her in the passenger seat. Charlie was sitting behind Anna, wondering when would have been the last time he had sat in the back of a car.

It's nearly impossible to not have a pleasurable trip to Collioure. The narrow, pedestrianised streets, the artisan shops and art exhibitions, the bars with their tables set out overlooking the pebble beach. Ramparts, the Mediterranean and numerous eye-catching people add to the many reasons why visitors tend to look around them rather than chat to their companions.

Katerina took special pleasure in browsing a shop which sold a range of women's clothing, most of it linen, and all of it white. Anna insisted on buying her a white, knee-length, linen, smock dress with silver piping around the neckline. "You'll need to wear pretty lingerie under that, Katya. It's see-through when the light's behind it".

Anna didn't leave empty-handed either as she couldn't resist a seersucker shirt which also appeared to be see-through. She intended to wear it, possibly without a bra, when they next stayed in Barcelona. She told herself that she didn't have Guillem in mind.

Katerina bought ice creams, pistachio for Charlie, Belgian chocolate for Anna and vanilla for herself, and they were enjoying them while sitting on a bench overlooking the beach, when Anna said, mischievously, "I think you've got an admirer, Katya". She nodded towards a waiter who was serving at the nearby bar. "I do believe his tongue is hanging out".

There was little doubt that, as he was moving around the tables, trying to appear busy, he was taking every possible opportunity to gaze at Katerina.

"Do you really think so?"

Charlie laughed. "I'm not an observant person, but even I can tell that the poor guy is in a desperate state".

Katerina looked down, attempting to hide her pleasure. Anna watched Katerina as she finished off her ice cream: was she siting up straighter; was she touching her hair; was she sucking her spoon even after the ice cream had disappeared from it? Anna was convinced she was. This reinforced

Anna's conviction that Katerina was benefitting greatly from Anna's guidance and Charlie's skills.

"Right, let's leave the lad to wallow in sorrow and regret. Banyuls next," said Charlie. Anna noticed that Katerina couldn't resist a glance behind her as they walked away from the bar. She was relieved to see that she was still being ogled.

Banyuls sur Mer is a totally different resort to Collioure. The town is long and straight as opposed to higgledy-piggledy, and the beach is large, better suited for sunbathing and playing in the sea. It attracts families and was thereby considerably busier and nosier than they were used to. "Maybe not such a good idea after all," admitted Anna.

"Not to worry, let's plonk ourselves down at an outside table, let Katya experience her first ever glass of Banyuls and bitch about anyone who particularly annoys us".

"Ooh, I love games like that," chuckled Katerina.

After playfully ripping to shreds many of the holidaymakers who were at the resort simply to have a good time, the three decided to make their way back to Le Racou, and to stop off somewhere for an early dinner rather than eat a late lunch at Banyuls sur Mer. "Let's go to Amelie les Bains and eat there," suggested Anna.

"Yes, good idea. It's a very pretty little town Katya, inland from the villa. You'll get a great view of Canigou as you drive past Ceret, and there's a lovely restaurant that serves an incredible duck dish".

"I've never eaten duck, I don't think. Sounds good to me," and she lost herself in her thoughts as Anna weaved the car out of Banyuls sur Mer on the way to join the northbound dual carriageway. Once Anna had changed into sixth, Katerina unconsciously took Anna's right hand away from the steering wheel and held it between her hands on her lap. Anna glanced to her right; Katerina was deep in thought, an almost imperceptible smile enlivening her dreamy appearance.

Once they had all finished the meal, Anna said, "Katya, how do you feel about everything? What did you enjoy last night? Do you want to continue, or would this be a good time to stop? Don't get too carried away with your response, there's people about!"

"No, I'll keep it down," promised Katerina. "Last night was truly amazing. I loved everything Charlie did to me. Everything. He made me feel special, desired, before we even started to do anything. The way he encouraged me to take my clothes off in front of him made it natural, and I wasn't at all embarrassed. I wanted to please him. I felt good about myself standing in front of him. Maybe it was because I was getting naked to enable him to give me pleasure rather than because he wanted to do something for his own satisfaction. Whatever was happening I felt wonderful. And the outcome, well, it was simply out of this world".

Anna looked at her and smiled. Charlie put his arm around her and gave her a hug.

"So, do you want to find out more?" asked Anna.

"Yes. Very much so".

"Are you sure? You do know that if you want to continue it will be Charlie's body, rather than yours, which will be the centre of attention. Your attention. Think about it carefully now, Katya, while you're still in control of your senses".

"I have thought about it. A lot. After what I've experienced with Charlie, it's obvious that, if we are to continue, I will be learning how to give a man pleasure rather than the other way round. I want that to happen, but only if you're comfortable with it, Anna," she looked Anna in the eye as she said this, "and you too, Charlie," she added, turning to face Charlie.

"I'm happy for Katya to experience more, Charlie, if you are".

"As long as it's what Katya wants and feels she needs, and you are comfortable with it, Anna".

Anna reached across the table and invited them to each take one of her hands in theirs. "That's settled then. Katya, you now need to find out more about a man's body. You know now the least a man should do for your pleasure. You know that sex is two-way. A man cannot simply think of you as someone who can provide him with gratification. If you're with the right man, and you're confident that he's not going to be selfish with the intimate side of your relationship, then you will both get far greater pleasure from the experience if you know what you're doing. Does that make sense?"

"It does. Until now I've been a bit terrified about a boy's body, and what it can do. As you know, Anna, I've no experience of what happens after the stage when a boy gets an erection. If I knew, I'm sure I wouldn't be so worried about what's going to happen to him, and how it's going to affect me".

"That's what we'll do next, then. Not tonight, but maybe tomorrow".

Chapter 12

There was tacit agreement the following day that they would revert to their routine. The three had larked together in the sea and Charlie had said that he was ready to leave to return to the villa for breakfast.

"Just a few more minutes," pleaded Anna. "It's so lovely. You'll keep me company, won't you Katya?"

"Of course".

"No problem. I'll dry off and wait for you on the beach. We'll go back together, and you can choose what you want for breakfast".

Once he had left them, Anna said to Katerina, "What I suggest is that we eat out tonight. Wear your new floral dress; Charlie hasn't seen you in it yet and he'll love it".

"OK. Why that in particular?"

"Clothes have a power, don't you think? I can put something on to wear and for some reason I don't feel right. I can change into something else and feel altogether different. Men give the impression that they believe females wear clothing to arouse them, but, for me, that's rarely the case. In fact, I think we are more concerned about impressing our own sex than we are enticing men. Whatever I wear, I simply want to feel good about myself. My thinking is that by wearing that dress you'll feel self-confident, and you'll soon realise that the control you have over Charlie, because of his appreciation of how you look, is boosting your self-esteem. If you do tonight what I'm going to talk you through during the day, when we get an opportunity, you'll be amazed at what you'll achieve and how it makes you feel".

"OK, I'll wear the dress, and I'll try to do whatever it is you're going to advise me to. I hope I don't let you or Charlie down".

"You won't".

After a wonderful day spent sunbathing, chatting, reading, swimming in the pool and dozing in the shade, it was finally time for them to get ready to go out for dinner. Charlie was the first to shower, change and return to the garden. Before too long, Anna joined him; she was wearing a pair of linen trousers with a loose fitting short sleeved blouse, deliberately chosen so that Katerina would stand out in her floral dress, with its tight-fitting bodice accentuating her bust, and the short, flared skirt drawing attention to her legs. As Katerina walked slowly across the garden, Anna knew immediately that, rather than feeling nervous, the girl was confident and in control of herself.

"Wow, some dress that, Katya," said Charlie, in genuine appreciation.

"Perfect for her, isn't it? Katya, you look stunning, you really do".

"Thank you. It does feel great on".

"If you'd had it made to measure, it wouldn't fit you better. And how your legs have browned-up over the past few days. Come on then, let's go and eat. You two lead the way, and I'll lock up".

As they headed towards the gate, Anna noticed that Katerina had slipped her arm through Charlie's, and they were striding out like a couple of young lovers. They allowed Anna to catch up with them as they turned into the main street, and Katerina slipped her other arm through Anna's so that, as they approached the restaurant, they were walking three abreast, each of them content within their own thoughts.

The food was pleasant, and the conversation flowed. However, there was a palpable tension, not uncomfortable, but strong enough to impact on their behaviour. For his part, Charlie was conscious that Anna and Katerina had shared several private conversations in the garden that afternoon. It was clear that Anna was preparing Katerina for the evening ahead. Charlie had no doubt that, whatever Katerina was going to do to, and with, him, it was going to be because of his wife's tutelage. Therefore, he didn't have to concern himself with whether he may do something which either Katerina or Anna took exception to.

Katerina was also engrossed in her thoughts. She had seen how Charlie had looked at her when he first saw her in her new dress, how he was continually glancing at her thighs at the table. The odd thing for her was that she knew it was lust, but it took a different form to that exuding from the boys she knew back at home. Theirs was lecherous, whereas Charlie's communicated longing and admiration. Already, she was feeling in control of events, as Anna had assured her that she would. She delighted in the knowledge that Charlie liked her as a person (she had been aware of that for some time) and that he desired her physically. That part wouldn't be a problem; she simply had to remember what Anna had been telling her about what to do and when and how to do it. She felt that she had performed the role well so far that evening, but that had been the easy part, wearing flattering clothes with confidence, and being attentive to Charlie.

Anna had been watching the two of them closely from the time Katerina had walked towards her and Charlie in the garden. Katerina didn't appear to feel intimidated or anxious, and Charlie was behaving as she had expected he would: appreciative of Katerina's physical appearance and respectful of her keenness to get things right.

The point was reached when all three, for their own reasons, felt it was time to return to the villa. The walk back was decidedly quicker than it had been when going out earlier. During the afternoon, Anna and Katerina had agreed that, rather than Anna being inconspicuous in the shadows, as she had been when Charlie was giving Katerina attention, she would, that night, be more visible, making suggestions to Katerina if she felt that they would be helpful.

Charlie faced Katerina in the middle of the room and drew her towards him. They kissed. Charlie's right hand slid down Katerina's side and worked itself up her skirt, first on the outside of her left thigh, and then on the inside.

"Charlie," she said, "I really want to see and touch you. Get naked for me".

She stepped back and watched as he removed clothing: loafers, shirt, trousers. The bulge in his boxer shorts took her by surprise; he appeared to be aroused already, something she hadn't anticipated. Katerina glanced towards Anna, who mouthed, "OK?" She turned back to look at Charlie, this time his face.

"I want to give you pleasure," she said.

From Charlie's movements and exclamations, there was little doubt that he had, indeed, received pleasure from her. Anna sat on the bed next to Katerina and put an arm around her. "Marks out of ten, Charlie?"

"If Katya was experienced sexually, and had done that numerous times, I would score it ten out of ten. As it was her first ever time, I'll have to give it fifteen".

Katerina knew that she was being humoured a little, albeit with the best of intentions. Nevertheless, the praise further enhanced her feeling of pride and well-being.

"And, as they say, how was it for you Katya?" asked Anna, warmly.

"I loved it. I had no idea that the girl gets the enjoyment I just experienced. I thought it was just for the guy's benefit. I loved everything about it".

"And do you get what I said? About empowerment?"

"Absolutely. I felt that Charlie had become totally dependent on my role as the provider of his pleasure. It's amazing".

Anna smiled, and hugged her again, in genuine affection.

"May I ask if you sunbathe naked? I noticed, of course, that Charlie doesn't have any white lines".

"Yes, we both do," answered Anna, "but only when we're on our own".

"OK. And Anna? Charlie? Before I leave to return home, I think I want to try doing it with my mouth. I think I'd like to give it a try. It's an opportunity I feel I shouldn't miss".

"We'll chat about it, Katya. If you still feel the same way, I'll talk you through what to expect. Be aware it's a bit more demanding than what you've just done. Charlie and I will discuss it too, just to make sure we're also comfortable with you doing it".

"OK. Thanks Anna".

"So, after all I've explained to you, you'd still like to try it?"

"Yes. In time, I want to try everything, and I'm still convinced I must make the most of the opportunity you and Charlie are providing for me".

"Fair enough. One final thing you should know, although it won't happen with Charlie tonight, be aware that men sometimes like to hold on to the back of your head to prevent you from pulling away from him, or they start pumping their hips. If either happens, and you don't like it, just stop. Stop what you're doing and tell them that, if they persist, they'll lose out. Once again, your terms or not at all. Actually, there's one further thing you need to be aware of. A gentleman will let you know in advance of it happening, but most guys won't want to risk you moving away from them, so you may be taken by surprise. Not every female enjoys the experience so you're usually going to have to work it out and decide for yourself".

"OK, thanks. By the way, when we go out for dinner, I was thinking of wearing the short skirt with the blouse. And I wondered about not wearing a bra. What do you think?"

"I think you're getting to the stage when you won't need any advice from me. Perfect. Go for it".

They found themselves to be much more relaxed in the restaurant than they had been the previous night. Once again, Charlie had complimented Katerina when she first appeared, and his appreciation increased, although he did not voice this, when he discerned that she was bra-less. There was absolutely no reason why she shouldn't be: she had pert breasts which didn't require support, and the blouse was opaque. Her bust simply formed an attractive, shapely appearance under the material.

She sat next to him in the restaurant and his glances in her direction, whilst the three of them were chatting, provided him with further opportunities to admire her thighs. The conversation was animated, Katerina being in great form. On several occasions, Anna burst into giggles, amused by Katerina's wit and observations.

Anna acted immediately on entering the villa, leading them upstairs and into the main bedroom. She turned on a lamp on the bedside table and draped a silk scarf over it. She then strolled across the room to sit on a chair placed in a corner. Katerina looked a little lost, unsure of herself, as she stood in the middle of the room, facing the bed and with her back to Charlie.

"Would you like me to take my clothes off?"

Katerina turned to face him, and her features relaxed. "Yes please, Charlie. Then lie on the bed with your head on the pillows". Katerina did not take her eyes off him, nor did she move. Once he was settled, Katerina unbuttoned and removed her blouse, knelt on the bed between his legs, leaned forward and slipped her lips over him, her breasts resting on his thighs.

She raised herself from him but neither Anna nor Charlie moved. It seemed to her that Charlie had passed out, and she couldn't even tell if Anna was still in the room. She started to get pins and needles so had to change position. She curled up beside Charlie and rested her cheek on his stomach. His limp penis faced her. She took it in her mouth once again, just for a short while, simply because she was sure that this would be her last opportunity, and because it felt right, comforting.

Anna walked towards them and sat on the side of the bed. She remained still and silent until Katerina pulled herself away and Charlie slipped out of her. "You're amazing, Katya. Truly amazing".

Katerina smiled dreamily. Charlie was unable to utter a sound.

The three of them remained on the bed for a further hour, forming a group cuddle. None of them felt ready to go to bed to sleep. After a while, Anna rose, walked off and returned carrying three dressing gowns. Anna was still fully clothed, and Katerina was yet to remove her skirt or knickers, so Charlie was the only one naked.

"Come on, let's go downstairs for a nightcap," said Anna as she started to undress. Katerina got off the bed and stripped off her remaining clothes. They were both in their dressing gown before Charlie got up and put his on too.

"Armagnac, Katya, or maybe a Baileys?"

"Ooh, a Baileys would be lovely, thank you".

"Armagnac for you Charlie?"

"Yes please".

With the three of them in the lounge, Anna and Charlie cuddled together on one settee and Katerina stretched out on another, Katerina asked a question that had been bothering her. "I was sucking a lot but didn't blow at all. Why's it called a blowjob?"

"Good question. I've no idea. Do you know Charlie?"

"I think it started in brothels in Victorian times. If a punter wanted oral sex, he told the Madame that he wanted a 'below job'. It got shortened to 'blowjob' over time".

"Well, I didn't know that. We've both learned something tonight Katya".

"I feel I've learned a lot tonight".

"A great deal has happened over the past few days, hasn't it?" asked Anna. "How are you feeling about it all?"

"Wonderful. I feel absolutely wonderful". There was a pause, and then Katerina added, "I think I'm done for the night". She walked over to where Anna and Charlie were sitting and kissed them both fully on the lips, first Charlie and then Anna. "Thank you. Thank you both so much. I love you both, I truly do. Good night".

"Good night, Katya. Sweet dreams".

"Good night. We love you too. Don't we Charlie?"

"We do".

Chapter 13

The following morning, as previously, there was a knock on their door before Charlie was due to rise, and Katerina walked in with their breakfast.

"Do you mind if I join you this time?"

"Of course not. Go and get yours too". Anna and Charlie waited until Katerina returned with a second, smaller, tray before they tucked into their drinks and pastries.

She sat on the end of the bed. "I meant what I said last night. I love you both".

"We know you meant it," responded Anna, warmly, "and we meant it too. You're a lovely girl. We are so fond of you. And when I said you're truly amazing, I meant that too".

Katerina smiled her thanks.

"You look troubled, Katya. Is everything OK?" asked Charlie, with concern.

"No, not troubled, but there are so many thoughts going through my mind. I was on the beach at 5 o'clock this morning. I woke early and couldn't get back to sleep".

"Do you want to tell us about it?" asked Anna.

"I do. And, just to put your mind at rest, I'm not troubled. Not in any way. Actually, I feel I'm the luckiest girl in the world".

Anna and Charlie allowed Katerina time to collect her thoughts.

"I didn't really know where I was when I came out here. Your invitation, so kind of you, couldn't have come at a better time. I'd finished my exams but, without wanting to sound big-headed, they hadn't really bothered me. I was confident that they'd go well. What I mean is that I didn't really know what type of person I was, and I had no idea what the future held for me. I've never been particularly bothered about other people's opinion of me, but I came to realise that Ilya and his mates, and the boys at school, had really got to me. I felt like an adult surrounded by children. Unfortunately, though, an adult who possessed no life skills whatsoever. Does Charlie know about Ilya and everything, Anna?"

"Yes".

"Well, that's how things were when I boarded the plane. The minute I got off it, into the sun, with the view from the tarmac of that wonderful mountain, Canigou, I felt totally different. At ease. Calm. And then you two were there to greet me, and you've both been wonderful from the first minute. You are the nicest people I've ever met, and it is just so obvious how great you are together and how much you love each other. Being around you would make anyone feel better about life".

"That's sweet".

"I mean it. You've both been so kind and considerate. And thoughtful. I've had the best holiday anyone could ever imagine. And I'm saying that without even considering what you've done for me with, you know, sex, and understanding my body. And getting to know about a man's body. It's been thrilling. Listening to you, Anna, when you've talked to me about what to expect, and how to act, well, it's something I suppose no one has ever benefitted from before. And yet I have. And Charlie, what you've done for me, what you've taught me and allowed me to experience. Just mind blowing. And you've been so mindful of me being this useless, inexperienced girl, willing but very far from able. Not only that but our chats have helped me to be even more at ease with being the type of person I am".

"Do you feel you will be better able to cope with the Ilya's of this world now?" asked Anna.

"It won't be a case of 'coping'. I feel 'coping' is trying to deal with a situation as best you can. No, when it comes to being with a boy or man, I won't ever now be coping. I feel confident that I will be capable of getting the best out of every situation, however experienced the guy may be. I just cannot tell you how fantastic that makes me feel. It's as though I've been huddled in a dark space trying to keep my head down, and now I'm out in the daylight, with my head up, looking for opportunities to better myself. Opportunities to enjoy myself".

"Funnily enough, Anna said that you were like someone who's been living inside herself. Like one of those Russian dolls".

"That's exactly it. I'm emerging. And to go with it, I've my new hair style, which I love. And new clothes. Not just the clothes, but the knowledge of what to buy, what to wear. What suits me, what reflects my personality. And, until the past few days, I had no idea how powerful the right clothes can be".

"Yes, Charlie's a sucker for short skirts, isn't he?" teased Anna, trying to lighten things a bit.

"Funnily enough, I've noticed that too! Would either of you like another coffee? Just to warn you, I haven't yet finished telling you what's been going through my head since 5am".

"Yes, I'll have a top up, thanks".

"Me too".

With Katerina out of the room Charlie turned to Anna and asked, "Is she OK?"

"Yes. Without question. More than OK, I'd say. I truly believe she's going to flourish once she returns to England".

"So," said Anna once Katerina had returned with three mugs of coffee, "keep going".

"I've got a job".

"Katya, that's brilliant news," exclaimed Anna. "What is it? How do you know? Come on, spill the beans".

"I received an email a couple of days ago. I didn't say anything because I didn't want to break the spell. To be honest, I was being selfish, being mindful of what Charlie and I would be doing, and I didn't want to risk anything getting in the way. There's a lady who's a member of Chrissy's Book Club. She owns a bookshop in Arundel".

"Salty!" interrupted Anna. "She was at my presentation. She was a hoot. Told us about giving her husband a blowjob".

"What?" exclaimed Charlie and Katerina in unison.

"Tell you later. Keep going Katya".

"Well, she owns a bookshop, and she plans to semi-retire in a year or two. She wants someone to come in and work with her until she packs it in, and then, if all works out OK, run it for her. She would still oversee it but wants someone else to be doing the day-to-day stuff".

"And that person is you?"

"Yes. Apparently, she's been talking to Chrissy about me for ages and she's also been making other enquiries. Don't know who else she's been talking to, but she must have heard what she wanted to hear because the job's mine if I want it. Probationary period, of course, but otherwise she seems to be convinced it's going to work out well for both of us".

"And it's what you want to do?" enquired Charlie.

"Yes. I can really picture myself in that bookshop, learning about buying and selling books and helping Mrs Yorke to maintain, and maybe add to, her loyal customer base".

"So can I," said Anna, with conviction. "You'll be brilliant at it. I'm so pleased for you, Katya".

"I'd say it's a match made in heaven. Congratulations Katya. When is she expecting you to start?"

"Well, that's the other thing, of course. Mrs Yorke wants me to start whenever I can, but she's told Chrissy that she knows I'm on holiday, and she doesn't want me to finish it early on her account. I can time it to suit myself, but, in fairness to her, I shouldn't keep her waiting too long. I'll have to get the train from Chichester initially, but once I've passed my test I may decide to drive there in my Mini".

"So, have you accepted?"

"I have. I've told her I'll let her know when I can start as soon as I've sorted things with you two".

"We're going to be sorry to see you go, aren't we Charlie, but what an exciting reason to have to finish a holiday".

"What have you got in mind, Katya?"

"Well, I was thinking of having a few extra days here, if that's OK with you two, and maybe going back early next week. What do you think?"

"Whatever you like, Katya. Do you want me to book a flight for you?"

"If you don't mind. I'll pay you back once I get home".

"You most certainly won't," insisted Anna. "Charlie, while you're sorting the flights, Katya and I can chat in the garden about how Katya would like to spend her last few days".

Charlie stepped out into the garden an hour or so later. Anna and Katerina were in the pool, playing with a ball, and he noticed that neither of them was wearing a bikini top. He walked across so that he could tell them about the flight booking and, as he stood on the side of the pool, it was clear that neither of them was wearing bikini bottoms either. He didn't comment.

"I've booked the flight, Katya. 3.10 Tuesday afternoon. The taxi is arranged too. Same guy as before, so just look out for him in the area he dropped you off".

"That's great, thank you".

"You coming in, Charlie?" asked Anna. "Katya will tell you how she'd like to spend the last few days of her holiday. Oh, and ditch the trunks. We're hanging loose from now on".

Katerina giggled as Charlie removed his swimming shorts and performed a dive, of sorts.

"Still crap," laughed Anna, while Charlie was out of earshot under water. He swam up to them and they stood together, at the shallow end, so that Katerina could confirm what she had been running past Anna: she didn't want to go out on day trips; she'd like to spend more time on the beach and in the sea and, when not there, in the garden and pool; she was going to try oysters in their favourite local restaurant (*"I told her the taste will now be familiar to her after last night!"*); she'd like them to have a barbecue on the beach, a late one, after everyone had gone, on her last evening.

"That's all very do-able, Katya. What about this evening. Will you want to eat out or shall I sort a barbecue here?"

"A barbecue in the garden would be lovely, thanks. I'll send an email later to let everyone know I'll be home on Tuesday and I'm ready to start work on the following Monday, or maybe the Saturday, if Mrs Yorke would prefer that".

"Do you want to tell Charlie the other thing you've asked about?"

"Er, could you?"

"No, I think you should".

"Anna, I'm a bit embarrassed".

Anna laughed. "How can you possibly be embarrassed now, Katya?"

Katerina conceded the point with a nod. "The thing is, Charlie, even after everything you two have helped me to experience, I still know next to nothing about having sex. Intercourse, I mean".

"I'm sorry, Katya, but Anna and I have already agreed that me having sex with you isn't an option".

"She knows that," responded Anna, assisting, "but she's asked if she can watch us. I think she was right when she told me that if she saw us making love, she'd be completing her knowledge. Katya says it would give her a lot of confidence for when it eventually happens for her. What do you think?"

Charlie hesitated, giving the request considerable thought. "Katya, would you mind if Anna and I discuss it first before deciding?"

"No, of course not. Come on then Anna, first to complete five lengths. Loser prepares lunch". And, without waiting for the challenge to be accepted, Katerina headed towards the deep end.

Later that day, while Katerina was clearing the table and carrying the remnants of the barbecue back to the kitchen, Charlie said to Anna, "Once I'd booked Katya's travel arrangements, I sorted the trip to Barca you said you wanted to do before we go back to England".

"Oh well done. What's happening?"

"A suite was free on the Saturday and Sunday nights after Katya goes home. I've booked a meal in the restaurant for the Saturday, but I thought we may like to keep Sunday free for now. What do you think?"

"Yes, sounds great. Let's not mention anything to Katya. I wouldn't want her thinking she's been cramping our style being here, or that we can't wait for her to go so we can go off somewhere".

"Totally agree. That's why I've waited to tell you. Now, do you really think it's a good idea for Katya to watch us having sex?"

"I'm thinking of it as an animated 'Joy of Sex' manual. Yes, we'll be making love to each other, the way we hope she will, once she's found the guy she wants to do it with, and she'll be watching us, but it will again be for her education, not because she wants a thrill".

"No, no, I understand that". A pause, then, "You make it sound a bit clinical, so does that mean I'm not allowed to come?"

"No, it doesn't mean that. But it does mean that you're not allowed to come until we've demonstrated at least two or three positions. I'm not going to simulate with a vibrator just because you can't control yourself".

"OK. But it's going to be difficult. You and me having sex while she's watching is going to be particularly horny, however altruistic the motive".

"Maybe so, but you'll just have to cope the best you can. Try thinking about how Dostoevsky's style of writing changed over the years. That should delay the inevitable for long enough".

The days ticked along, and Katerina continually told them how wonderful it all was. More time was spent at the beach than in the garden, and Katerina and Anna were in and out of the Med, behaving like a couple of school mates. When in the garden, they didn't bother with swimsuits, although Anna insisted that Katerina stayed in the shade during the hottest part of the days.

Finally, it was Monday, Katerina's last full day. They had already planned a late barbecue on the beach, so it was agreed that, once they had returned to the villa with their pastries for breakfast following their early morning dip in the sea, they would stay at home and enjoy the pool.

After a light lunch, Anna said, "Charlie and I will now try to behave as we often do when we're on our own here. We'll be having sex out here in the garden. The only difference is that you'll be watching, but we're going to try to put that out of our heads. I've laid out some towels on the grass under the trees and put some cushions on them. Just watch how and where you please. Does that sound OK?"

"Yes, of course".

Anna stripped off and rinsed herself in the shower by the pool. She used a spare towel to dry off, then lay under the trees. Charlie followed suit. Anna lay on her back and enticed Charlie to join her. They were soon embracing and commencing foreplay.

Katerina watched on in silence, their initiations now familiar to her. The couple's movements over the next twenty minutes were sometimes gymnastic, often balletic. On occasion, Katerina thought, 'This isn't sex, it's lovemaking. Beautiful'. Other times, 'This is sex, fucking'.

Arousal was inevitable and, without thinking or taking her eyes off them, Katerina stood up and removed her bikini. She began to masturbate, and, at one point, it was clear that Anna was watching her. Their eyes locked as Katerina lost herself to rapture. 'I need to get back in touch with Lene,' Anna thought, before deciding it was time to complete the performance.

"Harder. Come for me Charlie". As she said this, she winked at Katerina.

'This is power,' was Katerina's final thought before Charlie emitted a fierce growl as he climaxed.

Anna couldn't hold herself up any longer and collapsed forwards, with Charlie falling with her. He lay on top of her for a while before falling sideways to lie on his back. Anna remained on her front. Katerina didn't move in her chair.

"Jesus," said Anna.

"Incredible," said Charlie.

"Oh my fucking god," said Katerina.

The remaining time flew by. The barbecue on the beach, the midnight swim in the Med, the lie-in and late breakfast and even the time-killing period before the drive to the airport.

"Well, I'd better go through," said Katerina as the three of them stood together at the barrier leading to passport control.

"Yes," responded Charlie. "Unusually, it looks like the flight is on time".

Katerina released the handle of her new travel bag and hugged him. "Thank you so much. For everything".

She let him go and then re-embraced and kissed him before turning to Anna. "Anna, I just can't thank you enough". She couldn't add to this because she began to cry.

"Oh Katya". Anna pulled her into a hug. "We've had the most wonderful time. We're really going to miss you. Don't cry, please. You've so much to be happy about and look forward to".

"I know, I know. I'm not crying because I'm unhappy".

"Of course. Don't forget what we agreed: first holiday you're entitled to, you're out here, with us. We'll be here at Christmas if you want to join us. Now go on. And don't forget to let us know when you get home".

"I won't. Bye". She turned and raised an arm to convey a farewell wave. She didn't look back.

They watched her disappear through the door leading to the security area, then turned away. Charlie passed a tissue to Anna so that she could dab away her tears.

Shortly after returning to the villa, they simultaneously received a text:

Home safely. Good journey. Had the best time ever. Yearning already for: sunbathing under cerulean skies, warm Med, lengths in amazing pool, your beautiful villa and garden, barbecues under the trees, experiences, and discoveries. Even developed a taste for Oysters! Will miss you desperately. Love you both. Kxx

The following morning, they both received a second text, this one from Chrissy:

You must both come over for dinner as soon as you return. K hasn't stopped telling me about her holiday. Clothes and hair are fab! Want to thank you both in person. Fizz promised. Speak soon x

They seemed to go through the motions after reading this, as if the text had communicated bad news. Later that day, as they were drinking an early gin and tonic in the garden, Anna said, "I feel really flat".

"I know what you mean. Just as well we've booked the Barcelona trip at the weekend. Hopefully, it will spark us up".

"Maybe". She considered further, then added, "No, I don't think it will. Let's not go to Barcelona. Let's fly back".

"Seriously?"

"Yes. Look, Katya has really got under my skin, and she has yours too. It won't feel the same for either of us now that she's left. I quite fancy getting back to our England routines and I've realised how much I want to see Lene again. We can sort something with Katya, too".

"OK, no problem, I'll book the flights and cancel the room".

They returned to England the following day.

Book Three

The Adolescent

Chapter 14

The Saturday after Charlie and Anna's return from France, Chrissy took them out for a meal and a bottle of Champagne at Chichester's leading restaurant. "I can't get over it," she told them. "Katerina seems so full of enthusiasm and energy. The holiday was obviously great for her, and she looks terrific too; thank you both so much".

"We really enjoyed her company, didn't we Charlie? She was impeccably behaved and great fun. No doubt being able to put studying and exams behind her has enabled her to be herself once again".

"Plus getting a job so soon. She seems keen".

"Yes, that too, of course".

A few days later, Chrissy telephoned Anna.

"Anna, I need my chimney swept. It was chilly last night so I lit a fire. The lounge smells of smoke this morning so it must be the chimney. Can you give me the number of the guy you use?"

"Oh, right, yeah. It's Charlie's mate, Steve, but he was saying to Charlie recently that he's busy so you may be better off trying Dave Vowell".

"I've just called him, but he can't do it for six weeks and I don't want to wait that long. Do you think Charlie's mate would fit me in, being your sister?"

Anna felt somewhat flustered, recalling her Exocet discovery. "Not sure. Let me have a word with Charlie and I'll call you back later".

"Thanks Anna".

A while later: "Hi Chrissy. I've had a word with Charlie, who's phoned Steve. He said he's pleased to help, but can only do it first thing on Saturday, around 8am. Will that be OK with you?"

"That's great, thank you. Yes, tell him Saturday at 8 is fine. Thank Charlie for me, will you?"

"Will do. See you soon".

Since sending a text to Anna and Charlie on her return home from France, Katerina had focussed mainly on learning to drive and preparing for, and then embarking upon, her new employment in the bookstore in Arundel. She had also decided that she was keen to improve her French, determined to be able to converse fluently in the language when next visiting Anna and Charlie's villa. She had become aware that Anna and Charlie had returned to England, and that they had arranged an evening with Chrissy, but had felt that she wasn't yet ready to re-establish contact with them. For her, to go from the French idyll to routine behaviour in front of Chrissy and Ilya was too much of a stretch. She felt that the transition needed to be conducted in stages, and she believed that she could rely on Anna to arrange a meeting when and how it would be most appropriate. She trusted Anna implicitly. As far as Katerina was concerned, Anna always managed to say and do the right thing at the right time in the right way. If she could be anybody in the world, Katerina would choose to be Anna: attractive, classy, sexy, great company, wealthy, fun, modest and married to Charlie.

She had played the part with Chrissy, explaining the circumstances leading to the new clothes and radical hairstyle, and describing the holiday activities which she had enjoyed in France. She had established rapport with her new employer, Mrs Yorke, who insisted on being called Salty, and had quickly learned the rudimentary aspects of her new job role.

There was also a specific task which she had set herself. It wouldn't so much be revenge as a desire to quickly establish her new status, one born from the confidence and experience she had gained from her time with Anna and Charlie.

Ilya was entertaining in his bedroom the friend of his who had insulted her, and Katerina felt the opportunity had arrived. She went into her bedroom and removed her shorts, t-shirt, and underwear, then studied herself in the full-length mirror, as she had the day after her fourteenth birthday, and many times since. She had little doubt that boys (and men) would enjoy looking at her, and it struck her that she was excited by the thought of giving someone the opportunity. She climbed into her new, short, A-line skirt and looked again at her reflection. Even though she had lived through the transition, she was amazed at how the person looking back at her differed from the one who had boarded the plane at Gatwick. She climbed into her knickers then donned her bra, polo shirt and trainers. This was the Katya she had become, and she determined that never again would she be oppressed, belittled, or exploited.

Ilya's bedroom door was ajar, so she breezed in. The two boys were engrossed in Ilya's laptop screen and looked up only when Katerina gaily asked, "Hi you two, how's things?"

Ilya paid her little attention, but his mate stared at her with his mouth open.

"Nothing to say? You don't fancy me anymore then Glen, now that I've changed my hairstyle? Not going to ask your friend if his sister fancies tossing you off? Oh well, never mind. Shame though, I was considering it too. I expect Ilya will do it for you if you ask him nicely. Unless you're both bored now with doing it to each other! Must be off. Have fun".

She returned to her bedroom grinning. "Ha!" she said out loud before laying on the bed and streaming Nick Drake's 'Place To Be' through her earpieces, her favourite Nick Drake track, and a lovely reminder of her holiday, during which Charlie played a mix of Radiohead, Nick Cave, REM and Nick Drake (with the occasional sprinkling of Francoise Hardy—new to Katerina) whenever the three of them weren't otherwise engaged.

Since Anna left for France, Lene had simply experienced life as normal. It was busy enough, of course, being a wife, mother of two daughters and owner of a successful beauty salon, but it tended to be non-routine thoughts which buried themselves inside Lene's head. To be more precise, her thoughts were sexual.

Lene was adamant, when thinking about, and being with, Greg, that she would not give him any cause to complain. She loved and desired him just as much, if not more, than she ever had, so the afternoon with Anna and Charlie had not caused any damage in that respect. On the contrary, she had been far more attentive than usual as she felt in a continual state of sexual arousal. However, she could not deny to herself that Anna had triggered a strong emotion within her, one which, she was convinced, would not fizzle out. She was in love with her. Lene accepted that Anna may well have viewed their experience as a one-off, enjoyable but unlikely to be repeated. She would have to accept that, of course, and wouldn't dream of doing or saying anything which may damage their relationship. It would be very disappointing for her, though, if she were not able to enjoy Anna again in that way.

Lene considered Anna to be gorgeous, and she thrilled at what Anna's body had been able to do to her. She yearned for a repeat. 'It's up to Anna,' she thought. 'Totally up to her. If it's purely to be our friendship and her visits to the salon, that's fine. I'd love to have sex with her again, but only if she makes it clear that she wants me in that way. Yes, I'll leave it to her'.

Book Three: *The Adolescent*

Chapter 15

"I'm sorry I've been a bit of a bore since we came back from France," exclaimed Anna one evening, after they had finished supper and were appreciating the heat and comfort which was being provided by the log burner in the Snug.

"You haven't been a bore," responded Charlie.

"I think I have, and it's because I've been giving a great deal of thought to what you and I got up to during the past few months. I've tried to really challenge myself as to whether we've been wrong in what we did with Steve, Lene and Katya".

"And what conclusions have you come to?"

"Well, me wanking Steve was a bit of harmless fun. The afternoon with Lene went well and, afterwards, she assured me she had enjoyed it and was fine about it. I think I need to check her out again, but I can't imagine her relationship with Greg has been compromised in any way. And as for Katya, well, I can't say I've been feeling guilty about what we experienced with her. She was in control and I've no doubt she benefited from her time with us".

"What are you getting at?"

"I guess I'm saying that I don't feel any shame or guilt about any of it and I don't feel we've corrupted anyone. Steve was a drunken one-off, although I have to say the image will stay with me forever. Katya will now be getting on with her life, and I believe the three of us are now firm friends. And Lene and I will probably just carry on as before. Before The Spread Eagle, that is. She has, though, been on my mind quite a bit so I do need to get back in touch with her very soon".

"That's all good, then".

"Yes, I suppose it is". But even as she said it, her thoughts returned to Lene.

Anna knew it was early the following morning because Charlie had yet to return to their bedroom with their glasses of orange juice and mugs of coffee.

'Who on earth is phoning me at this hour?' she thought as she fumbled for her phone.

"Hello".

"I didn't wake you, Anna, did I?"

"Yes, you bloody did, Chrissy. What's going on?"

"I'm in love".

That woke Anna up! "What? Who with?"

"Steve".

"Steve?"

"Yes, Charlie's mate Steve".

"Chrissy, you hadn't even met him until he swept your chimney. How can you possibly be in love?"

"Don't give me that, Anna. How many times have you banged on about you and Mr Fucking Perfect falling in love with each other within a couple of hours of meeting up?"

"Yes, but…".

"But what?"

"Oh, I don't know. I guess I'm just mindful of your previous disasters".

"It's different this time".

"OK. Hang on a minute, Charlie's just walked in with the coffee. Charlie, it's Chrissy on the phone. She's in love. With Steve". Charlie nearly dropped the tray.

"So, how and when did it happen, Chrissy?"

"I've seen him a couple of times since that Saturday when he cleaned the chimney and, well, it's just happened. We get on great. I haven't felt like this since Ivan. In fact, I didn't even feel like this then. I'm telling you Anna, I'm in love. And I think he feels the same way".

"Have you been physical yet?"

"Physical? What are you, a biology teacher suddenly? If you mean have we had sex, the answer's no. But I think we'll be getting fruity soon. It's going that way for sure".

"You know his nickname at the rugby club was The Exocet, don't you?"

"No, how would I know that? Was he in the Navy, then?"

"No, he wasn't in the Navy (Charlie nearly choked on his coffee). The other teammates called him that because of his size".

"I know he's big, but it's not fat you know Anna. He's stockily built and very muscular".

"I don't mean big in that way, Chrissy".

There was a pause before Chrissy responded with, "Oh, I see. Hey, lucky me".

"Just be careful, that's all".

"Blimey, Anna, a big penis isn't going to kill me".

"Chrissy, there's big and there's big. From what I understand from Charlie, Steve is *very* big".

"Well, as I say, lucky me. So, are you going to congratulate me then?"

"Of course. Sorry Chrissy. You just took me by surprise, that's all. Well done you. The four of us will have to get together soon".

"Good idea. I'll have a word with Steve. Right, must crack on. Speak soon".

Anna stared at her phone, her mouth agape. "What the fuck?"

"Sounds like you'll be comparing notes soon".

"Fuck off Charlie".

"Hi Katya".

"Anna! Thank goodness".

"What? Is anything wrong?"

"No, not at all. It's just that I've been desperate to see you or at least speak to you. It's been ages".

"Yes, sorry. My fault. No excuse. How have you been?"

"Good. Really good. I've got so much to tell you".

"Well, I'm dying to hear about it all, but not on the phone, it's too important to me. What days do you get off work?"

"Every Sunday, and I can choose whatever day I want, Monday to Thursday".

"Right, can you take next Wednesday off?"

"Yes, I'm sure that will be fine with Salty".

"Good. Do that then. We're going to have a day at the races. Charlie's booking a box at Sandown Park, just the three of us. We'll pick you up around 10 on Wednesday morning. How does that sound?"

"Sounds brilliant. Can't wait".

"Great. Oh, and Katya?"

"Yes".

"We've really missed you".

There was silence and then Katerina's emotional response. "I've really missed you both too. Thank you so much for calling, Anna. You don't know how much it means to me".

"I can't wait to see you, Katya. I'll send you a text nearer the time as you may like a couple of ideas about what to wear and expect".

"Great, thank you. See you Wednesday".

"Good morning, Dani, it's Anna".

"Oh, hi Anna, how are you?"

"I'm great thanks. Hope you are too".

"Yes, all good thanks. Haven't seen you for a while. Been in France?"

"Yes, we've spent most of the summer there. How about you, have you been away?"

"Actually no, saving my money. Molly and I are aiming to buy somewhere. I'm sick of renting".

"Molly? I don't think I've heard you mention her before".

"Possibly not. We've been together for a while. To be honest with you, she was the reason I finished with Jonathan. Molly has wanted to keep things quiet, too. She's found it difficult getting her family to adjust to the fact that she has a girlfriend".

"Oh, I see. Are things a little easier now?"

"Thankfully, yes. Her parents and brother seem to have accepted that it's not a phase and that she is, in fact, gay. Shock, horror!"

Anna laughed. "A bit of an antiquated view".

"They're that type of family. Very nice, but I think they were anticipating their precious Molly marrying a Banker or Accountant".

"They must be appreciating things are real if you're aiming to buy a property together".

"Yes, we're getting there. Anyway, are you looking to book an appointment, or did you want to speak to Lene?"

"A quick word with Lene, if she's free".

"She's with a client at the moment, but she has some time before her next appointment so she should be fine to phone you in twenty minutes or so".

"That'd be great. Thank you".

"No problem. I'll let her know. See you soon, I hope".

"Yes, you will. Bye Dani".

A quarter of an hour later, Lene phoned.

"You never told me Dani was going out with a girl".

"No, sorry. She tends to keep things private, so thought it best not to".

"Of course, you were right. It just took me by surprise. I've known her so long, and I've heard her only speak about boyfriends in the past".

"Yes, she's had plenty of boyfriends. Most of her partners have been male. If things don't work out with Molly, Dani's as likely to hook up with a boy next as she is a girl".

"Quite a nice situation to be in. Widens the field".

"Indeed. Anyway, lovely to speak to you at last Anna. I was beginning to worry".

"About what?"

"Oh, I don't know. Whether you've struggled with what happened at The Spread Eagle I suppose".

"I'm so sorry, Lene. Nothing to worry about, for sure. And the only thing I may have struggled with is knowing how much I enjoyed being with you".

"I can't tell you what a relief that is. Anna, I need to tell you, you may not have been struggling, but I have".

"In what way?"

"With my feelings. For you. About you".

"Oh". A pause, and then, "Shall we meet up? Talk about it?"

"Yes, I think that would be a good idea".

"How about lunch on Monday? The salon will be closed, won't it? I'll pick you up around 11.30 on Monday morning and we'll drive out to the Downs and have a bite to eat somewhere. Maybe the Noah's Ark?"

"I'd love that. Yes, I'll see you on Monday. Thanks so much for ringing".

"Lovely to talk to you, Lene. And apologies again for leaving it so long".

Following this telephone conversation, Anna sat for a while, contemplating. Charlie was out so her thoughts were undisturbed. Disturbing perhaps, but undisturbed. What was Lene revealing? Anna felt it was obvious. Was she happy or worried about that? Flattered or on edge? Her main concern was that things had not been damaged between Lene and Greg. She hoped passionately that the afternoon she had enjoyed with Lene hadn't affected Lene's relationship with her husband or daughters. Anna decided that she wouldn't mention anything to Charlie for the moment, other than that she and Lene were lunching on Monday, and that she would try to put Lene out of mind until they talked things through.

The final phone call that Anna made was to Ralph Lauren's flagship store in New Bond Street. Anna's style of dress had changed little over the years but, since monetary outlay had become irrelevant, she tended to purchase from just a few select outlets. Ralph Lauren was her favourite for autumn and winter outfits. On this occasion she wasn't buying for herself, but for Katerina. The shopping trip in Perpignan had gone well, but that had been for summer clothing. Anna liked the idea of buying some winter attire for Katerina and the arranged trip to Sandown Park gave her the perfect opportunity. She had remembered Katerina's measurements—dress size, waist, length of leg, shoe size, bra fitting etc.—so felt confident that buying over the phone would cause few problems.

Before phoning, she studied Ralph Lauren's website and selected appropriate garments: knee length leather boots; ankle length leather boots; a herringbone silk-blend blazer; suede skinny trousers; a slim-fit cotton oxford shirt; a cashmere scoop-neck dress; an Aran-knit cotton jumper; a V-neck cable-knit cashmere jumper; a leather belt; a pair of 180 denier ribbed tights. All items were in brown, cream or beige. Once she'd completed the order, which the personal assistant had assured her would be delivered to Katerina over the weekend, she decided that another phone call was required as Ralph Lauren didn't supply the type of skirt she was looking for. Another quick call, this time to Burberry, and Anna was content that a vintage check, wool kilt, plus a pair of lambskin gloves, would also be in Katerina's possession in a day or two.

She looked at the clock. Not yet midday. 'It's amazing what can be achieved,' she thought, 'once you can be arsed'. She felt she'd earned an early lunch.

Ten minutes later, Charlie walked in.

"Good timing. I'm just making a chicken sandwich. Shall I make you one?"

"Yes please. Had a good morning?"

"Well, nothing to top Chrissy's bombshell, but, yes, there's been a bit going on. Did you get everything done that you wanted to?"

"Yes thanks. So, what's been going on?"

"Katya's up for coming to Sandown with us so you can confirm that box. I've also bought her some clothes as I doubt that she's earned enough yet to top up her wardrobe. Lene's fine and we're meeting up for lunch on Monday. Oh, one other thing, Dani is bi".

"Really? How do you know that?"

"She answered the phone when I was calling to speak to Lene. She said she's saving to buy a property with her partner Molly".

"Good for her. I'm sure, though, that she's referred to a boyfriend before now".

"She has. Hence the 'bi'".

"Good point".

"Right, chicken sandwiches done. Crisps?"

"No, just the sarnie is fine thanks".

On Saturday afternoon, Anna received a phone call from Katerina.

"I don't know what to say".

"Just say thanks, then tell me if I've made good choices and whether they fit you".

"OK. Thanks Anna. Thanks so, so much. I would never have dreamt of owning clothes like these. I've tried them all on and everything is perfect. Thank you, thank you, thank you".

"That's good. I did wonder if some of the stuff would be a little traditional for you, but I think you've got the carriage to make it work".

"Do you remember in France when I said I wanted my clothes to be like yours: classy, feminine and sexy?"

"Yes, I remember it clearly".

"Well, these new clothes are exactly that".

"Great. I'm so pleased you think so. Have you thought about what you'll wear on Wednesday?"

"I wanted to talk to you about that. Will we be outside? Is it going to be muddy or anything?"

"Well, first off, the weather forecast is good, a bit chilly, but dry and bright. We'll be parking near the entrance, so there'll be little walking, and then we'll go to our private box. There's no need to leave there if we don't want to. There's waitress service for drinks and lunch, and someone comes in to deal with your bets should you want to have a punt on a horse. Having said that, Charlie will choose to go outside. He likes to watch the horses in the parade ring, and he usually places his bets with the bookmakers. He'll come back to the box before each race, and we'll watch them together; the view of the course is brilliant. I'll probably stay in the box mostly, but you can decide what you want to do throughout the day".

"Sounds brilliant and I'm really looking forward to it. Do you still intend to pick me up at 10?"

"Yes, that's the plan. I'll let you know if it changes".

"OK, great, see you then. And Anna?"

"Yes".

"Thanks again".

"You're very welcome".

BOOK THREE: *THE ADOLESCENT*

CHAPTER 16

Anna chose to drive Charlie's Alfa Romeo 4C on Monday. As soon as she pulled up outside Lene's house, Lene came out and walked down the path towards the car. Anna watched her closely to try to detect her demeanour: she looked fine. As far as her attire was concerned, she looked better than fine. Ankle boots, mid-thigh skirt, a ribbed close-fit roll neck jumper, tucked in, and a short bolero-style jacket. Anna had selected to wear tight Armani jeans, a fitted shirt, and a blazer.

Lene opened the passenger door and climbed in before leaning towards Anna so that they could exchange a welcome kiss.

"You look sensational, Lene," said Anna, as she appreciated how much of Lene's legs were on view as she settled into her seat in the low sportscar.

"Do I? Thank you. And you look as gorgeous as ever".

"Scrub up OK for a couple of ladies approaching middle age, don't we? So, are you OK?"

"Yes, I'm fine thank you. It's great to see you again".

Anna pulled away and studied the road ahead. "It's great to see you too. We are fine, aren't we?"

"I'm sure we will be. I need to explain what I meant on the phone but let me do it after I've finished my first glass of wine".

"Of course. And Greg and the girls, are they OK?"

"Yes, everyone's good thanks". She paused, then added, "Christ, I'm so nervous".

Anna turned and gave her an anxious look. "Lene, please don't be nervous. You can say what you want to me. You can describe any feelings, good or bad. The only thing I wouldn't cope well with is to hear you say we can't be friends any more".

"There's no chance of me saying that, Anna". Another pause, and then, "Look, pull over when you can. Let me say what I need to say. We can deal with it in the privacy of the car and then we can have a more relaxed lunch at the pub".

Anna was driving down a county lane when Lene said this, and soon approached somewhere for her to pull in. She stopped the car, turned the engine off and faced her friend. They both undid their seatbelts. "Talk to me. Tell me what you meant when you said you had feelings for me and about me".

"Since our afternoon in Midhurst all I can think about is you. Your body, what you and I did, kissing you, everything. All you. It's been driving me crazy. I'm in love with you".

"Oh, I see. In love with me?"

"Yes".

"And has this affected you with Greg?"

"I've made sure that it hasn't. It's not been easy, but I'm confident that he's had no reason to wonder if there's something wrong with me. Or us. To be honest, I don't think anything that's happened has made me love or desire him less. It's just that you've been added to my life in some way. Without anything else being taken away".

"I'm so relieved to hear that. You and Greg are terrific together. And you're great parents to two lovely daughters. I couldn't bear it if I was party to anything between you all being damaged".

Lene just looked at her and smiled. She appeared to be too choked up to speak. Anna leaned across, put a hand behind Lene's head and gently pulled her forwards. Anna kissed Lene, a long, passionate kiss. On parting, they immediately sought each other again, and this time Anna's tongue explored Lene's mouth.

They finally separated and Lene said, "Oh Anna".

"Lene, you're so fucking hot".

Lene burst out laughing. "I don't know why I'm laughing. Through relief, I guess. We'll be OK with this, Anna, won't we? We'll be able to sort things out?"

"Of course we will. But one thing is paramount and non-negotiable: you and Greg are going to remain happily married and so are Charlie and I".

"Anna, as I've said, I've thought about little else other than you for weeks, months, but I've still functioned. Better than functioned. Greg has been delighted with the amount of time and energy I've committed to pleasing him. I would love it if I could continue with my role as a wife, mother, and businesswoman as if nothing had changed, but for me to also have opportunities to be with you".

"Like this, you mean? Lunches or evenings out?"

"If that was all, I'd gratefully accept it. But, in truth, I want more than this. I want to have sex with you again".

Anna considered this. Lene watched Anna as she formulated her thoughts. Finally, she said, "I would love for us to make that happen".

"Really? You mean that?"

"Yes, I do. I've been thinking a great deal about you, too, and since I saw you walk down your path, I've especially wanted to do two things. Kiss you and put my hand up that sexy skirt".

"Well, you've done the first of them. There's nothing stopping you doing the second".

Anna leaned towards her again so that they could kiss. This time, though, Anna's right hand slid up the inside of Lene's right thigh, and her fingers located Lene's most intimate area. It was another twenty minutes before they were able to continue their journey to the Noah's Ark pub.

They exchanged girly chit-chat while they ate their lunch and sipped their drinks. Once they had ordered coffees, Anna admitted that there had been an occasion in France when sex with Lene had been uppermost in her thoughts.

"Really? What was the trigger?"

"Charlie and I were having sex in the garden".

"And?"

"I was sitting on him and had a vision, one which reminded me how pleasurable it was being with you".

"Did you mention any of this to Charlie?"

"I told him I felt the need to see you. I tend to tell Charlie everything".

"Would that include telling him that you and I have said we want to see each other again, in that way?"

"Yes, I should think so. What about Greg, will you be telling him?"

"No, I won't share any of this with him. It's not his type of thing. No, he and I will continue as we have for many years, and it will be loving and caring and brilliant. I'll just have this added thrill of occasionally being with you. I would never be unfaithful to him with a man, but with you, rightly or wrongly, I believe it's different. Maybe because sex with you doesn't involve penetration. Not everyone would agree, but that's the way I view it".

"Yes, I can understand that. So, what would you like to do about this?"

"You obviously have more free time than I do. Shall I contact you when I know I'll be able to meet you for an hour or two? You can let me know if you'd like us to arrange something".

"Perfect".

Anna stopped outside Lene's house, and they exchanged a farewell kiss. Anna drove home and entered the cottage just as Charlie was making himself a cup of tea.

"Would you like one?"

"No thanks. I'm going to have a glass of wine".

"It's 3.30".

"So, you don't want one then?"

Charlie poured his tea away and opened a bottle of Collioure red while Anna located the glasses.

"Nice lunch?"

"Lovely. The Noah's Ark really is a great pub. And Lurgashall is such a beautiful village".

"Yes, I agree. We should go there more often".

"We should. How about Sunday lunch next weekend or the one after?"

"Good idea. I'll get something booked. How was Lene?"

"Yes, she was on good form. Sends her love".

"I bet she missed you".

"Yes, she said she did. Charlie?"

"Yes".

Anna's phoned pinged. A text:

'I'm so happy'

"Lene and I were chatting about our afternoon at The Spread Eagle, and we're both keen for us to meet again for some fun. Just the two of us. How do you feel about that?"

He pondered. "I don't see why that should be a problem".

Chapter 17

As soon as Charlie pulled up at the end of Chrissy's drive, and the two of them opened their doors to get out of the Land Rover Defender, the front door opened, and Katerina exited the house.

"Looks like we won't be seeing Chrissy before we leave," said Anna.

Katerina strode confidently towards them, smiling. Anna looked at her and decided that she had chosen her attire perfectly to suit the occasion: the suede skinny trousers tucked into the ankle boots, with the Aran-knit jumper worn under the herringbone jacket.

"Hello you two. So lovely to see you," shouted Katerina, fully twenty metres away from them. It was clear that she could not contain her excitement.

"Katya," responded Charlie, "great to see you too. You look absolutely fantastic".

Anna walked towards her and embraced her. They held each other close before Anna pulled away from her and looked her up and down. "I think Ralph Lauren have a new model for their Autumn range. Knock-out".

"Thank you". Katerina now turned her attention to Charlie, and their embrace communicated a relationship beyond mere friendship.

"Shall we go?" asked Charlie, at last.

"Yes, let's get off. I'll sit with you in the back, Katya, and you can start to get us up to date. I'm sure you've loads to tell us".

"I have indeed," answered Katerina as she climbed in. "Thanks Charlie". He opened and closed the door for her while Anna walked round the vehicle to get in the other side.

As soon as Charlie pulled away, Katerina exclaimed, "I'm going to have to find somewhere else to live".

Anna looked at her in horror. "Oh no, you haven't fallen out with Chrissy, have you?"

"No, we're fine".

"Ilya then. Has he upset you again?"

"Actually, no. Ilya's been great. This is the best we've been together since we were kids".

"Why then?"

"Chrissy's got a new boyfriend".

"Bloody hell, what's he done?"

"No, nothing like that. He's nice. I like him".

"Anna, I'm sure Katya will explain if you give her a chance," interjected Charlie with a chuckle.

"Well, Steve, that's her new boyfriend, stayed over on Saturday night and again last night. That's why I came straight out. They're still in bed".

"And?"

"I've had hardly any sleep. The noise coming out of the bedroom, well, what can I say? I've heard you two making love and you were rather vocal at times, but nothing like this. I've not heard Steve at all. It's all Chrissy".

Charlie and Anna remained silent.

"Chrissy's had plenty of boyfriends with her in the bedroom over the years, but I've never heard anything. But Saturday and last night! I couldn't work out if she was in ecstasy or being murdered".

Charlie couldn't help himself and he burst into laughter. Anna looked daggers at the back of his head and then she, too, started giggling.

"What? What's going on?" asked Katerina looking at one then the other.

"Well, how can I put this?" mused Anna. "Steve is an old friend of Charlie's. They played in the same rugby team for several years. Charlie has seen Steve in the showers. I understand that Steve is very well endowed".

"Don't misunderstand anything here, Katya," added Charlie. "Anna is not suggesting I've seen him with an erection, but she's right, he has a very large penis, and I would think that it would take some getting used to".

Katerina took this in. "Well, it appears that Chrissy hasn't yet got used to it".

Anna laughed until tears rolled down her cheeks, and Charlie forced himself to think of something else so that his driving wouldn't be impaired.

Once they had all composed themselves, Anna suggested, "Start with Ilya. Why the change? Has he finally grown up?"

"I confronted Glen when the two of them were together. Glen's the one who asked Ilya if I'd toss him off". Katerina continued to explain how she had belittled Glen.

"Brilliant. Good for you," was Anna's response to this.

"A couple of days afterwards, Ilya asked me if I fancied popping out for a drink. We went to the local, had a couple of pints, and he apologised. He admitted that he had treated me badly and asked if I'd forgive him".

"Did you make it easy for him?" asked Charlie.

"Actually, I did, but not before a bit of devilment".

"What did you do?" asked Anna in excitement.

"I said, "Tell you what Ilya, let me watch you masturbate and then I'll forgive you totally"".

"You didn't!"

"I did. Then I looked at him while he reeled in shock and embarrassment. I was determined that he would speak first, which he did. He said, "That was shameful of me. I'm very, very sorry Katerina". I said, "Quits?" and he replied, "Yes, quits". And that was it. In fact, we've been out again since, just the two of us, and it was great".

"I'm so pleased, Katya. Well done. Sounds like you couldn't have played that better," said Anna, admiringly.

"The three of us know that me handling it like that wouldn't have been possible without what you both did for me in France. I remember saying to you that I would no longer be just trying to cope with situations with boys but would be confident, with my head held high. That's down to you two, and I can't thank you enough".

Anna smiled at her and took Katerina's hand between hers. Charlie responded with, "It wasn't all one way you know, Katya. You made our holiday, and we loved having you there".

After a short period of silence, during which all three were visualising some of the events they had experienced together, Anna asked, "And how about your driving lessons? And work? How's that going?"

"I'll be taking my driving test soon. I've passed the theory part and Chrissy has been taking me out and feels I'm nearly ready. Work is going very well, thanks. Salty has been brilliant with me. She lets me get on with things and I've learned a lot".

"That's nice to hear".

"At first, I was reluctant to say anything when I thought things could be done differently, you know, a bit more efficiently. I did pluck up the courage to say about one thing which seemed blindingly obvious to me, and Salty couldn't have been more enthusiastic or receptive. She said that the store has been run in the same way for many years, and she really wants me to come up with ideas to modernise things. I really feel it's going to go well".

"For both of you, it appears," said Charlie.

"Yes, I think you're right. For both of us".

Anna wanted to keep things going, to try to get up to date before they arrived at Sandown Park so that, once there, they could concentrate on the racing, and all that goes with it. "Anything else we need to know?"

"Er, don't think so. Oh yes, just one more thing. I've got a boyfriend".

Anna admonished her with a mock slap to the back of the head. "You little tease. You should have started with that juicy bit of info".

Katerina laughed. "Sorry. Yes, early days. In fact, we've only been on a couple of dates, but it's promising. I like him". Anna pressed her for all the necessary information. Katerina relayed the events:

The customer approached her at the counter and asked if they had a copy of Nietzsche's Beyond Good and Evil. Katerina suggested he look in the philosophy section.

"I have, but no luck I'm afraid".

"That's odd, I'm sure I've seen a copy and I don't think we've sold it. Let me check for you".

They walked to the relevant section of the store and Katerina was disappointed to see that the customer had been correct. "Let's check in the Classics section," she suggested. "It may have been misfiled".

As they walked together, he said, "You know Nietzsche then?" and she replied, "Well no, not personally. He died more than a hundred years before I was born". He took that in then laughed heartily. Katerina laughed with him.

"Not here either. I'm afraid I can't check our stock on the computer because we're currently upgrading our technology. The abacus is being recycled as we speak. Let me have one more look in the philosophy section".

As they retraced their steps, Katerina glanced at a customer who was comfortably seated in the bay window reading a book. She felt she recognised the cover, so diverted so that she could say to him, "I'm so sorry to interrupt you, sir, but may I ask if that's Beyond Good and Evil".

"It is. I'm so sorry if I'm hogging it?"

"No, please, don't apologise. I don't suppose there's been anyone in this store for ages who's been after something by Nietzsche, yet I've got two customers about to have a duel over a copy of one of his books. Maybe the three of us can reach a philosophical outcome".

Both customers were delighted with the way Katerina was handling the situation, and the one who had been reading it said, "To be honest, I'm not intending to buy it. If the gentleman would like it, please do take it. Harold Robbins is more my style anyway. I was just trying to look intelligent".

More laughter, then thanks and finally Katerina completed the sale.

"His name is Louis, he's twenty-five, he's got some boring job in local government, but he's got a great sense of humour, which is probably essential if you work in local government. Good looking, calm and reasonably interesting. We've been getting on well. Nothing sexual yet so I've no idea whether he can rival Steve in the endowment department".

"Sounds ideal. You'll have to keep us updated," said Anna.

"I will. I promise".

"Any thoughts about contraceptives? You don't want to be caught out or rely on him".

"Don't worry, I sorted the Pill after I came home from France. As I told you while I was there, I felt I was ready to find a guy and have sex".

"Well, that all passed the time. We're here," said Charlie. "Let me locate our parking space then I'll give you your Day Membership Passes".

As soon as they were settled into their private box, which was designed to accommodate six people, the waitress who would be looking after them throughout the afternoon entered the room with a bottle of chilled Champagne, which she began to open.

"Er, I don't think I ordered Champagne," said Charlie, a little sheepishly.

"No sir, but we received a phone call from a young lady named Katerina. She has provided it for you. Shall I pour?"

"Yes, please do". Once the waitress had left the room, Anna and Charlie looked at Katerina and raised their glasses to her. "Cheers," she said, as the three of them chinked glasses. "Cheers," they replied, before Anna added, "To the lovely Katya. Our special friend. However wonderful our time with her has been, here's to even better times in the future. We love you Katya". Katerina beamed and downed half her glass in one.

"I gather from Anna that you've not been to a horse racing meeting before, so I'll just talk you through a few bits then you'll be free to do as you please this afternoon. I've arranged for our food to be brought in before the first race, which is at 1.55. They'll just lay it out and we can dip in as we please. There's a fridge over there with white wine, beer, cider, water, coke, and probably other stuff so help yourself when you want. There's red wine on the table. So, once they've brought in the food we won't be disturbed. I can buzz them if we want them to bring anything else".

"OK, cool".

"As for betting on the horses, we've each got a Race Card, and, on the table, you'll see three copies of the Racing Post, which gives a lot more detail, possibly too much as we're just here to have fun without taking it too seriously. As we said in France, Anna and I are pretty much creatures of habit. We usually go down to the paddock together to look at the horses parading. We'll choose what horse or horses we want to bet on. I'll go off to the bookies to bet then we'll watch the race from the box".

Katerina turned to Anna. "Didn't you say you tended to stay in the box?"

"Caught out, I did. I said it simply so that you had options to go outside with Charlie, or stay here, in which case I'd stay with you".

"Thoughtful as always, but I'd love to tag along with you to the parade ring and go with Charlie to place our bets with the bookies".

"Great," responded Charlie. "Why don't we have a mooch round now before it gets too crowded. Our badges allow us into all parts of the course".

They finished their drinks and walked together around the racecourse, with Charlie and Anna pointing out the paddock, the winner's enclosure, the bookmaker areas, the winning post and anything else in which they thought Katerina may be interested.

"Right, they'll be parading for the first race. Here are the Race Cards so take a look at the comments and the form guide as you spot them in the ring. Just to let you know, Katya, I make my selections by studying form, Anna does it by assessing the horses themselves and other people we've come with often just select names they like. A quick poll would indicate Anna's method is the most successful, then choosing horses you like the name of, then my approach of taking it seriously".

"He's not joking either, Katya".

"Right, I'll look at the names, hear what you have to say about the horses, Anna, and ignore anything Charlie may say". Katerina dug Charlie in the ribs as she said this, and he smiled with her.

Anna and Katerina chatted about the horses parading for the first race and both agreed that Bad Intentions looked fit and primed. "I like the name too," said Katerina. Charlie decided on a different one and then he and Katerina headed towards the bookmaker area while Anna returned to the box. Katerina slipped her arm through Charlie's, and they could be seen chatting and laughing like the best of friends.

"OK," said Charlie, "the trick is to stroll in front of the bookies and place your bet with the one offering the best odds. Look, he's offering six to one on your horse whereas the guy next to him is showing thirteen to two. So, which of those would you choose?"

"Thirteen to two. If I bet two pounds with him, I'd win thirteen pounds whereas it would be only twelve with the other guy".

"It sometimes takes me five races to get a first-timer to understand that. Right, before you go ahead, just have a quick look round to check if you can do better with anyone else. Be quick, though, because they update their odds and you may lose the chance".

"I'm going for the thirteen to two".

"How much are you betting?"

"Two pounds".

"Right, as Anna wants Bad Intentions too, could you place twelve pounds on it. Here's Anna's ten".

"So, what do I say to him?"

"Twelve pounds to win number three".

Charlie watched as Katerina successfully placed the bet and was pleased to note that she checked the betting slip before she walked away. Charlie placed his bet too and then they walked back to the box in the main grandstand. Anna was standing on the balcony, looking down at them walking arm in arm and chatting naturally. She smiled to herself, enjoying the affection she felt for them, and their relationship.

They watched the race from the balcony. Charlie's horse fell at the third hurdle and Bad Intentions kept himself in the middle of the main group of horses while the favourite in the betting surged ahead. With two more hurdles to jump, Bad Intentions' jockey started to galvanise his mount. Katerina began to get excited, her eyes glued to her selection. Over the last hurdle and it was still two lengths behind the leader, which appeared to be tiring.

"Come on Intentions, come on," called out Anna.

Katerina grabbed Anna's arm and started to jump up and down. "Go on, go on, go on".

Bad Intentions overtook the favourite just before the winning post and Anna and Katerina, in unison, shouted, "YES!" Katerina started clapping and Anna looked at Charlie and smiled.

"That was the most exciting thing I've seen since I watched you two having sex".

"Katya, you're incorrigible!" exclaimed Anna in mock horror.

"Sorry".

"No, don't apologise. It wasn't a criticism, I love it!"

"OK, Katya," said Charlie, "let's go and collect your and Anna's winnings, and then we'll stroll round to the parade ring for the next runners. Shall we see you at the same place Anna?"

"Yes, that's fine".

Anna stayed on the balcony and watched the couple make their way back to the bookmakers, again arm in arm. Charlie said something which must have delighted Katerina for she looked up at him as they walked, shrieked with laughter then kissed him on the cheek.

'I love that girl. I love that man too,' thought Anna.

Horses were chosen, bets were placed and viewing positions taken. The second race started and, once they had jumped the first, Katerina said, "That was a different fence to last race. Bigger".

"Yes," answered Anna, "there are hurdle races, like the first one, and steeplechases. This is a steeplechase".

"OK, got it".

Charlie was secretly delighted that his chosen horse won the second race. "I'll collect my winnings a bit later he said. Look, there's only three runners in the third race. I'm going to take the opportunity to stay here and have some eats. What would you two like to do?"

"I'm hungry. I won't be betting on a three-horse race, so I'll stay here too. What about you Katya?"

"I'll stay too if that's OK. Would you like me to dish up a selection for each of you?"

"That would be lovely, thank you. No peanut butter or apricots for me".

Katerina looked at him and smiled, realising he'd remembered her culinary dislikes. She went into the box while Anna and Charlie sat on the balcony.

"Charlie, you know you've been saying that, despite our lifestyle, our funds are growing rather than diminishing? Why don't we do a couple of things with it?"

"What have you got in mind?"

"The one which I'd most like to do is buy a property for Katya and Ilya to share. They will soon be getting to the stage where they would be thinking of moving out of Chrissy's, and a property would give them some freedom and a leg-up. We could put it in their names, 50/50, then they could sort it out from there".

"That's a big commitment".

"Yes, I know it's asking a lot, but think how hard it's been for all three of them. Chrissy has been amazing since Ivan left and deserves to concentrate now on her own happiness. Ilya and Katya, especially Katya, seem to have been uprooted time and again. They could finally feel they have a settled home, one which they're in control of".

Charlie gave this some thought, then smiled and said, "I'm happy for us to do that. What's the other idea?"

"Let's buy a racehorse. You, me and Katya as co-owners. How exciting would that be?"

"Well, that would certainly be a way to diminish the funds".

"Bad idea then?"

"Definitely. But let's do it anyway".

Anna got up, sat on his lap, put her arms around his neck and kissed him passionately. It was at that moment that Katerina returned, holding two plates of food. "Are you planning on demonstrating the other two positions?"

Anna released herself from her husband and laughed. "Oh yes, you watched us enjoy four sexual positions, didn't you, but I never did tell you what the other two main ones are".

"No, but don't worry, I've looked it up, so you can get off him now". Katerina gave them their food. "Now, are you going to behave while I go and get mine?"

"We will. Promise".

Katerina returned inside and Anna asked Charlie, "Do we say anything to Katya today?"

"If you'd like to then it's fine with me. Let's wait until after the last race, then we can relax and chat".

Katerina returned with her plate of food and sat on a spare chair. "Ooh, I forgot drinks. What would you two like?"

"White wine for me please Katya," replied Anna. "Will you have one with me?"

"Yes, I think I will. How about you Charlie?"

"A full fat coke please. No ice. Thanks".

The three of them chatted throughout the third race, and then resumed the paddock/bet/viewing process. No winners in the fourth or fifth races but, for the sixth and final race, Katerina selected a horse named Russian

Moll. "I don't care what it looks like or whether it's any good, I've just got to bet on that one". The best odds available to her were twenty to one, so a bit of a no-hoper.

With one fence to jump, the no-hoper galloped past several flagging horses in pursuit of the two leaders. "He's catching up, he's catching up," shrieked Katerina, once again jumping up and down. It took the lead with half a furlong of the race remaining.

"Keep him going," shouted Anna, in the hope that the jockey was listening out for instructions. It was visibly tiring and a horse from further back in the field started to close the gap. It was simply a case of whether the winning post would arrive in time. Anna and Katerina were statues, eyes fixed on the winning post. "And Russian Moll wins it by a short head," was announced by the course commentator. "He's won. He's only gone and won," cried out Katerina.

"You've had a good day, Katya," said Charlie once Katerina had calmed down. "I make it forty-seven pounds in profit".

"It's been brilliant. Thanks so much for bringing me. It's been such fun. Oh, and it's one hundred and forty-pounds profit. I was seven pounds up after five races, so I put that on Russian Moll".

"Well done you".

"Yes, nice work Katya," agreed Anna. "It's been a super day. Thank you for arranging it, Charlie. I think we should see Russian Moll coming into the winner's enclosure. Come on Katya, let's go and give him some adulation and pick up your winnings".

When they returned to the box, after Katerina had cheered in her new favourite horse and pocketed her money, Charlie said, "Look Katya, unless you're keen to get home, may I suggest that we stay here for an hour or so. We can tuck into any of the food that's left. I can arrange for them to bring more if you'd like. It will mean the crowds will clear and we should have a decent run home".

"I could stay here all night. Just tell me when you think we should be getting off".

"I'm going to have a coffee. Can I get you one Charlie? Katya?"

"Yes please," replied Charlie.

"I'll come in with you Anna. I think I'll have a little more wine".

"Shall we all go in? It's starting to get a bit chilly," suggested Charlie, so they all settled down with their drinks and some food inside the box.

"If you had a racehorse, Katya, what would you call it?" asked Anna.

"I was thinking about that when I saw Bad Intentions. I can't call it Russian Moll as that's already taken. I'd call it 'Place To Be'".

"I like that. How did you come up with it?"

Charlie got in before Katerina could answer. "Katya's favourite Nick Drake song".

"Yes, that's one reason. The second is that, whenever I play it, I think of my time in France where we listened to it loads. And the third reason is that wherever you both are, that's the place to be".

"Can't knock that for an answer," conceded Charlie.

"Well," said Anna, "how about you help us to source a young horseracing prospect? We'll buy it, call it Place To Be, register it as co-owned by the three of us, place it with a local trainer and cross our fingers. Charlie will pay the training and upkeep costs and the three of us will share any winnings".

"Are you serious?"

"Decision made," replied Charlie.

"Oh my god. Could life get any better?"

"Well, yes, it could".

"No, it couldn't Anna. How could it?"

"Because you're going to help Charlie and me source something else as well. We are going to buy a property for you and Ilya to share. Somewhere convenient for you both to live in, and one which you two can do what you like with as you get older, and your circumstances change".

Katerina looked at the two of them, her mouth open. She started to rise, presumably with the intention of giving them both a hug, but fell back in her chair, put her face in her hands and started to sob. Anna and Charlie gave her time, and before long she started to gain some control of herself. Anna rose, walked over to her, and embraced her. "It's something we want to do. No arguments. No feeling guilty. No feeling in our debt. It's something we can afford and is a way of keeping you close to us, so in some ways we're being selfish. It will be good for Chrissy too. So, there you are, as Charlie said about buying a horse: decision made. But don't say anything to Chrissy and Ilya just yet. I think it's important that Charlie and I run it past Chrissy first. Agreed?"

Katerina removed her hands and looked into Anna's eyes, her own still streaming.

"Agreed".

Katerina spend the next twenty minutes shaking her head, saying, "Oh my fucking god" to herself, hugging Anna, hugging Charlie, telling them in turn how much she loved them, sipping her wine, and drying fresh tears.

They walked back to the car three abreast, with Katerina in the middle, her arms pulling Charlie and Anna as close to her as possible. Anna again sat with her in the back, and the two held hands as Charlie pulled out of the car park. Whereas the journey there had been chatty and lively, the drive home was quiet, with all three lost in their thoughts.

BOOK THREE: *THE ADOLESCENT*

CHAPTER 18

They watched Katerina until she had opened the front door and disappeared into Chrissy's house, and then Charlie pulled away saying, "Lovely day, but it's turned out to be the most expensive trip to the races ever".

Anna, who had joined him in the front, laughed and said, "Yes, you're right. Betting on the occasional winner won't cover the cost of a property and a racehorse. Are you regretting it? Did I put you under pressure?"

"No, neither. Chrissy means a lot to you, and we're both extremely fond of Katya. And we couldn't think of not including Ilya, so the property purchase will be worth the outlay. As for the horse, that's just daft. But it's something I've thought about doing for ages so I'm all for it. It'll be fun for the three of us".

"Good. I feel the same way".

As soon as they entered the cottage, Anna said, "Come and have a shower with me".

"OK. You get it running and I'll follow you up with a couple of glasses of something. Armagnac or red wine?"

"Armagnac would be lovely, thanks".

By the time Charlie had poured the drinks, put the glasses on their bedside tables, taken off his clothes and entered the bathroom, Anna was standing under the stream of hot water. As he opened the shower door, Anna turned so that she had her back to him. He stood as close to her as possible and wrapped his arms around her so that he could fondle her breasts.

"I love you so much, Charlie". He didn't respond with words but with nibbling of her ears, shoulders, neck and upper back.

"Come on, let's go to bed. I need you badly". They left the shower, dried themselves and Charlie led Anna into the bedroom.

Afterwards, as they sat with their backs against pillows and the headboard, sipping their nightcaps, Anna said, "There's something I need to talk to you about. Something I'm trying to get my head around. Lene told me she's in love with me. I know you've said you're fine with me having some fun with her again, but I thought you should know".

"And how do you feel about her telling you that?"

"That's the difficult part. I think I've been avoiding admitting something to myself".

"What's that?"

"I think that I love Lene too". She swallowed hard and asked, a little tentatively, "What do you advise? I'm in a bit of turmoil, Charlie. To be honest, I feel confused. Should I tell her that from now on we must limit it to her being my beautician and best friend, nothing else? I can do that, I really can".

"Do you want to?"

"No. But then I don't know what I'm getting into. And I don't know your feelings about all this".

"Do you think you're heading towards having a relationship with her?"

"Yes, I'm beginning to understand that it's what we both want".

"And would that relationship create a possibility of any change of feeling you have towards me?"

"No".

"And if you were to have this relationship, would you be honest with me at all times, and never lie to me about what you're doing, where you're going or who you're seeing?"

"I will always be honest with you about everything".

"And, most importantly for me, if you ever felt that she, or you, were losing control, would you end things with her immediately, whatever the possible consequences to your relationship with her?"

"Yes".

"It wouldn't be acceptable to me if we were talking about a man, but with Lene, it's different. I trust you, Anna".

The following morning, after Charlie had left to go to his fencing club, Anna sent a text to Lene:

> *'Is it possible for us to meet. Don't worry, nothing has changed X'*

She then phoned Chrissy. "Hi Chrissy, am I interrupting anything?"

"No. Steve's just left. He stayed the night. Katerina seemed to have a great time at the races, and the clothes are fabulous. Thank you again for what you're doing for her".

"It's been a pleasure for both Charlie and me. You don't mind?"

"No, not at all. It's lovely to see her happy and doing so well".

"So, things are going well with Steve then?"

"What can I say? Anna, you know what you were saying, about Steve's reputation at the rugby club?"

"Yes".

"Well, it's true. It's fucking enormous".

Anna couldn't help laughing. "What, you mean it's somewhat bigger than any of your previous partners'?"

"No, I don't mean that at all. I mean that his cock is fucking enormous. Anna, however big you think it may be from me telling you this, it's much bigger, much, much bigger".

"I'm trying to imagine it".

"You have no idea".

Anna didn't respond to this but simply asked, "So, what have you done with it?"

"What do you mean?"

"Well, have you just rubbed it? Have you taken it in your mouth? Has it been inside you?"

"All three".

"And how have you coped with that, if it's as big as you're saying it is?"

"Don't doubt me. I'm not exaggerating. In fact, I'm doing it a disservice by describing it as fucking enormous".

"So, how have you coped?"

"Tossing him off was fine, although I could have done with four hands rather than two. Taking him in my mouth was like trying to digest a conger eel, whole, and I didn't do so well with that. When he put it inside me, well, I thought I was going to split in two".

Anna was laughing almost uncontrollably. "Oh god Chrissy, my eyes are streaming. I don't know whether it's from laughing so much or the thought of what you're describing".

"I wish I could share him with you, just for one evening, just so you could really appreciate what I'm talking about here. Anyway, I'm not going to, so I'll have to just tell you about it. Finally, after about five minutes of me saying, "slowly Steve, be careful Steve, Steve I'm not sure," and stuff like that, he was all in, well, as much as possible. I pleaded with him not to move too much until I got used to it. I came ridiculously quickly, and when he did too it felt like I had some sort of pumping machine inside me. Tell me, when you and Charlie have been getting carried away, have you ever said something like, "Ooh Charlie, I want you to spunk so hard inside me that I can taste it in my mouth"?"

"I have, yes".

"Well, when Steve came when he was inside me, he just about *was* inside my mouth. God knows how far up he was".

Anna was now on the floor. She couldn't speak and felt that she could be sick from laughing so much. After some time, she managed to ask, "So, was it pleasure or pain?"

"I can't say I didn't experience pain, but the pleasure was worth it. Well worth it. I'm always mindful of Ilya and Katerina being in the house when I've had a lover to stay, but I think with Steve I've been at risk of being noisy enough to be heard. I haven't had any funny or disgusted looks so I think I've got away with it".

Anna decided to change the subject before she wet herself. "Chrissy, there's something I'd like to run past you, Ilya and Katerina. Could you set something up for the five of us to meet, preferably within the next two or three days?"

"Yes, that shouldn't be a problem. How about you and Charlie coming round here for brunch on Sunday? Say around 10.30 or 11? I'll make sure they're both here".

"Great, thanks, we'll see you then. Now, you go off and order that lube you've been thinking about getting".

"It's not going up my bum, you know".

"Jesus, perish the thought. See you Sunday".

She received Lene's reply:

'You can pop into the salon this afternoon, around 4. I'm free from then'

Anna responded immediately:

'4 today is great. Don't worry'

When Charlie returned, Anna immediately said, "Right, three things: you and I are having brunch with Chrissy, Ilya and Katya on Sunday, you need to book a table for three at the Noah's Ark for Sunday week as we'll ask Katya to join us for the weekend so that we can start discussing the horse and the property, and, finally, I'm meeting Lene at the salon at 4 this afternoon so we can aim to get to grips with how things are between us. I have it in mind that the two of us will get together on Monday, if she's free, but I'd like to talk to her about it first. Are you OK with all of that?"

"Yes, I am. I'll contact the pub now to get the table booked. Will you be eating with Lene, or shall we have something together when you get back?"

"I doubt I'll be with her for long, so we'll eat when I get back. I can knock something up, we can sort a takeaway or we'll eat out. Up to you".

"OK. How about you pick up some fish and chips on your way back?"

"Good idea. I'll do that".

As Lene's beauty salon operated an appointment-only system, and she did not employ a receptionist, the entrance door was always locked so that customers were required to ring the bell on arrival. When Lene let Anna in, she was asked if Dani was working.

"No, I said she could go home early. We're often quiet on a Thursday prior to the weekend rush so it's no problem. Can I get you a coffee Anna?"

"No, I'm fine thanks".

Lene locked the door and sat on one of the chairs in the waiting area. Anna sat on another, facing Lene, who was fidgeting, almost trembling.

"You look so worried, Lene. I'm sorry if I've ruined your day. Believe me, there's nothing to concern yourself about. Look, I want you to be completely honest with me about something which has been on my mind. I'd like you to tell me exactly what feelings you have for me. And I'd like you to tell me how you view me in all this".

"I don't know what the last part means, so you'll have to explain that before I can answer it. As for my feelings, I thought I'd made them clear. I'm in love with you. It's obvious that I desire you, but maybe it's not so obvious that I love you too. As a person, as a lover. I love you the way a person loves someone they want to marry. Deeply, in other words, not just because of sexual desire".

"Yes, I thought that was the case. What I'm asking about how you view me is… Look, it's better if I backtrack a bit. The truth is that I've always been a feminine person. I like to wear feminine clothes and be looked after by my man. I've always considered myself to be quite short, quite slim, quite attractive to men. And then you and me together in The Spread Eagle turned all of that on its head".

"Really? In what way?"

"Because you arrived wearing that stunning, short, red dress which hugged your body. When you sat with us in the conservatory, you looked so defenceless. In control of yourself, sexy, with your skirt riding up and the gap between your thighs exposed, but defenceless, almost innocent. Then we got to the bedroom, and I saw you naked for the first time in so many years. You're still tiny, still beautifully in proportion. For the first time ever, I felt older and bigger than I'd previously viewed myself".

"Oh Anna".

"No, really Lene, I'm not feeling sorry for myself or anything, and I'm not saying I wish I looked any different to how I do. Maybe I have an old-fashioned view of female couples, but I've always thought that one is maybe the more dominant masculine one and the other the feminine one. I realise that I am probably slurring gay girls by saying this, but it's not through judgement but purely through inexperience and ignorance".

"And you're asking if I view you as the masculine one and me the feminine one?"

"Yes. But I'm not suggesting that you've done or said anything to encourage me to think that way. It's simply, as I say, you're shorter, slimmer, prettier and, oh I don't know, more girly I suppose".

"Really, I want to just stand up, walk over to you and hug and kiss you, and tell you off for being so silly, but instead I'll take your concern seriously. First, you are the most attractive, classy, and sexy female I've ever seen or met. In the many years I've known you, every male I've been with has followed you with his eyes and it has been obvious to me how much they fancy you. I'm not trying to flatter you when I say that your height, body shape, hairstyle, style of make-up, looks, everything, are things I've considered to be perfect, enviable. I've never seen anyone look better in clothes. And when I saw you naked at the hotel, I realised that clothes, in fact, do you an injustice. In my profession, I'm in contact with a lot of women and girls, of course. A small percentage are attractive, and just about all of those don't seem to know what to do with themselves".

"What do you mean by that?"

"Attractive females seem to want to draw attention to themselves— look at me, look at how pretty, or sexy, or beautiful I am. Look at my clothes and make-up. You're not like that, yet you are the most attractive of them all. Anna, everything about you exudes femininity and class. What's more, your naked body is incredible. I just wanted to wallow for hours between your breasts in that hotel room. I wanted to do whatever a girl can do to make love to another girl. Anna, you're desirable to me because you're a gorgeous female, and I want to enjoy every part of your female body. Does that make sense? Does it answer your concern?"

"It does. Thank you".

"Does it worry you that I've told you that I love you?"

"You said that you're *in love* with me".

"It's different, isn't it?"

"Yes".

"Well, it's true, I *am* in love with you. As I say, does it worry you?"

"It doesn't. The thing is Lene, I'm realising that I love you too; am in love with you too".

"Please don't say that purely because you think I may want to hear it".

"We're way beyond that, aren't we? No, I love that you love me, and, increasingly, I'm realising that I love you. What I need to come back to though is what you and I have agreed: that you with Greg, and me with Charlie, that cannot be threatened in any way. The first sign of it, however insignificant, and we must revert to being good friends. May I ask you to agree that with me?"

"Yes, of course. I honestly commit to continuing to love my husband and to be the best mother and businesswoman I can be. A loving and, hopefully, sexual relationship with you would be on top of that, not in replacement for any part of it".

"Wonderful. Now, if you're free, and want to, I can book an Airbnb house in Bracklesham, overlooking the beach, for Monday. They've agreed to let me have it from 11am. There's a locked box which has the key in it. The owner will text the code first thing on Monday. We can get there at 11 and you can leave whenever you like, to fit in with Greg and the girls. If we meet in the car park next to 'Billy's on the Beach' café a bit before 11 we can go to the house together. How does that sound?"

"It sounds incredible".

"Great. So, I'll get that confirmed and we can look forward to Monday".

"Can't wait. May I put in a request please?"

"Of course".

"I know it may not be the weather for it, but will you wear that lovely floral dress you wore to The Spread Eagle?"

"Yes, I'm happy to do that for you".

"And can we meet inside the café instead of the car park? Say 10.30? We can have a coffee and pick up some bits to take to the house, some sandwiches and beers, or whatever".

"Perfect". Anna stood up as she said this, and Lene followed suit.

"Actually, I said that your body is tiny but beautifully in proportion. Not quite true. There's one part of you which is beautifully out of proportion".

"Oh dear, which part is that?"

"Your nipples. They're so long and pronounced. I just cannot wait to take them in my mouth".

Lene emitted a barely audible gasp. They walked towards each other and embraced.

Chapter 19

Anna drove the Alfa on the Sunday morning, Charlie being happy to enjoy viewing the countryside as they sped through the lanes to Chrissy's house. Chrissy welcomed them and led them into the kitchen, where she had started to prepare brunch. "Sausages, bacon, fried bread, fried eggs, some hash browns and a few mushrooms. All healthy stuff. I'll just put it all on the table and you can help yourselves".

"Smells wonderful, Chrissy. It's making me really hungry," responded Charlie.

"Well, there'll be plenty of it, so that's fine. Ilya and Katerina are upstairs. I asked them to stay out of the way until I call them down. I guessed you'd want just the three of us to have some time first".

"Yes, we do," agreed Anna. "I'll get straight to it so that you can give us your thoughts before the food is ready to dish up. Charlie and I would like to buy a property for Ilya and Katerina to share. They can do with it as they please as it will be in their joint names, but it would be nice if they both decided to live there until either of them is ready to make individual plans".

"You want to buy a property, give it to the two of them, have it so they can move out of here, and arrange it so that it's their responsibility to sort as and when one of them wants a different arrangement?"

"Yes. Is that a problem?"

"A problem? It's an unbelievable thing for the two of you to offer".

"So, it's a yes, then? We can tell Ilya and Katerina about it this morning, and get things moving?"

"Absolutely. They'll be thrilled. It's so generous of you both". She hugged and kissed them in turn. "Thank you so much".

"It really is our pleasure," responded Charlie, wanting to ensure that Chrissy was aware that he was in total agreement with Anna's proposal.

"And there's an added bonus, of course".

"What's that?" asked Anna.

"I will be able to make as much noise as I like when Steve is splitting me in two".

"Oh god," said Anna, laughing. "Don't start me off again, please".

Chrissy called up the stairs, "Breakfast is ready guys. Come and get it before it gets cold". Katerina was the first down, and she gave Anna and Charlie a hug and a peck on the cheek. The four of them went into the dining room, where everything had been laid out. Ilya burst in shortly afterwards.

"Hi Anna. Hi Charlie. Great to see you". He walked over to Anna and embraced her in a manly hug, then turned to shake Charlie's hand.

"My god," exclaimed Anna, "what on earth has happened to you since I saw you last? You're so tall and grown up".

"All down to Chrissy's wonderful food," was his jocular response as he grabbed a plate and shaped to pierce a sausage.

"Hey, you," said Chrissy, with a hint of annoyance, "guests and ladies first".

"Sorry," replied Ilya, suitably abashed. "Anna, would you like me to plate up some food for you or would you prefer to help yourself?"

"I'll let you do it, thanks. I'll have a sausage, two slices of bacon, a hash brown, one piece of fried bread with a fried egg on top. Oh, and a few mushrooms please".

"Coming up. And what about you Charlie?"

"Thanks Ilya, but I'm happy for Katerina and Chrissy to take what they want, and then you and I can divvy up the rest".

"Sounds good to me".

The five of them sat around the table and tucked into their food while sharing news, teases, and old stories. Ilya informed Anna and Charlie that he was working at the water sports store in East Wittering and really loved it as it was a cool place to be and he was busy during most months of the year, catering for holidaymakers in the summer and kite surfers, wind surfers and surfers in and out of season.

"So, do you purely serve customers or do people expect you to provide advice and guidance with equipment?" asked Charlie, with genuine interest.

"Both, to be honest. As you probably know, I've done a bit of surfing during the past few years and mates of mine are into wind surfing, so I've learned a bit from them. Kite surfing is new to me, so I'm having to get to grips with what that involves, especially now that the unofficial season has started".

Breakfast continued in this vein until they all said they couldn't eat any more and Katerina had started to gather the dirty plates and dishes to carry back to the kitchen. "Come on Ilya, give me a hand," she said.

"No, don't worry Ilya, you tell Charlie more about the water sports stuff. I reckon there's a good chance you'll have a new customer. I'll sort this with Katerina".

"I'll help too," said Chrissy.

"No, you won't," insisted Anna. "You've done enough, preparing all this. Katerina and I will sort it, won't we?"

"Of course".

As soon as the two of them had carried everything into the kitchen, and Anna was loading the dishwasher while Katerina was doing some washing up, Katerina asked, "So, what do you think of Ilya?"

"I was genuinely shocked. He's grown up since the last time I saw him, which must have been April-time, I guess".

"He's very good looking, isn't he?"

"He is".

"Tell you what, if he asked me now to watch him masturbate, I might hang around until he finished".

"Katya! Like I said at Sandown, you're incorrigible. Come on, let's get these done then Charlie and I are going to talk to the three of you about the property. We're not going to mention the racehorse at this stage. Could you try to act as if this is the first you've heard of it?"

"No problem".

It was two hours before everything had been talked through and agreed, with initial plans formulated. Katerina and Ilya agreed that they would, together, produce a 'preference' list with regards to the proposed property purchase and that it would be Katerina who would be working with

Anna and Charlie to try to decide upon a short list of possible places to buy. Ilya would then join them to make the final decision, with Chrissy free to be involved as much as she wanted.

"So," summarised Anna as she and Charlie stood by the front door, about to leave, "Katerina will come to us next Saturday after work. One of us will collect her at six and then she'll stay with us until Monday morning when we'll drop her off at work. Hopefully, we will have made some progress narrowing down properties to have a look at. Katerina, don't forget to bring the preference list".

"No, I won't. See you on Saturday".

"Thanks again Anna, Charlie. It really is most awfully generous of you both".

"Honestly, Ilya, it's a pleasure. Thanks again for brunch, Chrissy. That was breakfast, lunch and dinner all in one," said Anna as she hugged each of them in turn.

"Yes, thanks Chrissy," added Charlie. "Come round soon, won't you?"

"I will. And thank you. These two are extremely lucky, and I can tell how excited they are".

They all exchanged final hugs, kisses, waves, and farewell wishes, and then Anna and Charlie began their journey home.

"Well," said Anna, "that couldn't have gone much better".

"No, guess not. But no real reason why it may have gone worse, is there?"

"No, I suppose not. Still, it's lovely to see the three of them so happy. I love the banter that goes on between Katya and Ilya. He clearly enjoys teasing her, but she deals with it so wittily. What did you think of him?"

"Ilya? I believe the traditional response would be that he's turned out to be a fine young man".

"Yes, very unlike the one who obviously gave Katya such a torrid time".

"Very good looking, too".

"He is. I wonder if he needs any guidance, as Katya did". She didn't look in Charlie's direction but could sense his eyes on her. "Only joking," she said, then paused before facing Charlie, a saucy grin on her face.

BOOK THREE: *THE ADOLESCENT*

CHAPTER 20

Knowing Anna was rarely late, Lene had ensured that she was seated in the café by 10.15. Anna drove into the car park at 10.25 and was quite surprised to see Lene's car already in a parking space. Although it was a bright, sunny day, and quite warm for the second half of October, there was a morning chill in the sea air, so Anna took the jacket she had brought with her and slipped it over her short-sleeved dress as she walked towards the café entrance.

Although the café was quite busy, Anna spotted Lene immediately, seated in the corner. Lene rose and waited for Anna to join her. As she reached the table, Lene pulled a chair away and guided Anna to take a seat. Before sitting down, Anna said, "Hello Lene," and they hugged.

Lene remained standing and said, "I haven't ordered anything yet. What would you like?"

"A flat white please".

"Would you like a cake or pastry to go with it?"

"I don't think I would, thanks, but don't let me stop you".

Lene smiled and walked to the counter to place the order. Anna's seat faced the window, overlooking the beach, so she needed to turn around to watch Lene, whose appearance was striking. She had chosen to wear a tailored, dark blue, trouser suit. Underneath the jacket, she wore a crisp, fitted, white shirt. In addition, a thin tie, with an impeccable Windsor knot. Her blond hair was swept back tightly off her face and was secured in a ponytail.

Lene returned and sat opposite Anna. "The waitress will come over to take the order. Thank you for wearing that dress. You look stunning".

"Thank you. And you, Lene? Wow".

Lene responded with a smile. The waitress joined them and had her pen poised over her notebook.

Lene looked at her and said, "Two flat whites please, one slice of your homemade Bakewell Tart, but please provide a knife and an extra plate. And could you also prepare us some food to take away please. Two ham and salad baguettes, no onion, two packets of salt and vinegar crisps and two cans of lager".

"Certainly. Would you prefer Stella or Carlsberg?"

"Stella please".

"And would you like any mayonnaise on your baguettes?"

"Not for me thanks. Anna?"

"No thank you".

The waitress returned to the counter and Lene asked, "I hope that's OK".

"It is. Thank you".

"It's a lovely morning. How are you feeling?"

"I woke up feeling happy. I then had a period of feeling nervous, which is unlike me, and now that I'm here, seeing you, I'm happy again".

"Have you brought any other clothes with you, should we want to have a walk on the beach later?"

"I have. I've a small bag in the boot".

"Me too".

"And what about you, Lene? How are you feeling?"

"As if I'm about to go in for an appointment with the most desirable dentist ever".

Anna laughed. "Anxious, but excited?"

"Yes. Any second thoughts?"

"None at all. You?"

"No".

"That's good then. And anxious excitement makes you feel alive, doesn't it?"

"I certainly feel alive".

The coffees and cake were served and then consumed whilst the girls chatted. Once they were both ready to leave, Lene said, "I'll just settle up and collect our lunch. Won't be a minute". Leaving the cafe, Anna took Lene's arm, and Lene led Anna to her car. "I'll follow you".

Within a couple of minutes, they had pulled into the drive, closed the double wrought iron gates behind them, Anna had extracted the keys from the lockbox, and they were inside The Terns, a modern, four bedroomed, detached house overlooking Bracklesham beach. They spent a quarter of an hour exploring the garden and the downstairs accommodation and then checked out the rooms upstairs, taking their bags with them.

"It's fantastic," said Lene.

"It is," agreed Anna. "And what a view," she added as she stood at the huge, floor to ceiling windows in the main bedroom. Lene stood behind her and enveloped her with her arms. She whispered, "I'm going to take off my jacket and then I'll sit down. You will then stand in front of me and do exactly as I tell you".

Anna faced her, with her back to the window. "Shoes off first". Anna removed her sandals.

"Now the dress". Anna undid the buttons, slipped out of the dress and cast it aside.

"Knickers". They were taken off.

"Bra". Anna was now naked in front of Lene. Eye contact had been maintained throughout.

"Lie on the bed and wait for me". Anna complied.

Lene opened the small case which she had brought with her and removed two sets of velvet handcuffs. Anna continued to watch her as Lene walked to the bed and passed a set to Anna.

"Handcuff your ankles to the bed". Anna did as she was told.

"Now lie back". Lene used the other set to secure Anna's wrists. Naked, legs spread and defenceless, Anna felt completely powerless under Lene's control. Her excitement and level of arousal made her shiver.

Lene stood by the side of the bed and removed her shoes and socks. Her tie and shirt followed. She had not been wearing a bra and her insignificant breasts were now exposed. As she gazed at Lene's nipples, Anna emitted an involuntary groan. Lene did not remove her trousers when laying on top of Anna. Anna longed to embrace her, but the handcuffs made this impossible. Lene kissed her, a passionate, sexual kiss, using her soft feminine lips and her tongue, which explored Anna's mouth.

Lene gradually slid down her lover's body. Her lips, teeth and tongue sucked, nibbled, and licked every inch of the front of Anna's upper body before Lene rested her face in the middle of Anna's chest. She then used her hands to position Anna's breasts so that they surrounded the sides of her face. The word she had previously used to describe what she was doing now was 'wallow'. She was wallowing in Anna's bosom. "Your breasts are absolutely magnificent," she said.

Lene was reluctant to leave them, so reluctant that her hands insisted on continuing to enjoy them as she slid herself further down, choosing to go no lower than the top of Anna's thighs. "Oh, the taste of you. Beautiful".

"Stop, please stop. Enough Lene, please". Lene relented and eased herself back up Anna's body until they were face to face once again. "I love you, Lene".

Lene re-secured Anna's wrist, which had come loose in her flailing, climbed off the bed, removed her trousers and knickers, and returned to her bag, from which she removed something which remained hidden from Anna's enquiring eyes. Lene climbed back onto the bed, knelt between Anna's knees and inserted part of something into herself. Then she leaned forward and eased the other part into Anna.

Slow, rhythmic momentum until, eventually, another plea from Anna. "No more. I can't take any more. Lene, please. Oh god, what's happening to me?"

Once she accepted that Anna had, indeed, taken all she could handle, Lene ceased her movements, yet she ensured their bodies remained connected. "I love you, Anna".

They maintained their positions for a while longer, before Lene withdrew from Anna and removed the toy.

"Give me a couple of minutes and then I would like to enjoy your body".

"Could you wait a while? How about having our lunch in the garden and then a quick walk on the beach? We can come back up here when we get back".

"I'd love that".

Lene loosened her hair from her ponytail, they both donned their practical clothes and then consumed their lunch in the warmth of the autumn sun, in a sheltered part of the garden. The waves breaking on the pebbles sounded like the shushing of a neighbour trying to quieten noisy people living next door.

"Thank you, Lene".
"For?"
"Reassuring me so beautifully".
Lene simply looked at her and smiled.
"That dildo. I've never seen one like that before".
"No, I hadn't either. I decided after we met last week to buy a strap-on. I did a bit of internet research and thought they all looked cumbersome and false. Then I saw that one and liked it. As a bonus, with half of it inside me, I felt part of the experience, as if I really was making love to you, and that was very, very arousing".
"As you may have gathered, it aroused me too".
"I've been wondering how it is that you and I have known each other for nearly twenty years, have been close but not living each other's lives, have been together while you've been practically naked when you've been receiving a treatment from me, yet it's now, only now, that we're sharing all this, feeling the way we do. And not just one of us, both".
"Who can explain love?"
"But we've never even had thoughts of intimacy, have we? Not since that freaky night at Uni. Until Midhurst, we've not even flirted with each other when we're pissed".
"I know. I can't explain it either. I just know that being with you like that at The Spread Eagle flicked a switch. Something became illuminated. Something previously unseen was suddenly so clear to me. Maybe the love wouldn't have happened without the sex. It probably wouldn't. I can't explain it either, but it's happened, and now we have to enjoy it and live with it the best we can bearing in mind our commitment to Charlie and Greg".
"Will you be able to continue with me like this without it affecting your love for Charlie".
"I'm determined to. And you must be determined too. And if doubts creep in, you must tell me, and then we must become just friends again. It has to be that way. I love Charlie, and I will not hurt him".
"I know, and I agree. I really do feel the same way as I've described, that you've been added to my life without anything else being taken away or compromised".

"Good. Now, I need to tell you, before we get intimate again. Your face and body are amazing. You're a thirty-seven-year-old mother, yet you still look like a teenager. I've no doubt that will still be the case during the next ten years or more".

Lene chuckled. "You know that little skirt I was wearing when we went to the Noah's Ark?"

"Yes. Loved it".

"Girls aged twelve from Next. And the red dress you've admired, the one I wore to Midhurst? Aged twelve to fourteen from River Island. I've another skirt you haven't seen me in yet. It's from Superdry's girls' section and it's tiny".

"I can't wait for you to wear it. And I have to tell you again: your nipples!"

"You like them, don't you?"

"They're like pistols aimed at me, and I have no option other than to hold up my hands in surrender," replied Anna, with a giggle.

"I'm delighted they give you so much pleasure, but from my point of view they're nothing compared to your breasts. I'd suggest a trade, but my frame couldn't support your bust; I'd continually topple forwards".

Anna laughed. "No need for us to trade. I'll continue to enjoy your nipples and you can make the most of my breasts whenever we manage to get together".

"Shall we have a quick walk on the beach, and then we can go up to the bedroom again?"

They were back in the bedroom a quarter of an hour later. They both undressed without requests or suggestions, and lay on the bed, side by side, with Anna's arm around Lene, holding her close.

"What would you like me to do?"

"You don't need to do anything. I would be happy to stay like this until I have to leave".

"But may I anyway?"

"Of course. My body is yours, in whatever way you want it. There isn't any part of me, inside or out, that doesn't yearn for a part of you".

BOOK THREE: *THE ADOLESCENT*

At 5pm Lene told Anna that she would need to go. Anna, not wishing to delay her friend, helped her to gather her belongings. They hugged by the side of Lene's car, both reluctant to let the other go. Anna finally stepped away and said, "It was one of the most pleasurable days I've ever experienced. Thank you, Lene".

"We'll do something again soon, won't we? Even just to meet up for a coffee or something?"

"Yes, of course".

"Bye Anna".

"Bye Lene," and she watched the car drive away.

Anna composed herself, then sent a text to Charlie:

> *'Lene has just left. I have the house until 11 in the morning. Why not drive over, bring a bottle of something, pick up a pizza and we can spend the night here?'*

Two minutes later a reply:

> *'Love to. Any particular pizza?'*
> *'Great, no anything thanks. I'll send you the address'*
> *'Should be there within an hour'*
> *'X'*

Chapter 21

Anna was sitting up in bed when she received a text from Katerina:

> *'I lost something yesterday'*
> *'Oh dear, nothing valuable, I hope'*
> *'Not valuable, but precious'*
> *'Aah, I think I see. Was Louis involved in the loss?'*
> *'He was'*
> *'And was he as you hoped he would be?'*
> *'He was'*
> *'Good. Tell us all about it on Saturday'*
> *'Of course. See you then xx'*

Anna looked at Charlie and said, "Katya had sex with Louis yesterday".

"Really? Good for her".

"Yes, good for her. It was the one thing which was missing. She can go on to rule the world".

"She's certainly a one-off".

"She's special. I'm so pleased she's in our life the way she is".

"It's lovely to think that, with the property purchase and the three of us owning a racehorse together, we'll be spending a lot of time with her. If she wants that, of course".

"She will. We must firm up on France. See if she still wants to join us while we're there over Christmas and New Year".

"Well remembered. Let's ask her at the weekend. We'll need to get the flights booked".

"I'll send her a text now. She'll have to sort it with Salty before we book anything".

"Good point".

> *'Just a reminder that we'll be in France Xmas & NY. If you want to come over, check what time off you can have. We*

will need to get the flights booked'
'I'd love to come. Will speak to Salty today'
'OK. Louis welcome too'
'Thanks, but if I'm able to come I want it to be just us three'
'OK, no problem'

"Right, that's done. Tell me, do you feel guilty at all that we've spent quite a bit of money on Katya and nothing on Ilya?"

"Not really. Three reasons: one, we're going to buy him half a property; two, Katya's given something, become part of what we're doing; three, I don't actually have a family connexion to him".

"Yes, that all makes sense. But you don't have a connexion to Katya either, and your natural fairness must encourage you to want to even things up a bit, surely?"

Charlie laughed. "Anna, I don't know why we're even discussing this. You've obviously thought about it and decided something. I'm happy for you to go ahead with whatever you've formulated".

"OK, thanks. We'll spend some money on him to balance out Katya's clothes. And maybe we should also let him know he's welcome to holiday with us in France if he wishes".

"Hang on, I'm not so sure about France".

"Why not? Katya's been and will be going again. We can't deny Ilya the opportunity too".

"I hope you're not considering a further episode of education".

"Furthest thing from my mind".

"That's reassuring, because it didn't seem to be on Sunday".

"You worry too much my darling Charlie".

"Whatever you say, Anna. I'm so soft, aren't I? I don't know why I always allow you to get your own way".

"Maybe it's because I provide the best head in the south of England. Or because of your obsession with these". On saying this, she slipped the straps of her nightie off her shoulders and revealed to him her breasts.

"Ratbag. Do you know, a part of me is looking forward to the day when my penis has hoisted the white flag, and your breasts are hanging down at your waist and I'm no longer interested".

"Won't happen. I'll still be going down on you when you're 90 and, by then, some scientist will be so horrified by his wife's sagging boobs that he will have devised some method of keeping god's greatest invention nicely pert without the need for pumping them with silicone. Now, are you going to enjoy them, or shall I put them away?"

"Just a few minutes, then".

Charlie was out for a few hours at the Fencing Club, and Anna had little to do, so she decided to drive into East Wittering to have a chat with Ilya. It just so happened that she selected from her wardrobe a short suede skirt which she wore with knee high, leather boots and a cashmere jumper. As she entered Shore Watersports store, a young man looked up and studied her as she walked towards him. Anna guessed him to be in his mid-twenties and would not look out of place on the beaches in California. Also, within the store, she sighted a girl who was rearranging clothing stock. She would be perhaps a little older than Katerina, strikingly pretty and displaying long, shapely legs in spray-on leggings.

"May I help you?" asked the lad.

"I'm looking for Ilya please. Is he working today?"

"He is. He's in our wetsuit section upstairs, but I'm very happy to help you. What is it you're looking for?"

Anna gave him one of her smiles and said, "That's very kind of you, but I'll pop up and have a word with Ilya". She headed for the stairs and the assistant's eyes followed her as she ascended.

Ilya was talking to a customer, so she had a look around the store while she waited for him to be free. She was impressed. Most of the downstairs floor space had been set up for clothing and footwear, catering in the main for holidaymakers, whereas upstairs was devoted to the enthusiast. Anna was surprised by how many options there were, how much choice. She took the opportunity to study Ilya who was now recording the details of a sale. He appeared to be providing an enthusiastic and informed service to the client.

"Anna," he said, once he was free, "how lovely".

Before she could respond, the guy she had spoken to when she entered the store appeared at the top of the stairs and said to Ilya, "I know you've been busy this morning, Ilya. If you like, I can assist the customer".

"Very thoughtful, Scott, but I can manage". Ilya waited for his co-worker to go back down the stairs then said to Anna, "I think you're in there, if you're interested".

"I'm fine thanks. It's a bit like Abercrombie & Fitch in here, isn't it? The owner will employ only very attractive people".

"A bit like Hooters—don't bother applying unless you're at least a C-cup".

"Exactly. Anyway, am I interrupting you or can you spare a few minutes?"

"No, I'm fine. I'll have to break off if a customer comes up but fire away".

"OK, I won't hold you up. I just wanted to check, you were talking to Charlie about surfing, which I gather you're into, and wind surfing and kite surfing".

"Yes, that's right".

"Are you planning to concentrate on progressing further with the surfing or do you also want to get involved in one of the others?"

"I'm very keen to learn how to kite surf. I can then do that in winter. Surfing is more of a summer activity".

"What's stopping you doing it?"

"I haven't got the equipment; I'm saving at the moment".

"What do you need?" Ilya started to run through a list of the required equipment, but Anna stopped him short. "Too technical for me. Look, will you do me a favour?"

"Name it".

"Whatever you need, order it, tell me how much it is and how and who I pay. Charlie and I want to set you up".

"No way. You told me only a few days ago that you're intending to buy a property for Katerina and me".

"Our plans haven't changed with that. This is in addition. Quite simply, we've helped Katerina with some summer and winter clothes and, unless you agree to this, I'll just have to ask her to give them back. Charlie and I are not going to allow purchases for her but not for you".

Ilya looked at her, frowning.

"You're not going to have a scene with me, are you? Just say yes, Ilya, and let's get it sorted. We're all level then and can look one another in the eye".

"Well, then thank you Anna".

"Our pleasure. And don't go choosing rubbish stuff just to save a bit of money. I hate that. Choose what you want and get it ordered".

"That is extremely kind of you. And Charlie too. Thank you".

"Right, I can hear someone coming up the stairs, so it may be time for you to try to make another sale".

"Thanks again. Oh, and by the way".

"Yes," said Anna, looking at him intently.

"Scott has excellent taste".

"Thank you, Ilya. And you can rest assured that if any female came into this store looking to attract one of the male assistants, however good looking he may be, it wouldn't be Scott who she'd aim to flirt with. See you soon. Don't forget to tell me what I'm to pay and who to pay it to". Anna headed for the stairs and then turned to smile and wave. Ilya smiled and waved in return.

"Right, I'll go and collect Katya from Arundel. Anything you need me to get while I'm out?"

"Don't think so, thanks. See you in a bit".

It's a lovely drive from their cottage to Arundel, and it was a pleasant late afternoon, so Charlie selected the Alfa keys. He parked at the pre-arranged place in Arundel and stood by the side of the car waiting for Katerina. A little after six he spotted her striding towards him. "Hi Charlie, thanks so much for picking me up," and she went on tiptoe to kiss him on the lips.

"Hello Katya. It's no problem. Here, chuck your bag in the boot". He opened the passenger door and held it for her to climb in, which she attempted as discreetly as possible, considering the length of her skirt, how low the Alfa was to the ground and cramped the passenger area. Charlie closed the door then walked around to get into the driver's side.

"Did you choose this car deliberately so that every time Anna gets in it when wearing a skirt, you can see what she's had for breakfast?"

"That wasn't the only reason. I also like the colour". He pulled away then added, "Great outfit Katya. New?"

"Thanks, yes, I used my Sandown winnings to buy myself some work clothes".

"I particularly like the skirt".

"Why is it that when men say they like your skirt or dress they're not really complimenting the garment but how much it reveals?"

"Oh, I think that's a bit unfair".

"Really? So, in France, did you prefer me to wear the short A-line or the knee length pleated?"

"The A-line. But that was because I liked the colour".

Katerina laughed.

Charlie continued with, "Haven't you ever heard the term 'less is more'?"

"I have, but if less is more, think how much more more would be".

"I hate it when you throw Nietzsche at me".

"It seems that the less material a skirt has, the more you like it. That's an oxymoron, isn't it? Or is it a paradox?"

"Paradox. Hey, 'Oxymoron' would be a great name for a band. You and I should form a duo and call ourselves that".

"That may be a reasonable idea other than the fact that neither of us can play an instrument and neither of us can sing".

"How do you know I can't sing?"

"Charlie, I've heard you trying to sing along to 'Karma Police'. And you've ruined one of my favourite songs ever. I used to love listening to Nick Drake sing 'Magic' but now my head only hears you wailing it out in France".

Charlie laughed. "Look," he said, "not being able to sing or play an instrument didn't stop Sonny and Cher earning a fortune with 'I got you babe'".

"You may be onto something there. If I remember correctly, Cher was sexy, and Sonny looked like an idiot".

"OK, bad example".

"And didn't he knock her around a bit? Or was that Ike and Tina Turner?"

"Could well have been both. It was a 60's thing".

"With the Oxymoron name suggestion for our duo, I see where you're going with the 'moron' part but how does 'Oxy' relate to me?"

"It's Greek for 'precocious adolescent'".

They drove on, both chuckling to themselves.

After a while, Katerina shuffled around in her seat and asked, "How on earth do you two manage to have sex in here when you pull off into a layby?"

"We don't pull off into a layby to have sex".

"Would you like me to pull *you* off in a layby?"

"See? Precocious adolescent".

"What's the matter, Charlie, don't you fancy me anymore, now that I'm no longer a virgin?"

"How much more evidence are you planning on providing? You'll never go to heaven, Katya".

Katerina laughed mischievously then said, in a serious voice, "I don't believe in any of that nonsense, and I know you don't either. I read a great quote by a main character in a book once: 'No plumb line could fathom the depths of my faithlessness'".

"William Boyd's Any Human Heart?".

"Do you know, I think it may have been. You're so smart Charlie".

"Still clinging on, trying to keep level with you. So, what if you're wrong? About heaven, I mean".

"Well, if I get there, I guess God will say to me, "Sorry, do I know you?" and I'll have to come up with something plausible before he kicks me out".

They entered the cottage, laughing, and Anna called out, "Hi Katya, I'm in the kitchen, come on through". Katerina and Charlie joined her, and the girls embraced. "What were you two finding so funny?"

"Nothing in particular. Katya's been on good form the whole journey".

Anna, smiled. "Katya, I love your clothes".

"Thanks. I was telling Charlie, I bought myself some bits to wear for work. Used my winnings. Charlie said he particularly likes the skirt".

BOOK THREE: *THE ADOLESCENT*

Anna turned to look at her husband and shook her head. "I bet he does. The skirt or Katya's legs, Charlie? Even your predictability has become predictable".

Charlie didn't rise to it but said instead, "Drink, Katya?"

"Yes please".

"G&T, wine, beer, cider?"

"Wine please".

"Red or white?"

"White please".

"Sauvignon, Viognier or Picpoul de Pinet?"

"Er, Viognier".

"2013 or 2014?"

"I'd prefer the 2013".

Charlie opened the fridge and extracted a three quarters full bottle of wine. "You're in luck. A 2015 Picpoul de Pinet from M&S". He poured some into a glass and passed it to her. "Here, drink this and be grateful".

Katerina giggled and thanked him.

"Glass for you, Anna?"

"Already got some thanks". Anna took a sip while adding the pasta to the boiling water.

Charlie poured a glass for himself and asked, "How long will the spaghetti be?"

"I don't know, I haven't measured it".

Katerina spat out a mouthful of wine as she tried to stop herself from choking. Once she'd finally finished spluttering, and could take in some air, Charlie simply said to her, "Serves you right". He then added, as if talking to himself, "This is going to be a long weekend".

Anna waited until they had finished eating their spaghetti Bolognese before asking Katerina about Louis.

"He's very nice. We've been getting on well".

"And you've had sex with him then?"

"Yes. Louis had some annual holiday entitlement left so he booked a day off for when I wasn't working. He picked me up and we had a nice pub lunch. He asked me if I wanted to go back to his place and it happened there".

"You sound rather matter of fact about it, Katya. I hope everything's OK," said Charlie, with some concern.

"Do you know, until I heard myself say it, I thought I'd been thrilled by what happened. For some reason it appears I wasn't".

"Why do you think that may be?" asked Anna.

"Maybe he's not 'the one'".

"To be frank, Katya, I don't think he should be. He is your first boyfriend. And you *are* only eighteen. Plenty of time and opportunity".

"No, of course you're right. I should see it as it was: I lost my virginity to a very considerate, attractive man who respected me. It was very enjoyable, and I'm sure we'll do it again soon. It just seems that something was missing".

"Was that your first sexual contact with him? Were you making love during your first sexual experience together?"

"Oh god no, Anna. I'd already tossed him off, and he's used his fingers on me. Haven't taken him in my mouth yet, but I probably would if things went that way".

Anna turned to face Charlie and feigned a disgusted look. "When I think of that young, innocent girl who walked through the exit gate at Perpignan Airport".

"I know. What have we helped to create?"

Katerina laughed but then insisted, "Stop it you two. You know perfectly well that the new Katya is far, far more at ease with herself than the pre-France Katya. In fact, we can refer to that girl as Katerina. No, believe me, if I'm open, yet discerning, about sex or anything else, it's because you two have helped me to be a more mature, selective, and controlled person. Joking aside, my life as Katerina was too challenging for me; I wasn't a happy person. My life as Katya is fun, optimistic, full of discoveries. I'm totally in control of my thoughts and actions and I couldn't be happier".

"That's lovely to hear," said Anna.

"Don't worry about what I've said about me having sex with Louis. If it had been sensational, it may have led to future love making being disappointing. That's one of the good things about me not having the option to have sex with Charlie in France: I'm sure nothing would compare".

"Charlie should be very pleased to hear that. Charlie, look at the satisfaction you've provided for an attractive young lady by *not* having sex with her!" She just managed to avoid the bread roll which had been thrown in her direction.

After everything had been cleared away, they settled into the Snug, where Charlie had lit the log burner. Katerina was sipping a Baileys and Charlie and Anna were each enjoying an Armagnac when Katerina asked, "May I be cheeky and ask you to either drive me home on Monday or let me stay Monday night too and get me to work on Tuesday? I'm not due in at work on Monday".

"We haven't got anything planned for Monday have we Charlie? I'm very happy for you to stay over until Tuesday".

"That's fine by me," confirmed Charlie.

"That's brilliant, thank you".

Anna then asked, "What about the property, Katya? Did you and Ilya get anywhere with your discussions?"

"It surprised us how difficult it was. We sat down one evening and put aside all distractions so that we could come up with a serious list, but it was tough".

"In what way?"

"I suppose it boils down to the fact that we won't be spending *our* money. One of us would say they wanted x number of bedrooms, and the other would reply that it would then become too expensive. Then one would say a town or village or area they would like to live in, and the other would then express concern that there are cheaper locations locally".

"I can see what she's getting at," said Charlie.

"Yes, so can I. Did you come up with anything at all?"

"Minimum of two bedrooms, Ilya doesn't want to sleep with me apparently, preferably some outside space but not a garden needing work and maintenance, modern if possible or at least a property which doesn't require lots of improvement or DIY. That's about it really".

"May I throw a few considerations at you? Could you answer for Ilya too?"

"Go ahead".

"Does it need to be somewhere lively, with a good night life?"

"Not really, but preferably not in the middle of the countryside or in a village that doesn't have at least a pub".

"Does it need to be somewhere equally convenient for you both to get to your places of work?"

"No, because travelling to Arundel from anywhere around Chichester will be fine for me, especially once I've passed my test. I think it would be better to be nearer to where Ilya works".

"Would you want to have two of anything, apart from bedrooms? I mean two bathrooms or two reception rooms so that you could entertain your friends separately if need be?"

"No, neither of those really bother us. I suppose, from my point of view, having a separate bathroom would be nice".

"Right," said Anna, firing up her laptop, "let's have a look on Rightmove".

Once on the website, she clicked through the filters, selecting only three: minimum two bedrooms; two bathrooms; within ten miles of Chichester. Eighteen properties were listed. Anna and Katerina worked up from the cheapest and several were quickly discarded for being too big, having too much of a garden or requiring a good deal of modernisation and/or upkeep. There was one property to which they kept returning.

Eventually Anna said, "That's the one to go for, surely".

"Is it within the price range you had in mind?"

"Charlie, what do you think?"

Charlie took considerable time studying the property details and photos. "I think Katya should contact Ilya as soon as possible and tell him to get online to take a look".

"I'll phone him now and email the link to him," responded Katerina.

"I think you should email it to Chrissy too".

"Will do".

Despite it being Saturday evening, within an hour Ilya had responded with nothing other than enthusiastic comments, and Chrissy had stated that, from her point of view, the property looked perfect for the two of them. Anna sent an email to the Agent requesting a viewing on Monday between midday and 2pm, during Ilya's lunch break. "They should be working in the morning so I'd expect to hear something tomorrow. As the property is empty, and is being sold by the builder, I can't see there being a problem with our request to see it on Monday".

"I'm so excited".

"Me too," confirmed Anna.

Twenty minutes later, Charlie rose from his chair and said, "I'm off to bed. Are you two staying down here a while longer?"

"What do you think Katya?"

"I'm ready for bed too, if that's all right with you Anna".

"Of course".

"We're out for lunch, leaving here a bit after 1. Do you fancy a lie in?" asked Charlie.

"If it's OK with you, I'll have my coffee when you have yours. I'm happy to make it and bring it in to you".

"No, that's fine thanks, I'll sort it. It'll be around 7.30. Too early?"

"No, that's great, thank you".

"Coffee, splash of cream, no sugar and a grapefruit juice?"

"That would be lovely, thanks".

As he did most mornings, Charlie woke with a semi erection. It tended to last until he got up and put on his dressing gown or boxers, and, if Anna noticed, she would say, despite knowing an early-morning erection rarely has anything to do with sexual arousal, something like, "What have you been dreaming about, or, more pertinently, who?" He glanced at his mobile phone. 'Blimey, 7.40. I've slept in,' he thought, and then, 'Katya's probably sitting up and wondering where the hell I am with the drinks'. He slid out of the bed and donned his dressing gown. Anna didn't stir.

Once the drinks were made and placed on the tray, he carried them upstairs. He knocked on Katerina's bedroom door and stepped in. She was sitting up, her Kindle in her hands.

"Good morning".

"Good morning, Katya, sleep well? Bit late this morning. Must have been the late-night alcohol".

"No problem. I wasn't awake until half seven anyway and it's been nice just sitting here thinking about that apartment and how you may be buying it".

"Still think it's the right one?"

"Most definitely. I'll be gutted if it's already been sold".

He placed the coffee mug on the bedside table and passed the glass of grapefruit juice to her. He found it impossible to not look at Katerina's upper body, which was visible above the quilt. She was wearing a pretty, pink nightie, the material of which was almost sheer. The shape and form of her breasts and nipples was apparent. His semi erection returned and this time it *was* due to sexual arousal.

"I'll leave you to it and take these through to Anna".

"Thanks Charlie. Let me know your plans for this morning and I'll tie in with whatever you decide".

"Will do". Charlie picked up the tray and returned to his bedroom, where Anna was also propped up against the headboard.

"Morning. I've just looked at the time. Not like us to be having our drinks this late". By the time she had finished saying this, Charlie had placed her drinks next to her and had removed his dressing gown prior to getting back into bed.

"You've normally lost that by the time you've made the drinks. Is Katya looking particularly fetching this morning?"

Charlie felt abashed, but still chose to answer the question honestly. "She's sitting up and she's wearing a nightie which is quite revealing". He turned to look at Anna. "A bit like yours, in fact".

Anna looked down. "Pretty, isn't it? Did Katya sleep well?"

"She didn't say, but she's obviously excited about the apartment. She said she'd be gutted if it were no longer available".

"We should know something before we leave for lunch. Hold on, I'll get Katya in here and we can talk about it again". Anna left the bed and padded across the carpet towards the door. Her nightie barely covered her bum; Charlie half hoped that Katerina's was longer.

"Should I put on some boxers?"

BOOK THREE: *THE ADOLESCENT*

Without providing an answer, Anna knocked on Katerina's door, opened it, stuck her head into the room and said, "Do you want to bring your coffee into us? We can discuss the apartment again if you like".

Charlie didn't hear the response but watched Anna return to the bed, standing beside it rather than getting back in. In a few moments, Katerina appeared. "Better get in this side," said Anna. "I didn't let on about this in France the times you brought us our coffee in bed, but Charlie never wears anything in bed, so he's staying covered up".

The three of them sat silently, side by side, Katerina in the middle, while they finished drinking their coffee. "Now, Charlie tells me you've woken up thinking about the apartment".

"I have. I got to sleep OK but once I woke up it was all I could think about". She then added, with a giggle, "Until you told me Charlie isn't wearing anything".

"Don't put yourself off your breakfast. So, now that you've had a good chance to think about it, tell us about the features which make this one so special".

"It's brand new. It's in East Wittering, which I love: shops, restaurants, cafes, and pubs. A bit too busy in the season, perhaps, but nicely lively. Three-minute walk to the beach. Not too bad a drive to get to work; Ilya can walk it in a couple of minutes, of course. It's a ground floor apartment in a block of only six. It's got a lovely kitchen. The lounge area isn't huge, but the doors open out onto its own little patio area making the whole thing appear bigger. It's got two bedrooms, so we'd have to manage things if one of us wanted someone to stay over, but they're a good size. The fitted cupboards and wardrobes are great. The fact that one of the bedrooms has an en suite bathroom is a bonus; I wasn't expecting that. Ilya has already said I could have that room. Only one designated parking space but that's OK. Easy to get to here, and to Chrissy's, so that's great. Can't think of anything else".

Anna and Charlie laughed together. "Haven't given it much thought then?" joked Anna.

"Just a bit".

"So, we'll wait for the Agent to confirm whether we can all view it tomorrow. If we can, and you and Ilya both agree that you want it, we'll tell the Agent and builder there and then that we'll pay the asking price and they must no longer market it. Charlie, could you sort the Solicitor?"

"Yes, that will be easy enough. I'll send an email this morning and get things moving".

"You two are brilliant".

Anna smiled at her, "Charlie, would you mind getting me another coffee?" Charlie turned towards her and stared, wordlessly.

"Katya, would you like one too?" asked Anna, ignoring Charlie.

"I'd love one, thanks".

Charlie hesitated then pulled the quilt off himself. Two pairs of eyes watched him walk across the room to locate and put on a pair of boxer shorts. Once he'd left the room, Katerina said to Anna, "I thought he wanted to be covered up. And you call me incorrigible!"

They had breakfast and were putting on some walking clothes when Anna's phone rang.

"Hello. Yes, this is Anna. Oh, hi. Yes, that's right. Oh really? Well, that sounds OK then. One o'clock is fine. Yes, see you there. Bye".

Katerina was staring at her, unable to ask.

"Viewing at one o'clock tomorrow. The Agent is working in tandem with the builder and is dealing with all the transactions on his behalf. The Agent will meet us outside and then show us around".

Before she could get to the end of saying this, Katerina was jumping up and down and then clinging onto Charlie. "Oh my god, I'm so excited!"

Anna looked at her and smiled. "All going according to plan so far," she said. "If you could let Ilya know he's to meet us there a bit before 1 tomorrow, I'll let Chrissy know what's happening and tell her she's welcome to come too".

They enjoyed an extremely pleasant walk along some of the footpaths near their South Downs cottage. Charlie had arranged for a taxi to pick them up at 1.15 to drive them to the Noah's Ark at Lurgashall, where they had a table booked for 1.30.

"I'm just wearing what I wore to Sandown. Is that OK?" asked Katerina.

Anna reassured her with, "Perfect. You look great and the clothes are ideal for lunch in an upmarket county pub. I did wonder if you'd go for the Burberry kilt".

"I thought about it but wondered if it may be a bit too much. Or little! I haven't worn it yet. I'll save it for another time I'm out with you and Charlie".

Anna chose the outfit she had worn when driving to East Wittering to see Ilya. As soon as Katerina saw her, she exclaimed, "There it is, exactly what I've been saying: classy, feminine, and sexy. I love those clothes, Anna. You look fantastic".

"Thank you, Katya. I do have some standards to maintain. My vanity simply won't allow all male eyes to follow you".

"Don't be ridiculous".

"Great meal," said Charlie. "Coffee? Another drink? The taxi isn't coming for another forty minutes, so there's plenty of time".

"Yes, I'll have an Armagnac to finish off please. I'll have a coffee when I get home".

"Just a coffee for me please Charlie".

"Would you like anything in it? Brandy or something?"

"Tell you what, I'll have a Russian coffee, for old time's sake. I haven't had one for ages and I like to remind myself of 'home', occasionally".

Charlie ordered the drinks, deciding upon a cognac for himself. "We haven't spoken about the racehorse at all, have we?"

"Are you still intending to buy one?" asked Katerina.

"Oh yes," responded Anna. "It's simply that we've been involved in a few things since Sandown and, of course, the property has been uppermost since you arrived yesterday. Shall we finish off here and maybe chat about it when we get home? Or would you rather wait until after the viewing tomorrow, Katya?"

"No, I'd love to talk about it later. There's nothing we can do about the apartment before we see it tomorrow and the racehorse will take my mind off it".

The taxi arrived and Katerina insisted on paying the lunch bill. "It's rather a lot, Katya," said Charlie. "There's no need for you to pay, honestly there isn't".

"I'd like to please".

"OK, well then thank you. It was a lovely lunch".

"Yes, thank you Katya. I need to get out of this skirt. I may even have to undo a button".

Within twenty minutes of arriving back at the cottage they were wearing loose-fitting leisure clothes and had an open laptop in front of them.

"Right," said Charlie, "I had some time on my hands this week while Anna was out with a friend, so I did a bit of research". He clicked onto a website and continued, "This trainer operates out of Findon. He's top notch and been operating for years. I think he should be our starting point".

"Findon. It's just the other side of Arundel, isn't it?" asked Katerina.

"Yes. Convenient, eh?"

"Seems ideal to me," confirmed Anna. "What do you think would be the best thing to do, Charlie? Arrange to go there and see what he has available?"

"Well, I think we should go there, but it's probably unlikely that they will have available a young, unnamed horse which is ready, or almost ready, to race".

"So, they'd find one for us?" asked Katerina.

"Yes, I think that's the way we should approach it. Tell them what we have in mind and see what they say".

"What do you think, Katya? What Charlie's saying makes sense to me".

"You two know much more about it than I do but, yes, if that's what Charlie thinks we should do, I'm happy".

"Do you want to contact them, Charlie? See if you can get something arranged?"

"Yes, no problem. I'll do it in the morning before we leave for East Wittering".

The following morning, Charlie walked up the stairs, carrying the tray, just after 7.30. Once again Katerina was sitting up in bed, Kindle in hand. "Morning Katya. Big day".

"Yes, big day Charlie. The time will drag this morning".

"Not necessarily. Be with me when I phone that Trainer. You can help me get things set up".

"Great, thanks". She accepted the glass of juice and was reassured to see that Charlie was again enjoying looking at her.

He returned to his bedroom and Anna immediately said, "Ask Katya if she wants to join us again, will you Charlie?"

Charlie placed their mugs and glasses on their bedside tables and returned to Katerina's room.

"She said she'll come right in". He had taken off his dressing gown, returned to the bed and had covered himself up with the quilt before she arrived.

"Get up for the girl, Charlie. How can you expect her to clamber over us?"

"Excited?" asked Anna, once Katerina had joined them.

"I am. Slept well though".

"I'm excited too. I hope we're not disappointed".

"I'm confident that we'll like it as much as we think we will. I'm more concerned about whether they'll sell it to us".

"Charlie will sort it, won't you Charlie?"

"I'll do my best".

The conversation turned to the impending contact with the racehorse trainer and when Katerina may next be available so that she could accompany them to Findon.

"I won't be able to get a day off before next Monday at the earliest. If you two want to go on your own for the first meeting with them, I'd quite understand".

"What do you think, Charlie? There's no rush, is there? I think it would be nice if the three of us went".

"I agree. Katya's going to be with me when I phone them this morning so we'll see what we can do".

By midday, Charlie and Katerina had arranged an appointment with the main Trainer himself at the racing stables in Findon for the Wednesday of the following week at 8am. Katerina said she would book the day off, and it was agreed that it would be best if she stayed at the cottage on the Tuesday night as they would be having an early start the following morning.

At 12.30, they piled into Anna's Defender and set off for East Wittering, where they met up with Ilya and were greeted by the Agent. Chrissy had said that she couldn't make it but had no problem with them deciding without her, so it was the four of them who, after the viewing, left the property and followed the Agent as he led them to his office. By 2pm the deal was done, and it was left to Charlie to instruct the Solicitor on behalf of Katerina and Ilya.

As soon as they came out of the office onto the pavement, Katerina and Ilya hugged and danced, then turned their attention to Anna and Charlie in a desperate attempt to try to convey how grateful they were. Ilya returned to the store, and Anna, Charlie and Katerina headed for Drifters café and bar, where they had decided to have a light lunch. Katerina was so thrilled she could barely eat. By 3.30 they were back at the cottage and Charlie was providing full details in an email to the Solicitor.

Once he had pressed 'send' he said, "A good day's work I'd say".

"Let's celebrate tonight," suggested Anna. "Let's eat out at a nice pub. We could down a bottle of Champagne before we go, then have a meal and some drinks".

"Great idea. I'll book a table and a taxi. We're paying for this one Katya, by the way".

The following morning, when Charlie returned upstairs carrying the tray, he noticed that Katerina's bedroom door was open. He walked into his and Anna's bedroom and saw that Katerina was already in their bed and the two were chatting.

"We're planning Katya's France arrangements".

"I've told Anna that Salty needs me to work up to the 24th, and then again on the 27th. She said I can take time off after that because they're normally quiet. I'm needed back for when she starts her Sale on the 4th".

"So, you could come 28th to the 3rd?"

"I could, but don't feel that you have to have me there for that long".

"Won't you want to see Louis during that time, Katya?" asked Anna.

"No, I don't think so. He'll be going back to the Midlands to see his family for Christmas and I've no doubt we'll do stuff together during the week before he goes".

"Shall I book the flights then? 28th and 3rd?"

"Yes, do that," replied Anna, "if those dates suit you, Katya".

"They do, but on the condition that I pay for my flights".

Anna got in first. "The best we can do is we pay for the flight there and you cover the one back".

"Yes, good compromise," agreed Charlie.

"OK then. That's great, thanks".

"What time do we need to leave here, Katya?"

"Blimey, Charlie, in about half an hour. I'd better get moving. I'll dive into the shower now".

The three of them rushed about, sorting clothing, preparing, and eating breakfast, Anna and Katerina exchanging goodbye's and thank you's before Charlie and Katerina headed off for Arundel in the Defender.

Once Charlie had pulled away, Anna sent a text to Ilya:

'I haven't heard from you re k/s equipment'
'Have held back in light of property'
'Why'
'Too much'
'So, will it be you who tells Katerina she's to return the clothes or me'
'You're determined, aren't you'
'You've no idea how persuasive I can be when I want something. Warning—I always get what I want'

There was a couple of minutes delay before Anna received Ilya's final text:

'OK, convinced. Happy for you to rely on me to give you what you want'

Anna read this three times before laughing out loud.

As Charlie drove away from the cottage, he fired up his iPhone to play some music in the car. "Just listen to this," he said.

An eight-minute track blared from the speakers.

"That's fantastic. What a track! Who is it?"

"Up there with Radiohead for me. It's Ben Harper. That one is when he is with The Innocent Criminals. The track is called 'With my own two hands/War'. It's from a live concert he played at the Hollywood Bowl".

"That's being added to my favourite playlist as soon as I get home. I'll check out his other stuff too".

They arrived at Arundel, and Charlie pulled into a parking space near the bookstore. He turned to Katerina and said, "I'll let you know how things progress with the Solicitor, and I'll pick you up from here at six next Tuesday".

"Brilliant, thanks. And thank you too for a wonderful weekend and all that you're doing for me".

"Pleasure. Before you go, I need you to tell me if we're embarrassing you by asking you to join us in bed in the mornings, especially knowing I'm not wearing anything".

She considered. "Well, I love our chats. And it's not as if I haven't seen you naked before, is it? No, I'm not embarrassed at all. It brings back happy memories".

He smiled. "For me too. As I knew you would, you're developing into a very attractive young lady. You have so much to look forward to in your life".

"I feel that's true, about the future I mean, not me being attractive. I just can't express how much I feel in debt to the two of you and how enjoyable it is for me to be with you both. Bye Charlie. See you on Tuesday," and she was off.

Chapter 22

On the following Tuesday, as Anna and Charlie were eating their lunch, Anna said, "If you're not doing anything this afternoon, I thought maybe we could drive to Arundel and have a look around before Katya finishes work. We could browse the shops and eat there with Katya before we bring her back here".

"Yes, good idea. I'm up for that".

They arrived at Arundel a little before three o'clock so were able to dedicate three hours to exploring. Anna spent some of the time in a vintage clothes shop and bought for herself a 1970's 'midi' skirt: grey, tight around the hips then full, mid-calf length. "This will look great with black boots". She also couldn't resist a 1960's Biba mini skirt for Katya: brown and orange panels of increasing width from waist to hem. "We won't give this to her yet. I think she'll love it for parties and going out to clubs and I don't want her to think it's another article of clothing for you to ogle. I might save it as a Christmas present for her".

The clocks having gone back at the weekend, it was dark when they were leaning up against the Defender, chatting, waiting for Katerina to join them after she'd finished work. "Both of you! How lovely".

"Yes," responded Anna, "we've had a good look round and thought it may be nice to have a meal here to save cooking at home. Is that OK with you?"

"Of course. That would be lovely".

They walked up the hill to a restaurant spotted earlier, Katerina telling them about her day.

During the meal, Katerina asked, with a serious expression, "What do you think about you guys meeting Louis?"

"Hey, Charlie, the girl's getting serious. 'Meet the parents'".

"No, it's not that. It's more that I'd like your opinion".

"Are you having doubts, or is it a case of substantiating your positive thoughts about him?"

"Doubts, I think".

"OK. So, do you know what it is about him, or the two of you together, that is causing these doubts?"

"It's just a feeling. It's not him, he's been great with me from the outset. It's just me being me. You know what I'm like. I don't have any close friends, no-one at all that I've stayed in contact with from school. I've spent so much of my time, since Ilya and I grew up from being children, on my own, reading or playing music. Being in a relationship is alien to me and I can't seem to get to grips with how it's making me feel".

"Didn't you ever feel lonely, spending so much time in your own company, not going out with friends?"

"It has rarely been loneliness, Anna; loneliness to me is feeling empty. When I'm on my own, rather than feel empty, I usually feel fulfilled. I suppose that's the difference between loneliness and solitude, whether or not you feel empty or fulfilled. That's the issue, I think: do I feel more fulfilled in my own company or in Louis'?"

Charlie asked, "I understand where you're coming from, Katya, but does it have to be one or the other? Can't you do your swimming, read your books, and listen to your music when it suits you, and then see Louis when you feel ready for some company?"

"Yes, I can do that. I do that now. Louis has made it clear that he'd like us to see more of each other, but I often put him off. I don't feel that I should keep doing that unless I can explain to him why. And before I do that, I'd like you to tell me your honest opinion of him. I guess I'm wondering if he's worth the effort, which, I know, sounds cruel and self-centred".

Anna reached across the table and held one of Katerina's hands. "Of course we'll meet him and give you an honest opinion. I do wonder though, my darling Katya, if you're over-thinking it. Maybe you could just go with the flow and enjoy things as they crop up".

"I'm not really a 'go with the flow' type of girl, am I? I suggested to you both in France that I was dull, but you insisted that I'm not. It's only when I'm with you two that I'm not the intense-me but the carefree-me. I'm comfortable with them both, but it's just that it would be nice if I could be the carefree-me with my boyfriend, and I haven't worked out if that's possible with Louis. If it isn't, it may be a good idea to accept it and see where it takes me. God, I hope this is making some sense".

"It does to me," said Charlie.

"But you get me, Charlie. Anna is the most fun, outward looking, expressive and carefree person I've ever met whereas you have the capacity to be as intense as I am. What's so wonderful about you is that you can get pleasure from both: immersing yourself in some moody music or dark novel as well as taking advantage of Anna's exuberant personality. Maybe I'm a you and I need an Anna, as you do. Male version, of course".

Anna felt that she needed to convey some thoughts. "It's strange how other people view us, isn't it? Often differently to how we view ourselves. For me, it is Charlie who leads our relationship. I'm convinced that there is no-one like him in the world. I can recognise the Anna you're describing, Katya, and I like her. I like being me. But there's no question, I wouldn't exist as the person I am without Charlie. If I hadn't met him, I feel that I would have led a fairly eventless, traditional 'wife and mother' life, having sex on a Friday night. Nothing wrong with that, but, until I met Charlie, I didn't appreciate that I had a choice. No, the way I see it is that it's not an Anna you need but a Charlie. You won't get one like him, of course, because he's unique, and he's mine, but I feel that the right person for you, your 'Charlie', will bring all your amazing character traits, the ones that Charlie and I see every time we're with you, to the fore. You'll display them naturally, as you do when you're with us. There's been times when you've been engrossed in Tolstoy, or whoever, and Charlie and I have involved ourselves in activities without you, and we've all been comfortable with that. And we all know what fun we've had together at other times. Your 'Charlie' will provide opportunities to help you to make the most of all of your incredible characteristics. But Katya, you're eighteen. No rush, eh?"

"I felt eighteen when I was twelve and thirty now that I'm eighteen! There again, there have been times, Anna, when I've felt that both you and I are eighteen; we've had so much fun. At least, I have".

"I have too, I can assure you. So, shall we agree that Charlie and I will spend some time with you and Louis, and then maybe we could be in a better position to share some valid thoughts?"

"I think that would be a good idea," confirmed Charlie. "I'd like to meet Louis anyway".

"Great, thank you. Maybe a pub lunch one Sunday would be the easiest to arrange?"

"I agree. Have a word with Louis and agree a couple of Sundays when you know you'll both be free. Let me or Charlie know, and then we'll set something up".

They finished at the restaurant, returned to the car, and drove back to the cottage. Once they had settled in, Charlie asked, "Excited about tomorrow?"

"Definitely," from Anna and, "Can't wait," from Katerina.

"I've been thinking about what the Trainer may ask us tomorrow and I think I'm clear about most of the essentials, but there's a couple of things the three of us haven't discussed yet".

"What's that?" asked Anna.

"Firstly, our racing colours. We've agreed that the three of us will jointly own it, once we've found a horse we like, of course. And we'll name it Place To Be, if that's available. But we've yet to decide on our jockey's colours. Any preference?"

Anna was the first to reply. "We want colours that stand out; ones that you can spot from the grandstand".

"I agree," responded Charlie. "Some of the muted colours are near to impossible to detect from a distance".

"Red! Red, white and blue. Red is the best to spot. It's Russian, that's me. It's the Cross of St George, that's you two. Red, white and blue are the colours of the Union flag and the French tricoleur".

"Anna?"

"I like it".

"I do too. Shall we check what combinations are available?"

They thoroughly explored the Weatherby's and British Horseracing Authority websites; it appeared that the name Place To Be was available, and that they would be free to select racing colours which they liked and upon which they all agreed: red body with red and blue hooped sleeves and a white cap.

"I can just see that in the Winner's Enclosure at The Cheltenham Festival," said Charlie, as if he were already three quarters of the way to achieving it. "We also need to agree a name for our owner partnership".

They fussed around numerous combinations of their names before Anna wrote down 'Canya'. "Get it?" she asked. "Charlie, Anna and Katya in the name and a mock question 'can you?'".

Katerina picked up the pen and amended it to 'Can'ya?' They instantaneously agreed on The Can'ya? Racehorse Owner Partnership and hoped that the Trainer and the authorities would find it acceptable.

At 6.30 the following morning, Charlie knocked on Katerina's bedroom door and walked in, carrying her coffee and grapefruit juice. She was still tucked up under the quilt and only the top of her head was visible. "Hey, you," said Charlie, giving Katerina a gentle prod. She emerged, opened her eyes and said, "Is it morning already? Thank goodness".

Anna, on the other hand, needed to be coaxed into life but finally, after a bit of huffing and puffing from Anna, the three of them climbed into the Defender and set off for Findon, Katerina still munching on a slice of toast. They pulled into the horse Trainer's Yard ten minutes early, and the first impression they all gained was extremely positive. The weather was crisp but fair, and they all wore warm clothing, anticipating some time on the gallops with the stable staff, or the Trainer himself. At 8am they entered a room which was clearly marked 'Office' and were greeted by a middle-aged man who introduced himself as the Travelling Head Lad. They were informed that he would be conducting the initial discussions and that they would then drive out to the gallops before returning with the Trainer, who would help them through the decision-making process.

They didn't leave the racing Yard until after midday. On pulling away, Katerina, who was sitting in the back, said, "Oh my god, what just happened?"

"You've become a third-share owner in a racehorse, that's what," replied Anna, who turned round in her seat to face Katerina. They were both beaming. Charlie was driving, trying not to look smug. "That was far easier than I thought it would be," he said.

"When I think what my life was like three months ago," mused Katerina.

Katerina had been mesmerised most of the morning, especially whilst they were with the Trainer who was watching with a keen eye a string of horses exercising on the all-weather gallops. In contrast, Anna had been calm and in her element. A good deal of time had been spent viewing young horses being schooled, and they also had the opportunity to witness a vet visit to a mare which had injured herself the day before in at fall at Chepstow. "No lasting damage, but no work for a fortnight. I'll come and see her again in a couple of weeks," had been the vet's summary.

Registrations with the British Horseracing Authority had been concluded, as well as some online documentation with Weatherby's. "Right," the Trainer had said, "you're now registered owners and have racing colours. All you need now is a horse. What are you looking for?"

Charlie had answered for them. "We're new to this, as you know, so this may not be possible. Ideally, we'd like a young, un-named and un-raced horse with the breeding to suggest it may have a degree of success. We're not expecting you to source a Gold Cup winner for us, but we'd like to think we owned something which stood the chance of getting us into the winner's enclosure at a local track. We expect you to tell us that you don't have one available at present, but it would be nice to think you could help us to track one down".

"We're continually attending auctions, here in England, France and sometimes Ireland. We buy anything which we like the look of and believe will be of interest to owners we work with. I have two in a field that may be worth you considering. Both are unraced and un-named. The younger one, which is four, we bought in February at an auction in France. He was very green, almost unbroken, but we feel that we're approaching the stage when he may attract an owner. The other one is a year older. He was bought from a fellow trainer who didn't want to spend any more time on him. He had developed a cyst deep in a hoof and it's taken longer than expected to heal. The vet gave us the all-clear a few weeks ago, so we've started some serious work with him. Both are from good racing stock and are geldings (Katerina had whispered to Anna, "What's a gelding?" and Anna had whispered back, "Had his balls cut off"). The younger one is a dark bay and the older is a chestnut".

"May we see them?" Anna had asked.

They bought the four-year-old bay, whose stable name was Stroppy ("He was a right bugger loading up to bring him home"). The Travelling

Head Lad had promised them that it would be registered to race under their ownership with the racing name Place To Be, and that confirmation should be received within the following few days. The Training Agreement was also finalised after Charlie had authorised a Bank Transfer. "Don't expect to be seeing him on a track any time soon, but you are welcome to visit him and see him develop whenever you like. We love to have owners who wish to play a part in the less glamourous side as well as seeing their horse at a racetrack".

"Do you need notice?" Katerina had asked.

"Just a call or a text before you set off, if you can".

"And when do you think he may be ready?" Anna had asked.

"We're aiming for the Spring".

"So, what are we going to do to help us to come back down to earth, and then to celebrate? An afternoon at Petworth? What are your plans Katya, do you want to stay with us?"

"If you don't mind taking me to work it the morning, that would be lovely, thank you".

"Great. Charlie, how about heading for Petworth so we can pick up some cheese and goodies at that amazing deli? We can then decide if we want to stay there and eat at a restaurant or go home to eat".

"Yep, will do".

Once again, the three of them were settled in the Snug, enjoying the heat from the log burner and a night cap.

"Well, it's never dull with you two," said Katerina.

Anna chuckled. "It's you, Katya, you lead us astray. I meant to ask, how are you sleeping these days? Is Chrissy still keeping you awake, or hasn't Steve stayed there recently?"

"It's as bad as ever, but at least I now have the satisfaction of knowing I'll be moving out soon. I'm reasonably certain that Steve will move in once Ilya and I have left".

"Really? I didn't realise Chrissy was that serious. Has Steve said anything to you, Charlie?"

"No, we haven't crossed paths since I asked him if he could sweep Chrissy's chimney—Katya, behave—so I don't even know from him that they're seeing each other".

"Hey, don't tell Chrissy that I've said anything to you. If that's what they're planning to do she will probably want to tell you herself. Besides, it's only a feeling; she hasn't said that's what they're planning".

"We won't drop you in it, I promise. Charlie, how long will it be before Katya will have her own place? Do you know if there's a targeted completion date?"

"Well, I don't want Katya to rely on this, but I think it should be sometime early January".

"How does that sound, Katya?"

"Can't bloody wait".

"What do you and Ilya plan to do about furniture?"

"Well, as you know, not much is needed. Chrissy has said she'll buy it all and then Ilya and I will pay her back monthly".

Charlie was starting to say, "You do know that..." when Katerina interrupted him and said, "If you're going to suggest that you two are going to pay anything towards furniture you can stop right there. Ilya and I will not accept anything more from you. It's down to us now, and we'll be forever grateful to you for being so generous and thoughtful for buying the apartment. No, we cannot agree to any more from you. If Ilya and I can't afford whatever we want, we won't have it".

"OK, fair enough," accepted Charlie.

"What time do you need to get up in the morning?" asked Charlie.

"7.30 again should be fine. I need to leave here by 8.30. Is that OK with you?"

"Of course. The usual?"

"Yes please".

At 7.20 the following morning Katerina knocked on Anna and Charlie's bedroom door and walked in carrying a tray of drinks. Charlie had been preparing to rise whereas Anna was still barely visible under the quilt.

"Am I too early?"

"Fine by me, but you might not get much out of Anna for five minutes or so".

Katerina placed their drinks on their bedside tables and said, "I'll take mine back to my room and leave you to it".

Anna's crumpled face appeared. "No, climb in. I'll be awake in a minute".

Charlie got up and stood aside for Katerina. She smiled at him and said, "Thank you". He returned the smile. "You're welcome". Katerina removed her dressing gown and settled herself in the middle, between them, as Anna sat up and reached for her orange juice.

"I'll drive you to work this morning, Katya. I've been thinking about something I saw in that vintage clothes shop and have been kicking myself for not buying it. If it's still there I'll get it. Do you want to come Charlie or have you got things you want to do?"

As Charlie answered, saying he would stay to liaise with the Solicitor and book the Barcelona room, Anna left the bed, removed her nightie, and walked to the bathroom. Katerina watched her and whispered, just loud enough to be heard, "I wish mine swayed like that".

After Katerina had showered, dressed, and eaten her breakfast, she and Anna set off in the Alfa. Anna took the opportunity to ask Katerina again about Louis. "I know we've talked about this, and agreed that we're going to meet Louis, but I still feel somewhat unclear about what you feel is missing with him. You seemed to convey that you think it's more you than him, but I do wonder if you might get more out of him if you talked to him about how you're feeling. Maybe he's not being his true self because he, too, is feeling his way into a new relationship. His true self may actually be what you're looking for".

"No, I think he's straightforward. It's one of the things I really like about him. No bullshit, no pretentiousness, just a good guy. I'm not being fair to him, I know I'm not. When I think back to you and me talking in France, when I told you how fed up I was about being a virgin and having to put up with immature boys and their sexist behaviour, I appreciate how well things have worked out in a short space of time. I have a boyfriend who's seven years older than I and who is mature and sees me as an equal. I've also lost my virginity with him and can have sex whenever I want with an attractive man who is very considerate. How lucky am I? Yet I'm moaning about something being missing: a spark. I've never before considered myself to be a selfish person, but I'm now doubting that".

"I wouldn't consider it selfishness in recognising an emotion".

"I'm expecting too much, aren't I? I've got nearly everything I wanted in a boyfriend, and he's my first one, so I'm doing well. I'm expecting too much so I'm not enjoying what I've got. I'm doing myself out of pleasure and that's stupid".

"I must admit that I've wondered if Charlie and I have partly caused this, whether our privileged lifestyle has glossed over what's really important for a young girl starting out in life".

"I don't think that's the case. French villas and racehorses and wonderful meals are fantastic, and the pleasure I've had since you invited me to France has been indescribable, but I have no expectations regarding that type of thing. If I can continue to enjoy being part of your life, that will be incredible for me, and I appreciate that I will be extremely fortunate with what comes with that. Really, it's only your partnership which I envy. There aren't 'sparks' between you two, there are mini explosions. That's why I'm suggesting I'm expecting too much. I could live five lifetimes and not be in a relationship like yours, or couple up with a Charlie. If I'm going to be content, I must accept that".

"I think you're wrong and I encourage you to maintain your expectations. I think you're remarkable and will achieve amazing things. I believe you should strive for everything to be at the level you want, and I'm convinced that nothing is beyond you. The only caveat I'd add is that your ultimate achievements won't be attained today or tomorrow. Your soulmate won't be your first partner and my advice would be to enjoy as best you can what you have today, with a boyfriend and job, but continually strive and continually search. You'll meet your Charlie. Now, we're here. We'll see you soon, OK?"

"Yes, see you soon, Anna. Thanks again".

Katerina walked towards the bookstore and Anna to the vintage clothes shop. She was required to wait a few minutes before it opened but was relieved to see that the garment that she wanted was still on display. The owner unlocked and let her in, recognising her from her previous visit.

"The bustier corset, is it an original?"

"Yes, we only sell originals. Lovely, isn't it? It was made in the early 50s. Used but looks almost new. That's an exclusive lace design, and the suspenders are a permanent feature of the garment. I can provide unused silk stockings in their original packaging too if you'd like. Seemed or plain. I also have 50's knickers still in their wrapping. I'm sure that I could match the colour".

"Do you think it would fit me?"

"What size are you, a ten? What about bra size?"

"Yes, I'm a ten, but sometimes I struggle with clothes being tight around the bust. I'm 34C".

"I'm not sure then. I think that you need to try it on".

Anna assessed herself in the full-length mirror in the changing room. The cream bustier fitted her extremely well around the waist and hips but had been designed for a female with a smaller bust. Whilst her breasts felt comfortable in the garment, they spilled out rather more than the designer would have been happy with. Anna felt that this would not be too much of a problem, so she happily bought it, along with knickers and a pair of silk stockings.

Anna arrived home and produced two rolls stuffed with ham and salad. "Look at those babies," she said as she presented them to Charlie.

"They look great. What would you like to drink?"

"Just some water please".

They settled down to eat their lunch, and neither chose to speak until they had finished.

"Did you get what you wanted?"

"I did, thanks. And how about you? Barcelona sorted?"

"Yes. As you know, we fly out on the 15th. I've arranged the hotel in Barcelona for the nights of 17th and 18th. We'll eat in their restaurant on the 17th. I've also reserved a table for you and me to eat at Les Antiquaires in Perpignan for Christmas lunch on the 25th and also for the evening of the 31st with Katya".

"Well, that's great. Looking forward to that. By the way, I've been thinking of going to London on Monday to do some Christmas shopping. Time will go quickly, I think, before we leave for France. I might ask Lene if she'd like to come with me. Would you be OK with that?"

"Yes, of course".

"Good. I'll give her a call".

"Hi Lene".

"Hello Anna. Having a good week?"

"Yes, very good thanks, how about you?"

"Not bad thanks. Been thinking of you, of course".

"Doing anything on Monday?"

"No, nothing planned".

"Would you like to come with me to London? Some early Christmas shopping?"

"I'd love to".

"If we could get a train from Chichester shortly after 9am, once it's quietened down, there'd be plenty of time for shopping and eating before you needed to get the train back for the girls".

"To save putting us under pressure, I'll check with Greg to see if he can get home for when the girls get back from school".

"That'd be great if he could. I'll text you some train times and you can let me know what works best for you".

"Brilliant. Thanks for thinking of me. It'll be a lovely to have a day out with you".

"See you on Monday".

BOOK THREE: *THE ADOLESCENT*

CHAPTER 23

They were sitting side-by-side, in a First-Class carriage, on the 9.09 to London Victoria. The seat opposite them was free, which meant the table was clear for their belongings and they would be able to chat freely.

Lene, who had the window seat, took hold of Anna's hand, and said, "I've missed you. Have you been all right?"

"It's been quite busy recently so that's helped. I think about you a lot though".

"Same with me. I'll tell you something else: my need for sexual attention is through the roof. Since you and I were together in Bracklesham, Greg and I have been making love at least once every three days or so and I've masturbated most days that I haven't had sex. I even did it a few days ago in a treatment room, lying on a massage couch. Just slipped off my trousers and knickers and frigged myself. I was half hoping that Dani would walk in on me. She asked me if I was coming down with a cold when she saw me a bit later. I don't know what's going on, I really don't".

Anna giggled. "Much the same with us. Great, isn't it?"

They arrived at 11.15 and Lene walked towards the entrance to the Underground. "No, this way," said Anna. "Taxi's today. I'll pay for them, and you get the lunch".

"I don't know what it is about being in a black cab, but it always makes me feel special".

"I feel the same. Millions of taxi journeys are made throughout London every week, yet it still makes me feel a little decadent".

"Where are we heading first?"

"Selfridges".

The taxi driver looked in his rear-view mirror and asked, "Here for a day's shopping ladies?"

"We are," responded Anna. "We got married on Saturday and we're here to buy some clothes. We're off on a cruise on Wednesday for our honeymoon". She turned to Lene and gave her a kiss on the lips.

"Congratulations! Where are you cruising to?"

"The Norwegian Fjords. My wife is Swedish and has always wanted to cruise the Fjords," and she kissed Lene again. "Can't wait, can we darling?"

"No, can't wait," was all Lene was able to articulate while trying to stifle her giggles.

Anna bought a bottle of Chrissy's favourite perfume and a crazy game she thought Ilya and Katerina would like to have in the apartment to play with friends. A few clothes for Ilya too, although she was aware that she was taking a risk, having never previously bought for a twenty-year-old lad. She was delighted to locate a saddle cloth in the equestrian department which she knew her riding friend, Samantha, would love, plus she selected a limited-edition bottle of vodka for Sam's husband, Tommy. Lene had a successful couple of hours too, loading up with presents for her daughters.

"We need time out," exclaimed Anna as they attempted to enter the lift carrying their numerous bags. "Hot salt beef sandwich with sliced gherkins and sauerkraut for me".

"I've never had one. Do you think I'd like it?"

"If you don't, we'll get you something else and I'll finish yours. I could eat the whole cow".

Anna took her first mouthful, a large one, sat back in her chair, closed her eyes, and chewed ostentatiously. "I'd been beginning to forget how good that tastes".

"I feel the same way about you".

Anna opened her eyes to look at her friend. She was relieved to see a smiling face and twinkling eyes and not a vision of desperation. "Hey, I know what I'm going to get you for Christmas. They sell them here. You can have it early".

Lene had taken a bite of her sandwich so couldn't immediately respond. "I see what you mean; that's lovely. Anna, you and I don't do presents. We never have".

"My mind is made up. But you're not to buy me anything".

"You know I will".

"Yes, of course I do".

As they reluctantly finished the last mouthful of sandwich and downed their drinks, milk for Anna and diet coke for Lene, Anna led them back to the lifts.

"So, what is it we're getting?" asked Lene.

"I'm buying you a Lelo Sona".

"What's one of those?"

"It's incredible. I've got one, but I haven't used it for ages. Have you ever used a vibrator?"

"Yes, of course".

"What do you think of them?"

"I always enjoy it more than I think I'm going to".

"This one is different. It's not a vibrator as such. It doesn't go inside you like a Rabbit. It uses air to simulate oral sex. If you can't have my or Greg's tongue, you'll find it will keep you going until one of us can oblige".

"That sounds like a very thoughtful Christmas present".

"My pleasure".

Once Lene's present had been purchased, they decided to take a taxi to Knightsbridge, drop their bags off at the 'Radical Storage' facility and walk the short distance to Harrod's.

"Where to start?" said Lene as they entered the store.

"Daunting, isn't it? Let's just get lost until we decide we want a break or something to eat".

"I couldn't eat anything just yet. That sandwich was huge".

"Yes, but you will be able to in a bit. Come on, let's take a look at their Christmas Department".

A little before six o'clock they collapsed in one of the excellent Harrods' restaurants and Anna ordered two glasses of Prosecco to drink while they were studying the menu.

"Do you mind if I phone Greg? We'll be much later than I thought, so I'd better check that he and the girls are OK".

"Of course, go ahead. I'll send a text to Charlie too".

Anna chose a smoked salmon salad and Lene just a prawn cocktail starter-dish. They agreed that they also deserved a bottle of wine after a hard day, so a New Zealand Sauvignon Blanc was requested.

"It's been a great day, hasn't it? Thank you so much for inviting me".

"I love coming to London. And I love shopping too. But doing both, with you, has been brilliant. You're such a great person to spend time with".

"You don't regret marrying me then?"

They managed to climb aboard the 8.35 just before the whistle was blown and the train headed out on their return journey to Chichester. Getting along the aisle and into a seat wasn't easy as they were laden with bags. A thoughtful, elderly gentleman offered to move seats so that they had all four to themselves.

"Phew," said Anna, "that was hard work. What's happening about getting home? Shall we share a taxi?"

"Yes, if you don't mind. It'll be too late for Greg to leave the girls and collect me".

"No problem. Happy with your purchases?"

"I am. I don't think I've ever be so ahead of myself".

Anna looked around the carriage before resting her hand on Lene's thigh, regretting the thickness of the denim separating her palm from Lene's skin. Lene parted her legs enough to enable Anna to slip her hand between them.

"I can't feel much," said Lene, "but it's still lovely".

"Go to the toilet and change into the skirt you bought".

Lene considered Anna's suggestion, located the appropriate bag from the seat opposite them, stood up, slipped past Anna, and walked down the aisle. Anna stood to let her back in and watched her return the bag to the seat, this time containing Lene's jeans instead of her new skirt. Anna's hand returned to its previous location, between Lene's upper thighs, underneath the skirt. She turned to face Lene as she came to realise that the bag opposite contained Lene's knickers as well as her jeans. "That's a lovely surprise".

Book Three: *The Adolescent*

The following morning, Lene phoned Anna. "Hi".

"Good morning Lene. You OK this morning?"

"Yes thanks. Just a quick call to say thanks again for yesterday. I had such a great day".

"I'm just so pleased we went together. We'll go again some time. Maybe even to the theatre or something".

"Yes, that would be lovely. Just to say also, you got me so aroused on the train that, as soon as I got home, I enticed Greg into bed, and we had delicious sex. Afterwards he said that he wasn't complaining but wondered what had happened to me. I couldn't really provide him with a decent explanation, so I blagged it a bit. Anyway, he says he's loving it, so everyone's happy".

"That's great to hear".

Anna received a text from Lene on Wednesday morning; she was still in bed, finishing her coffee.

> 'My xmas present!'
> 'Decent 3rd choice?'
> 'Defo. Under pressure to get you something decent now'
> 'You'll think of something'

On Thursday morning, as she was eating a bowl of muesli, Anna received a text from Katerina:

> 'You two doing anything today?'
> 'I'm not. Not sure about Charlie'
> 'Fancy going to see Stroppy?'
> 'Great idea. When shall I pick you up?'
> 'I'll pick you up'
> 'How come?'
> 'Passed my driving test yesterday'
> 'You clever thing, you'
> '10.30?'
> 'Great'

'I'll text them to let them know we're coming'

Charlie cancelled a fencing lesson as he was keen to join them. Katerina pulled up in her Mini and Anna and Charlie went straight out to greet her. They hugged and congratulated her in turn before Charlie eased himself into the back and Anna sat next to Katerina in the front.

"Have you taken today as your day off?" asked Charlie.

"Yes, I worked through lunch yesterday as Salty said I could leave early for my test".

"You must be thrilled," added Anna.

"Yes, I am, but once again it's down to you two. I couldn't have afforded the lessons myself".

"We're pleased it turned out to be a good choice for a present, aren't we Charlie?"

"Yes. Your idea Anna. First time Katya, so that's really well done".

"Thanks".

They spent more than two hours at the racing Yard and were entertained by one of the stable lasses. It was reassuring to see Stroppy at work, and to hear that he was progressing well and was due to be schooled over hurdles the following week.

As Katerina drove away, she said, "How great was that? Our own racehorse. Won't it be exciting being part of his development as he's prepared to go racing?"

"Absolutely," replied Charlie. "Anna, with your expert eye, did you notice any changes since last time?"

"Without question. He's starting to show his definition as he gets fitter, and I love how alert he was and keen to do the work. Some of them can be lazy buggers, which must be difficult for the training team".

"What are we doing now?" asked Charlie.

"Do you want to drive us back and stay for lunch Katya? You can stay as long as you like, of course".

"That's great, thanks".

Chapter 24

"Katya phoned me earlier. She asked if I could meet her for lunch. I think she wants to chat something through," said Anna, as she was drying her hair.

"Did she sound OK?"

"Yes, she was fine. I'm driving over tomorrow".

"OK. I hope there's nothing wrong".

"I wouldn't worry. By the way, have you remembered the cinema on Saturday?"

"Yes. I'm looking forward to it. We haven't been in ages".

On entering the bookstore, Anna immediately spied Katerina, who was standing in front of a large bookcase further inside the building. Katerina looked up, smiled, waved, and held up five fingers. As she nodded in understanding, Anna heard someone say, "Well, if it isn't the sex guru".

"Hello Salty, how are you?"

"I'm very well, thank you Anna. I was so sorry that the Club never got around to arranging a follow up presentation. Anyway, here to see the delightful Katerina?"

"Yes. We're having lunch".

"I've always rated that girl, ever since I met her a few years ago. The more I got to know her the more I thought she'd be a great person to train to run this place. I'm usually a good judge of people, yet I've never been so sure about anyone as I am about her. And, since she came back from being on holiday with you in the summer, she's been exceeding even my expectations of her".

"She's a credit to Chrissy, that's for sure".

"That's true, although I wouldn't be at all surprised if you had something to do with the way she's blossomed over the past few months. Here she is. All sorted Katerina?"

"Nearly. Is it OK if I finish off after lunch?"

"There's no rush. We're very quiet so don't bother hurrying back. Have a good gossip and you can finish off putting away those books when you get back".

"Thanks, Salty. See you in a bit".

"Enjoy your lunch. Bye Anna, lovely to see you again".

"Bye, Salty. See you soon, I hope".

"Pop in any time".

"I will. Thanks".

Salty watched them leave the store, arm in arm.

"I'll sort this," said Katya as they entered the café. "What would you like?"

"Thanks Katya. I'd like an egg mayo sandwich on granary and a glass of milk please".

Anna sat down at a spare table and watched as Katerina ordered their food and drink at the counter. Once Katerina had taken her seat opposite her, Anna said, "Salty seems to be pleased with how it's going".

"Does she? That's good. Well, I'm still enjoying it and Salty is taking me with her to a prospective book purchase next week. A local lady has a large selection of books that she doesn't want now that her husband has moved into a care home. I get the sense that profits depend on this type of thing, you know, buying sellable second-hand books at the right price. Hopefully, Salty will decide soon that this is all she will do, as well as the money side of it of course, and then I can run the store, maybe with a part time assistant or a work experience person".

"Do you see yourself doing this long term?"

"Yes, I do. It's interesting, I'm not stuck in an office, I'm surrounded by books, there's loads to learn, and I get on well with the owner, who seems to want me to take on more responsibility. The only downside is some of the arsehole customers. Not all of them of course, but some of them are just thick or rude. What I love most is the concept of a bookshop. I watch some customers enter the store and see they're browsing, with no specific book in mind. They wander from row to row, look along the shelves, take down a book to glance through it, keep hold of it if they like the look of it, buy it, then hopefully read it. It might trigger off seeking out another book by the same author, or a different one in the same genre. It's the randomness, the uncertainty, the discovery that books and bookstores provide that I love".

Anna looked at her with affection and a degree of awe. "That sarnie looks great. Thanks Katya," she said, once the waitress had served their order.

"You're welcome. And thanks so much for driving over to see me".

"Is there anything in particular you wanted to run past me?"

"There is, but first of all, do you mind that I tend to share my thoughts with you rather than with Chrissy?"

"Whether you choose to talk to Chrissy or me is totally fine with me. I'm certainly available whenever you feel I may be able to help. And that goes for Charlie too. You're very important to both of us, and that will continue without hesitation".

"Thank you. That means a lot to me. You and Charlie will always be the first people I will turn to, and I'll always be here for you, too, should the need arise, not that I can envisage that happening".

"Thanks. You talk and I'll eat but eat too if you can".

"I've finished with Louis. I told him at the weekend. My first boyfriend and I'm using the 'it's not you, it's me' cliché. But that really is the case. It's not him at all. He's a really nice guy, and we get on well, but it just wasn't happening for me. You know when you're fifty pages into a three-hundred-and-fifty-page novel and you're thinking to yourself, 'this is OK but it's not really my type of thing. Rather than continue through the next three hundred pages maybe I should put it away and try something else'? Well, it's like that. Quite enjoyable but a bit of a waste of time when I know there's better out there. Well, maybe not better but certainly more up my street".

"How did he take it?"

"Philosophically, which isn't surprising bearing in mind his interest in Nietzsche".

Anna giggled. "You do amuse me Katya".

"I could have told you all of that on the phone. Sorry for messing up your day".

"You haven't messed anything up, and if you feel you want to see me, whether it's to share a problem or seek a second opinion or just for some company, just ask. I'll be here, whatever the reason".

"Do you think I've been rash? Should I have stuck it out and given it a chance?"

"It depends. If you were looking for experience, you know, finding out how men tick, or if the sex was giving you something you wanted or needed, or if you wanted the company because the alternative was having too much time on your own, then you would have had valid reasons to keep it going until you found someone more to your liking".

"None of those apply. As you know, I'm fine in my own company and I feel like I've had a crash course in finding out how men tick".

"And the sex?"

"I'm pleased with the way it went with Louis; he was a good guy to lose my virginity to. But I'm not desperate, or anything like that. I can do without it for a while. Mind you, I'd prefer to have it on-tap, as you do. And with Charlie too—lucky you! Before France, I had associated socially simply with boys and girls. Charlie was the first man to treat me as a friend. I know you deserve it but you're so lucky, Anna. I increasingly appreciate how exceptional he is".

Anna studied the girl while sipping her milk. All she said in response was, "Come on, eat up Katya, you've hardly touched that sandwich".

As Katerina consumed her lunch, Anna told her that Charlie was reasonably confident that the purchase of the apartment would be completed shortly after they returned from France.

"Brilliant," exclaimed Katerina. "Chrissy will be delighted too. And Steve. He'll move in the next day, without doubt".

"They're still getting on well then?"

"Almost to the point of it being unbearable to watch or listen to them".

"Young love! Hey, one thing I've been meaning to mention is your school uniform".

"Really? That's a bit random. What about it?"

"Have you kept it?"

"It's probably in my wardrobe somewhere. I know I haven't chucked it and I can't imagine Chrissy has. Why do you ask?"

"Just an additional tip: keep it. You'll have fun with it at some point with a future boyfriend".

"Role play, you mean?"

"Yes. Charlie's a sucker for me dressing up. In fact, most of my boyfriends were the same. And I love doing it too".

"Right, if I don't bag a new boyfriend soon, I'll advertise in the local paper: 'Young, reasonable looks enhanced by Twiggy-inspired hair style, classy wardrobe, sexually experienced, 50% homeowner, full driving license, original school uniform freshly cleaned and ironed'. Something like that".

"Good. Don't take too long to fill the vacancy".

On Saturday evening, at 7.15, Charlie was showered, dressed, and sitting in the kitchen sipping a glass of red wine. He had taken a glass up to Anna and she had shouted from the shower, "Just leave it in the bedroom. I'll be down soon".

She joined Charlie in the kitchen at 7.25 and he was surprised to see that she was already clothed for walking out to the taxi: Burberry mac and stilettos.

"Stilettos, wow! What's underneath? You haven't told me what you're wearing tonight".

"Not until later. Good timing. Here's the taxi".

Charlie grabbed his jacket and followed Anna out of the door. As they neared the taxi, Anna turned round and said, "You look great, by the way".

They were seated three rows from the back, just to the right of centre. The cinema was approximately one third full but, thankfully, no one was sitting directly in front of them or within six seats either side. Ten minutes into the main feature, Anna undid the belt of her mac and calmly opened the garment as if too hot. It was so natural that Charlie had no need to glance to see what she was doing. However, following a dramatic scene, he turned to her to check her reaction. It was clear what she was wearing underneath: above her stiletto heels, silk stocking held up by suspender tags fitted to her bustier corset. Knickers were being worn beneath the suspender straps, which would need to be undone before her knickers could be removed. Her breasts were barely contained. Nor was Charlie's excitement. For the next few minutes, he barely looked at the screen. She turned to whisper in his ear, "I hope you're enjoying the film, Charlie".

Chapter 25

The holiday to France was approaching, and Anna wondered whether she would be seeing Lene before then. Eventually, she received a text:

'I'm free Monday if you are'

Anna read it, closed her eyes to compose herself, took a deep breath and then sent her considered response.

'I am. Any thoughts?'
'Anything/anywhere'
'I'll come back to you'
'OK'

"I'm meeting up with Lene on Monday, if that's OK with you".
"Just as friends or as friends and lovers?"
"Both, I should think. You OK with that?"
Charlie contemplated. "I guess so".
"You sure?"
"Where will you be meeting her?"
"We haven't sorted that yet".
"She could come here, I suppose. I've some Christmas shopping to do, and loads of other stuff, so I can make myself scarce for the day".
"You wouldn't mind?"
"I'll leave it with you".
"OK. I'll let you know".

Anna sent a text to Lene shortly afterwards:

'Charlie out all-day Mon and has suggested you may like to come here?'

A couple of hours passed before Anna received a response:

'That would be lovely'
'Good. Come as early as you like'
'10-ish?'
'No problem'
'Great. See you then x'

"Come in, Lene. It's so cold, isn't it?"

"Freezing".

Anna closed the door, and the friends held each other in a strong embrace.

"Let me take your coat then you go and stand in front of the log burner in the Snug to warm up. I'll bring some drinks in. What would you like?"

"May I have a coffee with a splash of milk, or cream, if you have it? I wouldn't mind a glass of water too please; my mouth is dry".

"Anxious excitement again?"

"No, no feelings of anxiousness. It's more than just excited though. It's a determination that I must savour every single second and, if I don't, I'll be cross with myself afterwards. I don't think you have any idea, Anna, quite what you do to people".

"We'll both savour every second".

They kissed, separated, kissed again, more passionately and for longer, then Anna went into the kitchen to prepare the drinks.

After they'd placed their empty mugs on the draining board, Anna took Lene's hand and they headed for the stairs, Lene picking up her handbag on the way.

"It's lovely and warm in here," said Lene, as Anna led her into the bedroom. "So, is this where you and Charlie sleep?"

"Yes. Does that concern you, us being in here?"

"No, it doesn't. Before we undress, I'd like to give you your Christmas present". Lene reached into her handbag and extracted a small package. She passed it to Anna, who slowly removed the gift wrapping. A box was revealed, and Anna opened the lid. Inside, she saw two orange-coloured, pear-shaped earrings. She removed one and studied it.

"They're not precious, Anna, so I haven't gone overboard. They're made from Carnelian, which is the Swedish National gemstone. I had them set in gold for you, but just have them as a keepsake if you can't see yourself wearing them. I won't mind at all".

Anna took the second earring out of the box. She placed them both on a chest of drawers, removed the earrings she had been wearing and then took off every article of clothing. She inserted her new earrings and stood directly in front of Lene.

"I'll treasure them forever". Tears were seeping from her eyes.

"Oh god Anna, don't start me off. You know what I'm like".

The girls hugged, partly through affection but also to save the embarrassment each knew the other was feeling.

"Now, get those clothes off before I go crazy".

Throughout the remainder of the morning, there were periods when desire for each other triggered frantic action and passion, but there were also numerous moments of tenderness, when they simply wanted nothing more than to cuddle and kiss each other. There was no need for communication, instruction, or request. Somehow, they each knew what to do, and how and when to do it. Eventually, they reached the point when they both felt they should take some time out to re-establish stability.

"Cheese on toast?"

"Perfect, thanks".

"Diet coke?"

"Yes please. Shall I come down with you?"

"Oh no, stay here, please. I won't be long. Stay in bed and wait for me".

After Anna had cleared away, they lay side by side, facing each other. Anna kissed Lene on her lips and the end of her nose, and then rolled onto her back. Lene climbed off the bed and picked up her handbag, which she placed on the floor at the foot of the bed. Anna watched her remove a tube from her handbag before climbing back onto the bed to kneel between Anna's legs.

BOOK THREE: *THE ADOLESCENT*

"Trust me". With considered preparation and slow, careful determination, Lene took Anna to a place to which she'd never previously been, in a way never previously experienced.

Once Anna's convulsions had ceased, and she stilled, Lene removed her phone from her handbag and took a photo before slowly, carefully and in stages, beginning to remove herself. Lene nestled herself into Anna's embrace and they remained silent, both engrossed in thought. Lene fondled Anna's breasts, feeling convinced that every single person in the world, in finding themselves in Lene's position, man, woman, boy, girl, old or young, would do the same. As for Anna, she was formulating the next words to be spoken.

"Lene, I need you to know that, however fantastic my sex life has been with Charlie, I have never experienced sensations like that. Whatever happens between us, I will forever treasure the memory of it in the same way as I will treasure my earrings. And there will never be a time when I'm putting the earrings in when I won't be thinking about today. With you, doing that, something which I didn't really think was possible".

Lene didn't respond with words but with a squeeze and a kiss. She then said, "Would you like to see the photo?"

"I didn't know you'd taken a photo".

"That doesn't surprise me. You were in another world".

"I was. But you were there too. Come on then, let's see it".

Lene located her phone and they both studied the photo. "My god," said Anna, "that's unbelievable. No wonder I felt the way I did".

"It was lovely to do and incredible being able to watch myself doing it. I felt sure that you'd like to see it".

"That is the horniest photo ever. You must forward it to me".

"I'll send it now". They both heard Anna's phone ping.

Further silence, and then Lene plucked up the courage to ask, "How long can we carry on like this, Anna? Do you think we should use the next few weeks, when we won't be able to see each other, to try to return to something approaching normality?"

Anna contemplated for a while and then answered, "Do you want to?"

"No. Do you?"

"No".

"Do you think we should?"

"I don't know. Do you?"

Lene didn't respond. Anna studied the ceiling. "I think maybe we should try. While we're still in control".

Lene rested a cheek on Anna's right breast. "OK".

"It makes sense, doesn't it?"

Lene fondled Anna's left breast. "I guess it does. I'll try".

BOOK THREE: *THE ADOLESCENT*

CHAPTER 26

Anna and Charlie found themselves rushing around prior to the day of their flight to France. There were further Christmas presents to buy and they all needed to be wrapped and delivered. They had mutually decided that they would not buy each other a present, preferring, instead, to treat themselves to something special during their upcoming visit to Barcelona.

"Right, Garibaldi is sorted so I don't have anything further to do at the stables. Presents have been delivered, other than to Chrissy and Ilya. I'm driving over to Chrissy's later this morning to drop them off. I was hoping we'd manage to fit in a visit to Findon, but I think we'll run out of time, unless you want to go while I'm at Chrissy's".

"Yes, I think I will. I'll send them a text to let them know I'm coming. I'll also check with Katya to see if she's free to join me. She might be able to get a couple of hours off".

"I had a quick chat with her yesterday on the phone. She was saying how busy they are in the shop, so it's doubtful".

"That would be disappointing. I'll try her anyway, just in case".

Anna arrived at Chrissy's house just as Chrissy was preparing a light lunch for the two of them. Gifts were exchanged, and Anna explained that Katerina's would be given to her when she joined them in France. "I've taken a punt with Ilya's. Clothes! Don't know what I was thinking really as I haven't a clue what he'd like. I just saw them in Selfridges and thought they were cool".

"You normally get things right, so don't worry too much about it. If he's disappointed with your choice, he can console himself with half an apartment in East Wittering".

"There's the Cat and Rabbit charity shop just along the road from the apartment. He can always drop them off there if he doesn't like them".

"Would they fit?"

"Who, Ilya?"

"No, a cat or a rabbit, if Ilya doesn't like them".

"Idiot".

Chrissy laughed. "So, all packed and ready to go?"

"Nearly. What are your plans for Christmas Day?"

"I'm really looking forward to it. It's going to be the four of us having a traditional Christmas. Katerina has agreed to go with Ilya to Shore Road Watersports' Christmas get-together on Christmas Eve. All employees are allowed one guest, and Ilya has asked Katerina, which is nice. I just hope they don't drink too much and ruin Christmas Day".

"I'd be surprised if either of them did. So, Steve's joining you?"

"Yes, but not until Christmas Day morning. He'll be with family and friends up to Christmas Eve".

"But he'll stay Christmas night?"

"Oh yes. He says he won't be working until the new year, so he'll stay several nights".

"I'm so pleased it's going well for the two of you. I've always thought he's a really nice guy and haven't been able to understand why he has never had a long-term relationship".

"It's because of his penis, I'm sure it is".

Anna tried to remain emotionless. "Do you really think it's been that much of an issue?"

"I do, yes. Think about it, Anna. Most girls in their twenties and thirties want to enjoy sex with their partner, so it would be a big deal if something major put them off. Let's face it, if a girl loved her guy but he farted every time they fucked, she'd pack it in, wouldn't she?"

Anna laughed. "Yes, I suppose she would".

"Or if he always shouted out, "Geronimo," at the point of ejaculation, she'd soon tire of it".

"Yes, I get your point. So, his penis isn't an issue for you then? It's not putting you off?"

"No. I love it. Maybe I've an extra-large fanny".

"Jesus, Chrissy, pack it in. That's not something a sister particularly wants to hear".

"Don't talk crap. I've always been able to say anything to you, ever since we were both first able to talk. No, I mean it, I must be made differently to his previous partners if they've finished with him purely because he was too big for them. It's a tight squeeze getting him all in, I'll admit to that, and he has to be mindful of not being too forceful, but he's never let me down yet. I orgasm every time, whether or not we have any foreplay. I don't have to rub myself or anything like that, it comes solely from him being inside me. That makes me extremely fortunate in my opinion".

"That aside, you like him too?"

"I really like him. We get on so well".

"That's great. Long term?"

"I think so. He'll move in as soon as Ilya and Katerina move out. To be frank, much as I've loved bringing them up and living with them, I'm really looking forward to the next stage of my life".

Anna pulled Chrissy into her body and wrapped her in a loving embrace. "I'm so happy for you Chrissy. Nobody deserves it more".

"Thanks Anna. I'd love it if the four of us could get together once you get back from France".

"Definitely. We'd love it too".

"Great. We'll wait until Ilya and Katerina are settled in, then you must come over for dinner and stay the night".

"Lovely idea. I'll leave it to you to come up with the date so that we do it when Steve isn't planning to work the following day".

Later in the day, Anna conveyed this information to Charlie, and he described his trip to Findon, which Katerina had been unable to make. "They're clearly delighted with him and said he'll be ready to have his first run before the end of March. A maiden hurdle race at Fontwell has been targeted. I've already messaged Katya to advise her to block out the day. Anything else going on?"

"Can't think of anything".

The flight to Perpignan had been uncomfortably bumpy and they were more pleased than normal to enter their villa in Le Racou. As always, Camille and Thierry had prepared everything according to their wishes: the log burner was roaring, the fridge and freezer were fully stocked, and the entire interior was clean, fresh, and welcoming.

They spent languid days before they drove to Barcelona, where they checked in at their beloved hotel, dropped off their bags and then strolled around the city. Their main objective was to visit a local art dealer who, they felt sure, could source a limited-edition Joan Miro print, which they had chosen to be their joint Christmas present.

That evening, they were eating in the hotel restaurant. Anna had chosen to wear a knee-length, straight, charcoal-grey skirt with the seersucker shirt she had bought in Collioure in the summer. As planned, she had decided to not wear a bra.

"You know your nipples can be clearly seen, don't you Anna?"

"Of course. Wouldn't be much of a special treat for you otherwise, would it?"

"Guillem will combust".

"As long as he's not expecting me to clear it up".

That evening was the first time in their experience that the table service was less than perfect. Guillem managed to miss Anna's glass when pouring her wine, and also dropped a roll after she'd asked him if she could have a second.

"I don't know whether he's going to be devastated or relieved when he finds out we're not eating here tomorrow evening," claimed Charlie.

"We'll have another special night tomorrow before Katya comes. It'll be one where you play a part, too".

She was sitting alone in the main bar of Hotel 1898, a small glass of local Cava on the table in front of her. She had decided to wear the dress that she had bought in Perpignan in the summer; it was its first outing. Its style was business-like: hem finishing just on the top of the knee, short sleeved, tailored, burnt orange in colour. It was the neckline which would have caused some raised eyebrows in a meeting room: a wide, deep, V-shape which revealed a considerable expanse of cleavage.

Absentmindedly, she fingered her orange, pear-shaped earrings as she assessed the other people in the bar area: mostly couples who were having a drink pre- or post-dining, plus groups of men, perhaps attending a retirement event for a work colleague, or a remembrance gathering for an old friend.

Finally, the arrival of a male to interest her. He was on his own, very smartly dressed: Armani was her assessment. Handsome, slim but with wide shoulders, expensive haircut, probably mid to late 30s. She guessed that he would order something 'grown-up': bourbon with ice or a James Bond style Martini as opposed to a pint of lager or a beach-bar cocktail. It turned out to be an 'Old Fashioned'. As he sipped his drink, while leaning against the bar, his eyes roamed the room. There appeared to be little to interest him until he spotted her. She returned his gaze. The length of time their eyes were locked would have made some people feel uncomfortable, but not either of them, apparently.

He walked over to where she was sitting. "Do you speak English?" he asked.

"I *am* English".

"Am I interrupting? Are you waiting for someone?"

"No, neither".

"Then may I sit with you? Please say if you'd rather I didn't".

"I'm happy for you to join me".

"Thank you. May I get you another drink?"

"No, I'm fine with this one, thanks".

They chatted for a while and before long, he said, "Have you eaten? I could ask to see the menu. We could eat in the restaurant, or here, if you prefer".

"Well, I had planned to leave after I'd finished this drink, but I don't have any plans for the evening so yes, thank you, it will save me seeking out a restaurant in the city and eating alone".

They decided to remain at their bar table, and a selection of tapas dishes was served to them. During the meal, she was able to get him to talk about himself. He told her he was in Barcelona on a business trip, being an investment fund manager assessing Catalan companies in which the Fund was considering investment.

"And how about yourself?" he asked. "Is this a business trip or leisure?"

"My husband and I love Barcelona. We are considering buying an apartment here. I'm spending a few days researching what's available. We'll come back together when he can spare the time".

"And why did you choose here for your drink? I assume from what you said earlier that you are not staying here".

"No, but I think I will next time. This appears to be a nicer hotel than the one in which I'm staying. I came in because my feet hurt after a long day, and it was the first I came to after I'd decided to end my research for the day. Have you stayed here before?"

"Yes, many times. Your husband is a busy man, then?"

"Oh, yes. He should have retired years ago but he's in great demand. He's seventy-five, now, and we don't need the money. It's purely his ego, in my opinion".

"Do you work?"

"Not now. I used to be an escort. It's how I met my husband. I'm starting to really miss it".

"What aspect are you missing?"

"Oh, the sex, of course. I mentioned my husband's age".

After conversing further, she said, "I'm ready to leave now. Would you mind walking me back to my hotel please?" They stood and walked out of the bar towards the hotel exit. Before they could get there, he took her by the hand and led her to the lifts. As they sped upwards, he pressed her against a wall of the lift, and they kissed with such passion that they appeared to be eating each other. Before the lift reached the floor of the suite in which they were spending two nights, the zip at the back of her dress had been lowered, one of her breasts had been manoeuvred out of the garment and a nipple was being fed into his mouth; she had not been wearing a bra. They stumbled along the passageway and, by the time they reached the door into the suite, the top half of her dress had been lowered to her waist and both breasts were on display. Her back was now up against the door, he was roughly fondling her left breast with his right hand, their kissing was even more intense than it had been in the lift, and she was frantically trying to undo the button at the top of his trousers and lower the zip of his fly. He was only able to get the plastic key into the slot once she had given him some room, which she did by kneeling on the floor in order to take him into her mouth. They were oblivious to movement further down the corridor as another couple exited the lift to return to their room. The door opened and they spilled in. He tore off his shoes, socks, trousers, and boxers, and she her knickers, before he managed to close the door and provide them with some privacy. He fucked her up against the door.

Anna and Charlie did very little at the villa in the run up to Christmas, preferring to idle away the days reading, snoozing, wandering around the village and sitting on the beach with a flask of coffee and a pack of sandwiches. The highlight was an excellent lunch at Les Antiquaires in Perpignan on Christmas Day.

During the evening prior to Katerina's visit, as they were cuddling on the sofa in front of the log burner, drinking Armagnac, Anna said, "It's been a great year".

"Yes, very enjoyable. Do you think next year will be much the same?"

"I've no idea what next year is going to bring".

He raised himself to look at her. "I may have got this wrong, but the way you said that suggests that you're worried about it in some way".

"Yes, I think I am".

He became concerned. "Bloody hell, why?"

"Lene, for a start. And then there's Katya".

"Explain".

"Well, for one thing, it probably hasn't escaped your notice that Lene and I have greatly enjoyed our times together. I think it may have to stop to save it from getting out of control".

"Out of your control, or hers?"

"Hers primarily, but maybe mine too".

"You've assured me a number of times that you'll put an end to it before that happens".

"Yes, I know".

"And I've told you I'm fine with the two of you getting together as long as it doesn't threaten relationships".

"Yes, I know, Charlie. You don't have to remind me".

"So, I'll leave you to get on top of that one. Why does Katya worry you?"

"I wouldn't be at all surprised if Katya discovers something about herself fairly soon".

"And that would be something for us to worry about?"

"It would, yes".

Charlie waited for Anna to expound. When she didn't, he asked, "Are you going to enlighten me?"

"Well, either I'm wrong, in which case we'll both forget I said anything, or I'm not, and then you'll see for yourself".

"Is that all I'm getting?"

"Yep".

She was the first one through the doors, spotting them immediately. She beamed and waved. "Oh my god," she said as she hugged and kissed them, "I can't believe I'm here. It's been such a long wait. How are you both? Did you have a nice Christmas? Canigou—wow. It looks stunning, all covered in snow".

Anna laughed at Katerina's exuberance. "We're both great thanks, and we've had a lovely time. How about you? How did Christmas Day go?"

"Shall we talk and walk?" suggested Charlie. "Here, Katya, let me take your bag".

"No need thanks Charlie, it's fine on my back. Yes, Christmas Day was great, thanks. Steve was good company and did most of the washing up, so that certainly did me a favour. Did Chrissy a favour too on Christmas night from the sounds coming from their room. Chrissy broke all records that night. God knows what they were doing".

"Here, you get in the front, Katya," said Anna, laughing, "and I'll jump in the back". Katerina placed her bag in the boot of the BMW, stepped into the car and they set off.

"How was your trip to Barcelona?"

"Really good thanks," answered Charlie. "Did you get any good presents?"

"Ilya bought me a TV for my room, and I bought him one for his. And Chrissy bought us both one for the lounge so we're TV'd out. Stupid thing is neither Ilya nor I watch much television. Steve was very generous. He bought something for Ilya to add to his kite surfing kit, don't know what it was, and he has bought me a spa treatment at The Spread Eagle in Midhurst".

"That's a lovely present," responded Anna. "That's one of the best spa's I've ever been to. Did you buy anything for him?"

"Yes. Ilya bought him a new shovel for his work; very exciting. Chrissy and I clubbed together and are paying for him to have a penis enlargement operation".

"I think you're getting worse, what do you think Anna?"

"I've said it before, and I'll say it again—incorrigible".

Katerina giggled. "What did you give each other? Other than multiple orgasms, that is".

"A print from an art dealer in Barca," said Anna. "Unfortunately, it won't be delivered until after we return to England".

"Don't tell me, don't tell me. I'd say it was either a limited-edition Picasso, or a Matisse. No, no, not either of those. I'm going for a limited-edition Miro".

"You're getting to know us too well," said Charlie with a shake of his head.

They were nearing the villa. "Le Racou," said Katerina, wistfully, "how I've missed you". They drove through the entrance gates and Katerina studied the house name sign. "L'Aubaine. The Windfall. You two are my windfall".

Anna cooked them an early meal as Katerina had admitted that she was tired. "It's been really busy at the store, and I've been working extra hours. I've also had a couple of late nights. That's my excuse, anyway".

"Good late nights?" enquired Anna.

"I went to Ilya's work's Christmas do on Christmas Eve. It was lovely of him to ask me to go with him and I had a great time".

"What are his work colleagues like?" asked Charlie.

"His boss seems decent. I spent a fair bit of time with a girl who works there. She's lovely and we got on well. There's a guy who works there who has obviously struck up a friendship with Ilya. I had a bit of a job keeping him at arm's length".

"Scott," said Anna.

"Yes. How did you know that?"

"Oh, I just remember him when I popped in to see Ilya when I was arranging for him to buy the kite surfing equipment".

"What did you think of him?"

"Can't remember much about him, to be honest".

"I don't believe you".

"Oh, OK, if you must know I thought he was very good looking and a typical surfer".

"That's more like it".

"I take it you think he's good looking too".

"Well, whilst I was trying to keep him at arm's length, I was trying to reel him in too!"

"Sounds interesting".

"I felt some sparks".

"What, as in sparks which were missing when you were with Louis?"

"Yes".

"So, anything further arranged? Are you seeing him again?"

"He asked for my number, and I said I'd text it to him, which I haven't. He wrote his on a scrap of paper and insisted I kept it. He asked if I'd give him a call when I got back to England".

"And what did you say?"

"I didn't say anything. I just smiled at him and turned back to talk to Katie".

"Is she the girl who works downstairs? Very pretty?"

"Yes, that's her. She's lovely, isn't she?"

"Very".

"I think that Ilya's smitten. Scott doesn't seem that interested. Maybe she's already re-buffed him".

"Or attractive Russian girls with a Twiggy haircut is more his thing?"

"Maybe. We'll see. Anyway, if you don't mind, I'm off to bed".

"It's all laid out for you, Katya," said Charlie. "Are you having a lie in?"

"I think I might, actually. You go ahead with your usual routine, and I'll sort myself out. I'm sure I'll be raring to go after a good night's sleep. Goodnight". She kissed them both and left the room.

"I think she likes him," said Anna, with a smile. She felt relief flood through her.

The days passed extremely pleasantly. The three of them were always together, whether it was walking on the beach, playing board games in the villa, having a drink in a local bar or sitting in the winter sun, in the garden, with a 'throw' over their legs. At 7.20 on New Year's Eve morning Katerina knocked on their bedroom door and walked in carrying a tray. "Morning! Not too early for the drinks, is it?"

Charlie had been sitting up, reading, and said, "Not too early for me Katya. Can't speak for Anna, though".

Anna's head appeared. "I'm OK. Well, I will be in a minute. That juice is welcome. I'm thirsty this morning".

"I was too," said Katerina. "I think it was from that Chilli I made".

"Maybe. Worth it though. Do you want to get your coffee and jump in with us? The room hasn't warmed up properly yet".

Katerina left the room and returned carrying her mug. Without being asked, Charlie got out to allow Katerina to climb in. They looked at each other but didn't speak.

"Anything in particular you'd like to do today?" asked Anna. "Don't forget, we're eating out in Perpignan this evening".

"I would really love to see that town you've talked to me about. The one in the mountains that you sometimes walk from".

"Prats de Mollo," said Anna. "Yes, I'm up for that. What do you think Charlie?"

"Great idea. Why don't we drive to Prats, have a coffee and a pastry, then drive over the top of the mountain and down into Spain? We could go to Camprodon, have a look round and buy some of their speciality cured meats".

"Perfect. Let's do that. Now, Katya, we haven't given you your Christmas present".

"No, I have to say I've been wondering about that. Half an apartment and a third of a racehorse is unreasonably miserly".

"You're not going to bring that up every time, are you? I'll go and get it". Anna climbed out of bed and both Charlie and Katerina watched her walk across the room. She opened a wardrobe door, grabbed hold of a parcel and an envelope, and carried them back to the bed.

"I wish my breasts swayed like that," said Katerina, not for the first time.

"Here, open this first".

Katerina took the parcel and removed the wrapping paper. She held up the skirt which Anna had bought in the vintage shop in Arundel. "I love it! It's so different".

"It's an original 60's skirt from Biba. I just hope it fits".

"I'll try it on". Katerina stood up on the bed. The nightie she was wearing barely covered her, and the sight of her caused Charlie to reminisce about the summer. Katerina climbed into the skirt, which she did up over her nightie, and exclaimed, "Fits perfectly".

"Not too short, is it?" asked Anna.

"I don't mind wearing it this short. What do you think Charlie?"

"You're wasting your time asking him".

"I like the colour," was all they could get him to say.

"Charlie, you give Katya the other present," said Anna, as she passed him the second gift.

"Merry Christmas. We hope you enjoy it".

Katerina thanked him, removed the skirt then began to open the envelope, which revealed an A4 sheet of paper and two event tickets.

"Radiohead! Old Trafford Cricket Ground in June. I don't believe it. And they're VIP tickets. Oh my fucking god that's unbelievable. How did you get them? They're gold dust". She unfolded the sheet of paper and read the contents. "Two nights at The Stock Exchange Hotel in Manchester plus limousine transfer to and from the venue". She hugged them both in turn. "Thank you, thank you, thank you".

"It's our pleasure," said Anna.

"Charlie, will you come with me? Will you have the second ticket?"

"No, thank you but no. It's your treat and you must take with you whoever you want at the time".

"What if I want you at the time? It's Radiohead! I don't know anyone else who likes them".

"We'll talk about it nearer the time. I'll be the last resort".

"Radiohead. Live! Six months to wait".

"They'll fly by".

"They will, especially with so much going on with the apartment and Stroppy. Right, time for your present". Katerina jumped off the bed, her nightie disarranged, and flew off to her room, returning with a small package. She climbed back into bed and passed the gift to Anna. "What do you buy the couple who has everything? Not much, I'm afraid, but I hope you like it".

"Thanks Katya," said Anna as she began the unwrapping. It was a box. Anna removed the lid, and two generously sized pewter hip flasks were revealed. Anna removed them and noticed an inscription on each: *To Can. Wherever they are is the place to be. Love, 'ya xx*

"I love it. Perfect for when we watch our pride and joy winning his first race. What do you think, Charlie?"

"That's a great present, Katya, thank you. Very thoughtful and very personal".

"Come on then, we need to get going if we're going to spend the day out before this evening's festivities," said Anna as she climbed out of bed and headed for the bathroom. Before reaching it, she paused and turned to face the couple still sitting up in bed. "I think it's time for you two to be a bit more discreet when the three of us are together. Charlie, you'll need to wear some underwear or pyjama bottoms before Katya joins us in bed. And Katya, playtime with Charlie is over. I know he's seen it all before, but we've moved on from that". She disappeared into the bathroom before either had a chance to react.

They arrived back at the villa in plenty of time to get ready for their evening at Les Antiquaires. Anna wore the grey, calf length, midi skirt, which she had bought in the vintage shop, together with long black boots and a white cashmere top, which she tucked into the waist of the skirt. On looking in the mirror she appreciated that the outfit made the most of her shape, enhancing her bust and narrow waist. She wondered whether Katerina would decide to wear the Biba skirt and, on meeting up with her in the lounge, was pleased to see that she had, instead, selected a straight, black, knee-length skirt coupled with a red polo-neck jumper.

"Great outfit. Is it new?" asked Anna.

"Thanks. Yes, I bought it in Chichester last week".

"And you look very smart too, my darling husband". Charlie was wearing her favourite grey Armani trousers and a black John Smedley long sleeved polo top.

"We all look OK, don't we?" suggested Charlie. "Glass of bubbly before the taxi arrives?"

As they were drinking their fizz, Katerina asked, "Would you mind if I took my phone with me? Ilya warned me he was planning on sending his Happy New Year texts early in case he's had too much to drink by midnight. If he sends one, I'd like to reply".

"That's fine, of course you can," Anna reassured her. "I can't imagine there's any other eighteen-year-old who would even think of asking".

As it turned out, Katerina's prediction had been correct. Ilya's goodwill message was received while they were eating their desert:

> *'HNY K'*
> *'Happy New Year to you too Ilya. Nice evening?'*
> *'Early yet but good start. With Katie'*
> *'Your new girlfriend now?'*
> *'Looks like it!'*
> *'You've surpassed yourself'*
> *'Gee thanks'*
> *'I mean it. I thought she was a lovely girl when I met her. Very pretty too. Treat her well Ilya'*
> *'I will. I promise'*
> *'The new Ilya not the old one'*
> *'I said I promise. Good time there?'*
> *'Brilliant thanks'*
> *'Say HNY to A & C for me'*
> *'Will do. And Ilya?'*
> *'What?'*
> *'In your moments of abandon, be careful when you exclaim the name of the girl taking you there—very similar to mine!'*
> *'Good point. That would take some explaining'*

"Ilya?" asked Anna, once Katerina had returned her phone to her bag.

BOOK THREE: *THE ADOLESCENT*

"Yes. He's spending the evening with Katie, so the year has ended very well for him. He asked me to wish you both a Happy New Year".

"That's thoughtful of him, especially bearing in mind he's probably concentrating on other things," joked Charlie. "Shall we have one more drink before we leave?"

Before the taxi arrived, Katerina's phone pinged again.

"Do you mind if I check who that's from?"

"Of course not," answered Charlie.

She removed the phone from her bag once again and read the text which had been sent to her.

"Is it OK if I answer? I know it's a bit rude when we're having a lovely evening together".

"Katya," said Anna, "it's New Year's Eve. Please, don't even think about it if you want to message people".

"Thanks". For the next few minutes Katerina was either reading or typing a text response. Once she was satisfied that the conversation was finished, she placed her phone in front of Anna and Charlie so that they could read the exchange:

> *'I know it's not midnight here yet but it's approaching it there. Happy New Year Katerina'*
> *'It's Katya. Who's this'*
> *'Scott'*
> *'Hi Scott. Sorry, didn't put your number in my phone. HNY'*
> *'Just wondered if you'd like to meet up once you're back'*
> *'What do you have in mind'*
> *'Drink, meal, whatever you like'*
> *'Yeah, I guess we could meet for a drink'*
> *'When r u back'*
> *'3rd'*
> *'Will call you. We could talk about me teaching you to surf in the Spring'*
> *'Spring? You said a drink. Not sure I'm looking for a long-term relationship'*
> *'See how it goes. Say Hi to Anna for me'*

'And Charlie?'
'Her husband?'
'Yes. It's neither or both with Anna and Charlie. So, neither or both?'
'OK. Say hi to them both'
'OK enjoy the rest of your night'
'You too x'

They finished reading, looked up and couldn't determine from her smile and contradictory shrug whether she was excited or indifferent.

They arrived back at the villa at 11.45. "I'll open some fizz," said Charlie. "We'll do the new year stuff and then I'll put on some music".

At midnight, they exchanged Happy New Year wishes and toasted The Can'ya? Partnership as well as Katerina's move into her own apartment.

"Here's to what I'm sure will be a great year," exclaimed Charlie, with certainty.

They clinked glasses and the girls echoed his good wishes and optimism. "Music, Charlie. I want to dance," requested Katerina.

Anna sat on the sofa and Charlie sat next to her as he selected Katerina's favourite Radiohead playlist. From the speaker, 'Pearly'. Katerina immediately responded to the music. Then 'There, There'. Her movements flowed. 'Creep', then 'Weird Fishes'. As each song developed into the more frantic passages, Katerina's dancing became increasingly liberated. As she watched her, with her right hand clenching Charlie's left, Anna wondered if there was anything which better communicated freedom and spirit than a young, athletic, girl dancing with abandon: a lithe body, all arms and motions, closed eyes, rocking head, slinking legs, extended fingers. Feet on the ground, yet floating. Katerina was the centre of attention, and she was fully aware of it. Yet she was utterly within herself, without any semblance of embarrassment or self-consciousness.

"Dance with me, Charlie". '2+2=5' began to play and Anna watched intently as they mooned about playfully before going crazy when Radiohead exploded into the finale.

BOOK THREE: *THE ADOLESCENT*

A couple of slower numbers, during which the two bodies merged. 'Karma Police' next. "Come on Anna". Katerina held out her hands to entice Anna to join them. They moved together, sang together, even Anna knowing most of the words. They linked arms, danced and swayed, becoming one body in motion.

Thom Yorke, Charlie, Anna, and Katerina singing the chorus:

For a minute there I lost myself, I lost myself

Book Four

Crime & Punishment

Chapter 27

Whenever Katerina dropped her guard and thought about Charlie and Anna, she said, "Shit", and busied herself. She hadn't realised that she had been saying the word out loud until Scott had said, "What's wrong?" "Nothing, why?" "You just said "shit"" "Did I? I think it was because I've just remembered that I forgot to do something at the store before I left last night" "Will it still be OK if you do it this morning?" "Oh yes. I'm just pleased I remembered".

She was in trouble, and she knew it.

As her relationship with Anna and Charlie had developed, she realised that she loved them both. She had told them that she did, and they had both told her that they loved her too. It was a warm, cosy, unthreatening, shared, open, comforting love. That is, until she woke up on New Year's Day realising that she still loved Anna but that something had changed with regard to her feelings for Charlie. On the plane at Perpignan airport, she managed to quantify how she felt. She was truly, madly, deeply in love with him. She yearned for him.

Katerina knew her music, she knew her novels. When she listened and read, she immersed herself. She had no interest in background music: it was to be listened to, not merely heard. She wouldn't dip in and out of a book: it either engulfed her or she discarded it. She read her favourite books time and again.

She didn't read about Anna Karenina, she *was* Anna Karenina. Emma Bovary had fascinated her from the second she had been introduced into her life. She didn't watch from a distance the misfortunes of Tess of the d'Urbervilles, she lived them. Thom Yorke's lyrics stretched her; she needed to know where he was coming from. With every Nick Drake song, she tried to plot the descent into his suicide. *'Oh so weak in this need for you'*, words from her favourite song of his, Place To Be. How resonant now. Charlie had introduced her to Ben Harper. One of her favourite songs was Amen Omen. Since her return to England, she cried every time she listened to it through her headphones. He wrote heart breaking lyrics for the song and, although they were written in a different context to the one in which she found herself—the singer was losing somebody, she had found someone—they had lived with her to the point where she could hardly bear to play the song: *'I put, I put your world into my veins'*. Charlie's world was in her veins, and it felt as if she was dying from blood poisoning.

Katerina was definitely in trouble.

"What's the matter, Katerina?"

"Nothing, Salty. Why do you ask?"

"Katerina, there were two acceptable responses to my question, either to tell me to bugger off because it's none of my business, or to tell me what it is that's causing you to feel the way you obviously are".

"I'm fine, honestly I am".

"I'll take that as the bugger off response. Look, sweet girl, I've known you for a long time. I knew you when you were experiencing the standard puberty issues. I was aware that you were struggling with attention from boys once you became desirable to them and I'm convinced that you're currently carrying a heavy weight on your shoulders. I hope you manage to resolve the problem, whatever it is, because you're lovely and you deserve to be happy. If you want to talk to a fusty old maid who's seen it all before, I'll always be ready to listen. If you need time off, just let me know. It won't be a problem".

"Thank you Salty. You're very kind and considerate. I'm OK, don't worry. Look, I really want to get this software set up. It's taking me longer than I anticipated".

"I'll take that as another bugger off. Tell me when you've got it up and running and we'll talk about how we'll start to record our stock".

"Will do".

"Are you OK?"

"Christ, don't you start".

"Have I done something wrong?"

"For fuck's sake, what is it with everybody? I'm fine Scott. No, you haven't done anything wrong. If being with me is getting you down, go home and leave me to my own company. At the moment, I'm the only person who doesn't piss me off".

"Well, it sounds like that person is pissing other people off, me included. You're a moody bitch. Call me if you stop being one".

"You really should have fucked off before you called me that".

He downed the last of his beer, collected his phone and wallet from the bedroom, picked up his jacket and silently left the apartment.

"Shit. Shit, shit, shit". She could do without this. She felt it would make sense to eat some humble pie, simply to give herself some breathing space to stabilise her feelings.

> *'I'm sorry. You're wrong to say I'm a moody bitch but maybe you'd be right to say that I'm currently behaving a bit like one. Not like me though, is it? It's not you, it's something else. Nothing for you to worry about. I'll be back to normal soon. Come back as soon as you feel like it. Kxx'*

It was over ten minutes before she received his reply:

> *'How long til the 'something else' is sorted and you're back to normal?'*
> *'Hard to say'*
> *'Can I help?'*
> *'Afraid not'*
> *'If I come back, how much crap will I have to put up with?'*
> *'Hardly any'*
> *'But some. Will there be any compensating factors?'*
> *'Maybe. What have you in mind?'*
> *'I've seen a very short kilt in your wardrobe. Wear it for me and be a hooker'*
> *'No, that skirt is special. But I've an alternative suggestion'*
> *'What?'*
> *'I'm sitting here on my own. Just back from school. Haven't changed out of my uniform yet. Hoping my big cousin*

Scottie will be coming round. I'm so innocent…'
'How innocent?'
'Totally'
'Hmm'
'But if Scottie decides to make the most of it I'd be allowed to carry on being moody'
'But you don't know how long that could be'
'No'
'Hmm'
'I feel for you. Tough decision'
'OK, decided. You can be a moody bitch whenever you need to be. But you'll have to comply with Scottie's demands'
'It's all a mystery to me. I'll do whatever cousin Scottie wants. I won't know any better'

Lene had deliberately refrained from contacting Anna since they had been in bed together at Anna's cottage, just before Christmas. Over six weeks, but Lene didn't know whether she should be congratulating or admonishing herself. The girls were at school, her husband, Greg, was at work and she was sitting at the dining room table, sipping a diet coke, and wondering how Anna had dealt with the prolonged period of absence and abstinence. Better than she had, Lene felt certain. Christmas had been wonderful. Greg had been loving and attentive, her daughters had been a pleasure to be with throughout their school holiday, and business at her salon had been thriving as clients prepared themselves for festivities and had indulged themselves after the period of continual preparation, cooking, entertaining and clearing up. Lene was aware that she had every reason to be happy, thankful, and optimistic.

Instead, she felt hollow and incomplete. Time, she had to give it time. Six weeks was nothing, no period at all in the big scheme of things. Yet it was an eternity. Too long to endure, not long enough to make the difference that was necessary. She decided to give it until after Valentine's Day and then send Anna a simple, *'Hi, how are you?'* text. She could send that now, though, couldn't she? What harm would it do? Just, *'Hi Anna, hope you had a great Christmas and New Year'*. She picked up her phone and unlocked it. She noticed that her hand was trembling.

"What should I do? What should I do?" She said this to her phone. It didn't respond, didn't even provide a suggestion, a reassurance. Not for the first time, she sobbed. And, once again, she realised that sobbing is pointless when you're on your own.

She knew she would have to try to pull herself together. She decided to make a serious effort, starting with a text to her husband:

> *'Hi Greg. How's the day going?'*
> *'Busy earlier but not too bad now. You OK?'*
> *'Of course. Just wanted to let you know that I'm aiming to give you some pleasure tonight'*
> *'Are you now?'*
> *'Yes. Any specific requests?'*
> *'There's so many it's difficult to choose'*
> *'Would you like me to surprise you?'*
> *'That would be lovely'*
> *'Will be my pleasure. We'll get the girls off to bed as early as we can'*
> *'Can't wait'*

'Well,' she thought, 'that's a start. I won't contact Anna yet but will send her a card for Valentine's. I'll see how she responds to that and then decide what I'm going to do'.

However desperate a situation appears to be, a plan of action can make an immediate impact. Lene felt better and decided she now had to concentrate on how she was going to pleasure her husband; she wanted to come up with something good.

Anna was demanding similar resolve from herself. She told herself that nothing had changed, that she still loved Charlie and that he had given her no reason to believe that he no longer adored her. Charlie had behaved as normal with Katerina whilst in France, on the journey home and throughout the period of Katerina moving out of Chrissy's house and into her new apartment, during which time Anna and Charlie had shared her excitement and assisted with her arrangement of the furnishings. Katerina, too, had been her normal self, and neither she nor Charlie had referred to Anna's instruction on New Year's Eve that they needed to be more discreet in future. It appeared that it was only Anna's instincts which were making her feel the way she was.

She purposely didn't consider Lene. They hadn't been in touch with each other since the day they spent together before Christmas. It had to stay that way for a while, until her head was clearer.

To complicate matters, she and Charlie had agreed to a social visit to Chrissy's. Chrissy didn't know anything about the fun she had enjoyed with Steve, and there was no reason why that should change. Of more concern would be Chrissy finding out about Katerina's sexual initiations with her and Charlie. It was imperative that she never did.

She rose from the table and poured herself a glass of wine. Before her first sip, she heard the rumble of the Alfa's engine as Charlie pulled up outside the cottage.

Charlie had decided to stop off at a pub for a quick pint of Guinness on the way back from the fencing club, which was totally out of character. He sat alone at a table, taking occasional sips. He had a lot to think about. He wasn't sure if the thoughts were welcome or an intrusion. Who was he kidding? He knew full well that his thoughts made him uncomfortable, worried him. Nobody paid any attention to him but, if anyone did choose to spend any time studying the solo drinker, they would have detected a worried man. Two months previously they would have seen someone who appeared to be as happy as could be, without a care in the world.

He returned his empty glass to the bar, left the pub, and drove home to Anna.

On her drive to work one morning, Katerina decided that it was time to contact Anna and Charlie. They'd met up only at the time of her moving into her new apartment. None of them would consider that there had been any sinister reason for not having any contact since then but, because of the way Katerina had been feeling, she felt that contact needed to be made to avoid cause for concern or doubt.

She parked her car and started the text. She selected for it to be sent to them both:

'Just a quick text before work to check how you're doing'

It was Anna who replied, almost immediately:

'Great thanks Katya. Settled in?'
'Yes thanks. Home from home now. Loving it'
'I'm so pleased. How's it going with Scott?'
'Pretty good, actually'
'Sparks?'
'Enough to be going on with'
'Excellent. Work OK?'
'Really good. Am sorting a software system so we can record our stock'
'Clever girl'
'Just makes me the 'I.T. girl' whereas you're the 'it-girl!''
'But you have something that men crave'
'Thing, singular. It-girls have things, plural'.
'What you have is special and outweighs whatever I have to offer'
'I'm intrigued. What is it that you think I have?'
'Mystique. I know what effect you have'
'I don't know how to respond to that'
'We're at Chrissy's this weekend then we're considering going away for a week. Do you want to come over, eat with us and stay over after we get back?'
'Would love to, thank you, Hope you enjoy your holiday'
'I'm sure we will. We'll sort asap xx'
'XX'

Katerina chose not to consider the implications of the correspondence and, instead, opened the car door and marched off to the bookstore.

Shortly after her return home, she sent a text to Anna suggesting the last weekend of February for her visit, if that tied in with their holiday and other commitments. She advised she would not be working on the Monday so would be able to stay over on the Sunday night. The response from Anna thrilled, yet discomforted, her: Anna proposed that she drive to their cottage straight from work on the Saturday and stay three nights. She added that the three of them could go to see their racehorse, Stroppy, while she was there. Katerina replied that she was greatly looking forward to it, instead of which she troubled herself with wondering if Anna would suggest she join them in bed on the mornings she was there, as she usually did. If so, what should she wear? Would Charlie be wearing anything?

Discreet? Appearing shapeless and unalluring would come easily to her after four years of practice, but hiding her love for Charlie would be less straightforward.

Mystique? Katerina felt miserable, not mystical.

Book Four: *Crime & Punishment*

Chapter 28

The doorbell rang. "It's them. How do I look?"

"You look great, Chrissy. Calm down, you've been jumpy all morning".

"I can't calm down. I so want this to go well. Come on, you need to be with me when I let them in".

Chrissy opened the door just as Anna was pressing the buzzer again. "Jesus, Chrissy, it's fucking freezing out here".

"Sorry Anna. Hi Charlie. Come in, come in. This is Steve. Of course, you know that. Steve, Anna and Charlie".

"Yes," said Steve with a laugh, "it is indeed Anna and Charlie. Hi you two. How'ya doing?"

"Great thanks Steve," replied Charlie as the two men shook hands.

"Lovely to see you again Steve," said Anna as she stretched up to give Steve a peck on the cheek.

"Lovely to see you too. It's been too long".

"It has," agreed Chrissy. "My fault. I should have arranged this ages ago".

"We've all been busy Chrissy. It's no problem".

"Let me take your coats. What have you got there?" Chrissy took a bag from Charlie as he began to slip off his jacket to pass to Steve.

"Just some wine and bits from the deli in Petworth".

"That looks great. Thank you. Steve, can you sort the drinks? You two go on through to the lounge and we'll be with you in a bit".

"Is there anything I can do to help?" asked Anna.

"No thanks. All under control".

"What can I get you? Alcohol or hot drink?"

"Black coffee please, Steve," said Charlie.

"May I have a hot chocolate please".

Anna and Charlie walked into the lounge and were joined by Steve a few minutes later. He handed out the drinks and then said, "You're looking well Charlie. And Anna is as ravishing as ever".

"You're looking good too, Steve," said Anna. "It seems clear that security and domestication is suiting you well".

"I'm very lucky to have met up with Chrissy. She's the best thing that's happened to me in quite a while".

"That's great to hear," responded Charlie. "I have to say, you both seem to have hit the jackpot".

"I've never seen her so happy," agreed Anna. "You must have a special something". She smiled at him sweetly.

"I don't know about that, Anna. There's nothing special about me, you know that". He grinned back.

"How's it going?" asked Chrissy as she burst through the door. "All getting on OK?"

"Chrissy has been frantic all week. For some reason she is on edge that we won't get on, even though we've known each other for years".

Anna slipped her arm around her sister's shoulders. "Nothing to be frantic about. We're great friends and all have fond memories and no secrets. That's right, isn't it lads?"

Steve responded with, "Great friends. Fond memories. No secrets. Well, none that any of us will admit to. Let's drink to that".

Chrissy's shoulders noticeably relaxed. "Food won't be long".

The rest of the day passed extremely pleasantly. Chrissy tended to dominate the conversation, which suited the others very well. At a little after midnight, Anna stood up and said, "I'm off to bed. Stay longer, Charlie, if you'd like to".

"I'm about done too, to be honest. I've eaten too much and drunk too much and am ready to crash out".

"Don't tell me this is going to be one of those rare nights when you two don't have sex".

"Tell me more," said Steve.

"My sister and her husband of nearly ten years can't keep their hands off each other. You must have noticed. I recall Anna once saying to me, "It's something I'm really good at, it provides the greatest of pleasures, it's free and the variety is limitless with an imagination like mine". I've never forgotten it. Do you remember saying that, Anna?"

"I do. I think I was thirteen at the time".

The others laughed and then Chrissy added, "Actually, thinking back, you weren't much older than that. Do you remember borrowing those monthly magazines from that older girl you made friends with? I think it was Cosmopolitan. You read all the articles associated with sex and always completed those questionnaires. I think you routinely fell into the 'Potential Nymphomaniac' category. I've always wanted to ask, Charlie, is she as good as she's cracked up to be?"

"Without doubt".

"And, after all these years, do you think she was right when she said the variety is limitless?"

"I'm not bored yet".

"Well, I've always envied you both. I no longer need to, now that I've got Steve. They're our role models, Steve. Do you think we'll be as happy together in twelve years as they are?"

"Well, it sounds like the magic formula includes sex nearly every day and plenty of variety. Fine by me if you want to follow the recipe".

Chrissy stood up. "Or maybe just having Anna as your partner! Anyway, come on Steve, we've some catching up to do".

"Keep the noise down," shouted Anna as she headed for the stairs.

Chapter 29

Katerina was lying on her back, having enjoyed the wonders of Scott's tongue. Once she had calmed, she decided that Scott merited some pleasure himself. She believed that he would assume she would be using her hands only because, until then, she had shown no enthusiasm for oral sex. This hadn't surprised him as he'd experienced the same frustrations with previous girlfriends, and, after all, Katerina was only eighteen so probably had little understanding of the arts and delights of fellatio.

She utilised all her newly discovered techniques and they soon reached the point at which Scott should have given her a warning. He didn't, of course, but she was happy to see it through.

As they settled into a cuddle, he asked, "How many boyfriends did you say you had before me?"

"One".

"And you went out with him for how long?"

"Oh, I don't know. A couple of months or so? Why?"

"You are unbelievable".

She smiled. "Why do you say that?"

"How on earth did you learn to do it like that?"

"Long story".

"Maybe you'll tell it to me some time?"

"No, I won't be doing that".

"Go on, I'd love to know. You've a skill set there, and I bet the story behind it would be worth listening to".

"Still a no, I'm afraid".

"Suit yourself".

Scott slept but, once again, Katerina was unable to drift off. She had never been in love before. Most eighteen-year-old girls haven't. They may think they have, but that's because they've misunderstood infatuation. Unfortunately for Katerina, she *was* in love. As she lay there, she summoned up the memory of lying on a sun bed next to Anna. They were talking about

Anna's early days with Charlie. "How did you recognise you were in love with him?" "When it happens, you know. It's like having an orgasm. If you're wondering if you've just had one, you haven't. If you are wondering whether you're in love, you're not". Katerina was beginning to discover that being in love isn't entirely pleasurable. It triggers unhealthy thoughts: jealousy, uncertainty, a longing for reassurance, desperation that it was unrequited, fear of its fragility. Of greater concern for her was that she felt alone in her love. There was no hope for her. But there again, she thought, you can't control hope. When hope lets you down, it's devastating. You wish to fuck it had never visited you in the first place.

'I'm going to have to tell him,' she thought. 'I need help, and only he can provide it'.

Anna and Charlie had arrived at the Anassa Hotel in Cyprus, which is situated on a cliff, overlooking the Mediterranean Sea, between the Baths of Aphrodite and Latsi. Whilst there, they didn't see any benefit to leaving their perfect location, so they simply relaxed and indulged themselves. By spending the time together without mentioning Katerina or Lene, the tension which had built between them since they had returned from France eased, and by the time they arrived home, they were a loving couple once again.

Charlie put the kettle on, and Anna collected the post from the box by their front gate.

"Well, a bit of boring stuff but some Valentines cards too. All for me, I'm afraid". This happened every year, with friends and admirers wishing to communicate their affection for her, sometimes anonymously. Charlie had often been inquisitive, but never jealous.

"I've no idea who this one is from but, from the wording, it appears that he or she has a sexual crush on me".

"How can you tell?"

"Whoever sent it has written, *They say forbidden fruit tastes sweeter. I'd love to use my tongue to find out if that's true*".

"And you've no idea who will have sent it?"

"None at all. Well, I know who this one's from," she said, as she opened her next card.

"What does it say?"
"*I need it still. Do you?*"
"Lene?"
"Yes".
"What will you do?"
"I haven't seen her for weeks".
"Do you need it still, too?"
"Perhaps I should meet with her and see how we both feel. I'll let you know".

Anna couldn't immediately get to grips with the emotions she felt. Relief? Certainty? Commitment? Worry? Confusion? That night, just before getting into bed, while Charlie was in the bathroom, she sent a text to Lene.

Lene had bought the Valentine's card when choosing the one which she would be giving to Greg. She had written Greg's immediately and had put it in a drawer ready to give to him on the 14th, together with the giant Toblerone, which was her standard Valentine's and Anniversary gift. Anna's remained unwritten until the 13th.

Lene was unaware that Anna was abroad so, on the 13th, she panicked, accepting that she either wrote and posted it, or threw it away. Finally, she decided to send it, but she then had the dilemma as to what to write. She considered sending it without an inscription but the will to communicate something resulted in her deciding upon the true message she wanted to convey. She simply couldn't carry on living as she was.

She stopped off at the post box on the way to the salon. She decided against dropping the card through the opening and returned it to the passenger seat. At lunchtime, she told Dani that she was popping out to get some diet coke, retrieved the card from the car and walked to the newsagent shop, outside which she knew there was a post box. She returned to the salon with the coke and the card.

During the afternoon, Dani told her that she had forgotten to ask Lene if she could buy some milk while she was out and, as they didn't have any for teas and coffees for clients, she would run round to the newsagent to get some. "Sorry, I should have thought of it earlier. Oh, Dani, would you mind posting this letter for me?" It was out of her hands. It was going to be sent.

On Valentine's Day, she and Greg exchanged cards just before he left for work. As she was about to leave to drive to the salon, the postman arrived: junk mail and a card. She opened the card with trembling fingers. '*x*'. That's all. She put it back in the envelope, placed the envelope in her handbag and left for work.

A few days later, she was frantic. Her message had annoyed Anna; it had upset her. Anna had shown Charlie and they had exchanged sympathetic shrugs. No, they had both shaken their heads in irritation. Anna had read it, laughed, and put it in the bin. Why oh why had she sent it? Lene had no thought that the reason Anna hadn't responded was that she was away on a celebration trip.

"You've hardly touched your dinner. Are you feeling OK, Lene?" Greg asked.

"Yes, fine, I had one of those torpedo rolls for lunch. Dani was out shopping and brought it back from Gregg's. I should have known better than to eat it all".

"Are you sure you're not coming down with anything? You've been rather subdued recently. Even one of the girls mentioned it".

"Sorry, I didn't realise I'd been quiet. Maybe I am starting a cold or something".

"No need to apologise. I'm just concerned that you're feeling all right. Why don't you have an early night? I'll bring up a brandy".

"You're such a wonderful husband, Greg. Thank you. Yes, I will go up and a brandy would be lovely. Bring one up for yourself, too, and we'll chat".

"I will. Go on, off you go. I'll clear all this up and come up with the drinks in twenty minutes or so".

She stood, walked to him to hug and kiss him, interrupted the girls' TV viewing by telling them she felt a little unwell so was going to bed, undressed, got into bed and then curled in a ball under the covers and sobbed. By the time Greg appeared, she had begun a fitful sleep.

She and Greg were dropping off to sleep the following night when her phone pinged.

"Bloody hell, who could that be at this time of night?" asked Greg.

She looked at her phone. "My first appointment on Tuesday morning. She needs to cancel".

"Bit inconsiderate sending it this late. Could have sent it tomorrow".

"Yes, sorry, she's a bit like that".

Lene looked at the message again. It said, *There's no way this can finish now.*

BOOK FOUR: *CRIME & PUNISHMENT*

CHAPTER 30

"Good day, Steve?"

"Really good thanks Chrissy. I finally finished that job over in Selsey, so I can now move on to the project in Arundel that's behind schedule".

"Were they pleased with what you did?"

"Very. They've promised a very complimentary review, so that's a bonus".

"Great. Well done".

"How about your day?"

"I'm not sure, to be honest. I phoned Katerina during her lunch break as it's been a while since we've spoken, and she wasn't her usual self".

"She's probably got a lot on".

"I phoned Salty this afternoon to ask if she had noticed anything and she said that she felt Katerina has had something troubling her for a few weeks. I feel really guilty now for not spotting it and finding out if I can help".

"Did Salty give you any idea about what may be causing it?"

"She said she didn't know but felt confident it's nothing to do with the bookstore as Katerina has been even more dedicated than previously, and I've told you how delighted Salty has been with her".

"Boyfriend trouble?"

"Well, after I'd talked to Salty, I phoned Ilya to see if he could throw any light on it. He said that, as far as he knew, Katerina was getting on well with Scott. He said that Scott has given him the impression that he and Katerina are having a lot of fun together. It's worrying me".

"Look, I obviously know very little about eighteen-year-old girls, but I would have thought that they have any number of issues to deal with. They're probably ones which seem insurmountable at the time yet miraculously dissolve".

"I thought you knew Katerina better than that".

Steve considered this. "You're right. If she's troubled, then it will be something which would trouble anybody. I've never met anyone as collected and self-assured as she is, whatever age, male or female".

257

"Exactly. I need to find a way of seeing her without it seeming as if I'm prying. How about inviting her and Scott over for a Sunday lunch?"

"Lovely idea. I could pop out for a pint with Scott so that the two of you have some time together".

"Yes, that would work well. Thanks. I'll let you know what's been arranged. Are there any Sundays when you won't be free?"

"No. Whenever suits is fine by me. And how about Ilya? How did he seem?"

"Cocky little sod".

Steve laughed. "Good, no problems there then. Some cocky little sods need a slap, but you can't help loving Ilya for being that way".

"People say to me how can a brother and sister be so different, and I have to remind them that there is no blood tie between them, nor between either of them or me. However many times I tell people, it still seems to confuse them".

"Do you know why that is?"

"Why?"

"Because it's confusing! Do I remember this correctly: Katerina doesn't know her father at all, her mother died a drunk, Ilya's mother also died, and his father became Katerina's stepfather but, after the three of them moved to England and he formed a relationship with you, he returned to Russia and neither of them have heard from him in a while. You have never had children but have raised Katerina and Ilya for several years, most of that time on your own. Is that right?"

"More or less. Sometimes, I can't exactly remember it all myself. In fairness to Ilya's father, Ivan, he did keep sending the money through until Katerina turned eighteen, so he provided some support, even though she's not his daughter".

"I should think so too. I honestly don't know how you did it all. By the way, is Ilya still with that sweet young girl? Katie, isn't it?"

"You know very well her name is Katie. You're like a council estate mongrel whenever she's around".

"Oh to be young again".

"Well, thanks very much".

"Sorry Chrissy, you know I don't mean it. She's a sweet girl, that's all".

"It's just as well you're not young again".

"Why's that?"

"Even with my years of experience of entertaining several lovers, it still takes willpower and dogged determination to accommodate that weapon of yours. For that poor wee girl, it would be like a polo mint trying to accommodate a hot dog".

"How are you feeling at the moment? In terms of willpower and dogged determination, I mean".

"I suppose I could summon up the courage in the time it takes you to have a shower".

"I'll go and have one now". Steve left the kitchen chuckling. "You know you love it really," he threw over his shoulder while he was still within earshot.

He just about heard her response. "I used the wrong word. It's a cannon, not a weapon. And yes, I love it".

They finished making love, Chrissy taking the standard ten minutes to lie flat so that her legs wouldn't give way as soon as she climbed off the bed. They ate their evening meal and, while Steve was doing the washing up, Chrissy sent a text to Katerina:

> *'Lovely to speak earlier. Fancy you & S coming over for Sunday lunch?'*
> *'Nice idea. Will need to be next month'*
> *'That's OK. 5th?'*
> *'Should be fine. Will let you know'*
> *'OK. Take care xx'*

Chrissy felt disturbed. It appeared that Katerina had reverted to her previous self, the one that was transformed during her summer holiday in France at Anna and Charlie's villa. It was unexpected. However much she thought about it, she simply couldn't identify what could have happened to dislodge a girl who had seemed so at ease with her job, her boyfriend, and her independence. She needed to find out, and then see if she could help.

"Well, you're obviously feeling better," said Greg as he watched his wife skip up the hall to welcome him home from work. He bent down to give her a kiss and then laughed as he watched her skip back to the kitchen.

"The girls are on a sleepover. They're all off on a field trip tomorrow, the whole class".

"Did I know that? Must have forgotten. What's for dinner?"

"You're taking me out".

"Did I forget that too?"

"No, I only decided this afternoon. Here, I've poured you a glass of wine. Drink that while I go and change. I'll drive," and she slipped off up the stairs. Ten minutes later she sped back down and shouted, "Ready". He walked out of the kitchen and saw her waiting for him by the front door.

"Lene, you look fantastic". She was wearing ankle boots and a short denim skirt. Between them, her legs were bare. "Won't you be cold?"

"I'm wearing a jacket too".

"No, I meant the bare legs".

"It's colder in Stockholm".

He laughed.

"Shall we go?"

"Just a minute". He walked up to her and put his hand up her skirt while kissing her.

"Are you checking if I'm wearing knickers?"

"No, I just couldn't resist the temptation".

"I'll take them off if you like. Go out without wearing any, I mean".

"You *are* feeling better, aren't you? It's lovely to have my Lene back".

"Sorry Greg. I must have been under the weather without knowing it".

"I think you'd better keep the knickers on. It's February and we don't want you coming down with something again".

"Greg, in all seriousness, how have things been for you over the past few months?"

"How do you mean?"

"With me. Us".

"I've been a bit worried about you since Christmas, but other than that, you, and we, have been great. The sex especially. I don't know what happened, Lene, but you and I got rampant suddenly. Late summer, wasn't it, when we found out we were teenagers again. I'm intrigued to know what sparked it off".

"Odd, wasn't it? Not complaining though".
"Me neither. Tell you what, if the offer's still on, take them off".
"You sure? This skirt is very short".
"If you'd rather not".
"Wouldn't you mind, knowing what other people may be able to see?"
"No".
"Do you like the idea?"
"Yes. Is that awful?"
She removed her knickers, put them in her handbag, picked up the car keys and led him out of the house to the car.

She'd been dying to respond to Anna's text and, because she'd felt decadent all evening, in the restaurant with Greg, them both knowing that, if she wasn't careful, she'd be on display, she decided to do just that, while Greg was visiting the Gent's.

'What/how/when?'

She hoped she'd receive a response before Greg returned to the table and she did.

'Soon. I'll let you know. You at home?'
'No. In a restaurant with Greg'
'When you get home, use your Lelo, my present to you. Imagine it's me licking you'
'Greg wants me tonight. He's already told me'
'Ask him to watch you. He'll love it'
'OK I will'
'Think of me'
'I will. I thought it was over'
'It's not. We'll meet soon. Enjoy your night xx'

"Received a text?"

"Yes, just checking on the girls". She hated herself and felt on top of the world, both feelings fighting for dominance. "Come on, let's settle up and go home. I've got something I've been wanting to show you".

As soon as they arrived home, Lene wasted no time. She held Greg's hand and immediately led him upstairs to the bedroom. "Stand at the end of the bed and watch". She opened the top drawer of her dressing table, rummaged through her underwear and extracted her Lelo Sona. She placed it on the bed and removed her cardigan and blouse. She had not been wearing a bra, and her nipples stood dark and proud, as usual. She kept on her boots and skirt and lay on her back. She pulled up the skirt, turned on the Lelo and positioned the pulse. She began to moan immediately. Greg watched, silently.

"I'm being licked Greg. Watch me. I'm your wife and am being licked by someone, and you're watching".

"Yes. I'm watching it happen, Lene".

"Who is it.... oh god.... who is it?"

"Who do you want it to be?"

"No, tell me. Quick before I come. Jesus that's good. Tell me Greg, I want to picture it".

"I want it to be who you want it to be".

"Oh, that's beautiful. A girl, Greg, I want a girl to be licking me. Tell me who it is so I can picture her doing it".

"Dani. It's Dani".

"Oh yes Dani. That's beautiful. You're going to make me come. Tell me Greg".

"It's lovely. She's doing it for you, Lene".

Lene threw her head back and her hips came off the bed. Greg watched his wife thrash about and heard her moaning and swearing.

"She wants to give you another one. Tell her she can".

"Don't stop, don't stop". She forced her legs apart and focussed once more on the pulse. "Christ, here it comes".

"Enjoy it Lene, then you must watch me make love to Dani. It's my turn next".

Lene forcefully threw the Lelo to the side and allowed the orgasm to pulsate through her body. Finally, it ended, and she stilled.

Greg didn't move or say anything. Eventually, Lene said to him, "You said it's your turn, Greg. Lene has told me what you do to her. Do it to me".

He wasted no more time. He stripped off his clothes and dived onto the bed. "Is this how you want it, Dani?"

He lay on his back, his arm around her. Her head rested on his chest. "That was sensational," he said.

"It was".

"Where did that come from?"

"What, the vibrator thingy?"

"Well, yes that, but what I actually meant was you choosing for it to be a girl who was licking you".

"Don't know really. A bit different, I suppose".

"We've done a few things like that before, but you've never mentioned picturing being with another girl".

"To be honest, I have thought about it but never had the courage to suggest it".

"The courage?"

"Yes, I haven't wanted to disgust you".

"It wouldn't have disgusted me".

"Would it have turned you on?"

"Well, it did just now".

"You liked the idea of me being licked by a girl then?"

"In the fantasy, yes".

"Wouldn't you like to see me with a girl in real life? Most men seem to be turned on by the girl with girl scenario".

"Why, would you like to?"

"You're not getting out of it that way. Don't avoid the question".

He laughed. "OK. Um, yes, I guess it would be sexy, but I've never even considered it or imagined it before".

"Why not?"

"Because our sex life until recently has been straightforward, I suppose. When we've gone out of ourselves, it's still been you and me, just in a situation outside our normal life together".

"But you enjoyed it?"

"Yes, I must admit, I did".

"Why Dani?"

"What do you mean?"

"You could have chosen anyone. Why Dani?"

"Oh, I don't know. I couldn't think of anyone else on the spur of the moment and I suppose subliminally I recalled you telling me she's bi".

"Do you fancy her?"

"Never thought about it really. Yes, she's cute. She works with you, and that's the only way I've known her, so I've never really considered whether or not I fancy her".

"Come on then, who *do* you fancy? There must be someone you and I both know who you've been attracted to".

"The only obvious one is Anna".

"Ah, Anna. Everyone fancies Anna".

"Would you have preferred me to have selected Anna for you to picture rather than Dani?"

"No, not at all. Dani certainly got the job done, didn't she? For both of us".

He laughed again.

She added, "Would you like us to role play like that again soon? Next time, though, we'll be with Anna. You can picture the two of us entertaining you".

"Well, Dani proved herself to be a very talented girl, but I'd have no complaint being in a fantasy threesome with you and Anna. Anna licking you to orgasm would be an arousing scene to visualise. Thinking about it, you were seeing quite a lot of Anna before Christmas. I haven't heard you mention her for a while. You haven't fallen out, have you?"

"No, of course not. Our paths haven't crossed, that's all. Funnily enough she recently sent me a short text suggesting we meet up again".

"That's good. I know you like each other and have fun when you're together. Anything planned yet?"

"No, we simply agreed we should meet soon. When we went to London that time, to do the Christmas shopping, she did say we should go again, maybe to see a show or something. Trouble is, that would involve staying overnight up there".

"Well, why don't you do it?"

"What about you and the girls?"

"That's not a problem. I'm quite capable. I'd simply arrange my work hours around them. Go on, get it sorted, it'll do you good".

"You sure you wouldn't mind?"

"No, of course not".

"I'll see what she says".

"So where *did* the vibrator thingy come from?"

"Oh, I read about it somewhere and the reviews were very positive. Believe it or not it was bought from Selfridge's". Once again, she felt a mixture of guilt and excitement.

They were just dropping off when Greg pulled back the quilt and said, "Sorry, I need the loo". While he was in the bathroom, Lene sent a short text to Anna:

'London? Stay over?'

She locked her phone and closed her eyes before Greg returned to the bedroom. She tried to stay awake in case she received a response, but she couldn't manage it. When she woke up the next morning, she saw that she was yet to hear back from Anna.

Once the girls had left to catch their school bus, and Greg had driven to work, Lene sat down with a cup of coffee and thought things through. How could she even consider it? What a great night she had shared with Greg. He gave her everything she wanted. She loved him. He didn't deserve it. She sent a text:

'Second thoughts. Let's meet for coffee'

She finished getting ready and then picked up her phone. She had received a text while fetching her coat.

'That's a shame. I've already started researching trains and accom'

Lene stared at her phone as if it had insulted her. She took off her coat and sat down again. She accepted that she was at risk of being late for her first appointment, but she felt that she needed to get things sorted before she went mad. After ten minutes of turmoil, she put on her coat again and picked up her phone and car keys. She reached the front door before stopping dead and remaining motionless. She took the phone out of her handbag and sat on the stairs. She typed out:

'Sorry to mess you around. Yes, please let me know suggested day/time/accom details. I'll then check with G'.

She pressed send, put the phone back in her handbag and left the house. When she arrived at the salon, she was shocked: she couldn't remember one thing about the journey.

"Lene has suggested a trip to London and maybe stay a night".
"Does this fit in with the Valentine message?"
"Yes, probably. How do you feel about that?"
"Has anything changed?"
"I wouldn't have thought so. You and I aren't at risk, but it may be wise for me to test the water to find out if everything's OK between Lene and Greg".
"Yes, I think you should. We'll discuss it when you get back".
"You sound a bit tetchy, and you've been on edge since we got back from France. What's up?"
"Nothing. Anyway, it seems you really want to go to London with Lene, and it's clear that she wants to maintain her sexual relationship with you. If you're satisfied that there's no reason for any of us to feel differently about this, then I guess I'm still fine about it".
"You're sure? There's no chance that you're trying to find a way to get back at me for telling you and Katya you need to behave better?"
"Is that what you were telling us?"

"Don't you agree that her seeing you naked, and flashing what she's got to you needs to be stopped?"

"You didn't seem to think like that a few weeks ago".

"Maybe I do now".

"I'll wear boxers, Anna, and, knowing Katya, I've no doubt she'll take account of what you said".

"I hope she does".

"Well, you sort things with Lene and then, as I said, we can discuss the two of you when you get back".

Charlie eventually decided, after suffering conflicting thoughts and emotions, that it would be a good idea for him to contact Katerina before the weekend of her visit. At the very least, she needed to know Anna had been serious about the two of them displaying more discretion. He called her and, when she answered, his opening words surprised him as much as they evidently did her.

"I'm sorry to dump this on you, Katya, but I need to tell you something. I love you".

No response. A silence so loud he felt the need to pull his phone away from his ear. "Katya?"

"What do you mean?"

"I'm sorry, but I felt I should tell you. I thought you need to know". A pause before continuing. "I know I'm being unfair, but I just thought that you need to know that if I behave oddly while you're with us, it's because I've fallen in love with you. You don't need to worry about it, I'll sort myself out. I promise I won't embarrass you or worry Anna. Everything will appear as normal".

"Oh my fucking god".

"I'm so sorry Katya. I'll sort it out. There's nothing for you to worry about. Things will still be the same between the three of us".

"They won't. Don't you see, I love you too. You must have known that".

"What are you talking about? What do you mean I must have known?"

"It's been seeping out of every pore of my body since New Year's Day. It's all I can think about". She started to cry.

"Are you OK?"

"No". It came out more forcefully than she intended.

"I love you Katya. I had no idea you feel the same". He could hear her crying. "Don't you want that?"

She sobbed into the phone, "Of course I do. And of course I don't".

"What are we going to do?"

A scoff and laugh combined. "It can't be left to me. I'm an eighteen-year-old Russian girl. Read the books. A tragedy is the inevitable outcome in situations like this. Whose heart would you want me to break?"

"Not yours".

"It would have to be Anna's then. You'll have to phone me back. I can't cope with this at the moment".

"Katya".

"Phone me back. In an hour".

The line went dead.

He phoned back in an hour. She answered after one ring.

"Anna knows," she said.

"I don't think that's the case. I think it's simply that she believes it's time that we behaved as normal friends would. That's why we should wear things when we see each other. It's probably wise".

"Charlie, trust me, Anna knows. She knew before even you or I did".

"She hasn't let on".

"She will".

"We have this weekend together. The three of us".

"Don't imagine that my thoughts haven't been dominated by that".

"Perhaps we should put it off".

"Until when? Is this going to go away, do you think?"

"No".

"Tell me again how you're feeling. Truthfully. Do you love me because you want me?"

"I most definitely want you. But that's not it".

"So, what is it?"

"My cock makes me desire you, my heart makes me love you but it's my brain which makes me want to be with you".

"Your brain? Your biggest organ? Even bigger than Steve's penis? Face it, Charlie, you're fucked". Despite himself, he laughed. "But Charlie, you have Anna. She's gorgeous. She's wonderful. You love her".

"I know, Katya. I know".

"I need to go. I'll see you on Saturday. Don't worry, I'll bring a jumpsuit to wear in bed".

The line went dead again.

Thirty seconds later, she phoned him.

"What's that chess word that means any move you make worsens your situation?"

"Zugzwang".

"I'm zugzwanged".

The line went dead for a third time.

Chapter 31

'Suggest train to London early Sun 5th. Back eve Mon 6th. Let me know if suits'

Anna telephoned the racing Yard and tried to arrange for the three of them to see Stroppy and to chat to the Trainer on the upcoming Monday. She was told that they would all be too busy as they had several horses racing on that day, at various tracks. It was agreed that, instead, they would visit on Sunday.

"We're going to Findon on Sunday morning. Might be nice to have a late Sunday lunch somewhere".

"That would be lovely. I'll book a table".

"I'm looking forward to seeing Katya again. So much seems to have happened since the three of us got back from France".

"Yes, it will be great. I expect she'll have a lot to tell us".

"Despite what I said, I'd still like her to join us in bed in the mornings. We love chatting together, and we've formulated so many plans that way".

"Why *did* you say what you said?"

"Because of how you two now feel about each other".

Charlie didn't respond.

"To be honest, I don't blame either of you. I'm at fault for not doing something about it earlier".

Charlie simply looked at her.

"I still love her, and I think she still loves me. But I don't know if Charlie and Katya are now putting Charlie and Anna at risk".

"I don't want that to happen".

"Neither do I. But nor do I want Katya to be excluded from our lives. I said in France last summer that she'd got under my skin. Since then, she's become even more precious to me. I suppose it seems to be working with Lene, doesn't it? Maybe it could work with Katya too".

"Do you mean that Lene's in love with you, and you with her, yet you feel that you and I are not jeopardized?"

Book Four: *Crime & Punishment*

"Yes".

"Are you two discreet when you're together?"

"Don't be a shit, Charlie".

He stared at her, then simply said, "I'll phone about that table".

"Greg, are you still OK about me going to London with Anna?"

"Yes, of course. Have you set something up?"

"Only provisionally. I told Anna I need you to be comfortable with my staying up there for a night and whether you could arrange work hours around it".

"What's the provisional date?"

"Sunday and Monday week. I think that's the 5th and 6th".

"Well, the Sunday's no problem as I've nothing planned. I'll simply make sure that, on the Monday, I'm home for the girls leaving for school and for when they get back. You can get whatever time train back you like".

"That's great, thank you. I'll let Anna know".

"No problem. Right, to save you cooking tonight, shall I bring fish and chips in with me?"

"Lovely. The girls will be pleased".

"Haddock?"

"Yes, for me, but the girls will both want cod".

"OK. I should be back before 6.30 so get the plates and sauces ready".

"Will do. Have a good day".

"You too".

She phoned Anna from the car, as she pulled up in a space near the salon.

"Hi Anna".

"Lene. All OK?"

"Yes. I can make the 5th and 6th".

"That's terrific. I'll book the train tickets. What times are best for you?"

"It doesn't matter. Greg has said he'll be there for the girls, whatever we arrange".

"That's good of him. Is there anything in particular you'd like to do in London?"

"No, anything. I just want to be with you".

"I feel that way too. How about I book somewhere nice for a meal on Sunday evening but otherwise leave things open?"

"That would be lovely".

"Are you OK?"

"It's been difficult, but I'm feeling better now".

"Are you going to enjoy this or are doubts going to get in the way?"

"I'm going to enjoy this. I cannot wait".

"Neither can I. Thank you for ringing. I'll send you a text with the train times".

"Thanks Anna. See you soon".

"Yes, see you soon".

"That was a great fish supper. Thank you for suggesting that".

"I'm stuffed. Bought too many chips again".

"You didn't have to finish them all!"

"I don't have your discipline".

Lene pondered this before saying, "Anna has confirmed the 5th and 6th. Is that still OK?"

"Sure. Do you know what you'll be doing?"

"I don't, actually. Anna knows the London scene so much better than I, so I've left it to her".

"She'll make sure you have a lovely time, whatever you do".

"Yes, I'm sure she will. I'll get some easy meals for you to have. You don't want to be worrying about what to eat and how to cook it".

"Great, thanks. Some things I can heat up which you know the girls like".

"That's easy enough. Thanks again Greg".

"For the fish supper?"

"No, for being so considerate about my trip to London".

"Don't be silly. I'm hardly making a sacrifice, am I, and it will be good for you to spend some time away from the house and salon routine".

"I do love you".

"I love you too. Right, let me clear this mess away, then we can settle down in front of the TV".

"I'll help".

"No need. You go on through and spend a bit of time with the girls before they go to bed".

"OK. Thanks".

Chapter 32

"Fancy a pint once we've closed up Ilya?"

"Yeah, don't see why not, Scott. Katie's at her dad's so I'd be on my own. The Shore?"

"Might as well".

"Doom Bar?"

"Yes please mate".

"Crisps or nuts?"

"Dry roasted nuts please".

They were the only customers so decided to sit on bar stools to chat.

"So, tell me all about Auntie Anna".

"Who's Auntie Anna?"

"Auntie Anna and Uncle Charlie".

"Christ, does no one ever pay attention? Let me spell this out, once and for all. My last name is Andreev. I'm Russian, as is my father and my mother before she died. Katerina is also Russian, and her last name is Pimenova, which was her mother's name. Chrissy is English and her surname is Swift, and that, too, was Anna's maiden name; she's also English, by the way. Anna married an English man, and her surname now is Knightley. I would have thought any idiot could see that there is no connexion between Anna and me or Katerina, but obviously not. I do have an aunt, though. Her name is Svetlana Pavlyuchenkova, she lives in an apartment block in St Petersburg, and I spent a lot of time with her there when my dad was working. We lost touch when I left Russia. So, have you got it at last?"

"OK, calm down. How do you refer to her then?"

"Anna".

"What she's like?"

"Why do you want to know?"

"I find her interesting. Don't tell me you don't".

"She's fun, lively, generous and considerate. There, that should do you".

"And fit".

"I guess she is".

"Fuck off Ilya".

"Is this why you wanted a pint? So that you could find out if she'd be up for it?"

"I'm just asking you to tell me a bit about her. Katya's with her and Charlie this weekend, and she was pretty clear that she didn't want me muscling in".

"Katerina and I have known her for years. She's been lovely to us, especially recently. Katerina gets on very well with both of them. She's stayed with them in France a couple of times. If she isn't inviting you when she meets up with them, I wouldn't go thinking there's any sinister reason. In fact, bearing in mind Katerina is supposed to be your girlfriend, I think you're out of order asking me about Anna".

"Calm down. No harm intended. If we were in a bar in Russia, would you have taken your glove off and slapped me round the face to challenge me to a duel?"

Despite himself, Ilya laughed. "Yes, that's how it would have worked. It would be up to you to choose the weapon".

"Against you, I'd choose cocks. I'd win easily".

"Wanker".

Ilya walked home and Scott decided to have another half before driving home. "Tell you what, could you do me a pie and chips too?" While he was sipping his drink and waiting for his food, he thought about his card to Anna. Why had he referred to her as 'forbidden fruit'? Was it because she is married? Or because she's the sister of the lady who had brought up Katya? Or because he had a girlfriend and shouldn't be having carnal thoughts about an older lady? He didn't really know and didn't particularly care.

Katerina rang the doorbell a little after 6.30 on Saturday evening. Anna answered the door, and they studied each other for a few seconds before Anna stood aside to let Katerina in. After closing the door, Anna stepped towards the girl, held her face in her hands, kissed her, and then embraced her in a tight cuddle. Katerina responded by wrapping her arms around Anna's waist.

"Oh Katya, it's so lovely to see you". Katerina squeezed and tried hard not to cry.

Charlie was waiting for them in the Snug. Anna led Katerina into the room, holding her hand.

"Hello Katya. Lovely to see you".

"Hi Charlie. It's lovely to be here again. I've missed you both, terribly".

Charlie walked up to her, and Anna stepped back. "We'll have a lovely weekend Katya," he said. "Relax for now. You've had a long day, I should think. We'll have a quiet evening and then we have all day Sunday and Monday. Anna's arranged for us to visit the stables tomorrow".

"Charlie, could you pour the drinks and I'll finish preparing supper. I've made a chicken and mushroom pie. Is that OK, Katya?"

"Lovely, thank you. Not too much for me".

"We'll eat in here, on our laps, in front of the log burner. Charlie, would you mind bringing a glass of red wine to me?"

"Of course. How about you Katya?"

"Yes, a red wine would be very nice".

Anna disappeared into the kitchen. Charlie opened a bottle of Merlot and poured three large glasses; Katerina remained standing.

"I'll just take this into Anna. Sit down Katya. Or would you prefer to get changed first?"

"I'll get changed".

"Wait here and I'll carry your bag up for you".

When Charlie returned, he saw that Katerina hadn't moved. He walked up to her, put his arms around her and kissed her. He released her and stepped back. Katerina stepped towards him and stood on tiptoe. He kissed her again, more passionately.

"Help me, Charlie. Help me through this, please".

"I will. You were right, Anna knows".

"Oh my god, does she hate me?"

"She's been looking forward to you staying with us. Don't worry, it will be OK".

"How can you say that?" She paused, then swayed a little. "I think I'm going to be sick".

He went to her and held her. "Relax. It's OK, you're not going to be sick".

After a while, he released her, walked into the hall, picked up her overnight bag and proceeded up the stairs, Katerina following closely behind. He led her into the bedroom and placed her bag on the bed.

"We'll see you when you're ready".

"I love you, Charlie. I can't believe that you feel the same way about me as I do about you".

"This will be OK".

"Hold me".

"How is she?" asked Anna as she was dishing up.

"She's getting changed. She'll be down in a minute".

"She's suffering".

"Yes, she is".

"It's difficult for me. I cannot lose you to her, but she mustn't suffer. We must help her. We need to get the best outcome for her that we can".

"I think we're all suffering, one way or another".

"Yes, I guess we are. She needs to see that she can get something out of this. Neither of us can abandon her".

"We won't abandon her".

They heard Katerina call from the bottom of the stairs. "I'm ready. I hope I haven't messed you up".

"Not at all," Anna called back. "Just dishing up. Do you want to come in and grab your plate?"

Katerina joined them in the kitchen. She looked better than she had. "Looks lovely, thank you. I'll carry two in. Shall I come back for something else?"

"No, that's it. We're ready to eat".

The three went back to the Snug and didn't start chatting until they had finished their meals.

When Charlie woke the following morning, he sensed something was different. Anna wasn't lying next to him. Although he couldn't hear her in the en suite bathroom, he assumed that she would be there, using the loo. After a while he got up, put on his dressing gown, and padded downstairs. She wasn't there. He walked back up the stairs, knocked gently on the door to Katerina's bedroom and opened it. Anna was sitting up in bed, under the quilt, wide awake. She immediately put her finger to her mouth to shush him. He walked over to the bed and saw that Katerina was fast asleep alongside Anna. Anna indicated for him to lower his head so that she could whisper in his ear.

"I heard her in the night. She was in the bathroom, being sick. I stayed with her".

He whispered back, "Is she OK, do you think?"

Anna didn't immediately respond but, after a while, whispered, "Put my side of the electric blanket on and Katya and I will come in once she's woken up. Go ahead and have your coffee if you like".

"No, I'll wait". He left them and returned to his bedroom. He turned on the electric blanket, put on a pair of boxer shorts and got back into bed. He tried to read but couldn't concentrate. Twenty minutes later, they entered the room.

"Go on Katya, get in. Charlie's put the blanket on for us".

Katerina, wearing pyjamas, clambered into the bed, followed by Anna.

"OJ and coffee for me please Charlie. Katya?"

"Just coffee please. No juice".

"I'll be back in a bit".

Once the three of them were sitting up in bed, sipping their drinks, Charlie asked, "How are you feeling Katya?"

"I'm fine now, thanks. I must have eaten too much dinner".

Anna simply exchanged glances with Charlie.

"I'm pleased you're feeling better. Are you still up for driving out to see Stroppy?"

"Oh yes, I'm looking forward to it".

"Good. Well, we've plenty of time. We can sit here and relax for a bit".

"So, how's the software installation going, Katya?" asked Anna.

"It's taking a time. To be honest, the whole thing is outside my area of expertise, but I think I've got it sussed".

"What will you be able to do with it, once it's up and running?"

"It should do everything. It's specifically designed for a set-up like ours. Once we've recorded all our stock, and where the individual books are located in the store, we will know exactly what we've got, where to find each individual book, what we need to order, what's been selling well, you know, all that sort of stuff. It will handle the finances too, but I'm not sure that Salty will want to give up the way she's been doing it for decades".

"Recording the stock will be a big job," suggested Charlie.

"Yes, it will. If you fancy a part time job, just let me know".

Anna laughed. "It would take him too long. He'd be picking each one up to say, "This looks interesting, Katya, have you read it?" or, "God, I haven't read this in years. Katya, let me just find a passage which I thought was brilliantly written"".

Katerina smiled and said, "I agree. We certainly couldn't afford to pay him by the hour".

Anna jumped out of bed. "Right. Let's be decadent. Breakfast in bed. I'll get it". She walked across the bedroom to collect her dressing gown.

Katerina and Charlie watched her, and Katerina said, "I know I'm repeating myself, but I really do wish my breasts swayed like that".

"I think you're fine as you are. Now, what would you like for breakfast? Toast, muesli, porridge? We've got some cereal: Crunchy Nut Cornflakes, I think".

"Just some toast please".

"Marmite? Marmalade?"

"Just butter please. Anna, why don't you get back into bed and let me do it? You must be tired".

"Don't be daft. You stay there. Charlie, what would you like?"

"I'll have toast too please. With marmalade".

"Back in a bit. I'll make some fresh coffee too".

Once Anna had left the room Charlie asked, "Are you all right?"

"Yes, honestly, I'm fine thank you. She's so wonderful".

"Yes, she is". They held hands under the quilt.

Anna returned to the bedroom carrying a tray laden with plates and mugs. "Almost bit off more than I could chew there. This nearly went flying back down the stairs".

"Sorry, I should have given you a hand," admitted Charlie, guiltily.

"Instead of which you've been lying in bed next to the beautiful Katya". Anna leaned forward and kissed Katerina on the lips. "You OK darling girl?"

"I'm much better now, thank you".

"Good. Now, eat your toast slowly. We don't want it upsetting your tummy".

"Anna?"

"Yes?"

"Thank you".

"I'm not sure what you're thanking me for, but you're welcome".

"For tending to me while I was being sick".

"Katya, I need to tell you something. I'm not giving Charlie up to you, but I'm not going to lose you either. You're a combination of a daughter, a niece, a sister, a best friend, and a lover to me. I'm not giving up Charlie, but neither am I giving up you. I love you both and I need you both. Now, finish your breakfast and then we'll get going. I'm going to have a shower". Anna peeled off her nightie and walked, naked, to the en suite. Charlie and Katerina watched her right up until the bathroom door closed.

They seated themselves at their reserved table in the pub restaurant and Charlie said, "Well, that was a pleasant surprise".

"Shall we have champagne?"

"What the hell, why not. Is that OK with you, Katya?"

"A glass of champagne would be lovely, thanks".

"You'll need to have two. I can only have one as I'll drive back. Do you feel well enough for that?"

"Yes, I feel totally fine now".

"Great. Order what you like from the menu. We'll go big and not bother this evening. Good idea Anna?"

"Good idea Charlie. I know what I want already".

Both the Trainer and the Head Lad had been available to meet them when they arrived, which was unusual.

"Anna, Charlie, Katerina, great to see you again," the Trainer had said as they exited the Land Rover Defender in the car park. "Come on over to the stables and take a look at your horse". They had followed him across to the main stable block, with the Head Lad following in the rear. "I think you'll notice a difference".

They had indeed, even the inexperienced Charlie and Katerina.

"He's ready to race," the Head Lad had added. "Come on into the office and we'll talk you through it".

They were advised that Stroppy, racing under the name Place To Be, would no longer run in a maiden hurdle at Fontwell as originally planned.

"He'd romp it. The Handicapper would notice and so would the punters, plus the prize money would be poor. No, he's being targeted for a far superior race, to be run at Kempton in a few weeks".

"Why the change of heart?" Anna had asked.

"He's keeping up with some of our better, experienced hurdlers on the gallops. I've undersold him, and you've got yourselves a terrific prospect at a very good price. If he keeps sound, you're going to have a lot of fun with him".

"So are we," added the Head Lad.

"What's the date of the race?" Katerina had asked.

"Tuesday 21st March. Make sure you're there".

"We will," Anna had assured him.

That evening was little different to how things had been before Christmas. Katerina went to bed feeling somewhat happier than she had for several weeks, although she felt tired from having had little sleep the night before. She set off for bed early.

"7.30, grapefruit juice and coffee?"

"Great, thank you. Good night. See you both in the morning. Thank you for a lovely day".

"Good night, Katya".

"Yes, good night, Katya. Sleep well".

Chapter 33

Katerina woke a little after 6am and couldn't get back to sleep. She was pleased to be awake, and on her own, as it gave her an opportunity to consider matters. Even although she went over every detail of conversations and actions since she had arrived, she couldn't put her finger on why it would be that she had progressed from the state she had been in, so bad that it had made her physically ill, to the calmness she was now feeling.

She knew that Anna knew. That helped, as the fear of Anna's reaction had been overwhelming her. Anna hadn't slapped her, sworn at her, banned her from seeing Charlie or told her never to darken their door again.

As for Charlie, were there reasons to feel positive about the future, or was she simply feeling better because things didn't seem as bad as she had feared them to be? Was there any possibility that she and Charlie could have a life together? Did she even want that, knowing that it would mean that Anna and Charlie would be separating?

Charlie knocked on her bedroom door and walked in. "Good morning. Better night's sleep?"

"Morning Charlie. Much better thanks". She was sitting up in bed, the quilt pulled up to her waist, her pyjama top buttoned to her clavicle.

"One grapefruit and one coffee with a spot of cream".

"Perfect, thank you".

"I'll take these through to Anna and we'll see you in a bit".

He left her and returned to his bedroom. Anna was sitting up, waiting for him.

"Would Katya like to join us?"

"I didn't ask".

"I'd like her to, if she wants to".

Charlie returned to Katerina's room. "Coming in?"

"Is it OK with Anna?"

"She said she'd like you to".

Katerina left the bed, followed Charlie, who carried her glass and mug for her, and climbed in. Once they were all settled, Anna asked, "So, what are we going to do today?"

"Any preferences Katya?" asked Charlie.

"A walk in the Downs maybe? Or drive down to West Wittering and walk along the beach?"

"I'm happy with either of those. What about you, Anna?"

"Let's just enjoy this for a while, the three of us in bed together. We'll decide after breakfast".

They all sat, drank, and pondered. Eventually, Anna said, "What changed, Katya?"

Hesitation, and then, "What do you mean?"

"You know what I mean. With your feelings for Charlie".

Charlie interjected. "Anna, are you sure?"

"Look, there's no point in avoiding it. We've tiptoed around it so far but none of us want to tread carefully when we're together, surely".

"It was New Year".

"Yes, I know when it happened, but I'm asking what made it happen".

Katerina turned her head to give Charlie an anxious look. She then looked at Anna. "I'm not sure I'm strong enough to go on with this".

"You are. Come on, it's two adult females talking. I'm not coming across as angry or aggressive, am I?"

"No".

"So, what changed?"

"Realisation".

"Of what?"

"Of the growth of a feeling".

"Love for Charlie?"

"Yes".

"You said you loved us both. Why did your love for Charlie change but not your love for me?"

"Oh Anna, I don't know".

"Yes you do. Come on, why is your love for Charlie, and not your love for me, causing you to be in the state that you are?"

"He's a man".

"And he has a penis which he can put inside you?"

"I don't love him because he has a penis. I love him because he's Charlie".

"Yes, Charlie, with a penis. Not Anna, without one".

"This is really, really difficult, Anna". Katerina's bottom lip was trembling.

"Of course it is. For me too. And probably Charlie as well. Come on, you can do this. It must be because of how sex with him would be different to sex with me".

"Maybe. I love you, Anna, but I can't ever see myself wanting a sexual relationship with a female. Even you". Katerina looked to see how Anna was reacting and detected tears forming in Anna's eyes. "Last summer, I loved you both. I still do. You said to me yesterday that I'm a combination of sister, niece, friend, lover, and daughter. I've loved you much the same way as you're telling me you love me. But not as a lover. I only want a man as a lover".

"But not just any man, eh? It has to be Charlie, doesn't it?"

"Do you remember saying to me, when I said I needed to find an Anna, that it wasn't an Anna I needed but a Charlie?"

"Yes, I do".

"Maybe I realised that you were right, and that I'd found him".

"It didn't have to be my fucking Charlie, though, did it? I wasn't offering him to you".

Katerina reeled at the force of Anna's comment. She calmed herself and said, "I didn't plan it this way. I didn't want this, it just happened".

"So, tell me, what's the best outcome you could get?"

Charlie interjected again. "Anna, that's too difficult".

"Not for Katya it isn't".

"Are you hating me now?" Katerina asked, her bottom lip trembling again.

"Do I sound that way?"

"A bit, yes".

"Well, I don't hate you. Come on, hold back the tears, and tell me. For you, what's the best outcome you could get?"

"To be with Charlie".

There was silence then, "All the time?"

Katerina didn't answer.

"Where would I be?"

Still no answer.

"And how would we explain it to Chrissy?"

Katerina took a breath. "My best outcome would be for Charlie and me to live together and for you to be our best friend".

"When I said best outcome, you know I meant best *achievable* outcome, don't you?"

"You would be able to be our best friend if you, too, had a Charlie. A different one".

"If you remembered me saying you needed to find a Charlie, you'll also remember me saying not this one, that he's unique and he's mine".

"Yes".

"So how could I be with another Charlie, in this scenario of yours?"

"I don't know Anna".

"Would you lose me to be with him?"

"I wouldn't want to".

"Maybe not, but could you?"

"I'd hate it but yes, if I had to".

It was incongruous. The three of them were still sitting up in bed, side by side, holding their coffee mug.

"I don't think I've loved and admired you more than I do at this moment". This was Anna, to Katerina.

"What?"

"You're incredible Katya".

"What are you saying, Anna?"

"I don't know, really. I simply think you're remarkable. I should hate you, but I love you. I should fear you, but I want you to be part of me. I should want to belittle what you say yet I understand you. How fucked up is that?" She paused before continuing. "Right, I've decided. Breakfast, then down to West Wittering. Walk along the beach and then a meal in Drifters". She jumped out of bed, peeled off her nightie and walked into the en suite bathroom. Katerina turned her head to look at Charlie. Whatever the question her eyes were trying to ask, his mouth was incapable of providing the answer.

They parked the Defender in West Wittering Beach car park and strolled down to the beach. The tide was out so they had a vast stretch of golden sand available to them. They wordlessly chose to walk towards the sea before turning left along the shoreline towards East Wittering. Katerina found herself in the middle and Anna slipped her arm through hers. Katerina automatically linked arms with Charlie.

Occasionally, one of them stopped to pick up and inspect a shell, but it wasn't a day for lingering as a chill wind was blowing off the sea. By the time they reached East Wittering they were ready for a hot meal or drink.

Drifters café is reached before getting to Shore Watersports, where Scott and Ilya worked, and Katerina was relieved that Anna hadn't suggested that they should pop in to say "hello".

"I'll get this," said Katerina, as they were seated by the waitress. "Would you like a hot drink first and then choose something to eat?"

"Yes, good idea," said Anna. "I'll have a flat white please". Charlie chose an Americano and Katerina a Mocha.

"That was a lovely walk, but it got a bit bracing," said Charlie.

"Bracing, or bloody freezing?" asked Anna. "Ooh lovely thanks," she added as her steaming drink was placed in front of her. The three sipped their drinks while studying the lunch menu.

"Chilli for me".

"And me".

"Me too".

"What shall we do this afternoon?" asked Charlie.

"The three of us could go to bed," suggested Anna.

Katerina had been provided with yet another opportunity to simply look at Charlie. Charlie was the one who responded. "I assume that's an attempt at levity, Anna".

"No, I'm not in the mood for levity. What do you think, Katya? The three of us spending a cold afternoon snuggled up in bed. Quite tempting".

"What's this about, Anna?" asked Katerina, with a frown.

"The three of us love each other and it's all got a bit serious. We could lighten it up".

The waitress returned to the table to remove their cups. "Would you like to order something for lunch?"

Katerina requested three chilli con carne's, a bottle of Shiraz and a bottle of still mineral water.

Once they were on their own again, Charlie asked, "Anna, is this genuine or are you on the verge of being spiteful?"

"Have you ever known me to be spiteful?"

"Not previously, no".

"Do you love me?"

"Yes".

"And Katya?"

"Yes".

"I love you both. What about you, Katya, do you still love me?"

"You know I do Anna. I've told you".

"And we know that you love Charlie. So, like I was saying, we all love each other. Now, I know that Charlie desires both of us, and I'm excited at the thought of having sex with both of you, too. So, it's just you Katya. You obviously want Charlie. What about me? Do you want me too?"

"I've already said I don't want you that way. It seems to me that we should sort a few things before thinking of ways to complicate it further".

"What, like is Charlie going to leave me for you? Or will the three of us simply decide to live together like we're forming one of those American cults?"

"Anna!" exclaimed Charlie.

"I'm simply trying to ask what Katya thinks we should be sorting".

"OK Anna, that's fair enough," said Katerina, in a measured tone. "I've told you my best outcome. How about yours? And Charlie's?"

"I love a girl with spunk in her," said Anna, admiring Katerina's unwavering approach. "But maybe I shouldn't use that phrase in the circumstances".

The waitress brought the wine and water. Katerina asked her to leave the bottles on the table and advised her that they would pour their own.

"I'll tell you what I think is my best outcome. I'd like to stay exactly as I am with Charlie, and I'd like you to continue to be a wonderful friend".

Charlie responded with, "And in this perfect scenario, would anyone else be involved?"

Katerina looked at him and couldn't work out what he was getting at.

"Well, Katya would still be with Scott, of course". Charlie let her continue. "Charlie, not now".

"What's going on?" asked Katerina.

"I'll tell you Katya, but not at the moment".

"But it affects all of this?"

"No, it doesn't".

"Are you sure, Anna?" asked Charlie.

"Charlie, please".

"OK, I'll leave you to come back to it when you're ready. Now, where's that chilli? I'm starving". Thankfully, the waitress was leaving the kitchen carrying their meals, so they were able to concentrate on eating, which they did in silence.

They had walked to East Wittering arm in arm, but there was an acre of room between them on the way back. As soon as Charlie unlocked the car door, Anna climbed in the back. Katerina hesitated before joining Charlie in the front.

Nothing was said until they walked through the front door of the cottage. Just as Katerina was about to say that she would collect her things and drive home, Anna put her face in her hands and began to weep. She lost the strength to stand and collapsed onto her knees and then made her way to the stairs. She sat on the bottom but one stair and cried uncontrollably.

"Anna," said Charlie, moving swiftly to comfort his wife. Katerina looked on in shock. This lady, who had been in control of all situations since she had first known her, who had counselled her, instructed her, guided her, was desolate; Anna, who had led Katerina, hand in hand, into the most fun and enjoyable experiences she had ever had, was inconsolable. Charlie held her but Anna managed to summon up the strength to shrug him off.

"Charlie, get some water and brandy and take them into the Snug. Light the fire. Anna will join you soon". Katerina was calm, direct, and measured. She sat on the stairs next to Anna and put an arm around her shoulders. Anna allowed Katerina to draw her in close, removed her hands from her face, rested a cheek on Katerina's chest and pulled a tissue from her pocket.

She could finally control her breathing. "I'm sorry".

"It's me who's in the wrong. I hate myself for hurting you".

"I watched it happen and I could have stopped it. I *should* have stopped it. Instead of which I did things which encouraged it. I'm as much to blame as you are".

"I love you so much".

"Even now? After I've been such a bitch?"

"You haven't been. I think we've all done the best we can".

"Christ, Katya, what a fucking mess".

"We're smart enough to find a way out of it".

"You and Charlie are. You're both so brilliant and sharp and witty. I'm just the good time girl. The it-girl".

"Anna, don't be ridiculous. You're not the good time girl, you're the person everybody adores. We all love you. We all want to be with you. I've never met anyone like you. You're gorgeous and wonderful and smart. Knowing how to have a good time is simply an added extra".

"Will you help me?"

"In what way?"

"Either to keep Charlie or to live without him if he chooses you".

"Oh Anna". Katerina was the one who was now crying. They clung to each other, each trying to save themself, and the other, from plummeting.

Anna woke the following morning feeling exhausted. She hadn't slept well. She lifted her phone to check the time: 7.45. Why wasn't she sitting up in bed, Charlie by her side, sipping her morning drinks and checking social media for local horsey gossip? She propped herself up and saw that she was on her own. Was Charlie in with Katya? Had he been all night? She got up, put on her dressing gown, and left the room. Katerina's bedroom door was ajar. She peeped in. The bed and room were empty. She carried on downstairs. Charlie was sitting on a chair in the kitchen, an empty coffee mug in front of him. He picked up a sheet of A5 from the worktop and passed it to her.

> *I'm sorry I've left before saying 'goodbye' and thanking you for letting me stay. I thought it would be for the best.*
> *You were right, of course, Anna: he is unique and he's <u>yours</u>. I have no right to de-stabilise what you two have together.*
> *Don't worry, I'll be able to accept and deal with this. And Chrissy will never learn about any of this—not from me, anyway.*
> *By the time Stroppy races at Kempton I will have re-constructed myself so will still go there, with you both, as a co-owner and, from my point of view anyway, your friend.*
> *Please leave me to deal with this in the meantime.*
> *K xx*

Anna put the note down and made her way to the coffee machine. "Would you like another one?"

Charlie looked up at her. He answered with a shake of his head. As the machine performed its magic, Anna poured herself an orange juice.

As she walked past him, carrying her mug, she kissed him on the cheek. At the doorway, she turned and said, "I'll drink this in bed and then I'll go to the yard. I'll probably take Garibaldi out and have a ride on the beach. I'm not sure what time I'll be back but if it's not until later, don't worry. I hope you have a decent day, Charlie. It may be a good idea to get yourself to the fencing club. I'm sure you feel the need to work out a bit of aggression. Have a good day, and I'll see you later. I love you Charlie". He didn't see her again during the day, not until they walked through the front door at a little after nine o'clock that evening, by which time he had eaten and had poured himself a large glass of Armagnac.

Anna calculated that Katerina would finish work either early, because she didn't feel up to it, or late, because work took her mind off her troubles, so she ensured that she had parked her car before 5pm. Katerina's car was within eyesight, so Anna didn't bother to get out.

She was waiting for an hour and a half before she spotted Katerina, walking slowly from the bookstore towards her car. Anna got out and started walking towards her. Because Katerina was walking with her head bowed, she didn't notice Anna until she had almost reached her car. She stopped dead. "Anna?"

"I bet you've had a shitty day. Come on, let me buy you a drink," and, without waiting for a response, she slinked her arm through Katerina's and led her around the corner towards one of Arundel's many tourist-based pubs. As it was a cold, dark, winter evening, there weren't any tourists.

"What would you like?"

"Half a Kopparberg please".

"You'll need a pint. Do you want to grab that table in the corner? I'll just get these and join you. Crisps?"

"No thanks".

Anna placed Katerina's cider and her own white wine spritzer on the table and sat down. "This isn't how it ends. If it ends like this, Charlie will hate me, and everything will be lost".

"I couldn't think of another way".

"Nobody wins this way. You'll be desperately miserable, Charlie too, and I'll lose Charlie's love, your friendship and something else which is very important to me. There *is* another way. We just haven't thought of it yet. Do you have to rush off?"

"Not really. Scott said he may come round after dinner".

"This could take a while".

Katerina sent a text to advise she would be working late.

"I need to confide in you about something. Do you want the unadulterated facts or the abridged, pre-nine o'clock watershed version?"

"I don't want other information coming out later if you could have told me now".

"OK. Do you remember in the summer, in France, when I said that I believe it doesn't matter if we have sexual desires outside the norm, as long as no-one is being hurt?"

"I remember everything".

"You do, don't you? I've often wondered if you have a very high IQ".

"Yes, it is high".
"What is it?"
"154".
"Blimey".
"It's nothing to be proud of. I haven't worked at it or practiced or anything. I was simply born this way. Just like you being born with a face like yours. Except a face like yours will be a positive, but my IQ hasn't really worked to my advantage".

"If you didn't want to feel proud about it, why did you have it measured?"

"It happened in my last term at school. I was walking down a corridor and one of the teachers said, "Cheer up, it may never happen". I can't tell you how many times that's been said to me. Because the guy is OK, not a dickhead like most of them, I gave him a response. "I'm not miserable, I'm simply thinking". He stopped and said, "I bet it drives you crazy at times". I admitted that it did. He told me he reckoned it was caused by a high IQ and recommended I have it assessed, just so that I knew what I was dealing with. I went to one of those MENSA sessions".

"Who knows?"
"No one".
"What, not even Chrissy? Or Ilya?"
"No. You're the only person I've mentioned it to".
"Fair enough. So, back to France last year, when I admitted that I'd discovered I had some sexual desires outside the norm which I wasn't prepared to disclose to you at the time".

"You're going to disclose them now?"
"Yes".
"Why? Why now?"
"Because, as you'll find out, it's relevant to the situation the three of us are in. And it's a reason why you shouldn't fall on your sword so that I can claim the handsome prince. Why it's not that straightforward".
"OK, I'm listening".
"I've had sex with Steve".
"What?"

"Well, not sex, exactly. I've tossed him off. Way before he met Chrissy. It was something that just happened one evening when he was staying with us".

"Charlie was there?"

"Yes".

"Christ, Anna. I assume Chrissy doesn't know?"

"No. And what's more, she mustn't. She's so happy and it would ruin things for her".

"Had you always fancied him?"

"No, not at all. It simply happened after a few drinks".

"Well, I certainly wasn't expecting that bit of news. Is that what Charlie was referring to? In Drifters?"

Anna paused to consider. She was getting to the crux of why she had decided to meet up with Katerina.

"No. He was referring to Lene. My oldest, dearest friend and beautician".

Katerina waited for Anna to gather herself before explaining.

"Look, before I tell you all about Lene, will you please accept that I'm telling the absolute truth when I say that what Charlie and I did with you in France was purely born out of our love and affection for you, and you asking me for help".

"Yes, I don't doubt that for a minute".

"Good. Well, Lene. She and I have been sexual together. We had a fantastic afternoon in The Spread Eagle doing a bit of a girl-on-girl show for Charlie. It was an anniversary present for him. We role played it at first, which Charlie and I do a lot, and then got into it".

"I've role played with Scott too, so I know it can lead to something unplanned. I recently wore my school uniform. You were right about that".

"Did it go well?"

"Very. We both had fun".

"It was partly because of you that I took things a stage further with Lene".

"In what way?"

"You remember in the garden, when Charlie and I were performing together?"

"Of course".

"You did something".

"Yes, and you watched me do it".

"I thought then how beautiful it was and it occurred to me that I wanted to have sex with Lene again".

"And your sex with Lene is causing complications with Charlie? That's why he referred to her?"

"Yes. Although to be fair, the complications are for Lene and me rather than for Charlie".

"Because?"

"We've fallen in love with each other. It's not just sex and fun".

"Oh Anna. Do you mean different to the love you and I have for each other? Actually 'head over heels, I can't think of much else' fallen in love?"

"Yes".

"And Charlie's jealous?"

"Surprisingly, until recently he hasn't been. He's said that as long as what Lene and I are doing together doesn't damage my relationship with him, or Lene's with her husband Greg, then we could carry on and have fun".

Anna didn't continue until Katerina encouraged her with a raise of her eyebrows. "I think Charlie is now thinking that I'm trying to have it both ways: in love with Lene and having sex with her, being in love with Charlie and having sex with him yet getting prissy now I've discovered about the two of you. He's got a point too, hasn't he?"

"Have you discovered that you're bi? Is that why you've suggested you and I being intimate?"

"No, I don't think I'm bi. It's purely Lene. Something we've discovered about each other. It's probably been simmering under the surface for fifteen years or so, like a semi-dormant volcano. To be frank, Katya, that stuff about the three of us going to bed, well, Charlie was probably right, I guess I was being spiteful".

"I understand. Shame I'm driving. I could do with another one".

"Me too. How about driving back to yours so that you can pick up your overnight stuff and whatever you'll need for work tomorrow, then coming back to the cottage with me? We could pick up a pizza on the way to yours and eat it quickly while we're there".

"Yeah, OK".

He felt massive relief when he heard Anna call out, "Hi Charlie, I'm back". Relief turned to shock when Katerina walked into the Snug ahead of Anna. "Look who I picked up staring over the edge of Beachy Head".

"Hello Katya. Is everything OK? Are you all right?"

"Hi Charlie. Yes, I'm fine thank you. I'm staying the night".

He bent down to kiss her, then did the same to Anna. "All OK with you too?"

She hugged him. "Yes, thank you. Have you worried terribly?"

"Yes. Since early evening, anyway".

"I'm sorry, but we'll explain. Alcohol first, though. What do you fancy, Katya?"

"Charlie, would you mind making me one of those mixes. Rusty Nail, isn't it?"

"Coming up. What about you Anna?"

"Yes, I'll have one of those too".

"Would you like me to bring in something to eat?"

"No thanks, we've just shared a pizza".

Charlie returned with the drinks. "I didn't expect to see the two of you arrive together".

"No," responded Anna.

"I assume you didn't meet up by chance".

"No. I met Katya from work. We had a drink and a chat. I said we weren't to end things with Katya sacrificing herself for the good of you and me because it wouldn't work. I want to try to start the process of finding another way through this because I'm not convinced Katya making herself scarce will necessarily resolve our problems".

"Is there another way through this?"

"I don't know, but we've made a start, haven't we Katya?"

"Well, I don't think we got anywhere nearer to a solution but, as you say Anna, we've made a start".

"I've told Katya about Steve and Lene".

Anna watched Charlie blush for the first time since she'd met him.

"Really?"

"Yes, she knows about that evening with Steve and about Lene, your anniversary present and what it has led to".

"Why have you told her?"

"Because she needed to know. That scene in Drifters included reference to Lene, me and Lene, and I felt it wasn't fair for Katya to have heard all that and not known what it was about. If we're going to work together on this, she has to know".

"Well Katya, you couldn't have written us off after hearing our dirty secrets otherwise you wouldn't be here".

"I don't consider them to be dirty".

"Really?"

"No. They're unusual, of course they are. But you're not the standard couple, which is one of the reasons I've said wherever you are is the place to be".

"So, what next?"

Anna replied. "Well, I have a suggestion for you two to consider. It's only a suggestion, as I say, and I'm happy to hear you dismiss it or throw in an alternative".

"Go on".

"I've told Katya about my relationship with Lene but I've yet to tell her that Lene and I are going to London this Sunday and are not returning until Monday evening".

Katerina was watching Anna and trying to work out what she would say next.

"I think it may be a good idea for Katya to come here on Sunday, after I've left, and for the two of you to be together until just before I return".

Katerina looked stunned.

"In what way is that a good idea?" asked Charlie, incredulous.

"Let's face it, as Katya has said, it's complicated. There are five people involved and there are eight loves. I will spend the two days with Lene and you two would also be together. The four of us could spend the time trying to work out what it is we want. If I feel I can end it with Lene, then I will, because of my love for Charlie. I will also encourage Lene to consider whether she can end it with me, because of her love for Greg. If neither of us can, this is the time to find out. You two being together alone, for the first time, may clarify things for you, too. What your priorities are. I think that would help".

BOOK FOUR: *CRIME & PUNISHMENT*

"May I ask what you would expect of us Anna? Over the two days, I mean".

"I know you're not suggesting that I'm a fool, Katya, but if I said, "I'm not a fool," you'd know what I mean".

"Yes. I know what you mean. Charlie, I'll leave it to you".

"Let me think about it. I'll let you know my thoughts before we go to bed, or maybe first thing tomorrow morning. Now, it seems those drinks didn't touch the sides. Let me top us up".

They were in bed before midnight and were asleep within ten minutes.

The following morning, at 7.30 on the dot, Charlie knocked on Katerina's bedroom door. He opened it to see her propped up, as usual. "I'll carry these to our bedroom. Come in with us". He walked away before she had a chance to respond.

They had finished drinking the juices and were sipping their coffee when Charlie said, "Yes, OK Anna, if Katya would like to come over on Sunday, I'm prepared to do as you suggest".

"Katya?"

"I'd decided that if Charlie said yes, then I would agree to it too".

"OK," said Anna, "let's see how we get on".

Chapter 34

Chrissy was clearing up in her kitchen when she received a text from Katerina:

> *'So sorry Chrissy but something's come up at the weekend so can't make Sunday lunch. Rearrange? Apologies K xx'*

She didn't reply immediately to save herself from banging out a tetchy response.

> *'Shame. Good reason or not so good?'*
> *'Good. Sunday was their only available day to meet up'*
> *'Old friend?'*
> *'Sort of'*

Chrissy gave up. Katerina was clearly not going to give anything away.

> *'I'll check with S to see if following week is OK. Could you do that?'*
> *'Yes, but I'd also need to check with my S'*
> *'Pencil it in then'*
> *'Will do. Really sorry xx'*
> *'No problem. Take care xxx'*

She phoned Anna.
"Hi Chrissy, how's things?"
"Fine thanks. How are you both?"
"Not too bad".
"You sound a bit down. Is everything OK?"
"Yes, of course".
"Well, I'm just phoning to ask if you've been seeing much of Katerina?"

"A bit. Why, something wrong?"

"I think there may well be".

"What makes you think that?"

"Haven't you noticed anything?"

"She seemed fine when I last saw her. A bit quiet maybe but she's got a lot on at work. Installing a new software system and she says some of it is a bit outside her area of knowledge".

"How come she seems to tell you stuff that she doesn't tell me?"

"Because I'm nicer than you are".

"Anna, I'm serious. Do you think it's because I've been so wrapped up in Steve?"

"Christ Chrissy, is it really that long that he can wrap you with it? A bit like a boa constrictor I suppose".

"Well, it was a waste of fucking time phoning you, wasn't it? I'm concerned. I thought my sister would be astute enough to pick up on that".

Anna paused. "OK, sorry. Look, I'm sure there's no need for you to worry. Work is clearly going well, and I don't think there's any problem between Katerina and Scott".

"Maybe it's her health. Oh shit Anna, do you think there's something wrong with her and she's keeping it to herself? She'd tell one of us if it was minor, but maybe it's not. Maybe she has a health issue which she doesn't want to worry us with?"

Anna paused again. "She still goes swimming, doesn't she? The last time I saw her she drank alcohol and ate well. I feel fairly certain that she's not unwell Chrissy".

"Well, if it's not her health, her boyfriend or work, what could it be?"

"Your imagination?"

"Maybe. But I don't think so. Thanks Anna. Speak soon".

Steve didn't arrive home until after 7pm and Chrissy decided that it wouldn't be fair to lumber him with her concerns regarding Katerina until after he'd eaten and had a chance to unwind.

"Go and get changed. I've a stew in the slow cooker; it'll be dished up when you're ready to eat".

"Lovely, thanks. You can start plating up now thanks, I'll be down in a minute". He mounted the stairs two at a time and within a few minutes they were eating together at the dining room table.

"Just what I needed. Stuffed".

"You up for stuffing me later?"

"Yes, I should think so. How's your day been?"

"Katerina sent a text. She can't make this Sunday".

"Oh, that's a shame. She must have a good reason".

"Well, if she has, she didn't share it with me. She's seeing a 'sort of' old friend".

"You're still worried about her, aren't you?"

"I am, yes. Anna doesn't seem at all concerned but, oh, I don't know, something just doesn't feel right".

"Here's an idea. You know I'm working at Arundel at the moment. Why don't I tell Katerina I've got a job on near her, which I have, and would love to see this bookstore of hers, which I would. I could say I'll be finishing early on Friday so could pop in to fit in with her lunch break".

"Do you think that would do any good?"

"I don't know, but I'm obviously not as close to her as you, Anna or Ilya are. She may be prepared to run something past me that she wouldn't want to worry you guys with".

"Yes, I suppose that's possible. Thanks Steve. Yes, good idea. Thanks".

"Are you grateful enough for me to choose the position?"

Chrissy giggled. "Yes, go on then".

"Doggy".

Chrissy groaned. "Bloody hell Steve, you know that's a big challenge for me".

"I know, but when we get it right it's especially good, isn't it?"

"Yes, but when we don't get it right, I feel like I'm giving birth to twins, both at the same time".

"I'll take it slowly and gently".

"OK. But bear in mind I reserve the right to use the safe word".

"What is it again? Remind me".

"Jesusfuckingchrist".

"Oh yeah. I remember now".

BOOK FOUR: *CRIME & PUNISHMENT*

On Thursday morning, Lene sent a text to Anna:

'I'm so excited'

Anna sent a reply:

'Me too. 8.22 train too early?'
'That's fine'
'I'll order a taxi and get him to pick you up too. Be ready for 7.50'
'Will do. XXXXXXX'

'Hi Katerina. It's Steve. Would love to visit the bookstore while I'm working on a job in Arundel. Could I pop in lunchtime Friday? Buy you a sarnie too if you have time'

Katerina emitted a pronounced sigh.
"What's up Katerina?" asked Salty, in a concerned voice.
"Oh, nothing. I just need to reply to this".

'Hi Steve. If you can get here approx 1.30 I should be able to get out for a quick bite'
'1.30 perfect. See you Fri'

He walked through the door five minutes early. He couldn't spot Katerina so had a browse.
"May I help you with anything?"
"Oh, no thanks, I'm just having a quick look around while waiting for Katerina".
"Sorry, are you a customer or a friend of hers?"
"A friend. My name's Steve".
"Ah, Steve. Chrissy's new man? I'm Salty. I've known Chrissy for years".
"Pleased to meet you Salty. Chrissy has mentioned you several times. And Katerina has".
"Well, that's all good. She'll be with you in a bit".

"Thanks".

Katerina appeared. "Hi Steve. I won't be a minute".

"That's fine. No rush".

They were sitting in the café ten minutes later. After their food and drink had been brought to the table, Katerina asked, "Job going well?"

"Yeah, good thanks. I'm impressed with the store".

"Yes, it's great, isn't it? Salty's got it just right".

"And Scott? All going well there?"

"Yes, very well. I'm sorry we had to rearrange Sunday".

"That's OK. A better offer turn up?"

"No, nothing like that. It's just something which has to be this weekend or not at all".

"Something good, I hope".

"Yes, it should be".

They concentrated on their food for a while and then Steve continued, "Chrissy seems to think you've not been quite yourself recently".

"Really? Don't know where she's got that from. I'm fine".

"That's good to hear. I'll reassure her".

They finished their sandwich and drink and Katerina shaped to collect her bag, saying, "Well, that was great thanks Steve. I'd better be getting back. Friday afternoon deadlines and all that".

"Just another minute or two". He watched her put down the bag. "Are you sure there's nothing wrong?"

Katerina composed herself before replying, "Steve, tell me, what do you think of me?"

"Erm, well, I think you're lovely".

"Lovely? As in "that was a lovely cup of tea". Am I as lovely as a nice cup of tea?"

He smiled. "I simply mean that I'm very fond of you. You're a great girl. Why have you asked me what I think of you?"

"Because if you knew me, you'd know that I tend to deal with things, good or bad, in my own way. I've never understood the saying *don't worry about what you can't control*. I feel the opposite because I tend to not worry about things I *can* control. It's the fuckers lying in wait that bother me. Look, you've been around the block a few times. You're with Chrissy now, and you're making her very happy, but I should imagine that, at your age, you've had difficulties with a few partners. You will also have had ups and downs with your work".

"Yes, that's true, I have".

"Well, we all have our issues, some of which are good and some bad. Some people like to share their thoughts and others don't. I don't suppose you've shared all of yours. For example, I wouldn't be at all surprised if you've fallen in love in the past, unexpectedly. Maybe even the recent past, with someone you shouldn't have. Perhaps because of something which happened out of the blue. I bet you were a bit distant to friends at the time, but maybe they didn't pester you about it. I bet they just thought, 'That Steve. Another woman causing him trouble. He'll sort it out'".

Steve looked at her for a while, then smiled. She smiled back. "Yes, I'll tell Chrissy that, in my opinion, you're in good shape. As good as anyone I've met. Thanks for being candid".

"My pleasure. And thanks again for lunch. It was very thoughtful of you to take time out to see me".

That evening, while they were enjoying a bottle of wine, Chrissy said, "So you really think I don't have anything to worry about?"

"Chrissy, for the fourth and, I hope, final time, my belief is that you're right to think that Katerina is trying to deal with something. It may even be something very important to her. But I'm convinced that you shouldn't concern yourself about it. That girl can take care of herself".

"Thanks Steve. And thanks again for going to see her".

"Does this mean I get to choose the position again?"

"As long as it's not doggy".

"What's wrong with doggy?"

"Because we've already done it that way once this week. You know it takes me at least a fortnight before I can deal with it that way again".

"Fair enough. You sit on me?"

"May I finish my drink first?"

"Of course. No rush".

"Ooh I've been meaning to ask. What did you mean, that evening when Anna and Charlie were here? You said you three had no secrets that you would be willing to admit to".

"I don't recall what I had in mind at the time. Must have been some pranks that Charlie and I got up to in our younger days. You know, stupid rugby club stuff".

"And Anna would have known about it?"

"I guess so. You know those two, they've always shared everything".

"I know I shouldn't say this about my sister but with Anna's sex drive I wouldn't be at all surprised if they'd shared her too".

"What, a threesome?"

"I'm not sure that Anna would necessarily stop at three".

"If that's true, how does that affect the way you feel about her?"

"Oh, Anna's Anna. Everyone loves her. Everyone wants to fuck her too. I bet you would too if she gave you the come-on".

"Come off it, Chrissy".

"You couldn't resist it. She's gorgeous and extremely fuckable. It's something I've had to live with since she was about twelve. I don't hold it against her. It's just a fact that everyone loves her, and everyone wants to fuck her. I just thank god that I've got you in my grasp before Anna and Charlie tried to get you to join them. I bet she wishes she'd acted sooner now that she knows how big your cock is".

"She what?"

"She's my sister. I've always told her everything".

"Christ".

"Oh, don't go all coy on me. I bet you love the thought of her trying to picture your cock".

"Come on. Drink up. You've been making that glass last ages".

"See, she's got you all aroused just through us talking about her. OK, finished. I'll be watching you, you know. You'd better concentrate on the fact it's me sitting on top of you".

Charlie had been subdued for most of the week. Anna chose not to ask him to share his thoughts as she knew he would voice them when he was ready. Eventually, on Saturday morning, as he watched his wife pack an overnight bag, he said to her, "It might be a good idea to stop the process for a minute to check we both intend for the next couple of days to go as we've talked about. We could be making a massive mistake".

"Or we could be taking the first step in returning to normality".

"It has the appearance of a step away from normality".

"Charlie, answer these questions for me: do you and I love each other? Do you and Katya? Lene and me? Lene and Greg? Five people, eight loves. I don't see how maintaining the status quo will resolve anything. I believe we need to test those eight loves to find out if there are any chinks. See if something isn't all it's cracked up to be. Find out if doing what we're doing leads to guilt and regret. Decide what's most important to us".

Charlie spent the next few minutes trying to work out whether or not he agreed with her. Sometimes he did, and sometimes he didn't, which wasn't much use to him or anyone else. Finally, he came to a simple conclusion: if it was going to happen, which it clearly was, he may as well enjoy it.

"You're really excited, aren't you?"

"Sorry Greg, am I being over the top?"

He laughed. "No, not at all. It's lovely to see you looking forward to something so much. What's the plan, do you know yet?"

"Anna will come here by taxi then we'll carry on to Chichester station. We're catching the 8 something to London. What we're going to do when we get there, I've no idea. I told Anna I was happy to leave it all to her".

He laughed again. "If you don't know what you're doing, how can you get so excited?"

She blushed and smiled. "Childish of me, I know, but I'm excited by knowing I'm going to London. I'll be getting a black cab to somewhere. I'll be eating in a fancy restaurant and spending a night in a luxury hotel. A hotel breakfast, seeing the sights. It doesn't matter that I don't know the precise arrangements, it just feels like an exciting trip for me".

"Plus, a nice break away from the routine with a close friend".

"Yes, I suppose, but I love my routine with you and the girls. I'm not looking to escape from it but now that it's been arranged, I'm looking forward to it".

"That's fine. I think it's a lovely thing for you to be doing. I'm really pleased it's Anna you'll be going with. She's very capable and I know you'll be safe in her hands".

She held his hand and gave it a squeeze. She then said she was going to make a cup of tea, should he like one too.

Scott was waiting for her when Katerina returned home from work. "I'll just have a quick shower and we can chat while I'm getting dressed". They had arranged to walk to The Shore Inn for a meal and a couple of drinks. Scott sat on the bed and watched her as she put on her underwear and clothes. "So," he said, "tell me again why you've cancelled us going for Sunday lunch at Chrissy's tomorrow".

"I haven't cancelled, I've postponed".

"OK, postponed. Why have you postponed?"

"Because Anna is going away for a couple of days, and she'd like me to go and see Charlie".

"But why? Why can't he look after himself for a day or two? He's quite capable, isn't he?"

"That's not for you to decide. And if they ask me there, it's because they want me there and I don't suppose they feel the need to clear it with you first".

"How can you be arsed? Why would you want to spend all that time with Charlie? Anna's the one you're friendly with, surely? If he was going away for two days, I could understand you and Anna wanting to be together but not the other way round".

"They're both my friend, not just Anna".

"What on earth will you do there? He's a bit dull, isn't he?"

"It's strange how your mind seems to be working with this. First you seem to think that Anna and Charlie need to justify to you their invitation to me, and now you think that I need to justify accepting it. I don't have to justify myself, Scott. I don't have to explain my friendship with both Anna and Charlie. I can choose to spend my Sunday however, and with whom, I wish. You've always given the impression you have lots of options. You must have, a good-looking boy like you. Go and take one up. Or stay at home and sulk. Watch porn and masturbate if you like. It's up to you what you do on Sunday but, just to be clear, I've told Anna I'll go over to the cottage and that's exactly what I'm going to do".

"I'm not sure this is going to work between me and you, Katya".

"Why, because I've got a mind of my own? I think you've had your own way with too many people for too long. Let's be clear, if it finishes between you and me, it won't be due to me postponing a lunch because of a reason you can't fathom, it will be down to your inability to accept that I have a right to decide how I want to spend my leisure time".

"But why decide to spend it with Charlie when you could spend it with Chrissy and, more importantly, me?"

"There you go again, probing to get me to justify myself. Not only will I not explain my reasons to you, I'm also not going to try to get you to see why I have every right to make the decisions I make. Go get yourself a compliant girlfriend if I'm not prostrating myself enough for you".

"There's plenty who would welcome it".

"I don't doubt it".

"Do you want me to do just that?"

"I'm simply wondering why you're wasting time talking about it. It's Saturday evening. If you want to have female company when you eat your Sunday lunch, you'd best not take up any more time".

"This is a daft way for you and me to split up".

"In your opinion. For me, splitting up would be much more in keeping with my principles than compromising myself to satisfy your vanity and selfishness".

He stared at her. She didn't drop eye contact with him. He eventually got up and gathered all his belongings. She simply watched him from the middle of the bedroom. As he brushed past her, on the way to the lounge and then the front door, he said, "You really should grow your hair, Katya. You look like a dyke".

She laughed in genuine amusement. "A dyke who can provide an awesome blowjob. Is that an oxymoron or a paradox? Oh, what on earth am I asking you for, you haven't a clue, have you Scott? Go on, off you go so I can get ready to spend some time with a grown up".

He started to say something, thought better of it, and opened the front door. Before stepping out, Katerina called to him. "Scott, wait". He turned, smirking, and watched as she approached him, a hand offered in apparent surrender. "I'll need my key back". The smirk was replaced by an acid stare. "Thanks," she said as she received it from him. As she closed the door behind him, she thought, 'Now, what am I going to pack?' Before answering her own question, she received a text:

> *'You still OK about coming tomorrow?'*
> *'I'm looking forward to it more than Yossarian looked forward to completing his final combat mission'*
> *'Any time after 8am'*
> *'I'll see you at 8.01. Have the coffee brewing'*

Ilya walked into the apartment, followed by Katie. "I thought you were going out with Scott?"

"I was, but we've just split up, so I've made myself some marmite on toast".

"Bloody hell, what happened?"

"We didn't see eye to eye about something".

"Must have been something pretty serious".

Katie, who didn't normally interject when Ilya and Katerina were conversing, simply said, "He's a dick".

Katerina looked at her and laughed. "Funnily enough he called me a dyke, so we could have appeared in an American cartoon series 'The Dick and Dyke Show'".

Katie laughed with her. "You're far too good for him, Katya. Move on and be grateful, I say. Find yourself someone who knows how to look after girls and isn't motivated by his own appearance and desires".

"Yes, I agree," said Ilya, looking intently at Katerina. "Someone like Charlie".

"Yes," said Katie, who had met Charlie a couple of times. "Just like him, but a bit younger".

Katerina, who hadn't taken her eyes off Ilya, said, "Age doesn't bother me".

Ilya followed up with, "I wonder if Scott will make a move for Anna now".

The girls said, "What?" in unison.

"He took me out for a pint to ask me questions about her. I know for a fact that he sent her a Valentine's card with a personal sexual message".

"What did he write?" asked Katerina.

"I can't remember the exact words, but he was making it clear he'd like to perform oral sex on her. At least he had the sense to send it anonymously".

"Sick bastard," said Katie.

Ilya continued, "He fancies her like hell".

"Everyone fancies her like hell," said Katerina. "Even you Ilya".

"Yes, of course I do, but at least I'm discreet about it. She'd never find me ogling her or trying to find out from others any of her secrets".

"No, fair enough".

"Even I fancy her," piped up Katie. They all chuckled at this before Katerina added, "And me".

"Look, Katie and I were going to have a pizza delivered. Why don't I order a bigger one and you eat with us, Katya?"

"Is that OK with you Katie?"

"Yes, of course, it will be lovely. We can stay in and bitch about Scott while we're eating".

Later in the evening, Katie said, "I'm off to bed. If you two want to carry on chatting, that's fine by me. I'll see you in a bit Ilya".

"Thanks Katie. I won't be long".

"Good night, Katie. Thank you for being so sweet and thoughtful".

"Don't be silly. I simply don't understand why Scott didn't appreciate how privileged he was. Good night".

As soon as Katie had closed the bedroom door, Katerina asked Ilya, in Russian, "How did you know?"

"About you and Charlie?"

"Yes".

"The day we were moving into the apartment, I noticed how you were looking at him. It was clear to me that you're in love with him".

"Oh dear".

"Be careful Katya, I believe it was clear to Anna too".

"What made you think that?"

"I find it very easy to look at Anna. I saw her watching the two of you, how you were interacting and looking at each other. I'd say she drew the same conclusions as I did".

"Are you cross with me?"

"Not at all. He's perfect for you. From your point of view, though, there's Anna to think of. She's incredible, and they have a special relationship. Despite that, it's clear that Charlie loves you back".

"Is it?"

"Oh yes, as clear as day".

"What do you mean by 'he's perfect for you'?"

"Before you left home to fly to France last summer, you were an immature young girl. I didn't help with that, of course. You were innocent in terms of dealing with the outside world, but everyone knows that inside your head you are mature way, way beyond your years. When you arrived home from your holiday, it was clear that something dramatic had changed in a matter of a few weeks and you were no longer a child. You had become streetwise and, somehow, your body and behaviour caught up with your head".

"Yes, that's exactly what happened".

"The thing is though, Katya, from then until you went over to France again after Christmas, you had the delightful combination of young and vibrant together with being mature and wise. The young and vibrant part of you remained in France. You've been mature, wise, and concerned, and we've all been worried about you".

"But you clocked the reason I've been like that".

"Yes. You're in love with Charlie. The reason I say he's perfect for you is that I believe that he's the only person, apart from Anna maybe, who will, simply by being with you, provide whatever's needed for you to be the young, vibrant, mature, and wise Katya we all love".

"And there's me been thinking all this time that you're just a lad. A loveable one, though. I didn't give you the credit for being a sage".

"Forever underestimated!"

"I won't make that mistake again. Thank you, Ilya".

"I love you Katya. I've never said it to you before, I don't think. I'm always insistent that you're not my sister when people refer to you as that. I put them right because it's true, you're not my sister. But I love you as if you are".

"That means so much to me, Ilya".

"Well, come on then".

"Come on what?"

"You're supposed to say that you love me too".

Katerina laughed. "I love you, Ilya. You're a brother and a great friend. Not only that, but I'll also forever cherish the vision of you displaying for me your erect cock. I picture it often".

"Bitch".

She laughed and kissed him on the cheek. "Katie's very lucky. It's a decent size".

"Fuck off Katya," he said, laughing with her now.

"I told you at New Year to look after her, and you have. You look great together".

"I'm thinking of asking her if she'd like to get engaged".

"To you?"

"I'm going to slap you in a minute. Yes, to me. What do you think?"

"I think you're both far too young, and she's obviously way too nice, and pretty, to be stuck with you for the rest of her life, but you're asking someone who's in love with a man considerably older than she is and who is married to the most perfect female on the planet. What the fuck do I know about anything?"

"You know an incredible amount about most things. I'm serious, Katya, what do you think? I know that you'll tell me the truth. You like her, don't you?"

"I think she's the catch of a lifetime. Maybe I can relate to her more than some of the girls you've introduced me to because, like us, she hasn't had it easy, what with her Mum leaving her like that, when she was so young. Her Dad must be a good guy because she's faultless. Don't hesitate. If you're thinking long and hard about it, don't. A wise man once said that we've already made up our mind; the rest of it is simply justifying to ourselves the decision we've made. Don't try to justify it any longer, if you know in your heart that it's what you want. Find out if it's what she wants, too".

"Should I ask her now?"

"What's she like when she's been woken before she's ready? I seem to be able to hit the ground running, but many people are grouchy for a while".

"Well, it's only happened a couple of times, when I've had to wake her, but it's not been a pretty sight".

"I'd leave it then".

"Thanks Katya. By the way, do you really think it's a decent size?"

Katerina smiled and said, "I'm off to bed. Thank you for the chat, Ilya. I enjoyed it and it was helpful".

"For me too. Good night".

Ilya woke and got up to use the bathroom. He looked at the clock on the microwave and saw it was 7.40. Katerina's bedroom door was open and the room empty. He was quite surprised initially and then recalled something about her going to Anna and Charlie's. As he pee'd into the bowl he thought about Katerina, and where she may be heading in life. He was concerned. He also thought about when the best time may be to ask Katie if she'd like to get engaged to him. He really wanted things to work out between them; he could see himself marrying her, there was no doubt about that.

As he washed his hands, his thoughts returned to Katerina. He then considered how Chrissy would react if she found out Charlie and Katerina had a thing for each other. He felt it wouldn't be pleasant. Also, the thought of Anna and Chrissy becoming casualties distressed him for he was very fond of them both.

'No man would ever leave Anna,' he thought. 'She's fucking gorgeous'. He decided that if she were to split with Charlie, a queue would form extremely quickly. He walked briskly back to his bedroom, extinguishing any thought that he may be fighting for a place near the head of the queue.

Once back in the bedroom, he studied Katie before climbing back in. She was lying on her back, sound asleep. 'She's too young to think about marriage,' he thought. 'We both are'. As he lay beside her, he decided that he would wait before finding out her views on the subject.

When she woke at 8.45, her first words were the standard, "Good morning, Ilya. Sleep well?"

"Would you like to get engaged to me?"

She turned her body so that she could face him, leaned on her elbow and replied, "You what?"

"If I asked you to get engaged to me, would you say yes?"

"Why, is that what you're asking?"

"I'm wondering if you feel you're too young to commit yourself".

"I won't know until you ask me".

"Do you want me to ask you?"

"I don't think this is how it's supposed to work, is it?"

"What, should I be speaking to your dad?"

"No, silly, you should ask me, not ask me if I want you to ask me".

"Fair enough. Katie, would you like to get engaged to me?"

"Yes, I would".

Ilya sat up. "Really?"

"Yes, really. I'd like to be engaged to you Ilya".

"What, now?"

"Yes, now, if that's what you're asking. Is it?"

"Er, yes, it is".

"You don't sound too sure".

"Sorry Katie, yes, I'm sure. You've taken me by surprise, that's all".

"Start again".

"Katie, I'd like to marry you when you feel the time is right. Will you agree to being engaged to me?"

"Yes, that's wonderful. Thank you for asking, Ilya. Yes, I'd like to be engaged to you and to marry you".

"Bloody hell, what just happened there?"

She laughed. "Don't back out now. I want the ring first".

He laughed too. "I'm not backing out. I just can't believe it. Do you have any plans for today?"

"No. I thought we were going to spend the day together".

"Shall we get the train to Brighton and buy the ring?"

"What, today?"

"Yes, why not?"

"I'd like to get my nails done first. Shall we go one day this week. Take the same day off as each other?"

"Are you playing for time?"

"Ilya, if I'm trying on rings, I want my nails to look nice. I'm not going to change my mind in a week".

"Are you serious? You really want to be engaged to me?"

She slapped him around the head. "Yes. How many more times? Yes, yes, yes, yes".

He jumped up and bounced on the bed, his flaccid penis dancing from side to side.

"You mad fool," she said, laughing. "Get back in. We need to consummate the engagement".

"Do we tell anyone?"

"Not yet. Not 'til we've bought the ring".

"OK. Next week then". He kissed and fondled her, and then they rubber stamped the decision.

Book Four: *Crime & Punishment*

Chapter 35

Lene didn't head for the Underground entrance as she had on their previous visit to London. Instead, she and Anna walked arm in arm to the taxi rank.

"Where to, love?"

"The NoMad Hotel please," answered Anna.

"Have you stayed there before, darlin'?" the driver asked, as he pulled into the traffic.

"No. First time".

"I've only seen a bit of it, when I've been helping my passengers, but it looks a very cool hotel. Celebrating?"

It was Lene who answered the cabbie. "I've finally managed to persuade my wife to take time off from her busy schedule. Two nights in London, then three in Paris and two in Rome".

"Nice. What is it you do, love, making you so busy?"

Before Anna could answer, Lene jumped in with, "Don't you recognise her? Top model. You must have seen her".

"Don't go in for fashion much these days. All 'er indoors wears is tracky bottoms and a hoody".

"But you will have seen the giant ad in Piccadilly Circus. Couldn't miss it. It caused quite a stir. 'Follow and Wallow' was the banner headline".

"Oh yeah, I remember now".

"Thought you would. That bra she was modelling flew off the shelves and the ad caused four crashes apparently. The laugh is that men couldn't get enough of it, but they didn't know their fantasy girl has no interest in men whatsoever. Always makes us laugh that, doesn't it darling?"

"Yes, it does".

"Can't wait to tell my other cabbie mates. They can keep their film star and pop singer celebrities in the back of their cab, I've had the wallow girl".

He drove on, feeling smug, and Lene and Anna exchanged a kiss before looking out of the windows to regard the wonders of the city.

Once through the entrance, Anna said, "I've arranged for an early check in. Could you sort it while I have a word with the concierge?"

"Of course".

At the concierge's desk, Anna was asked, "How can I help you, madam?"

"What nightclub can you recommend? One that celebrities would choose if they wanted a night out?"

"There's one in Mayfair that comes highly recommended".

"Would you be able to arrange for my partner and me to go there tonight?"

The concierge studied Anna and then took some time appraising Lene, who was being assisted at the reception desk. "I'm sure I would".

"How much cash would you need, so that, when we get there, we could go straight in?"

"£350 should do it".

Anna took her purse from her bag. "Here's £400. Whatever's not required for our entry, please keep for yourself".

"That's very good of you, madam".

"What would be a good time to arrive there?"

"I understand that midnight until around 4am are the liveliest hours".

"Could you please arrange for a taxi to collect us from here at 11.45 tonight and to be waiting for us outside the club at 3am to bring us back. Here's another fifty".

"I won't be working at the time you'll be leaving so I'll ensure your club entry tickets are at this desk for you to collect".

"Thanks for your help".

"It's a pleasure madam. What name shall I write on the envelope?"

"Anna. Oh, one final thing, could you please arrange for a bottle of chilled Pol Roger to be brought up to our room immediately. The 2012 please. Just two glasses".

"Certainly".

Lene joined Anna and the two of them, together with a bell-boy, who was seeing to their cases, proceeded to their Parlour Suite.

Once settled into the lounge area of their room, sipping their Champagne, Anna said, "I need to ask, before we do anything together, why you sent me the message".

"On the card, you mean?"

"Yes".

Lene sat motionless for a while, trying to formulate her response. Finally, and with emotion, she said, "I tried so hard to wean myself off you, Anna, believe me I did. It was bearable at the start, but it became more and more difficult. I became miserable, and Greg thought I was unwell. I tried, Anna, I really did".

"Don't get upset, Lene, please".

"Are you cross with me? Have I made things difficult for you?" She was crying.

"How are we going to get through this if we can't handle two months?"

"I don't know, Anna," sobbed Lene. "It's so, so hard".

"If I told you that this weekend will be the end of it for us, not as friends, of course, but as lovers, would you feel a degree of relief?"

Lene couldn't hide her look of despair, but the shock of Anna's question caused composure. "No. I would understand, but I wouldn't be relieved. I'd be desperate. I'm sorry if that's not what you want to hear but that's the truth. I'd be desperate. I don't know how I'd get through life. I'm so in love with you".

"But what about Greg? How can you be happily married to him if you feel this way about me?"

"Why don't you believe me when I say you've been added but nothing's been taken away? How can I persuade you that Greg and I are still…?" She couldn't finish the sentence. All composure dissolved and she cried uncontrollably.

Anna held Lene's face between her hands and licked the tears from her cheeks. "I'm here, Lene. I'll always be here. I'm sorry that I put you through that, but I needed to know. No need to cry now. It's OK, I'm here. I'll be here for as long as you want me to be. I love you, Lene, I love you dearly".

Lene's sobs subsided. "Tell me again," she pleaded.

"I love you and I will be with you for as long as you want me to be. Come on, let's now enjoy our time together. I've been wondering if you've brought that tiny Superdry skirt that you promised you'd wear the next time we were together".

"Of course. I've been saving it for you".

"Thank you. OK, so what I suggest is that we have a bath together and then make love. A wander around Covent Garden, back to the hotel bar, and then dinner in the restaurant, before coming back to the room to get changed to go out. You must wear that skirt, and I'll be wearing something I think that you will like. We're going to have a wild night and a dreadful hangover in the morning".

"Do you really mean it, Anna? This is not the end for us?"

In an instant, Anna visualised the two paths which lay in front of her. If she took one, both she and Lene would suffer pain, but maybe they would find the will to endure it for the sake of their married lives. By taking the other, her fate would be decided by Charlie and Katerina: if their time together confirmed their love, Anna did not doubt Charlie's decision. How had her perfect life come to this, with her facing either loss and misery or loss and desolation? Quite simply, because she hadn't said no to Katerina, and neither Lene nor Charlie had said no to her.

She hadn't looked at Lene while these thoughts had been formulating. This was her decision to make, and she must not be influenced by the desperation bleeding from her lover.

Finally, she re-established eye contact with Lene and stated, as if her answer had never been in doubt, "No, it's not the end. I'd be desperate too. I, also, realise that I couldn't get through life without you. Now, get those clothes off".

He heard Katerina's Mini pull up outside the cottage at 8.01. He pressed the 'pour' button on the coffee machine and went to the door to welcome her. They kissed, then he took the overnight bag from her, saying, "I'll leave it here and take it up to the room later. Come on through. The coffee's ready". She followed him into the kitchen and watched him add a splash of cream to the mug. He passed it to her then proceeded to make a fresh mug for himself. She waited until he had finished and then sat with him at the table. He noticed that she was wearing tight jeans tucked into ankle boots and a cream Aran jumper.

It could have been a mere acquaintance joining him for breakfast. "This is odd," he said.

"Yes, it is," she agreed.

"Good odd?"

"Just a couple of months ago I was a desperate girl who had no thought that it could be possible for me to be here with you, like this. So yes, good odd".

"What would you like to do?"

"May I ask you something first? It may sound a weird question but the answer's important to me".

"Of course".

"It appears that you've had quite a year. Thrilling. When have you been the happiest during that time?"

He looked at her as he considered the question. As the time passed, it occurred to him that this was another reason why he admired Katerina the way he did: unlike most people, she asked a question and then waited to hear the answer.

He regarded her looking at him and finally said, "I'm happy most of the time. I have a privileged lifestyle so it would be ridiculous to not be. But I'd say I'm happier when I'm in France than when I'm here. Most of the time it's contentment rather than happiness. Maybe that's it, maybe I'm happiest when I'm content in France".

"Tell me about one time when it was clear to you that you were really happy, not simply content".

He mulled on this before answering with, "When I was driving you to the cottage, the first time I picked you up from work".

"That made you happy? The time when we joked about starting a band and calling it Oxymoron?"

"Yes".

"Wow. OK".

"Why 'wow'?"

"Because I originally believed that it was New Year when I fell in love with you, but then it became obvious to me that it happened earlier than that".

"Have you identified when it was, that you first realised you love me?"

"Oh yes. It was during that same journey".

Charlie couldn't prevent himself from wondering how things may have turned out if Anna had collected Katerina that evening. "So, what would you like to do?"

"I'd like us to do what would come naturally if we'd been together for five years or more. I want to go for a walk, stop off at a pub, decide while we're there whether we'll choose to have their Sunday roast or just a packet of crisps. I want to walk back, arm in arm with you, feeling a little tipsy. I want to sit next to you in the Snug, in front of the log burner and talk about books and music. Listen to some music too. If you decide that you'd like to make love to me, I want us to do it as if we've been together for five years or more. And, when we go to bed tonight, no matter what the time is, I want to read until I'm ready to go to sleep. Then I want to wake up next to you, have my grapefruit juice and coffee in bed and chat to you about what we're going to do for the rest of the day. That's what I'd like to do".

He smiled at her. "Let's do that then".

They decided upon a circuitous walk, one which they had completed with Anna several times, and ended up in a local pub, where they enjoyed a traditional roast dinner. They took their time, and it was mid-afternoon before they returned to the cottage. Charlie had yet to carry Katerina's bag to the bedroom and felt that this would be an appropriate time to ask her to join him upstairs.

"I'd like to make love to you now, Katya. I cannot wait any longer".

She took his hand and allowed him to guide her up the stairs and into the bedroom, where they both undressed. As they stood before each other, naked, she gazed at him and said, "Goodness, you *are* looking forward to this, aren't you?"

They lay side by side on the bed. He leaned towards her and sucked on her breasts and salmon-pink nipples before kissing her passionately on her lips. "It seems incredible that we've just made love for the first time. Somehow, it felt like coming home. As if I've been away for many months and have been homesick to the point of suffocation".

"It's clear to me now that I've simply had sex with Louis and Scott. What I just experienced with you was, as you say, making love; you making love to me. I'm sorry if my inexperience made it less pleasurable than you've been used to. I'll improve, if we have more opportunities, after these special days given to us by Anna. I'd do whatever you want to do".

"Katya, you mustn't think that way. You must never think about what it's been like between Anna and me. What I just experienced with you was beautiful. Please know that".

She propped herself up and said, "But I *am* terribly inexperienced. I feel I want to try to balance being your pupil with being your partner. I want the opportunity to learn from you so that I can provide sexual pleasure to match my love for you. That would be the case if we were together for eternity or only two days". She kissed him, and then added, "I love you, Charlie, and I want to demonstrate that in every way I can. The added benefit is that I will get a ridiculous amount of pleasure too. And, let's face it, what eighteen-year-old girl doesn't want to have a ridiculous amount of pleasure?"

"Have we only got until your nineteenth birthday then?"

She picked up a pillow and swung it at him.

"You had better not stop giving me pleasure otherwise I'll leave you for an older man".

They remained on the bed, with Katerina's head on Charlie's chest and with his right arm wrapped around her.

"What about Scott? Does he add to your complications?"

"He doesn't add to any complications. He is of no consequence. We are no longer in a relationship".

"Oh, when did that happen?"

"A few hours ago. In a different lifetime".

"Are you're not upset in any way? I thought you were getting on well".

"Scott Walker from The Walker Brothers means more to me. So does Scott of the Antarctic. Even Scott Joplin, despite my dislike of ragtime music".

"OK, I get the picture".

"Tell me about Lene".

Charlie paused before responding. "Well, she's lovely. She's just the sweetest girl you could meet. Very, very pretty, tiny, so Swedish she could be their poster-girl".

"What do you mean by 'tiny'?"

"Short. Shorter than you. Very slim. Not an ounce of fat. Chiselled facial features. Straight, shoulder length hair. Blonde, of course".

"How do you feel about Anna and Lene being in love with each other?"

"There are many feelings. They seem to be constantly evolving. One, though, has been a constant".

"Which is?"

"I don't want Lene to get hurt. Some people can take being injured. They can pull out the arrow or dig out the bullet, grind their teeth until the pain subsides, dress the wound as best they can and then carry on, even if the injury leads to an impairment. Lene couldn't do any of that. I don't want her to get hurt because she wouldn't be able to deal with it".

"She's different to Anna and us, you think?"

"Definitely. Of the four of us, it's only Lene who won't be able to cope with the fallout. This has to go the way she wants otherwise I truly worry about her".

"You don't worry about me?"

"Yes, I worry about you, but that's because I love you. It's not because I feel you'd be lost if things turn out badly for you. You'll thrive, whatever life throws at you".

"How can a man of your age and experience feel the way you do about a girl of my age and inexperience? Why is it you don't simply want a sexual adventure with a girl less than half your age? That would be a thrill for most men, wouldn't it?"

"But then it would only be my cock which would be satisfied. What about my heart and my brain?"

"Your heart could once again merge with Anna's and your brain could be saying to you, "Phew Charlie, that was a close one"".

"No. You have my heart and only you stimulate me in a way I've never previously experienced. I want that forever". He studied her as she listened to what he had said. "You seem to be on the point of asking something. Something important to you".

"Yes. It's a big one and it's time for me to ask it. Anna and I have voiced our best outcomes from the position we find ourselves in, but you haven't. What's your best outcome? Truthfully".

"To live in France".

He didn't add to this. Katerina simply looked at him until he had formulated what he wanted to say next.

"I want to live in France, with you".

A slight shake of the head was Katerina's only response.

"You don't want that?"

"Living with you hasn't been something I've considered a possibility. I'd accepted that I could never expect more than this, being with you occasionally. Now, you've made me hopeful and desperate. You've made me feel as if I'm carrying a baby across a tightrope and am terrified that the baby is making me unstable".

He looked at her and nodded.

"And what about Anna?" she added.

"It's clear to me now that Anna and I have got to a point from which we would be unable to return to where we were. If I can't be where I was with her, before all this, then being anywhere else with her would make me feel lost. I love Anna, of course I do, but for me, it was so special that any slight defect would make the whole thing too difficult to live with. Like owning a beautiful, expensive, classic car. Gleaming bodywork and exhilarating to drive but get a tiny scratch on it and that's all you can see. Also, I'm no longer comfortable about sharing her with Lene".

"Hearing you say these things makes me feel that my life could be about to make a turn with monumental implications. And I don't think I can influence in which direction it goes. I could end up in utopia or dystopia but nowhere in between".

"I understand what you mean. There's something my thoughts have been toying with".

"Tell me".

"Why it is that an attractive, vibrant, highly intelligent, knowledgeable, eighteen-year-old girl, with her whole brilliant life ahead of her, would want to commit herself to a man of my age who has been party to a devastating end to a perfect marriage?"

"Tricky one, that. Maybe for similar reasons to why a handsome, vibrant, highly intelligent, knowledgeable, experienced man, with an enviable lifestyle and a gorgeous wife, would want to commit himself to a girl of eighteen who, until six months previously, had no knowledge or experience of life and whose only achievements are A' levels and a full driving licence".

He smiled at her; she was already smiling at him.

She continued. "I'd say the only differences are that, for the man in question, his drivers are his cock, his heart and his brain whereas for the girl, the drivers are her vagina, her heart and her brain".

"You could well be right".

"So, are you ready to continue my lessons?"

Chapter 36

Charlie woke and checked his phone: 7.05. He could tell from Katerina's breathing that she was asleep but stirring. He lay still, not wishing to disturb her. She opened her eyes and saw the back of Charlie's head. She didn't know whether he was awake but decided he probably was. She shuffled towards him so that she was nestled into his back. She reached her arm around him to seek his penis. She took hold of it and discovered he was semi erect.

"Good morning, Katya. Do you always start your day like that?"

"Good morning, Charlie. No, I don't, but I've not woken up beside you before".

"You have an extremely sensual touch".

She began to rub. "Would you like me to continue?" she asked.

"Is an alternative on offer?"

She insisted on getting the drinks, so he was able to sit up in bed and contemplate while she was in the kitchen. He felt certain that she would challenge him about whether he truly believed that they had a future together.

They drank their juice in silence, but the inevitable topic was raised once Katerina had taken the first sip of her coffee. "What happens if Anna comes home this evening and tells you that she has decided that she will no longer continue the relationship with Lene? What if she says she has come to appreciate what is at stake? Or if Lene tells Anna that it was a wonderful experience, but she can no longer handle the guilt? Or if, in a week's time, or a month, Lene's husband finds out what has been happening and demands that she finishes it and remains faithful to him? What happens then?"

He turned to face her. "Answer something for me first".

"What would you like to know?"

"I'd like you to tell me how you felt when I told you that I wanted to live in France, with you".

"I was flabbergasted".

He laughed. "Flabbergasted?"

She laughed too. "Why's that so funny?"

"I just didn't expect you to come out with a word like that. I thought you'd be poetic or use a quote from a favourite Russian heroine of yours. Flabbergasted".

"Well, I was. You were telling me that you'd give up all that you have with Anna, your wonderful lifestyle, lived in two beautiful homes, that you'd turn your back on England, the friends you have here, to live full time in a foreign country with a foreign girl who has little to offer you other than her heart".

"And her vagina and brain".

She laughed again. "Yes, and those, too".

"Have you thought at all that living with me has some appeal, but you don't fancy the moving to France part?"

"No, I haven't thought that, not for a moment. They are both what I want".

"OK, so here's my answer to your question. I know you appeared to ask several but really it was just one: what will I do if Anna wants us to get back on track, to be the loving husband and wife that we've been, without Lene distracting Anna from her love for me?"

"Yes. What happens then?"

"I want to live in France, with you".

She stared at him and he allowed her the time she needed. Eventually, she said, almost as a whisper, "Let me just check, because this is extremely important. I do not want to misunderstand any aspect of this. Are you saying that, whatever happens now between you and Anna, you've decided that you'll no longer be with her? Are you saying that, if you are the one to determine the outcome, you will ensure that you will be living in France, full time, with me?"

"You have not misunderstood anything. Yes, that is exactly what I'm saying. I want to live with you in France. Move there. Live there. The only thing that can stop that happening, as far as I am concerned, is you saying you don't want that too. If you say you want to live with me, but in England, not in France, then I will still be ecstatic. If you say that this is purely a dalliance, then I will simply thank my lucky stars for the experiences I have had with you. I would then see if and how Anna and I could rebuild so that we are as close as possible to where we were, not too long ago".

"Right, now it's your turn to ensure nothing is being misunderstood. If what I'm going to say isn't clear, tell me. I will then say it differently. I will keep trying to get it right until you are able to say to me, "Yes Katya, I totally understand what you have said to me"".

"OK, I will most certainly tell you if I am in any doubt".

"This is what you have to clearly understand: Charlie, I want to live in France, full time, with you. Just you and me, living together, in France, with no thought of returning to England. The two of us. A couple".

"I totally understand what you have just said to me, Katya. I will now focus on the decision that you and I have made. We've made it together and separately. We have decided that we are going to France, and we are going to live there together, as a couple. That is no longer in doubt. The only matters to be worked on are how and when".

"Oh my fucking god". She jumped up and piled on top of him. She showered every inch of him with kisses. She proved that she was still capable of something very special to him, behaving naturally, as an excited eighteen-year-old girl would.

She stopped herself. "What about Stroppy? We can't abandon Stroppy".

"We'll be back to see him. We'll watch every one of his races".

She squealed, then kissed every part of him again. "Radiohead! I told you that I wanted you to be the one to go with me. You'll be able to now, Charlie, won't you? We'll go to the concert together".

"We will. And stay at the hotel. It's possible that we won't have moved to France by then but, if we have, we'll fly back and make a short holiday of it. Maybe a few days in the Lake District".

She sat astride his chest and stared down at him. "Are we going to live at L'Aubaine, or would that be too painful for you? Too many memories?"

"Where would you like to live?"

"That's the only place I've been to. I don't know anywhere else in France. After leaving Russia, I hadn't been away from England before my holiday with you last summer".

"There are many beautiful places in France. Our options are limitless".

"Why did you choose Le Racou?"

"The Med, the mountains, the climate, and being able to drive to Barcelona".

"I love it there".

"Is that where you'd like to live?"

"Yes".

"Would it be difficult for you, living at L'Aubaine?"

She considered this for a while. "What, because you and Anna have been so happy there? Because you may associate the villa with Anna?"

"Yes".

"Maybe".

"Would you like to live there at first, once we've moved from England? Give it a try, perhaps, and, if either of us don't feel comfortable, sell it and buy a different property?"

"In Le Racou?"

"Yes, if you want to stay there. Or we could spend the first few months driving to different parts of France. You may find you prefer somewhere different".

"But you did all that and decided upon Le Racou. It must be the place you like the most".

"Yes, it is. But that isn't to say I couldn't be happy living somewhere else".

"I don't want to live anywhere else. Can we live at Le Racou, Charlie?"

He smiled affectionately. "Of course. What about the idea of testing out living in L'Aubaine?"

"Yes, I think that's a good idea. I think I'll be disappointed if either of us decide that we wouldn't be comfortable living there together, because it's simply perfect".

"Well, we'll see".

"What about Anna? She may want the villa".

"Anna won't want to live there on her own. I will try to arrange things with her so that she keeps this cottage and I have the villa".

She froze, and then tumbled off him, onto her back. "She's going to get you to change your mind".

"Katya".

"She is. She won't want to live anywhere on her own. She'll want to live with you. Think about it Charlie, Anna always gets what she wants. Whatever happens between her and Lene, she will want to stay with you. She's going to get you to change your mind".

He propped himself up so that he could look at her. "Katya, please".

"You know what she's said. You're unique. You're hers. She'll want to keep you. She's irresistible. You won't be able to say no. Who on earth can say no to Anna? She'll convince you about how much she still loves you and how much you still love her. She'll get you to see that you're just having a man thing with a young girl, and that the novelty will wear off after you've been with me a while. She'll make it clear to you that she can give you so much more than I can. A young girl like me? What do I know about life? You'll get bored with me. I'm ordinary compared to Anna. Everyone is. She'll convince you that nothing between the two of you has been broken and that you'll soon be back as you were. Oh Charlie, I feel as though I've found you but know that you'll be lost to me in no time at all. Having something and then losing it is worse than never having had it at all. We have to finish this immediately. I can just about bear it now, but it will break my heart when you tell me you've made a mistake and you and Anna will be together again". She began to cry.

Despite her genuine anguish, he began to laugh. "I'm sorry, but you Russians simply don't possess the British stiff upper lip".

"Don't laugh at me. Please don't". She covered her face.

He gently pulled her hands away and kissed her. "Katya, stop now. No more tears. Once all that needs to be done has been done, you and I will be together. We're going to be living as a couple in France. As long as it's what you want then it will happen. And that's because I want it too".

"But Anna…"

"Yes, I know. I know what you feel could happen, but it will only happen if I want it to. But I don't. I want to be with you, Katya".

She held her arms open. He lowered himself into her embrace and she pulled him in, as tightly as she could. "I love you Charlie," she whispered.

"Katya, do you believe me?"

"Yes".

"Then be calm and patient. What you and I have said we want to happen, will. We will make it happen, despite the challenges we are going to have to face from Anna and Chrissy. Will you be able to do that, be calm and patient?"

"Yes, I think so".

"Trust me, Katya. I love you and I want to be with you. I see my future with you. The only thing which can stop this happening is you deciding that it is not a good idea, for you I mean. If you see that committing yourself to someone so much older than you is foolishness, or if throwing away a future in England for uncertainties in France is unnecessarily risky".

"It's going to happen, isn't it?"

"I truly hope so. Now, come on, we need to decide what we're doing today".

"Let me hold you a little longer".

Katerina still felt the need to discuss the upcoming, difficult period. "I know that you'll do whatever you can to make it as painless as possible for Anna. I want you to do that, however much that may delay us being together. And I know that you will continue to have sex with her. It won't be easy for me, but I must accept it. I do accept it, but you mustn't talk to me about it".

"I won't now have sex with Anna. That's over. I'll arrange things as painlessly for everyone as possible, and as quickly. You must continue to live your life in the meantime and not put anything on hold. It may take a while, but it's going to happen".

"My life will go on, while I'm waiting, but I won't be having another relationship during that time".

A further period of silence was once again broken by Katerina voicing her thoughts. "You're acting very calmly, bearing in mind you've decided to leave your wife and emigrate, to live with me".

"It's turmoil inside and I'm bound to be agitated when Anna gets home, and even more so when I tell her. God knows what state I'll be in on the way to tell Chrissy the news".

"I'll do it".

"No. Thanks, but no. It's for me to explain it to her and receive the flack".

"I've let her down terribly. Every time I think about it, I feel pain for her".

"You're not letting her down Katya".

"Oh, but I am. She will be devastated by this news. She'll hate you and accuse you of all sorts of things. She'll probably hate Anna too for a while for allowing it to happen under her nose. And she'll feel ashamed of me after all she's done for me since Ivan brought me over here and then abandoned us all. I don't have a mother or father, only Chrissy, and, from her point of view, I will be doing something far worse than taking drugs or stealing from the corner shop".

Charlie didn't interrupt.

"I've taken her for granted and so has Ilya. She took us on and has raised us on her own. If she was our mother, she could not have been any more attentive towards us. She doesn't love us as a mother would, of course she doesn't, but that makes her commitment and sacrifice even more amazing. This will be a terrible thing for her to have to deal with. After all she's done, she'll see me going away to France with her sister's husband. It devastates me that I've left it too late to tell her how grateful I am and how I feel about her. I'm ashamed of myself. It's similar, I suppose, to when a loved one dies and those left behind feel guilty that they didn't say, "I love you," often enough".

"You'll find a way to let her know. It won't need to be forced. Somehow, at some time, you will have the opportunity to say to her what you want her to know. And she will be very happy to hear you say it, despite how she may initially feel about you".

"Do you honestly think that?"

"I do. Now, come on, let's enjoy the day".

"It's pouring".

"Can't really go out for a walk. Unless you have anything else in mind, maybe you could light the log burner in the Snug. We could listen to music and have a read".

"Perfect".

"Do you know at what time our day will end? When's Anna back?"

"I don't know. She let me know that they'd arrived safely, but I haven't heard from her since. It won't be until this evening. We've plenty of time".

"I know the first tune I want us to play, once we've settled into the Snug".

"OK. I'll get the fire lit, have a shower and get dressed".

"I'll shower while you're sorting the fire". She kissed him on the cheek and left the kitchen to return to the bedroom.

Twenty minutes later they were entwined on the sofa. Charlie passed over his phone so that Katerina could select the tune she wanted them to listen to.

"'Forever'. Wonderful song. You're really into Ben Harper, aren't you?"

"I love listening to him. The acoustic love songs, like this, and the belters: 'Glory and Consequence', 'Better Way', stuff like that".

"I've given you my forever, Katya".

"Yes, but Ben goes on to sing that forever always seems to be around when things begin, but it never seems to be around when things end".

"Anna and me being a case in point".

"It was as if he had you two in mind".

"And who's to say it won't end that way between us, too?"

"Who's to say?"

"But you want to give it a chance? On the basis that we're both committed?"

"Oh yes, of course I do. Who knows, the person Ben is singing to may turn out to be his forever person after his previous disappointments".

"What else shall we play? I'll choose one, and then we'll select a Playlist".

Out of the speakers came the plaintive voice of Liam Fray. She listened intently. "Play it again," she whispered. He repeated the song. "And again". They heard it a third time: 'Last of the Ladies'. "That is beautiful. Is it for me?"

"Yes, just for you".

"Play it again".

As soon as they'd heard it for the fourth time, she straddled him and wrapped her arms around his neck. "I want it to be 'forever' Charlie. Please tell me it will be".

"I'll try my very best to make it so".

Several songs were played before they decided to resume chatting. "You referred to Yosarrian in your text to me on Saturday. I think of that book often. I've read it several times".

"I think it's the funniest book I've ever read. It's written by a genius".

"I've read somewhere that an interviewer once said to Joseph Heller, later in his career, that he hadn't managed to write another book as good as Catch 22. Heller replied that no-one has managed to write another book as good as Catch 22. I guess it may have sounded conceited, but I think he was simply stating a fact".

"Would you say it's your favourite ever book?"

"Hard to say, isn't it? It may well be. What about yours?"

"If I had to select only one book which would be available for me to read in Le Racou, it would probably be Anna Karenina. Or maybe Crime and Punishment. Or The Brothers Karamazov". She started to giggle. "Or Madam Bovary. But then it would feel wrong not selecting a Dickens. Or a Hardy".

"Do you remember us discussing our mutual love for Dickens? In the early days of your summer holiday with us? We've been holding hands since then, I think, without realising it until recently. Tell me, do you still read the Russian edition of Anna Karenina, or is it becoming more difficult, the less opportunity you have to speak Russian?"

"If I'm reading a book by a Russian author, it's always the Russian edition".

"Stick with Anna Karenina as your selection then. Cracking read plus Russian practice".

"Good thinking. Although it could be a Dostoevsky, of course. In fact, I've decided it *will* be Dostoevsky. Crime and Punishment and I'm not budging. So, what would your single choice be? Catch 22?"

"If it was my sole book, I would want it to be a long one, with plenty of characters and lots going on. I think I'd choose The Count of Monte Cristo".

"I've never read an Alexandre Dumas novel".

"I'm convinced you'd love it".

"By the time we move to France I want to be capable of reading the French edition".

"Bloody hell, Katya, that's a big ask".

"Maybe, but I'm making good progress".

"With what?"

"I started to learn French as soon as I arrived home from my summer holiday with you. I began with distance learning but since the new year I've been having lessons with a French tutor".

"You put us all to shame".

"Not really. I've had plenty of time on my hands and I wanted to be able to converse if I was able to go on holiday with you again. I've an extra incentive now. That's the goal then, to be able to read The Count of Monte Cristo in French".

"It's in your interests for the process to take a while then".

"Don't you dare!"

He laughed. "OK, let's agree that we're allowed three books, one in Russian, Crime and Punishment, and one in French, The Count of Monte Cristo. What shall we choose for the English book?"

They both gave this serious consideration, despite it being a hypothetical situation. Finally, they both confirmed it had to be Dickens, and Katerina offered Bleak House while Charlie suggested A Tale of Two Cities.

"Shall we push the boat out and take both?"

"What, and also the other two?"

"Yes. Let's take four, not three".

"You rebel, you. OK, I'll sneak one of them under my skirt".

"Why not down your front, instead?"

"Oh, don't tell me, A Tale of Two Titties, I suppose?"

"One step ahead of me again, Katya. Speaking of skirts, I notice you haven't worn one here, just jeans".

"It was a test. I wanted to know if you fancy me even when my legs aren't on show".

"Have I passed?"

"With flying colours. I deliberately chose to not pack a skirt, so I can't even wear one for you after lunch".

"Why, what's happening after lunch?"

"What would you like to happen?"

"I'd like us to make love".

"I was hoping that would be your choice".

They had lunch and then they went to bed. As soon as Charlie entered Katerina, she said, "Just keep it there. Don't move. Not yet. Wait until I tell you. I just want to feel you and talk to you".

"It feels good, Katya. It feels right".

"How has this happened? How is it that you have gone from loving Anna to deciding to split with Anna because you love me and want us to live together?"

He moved slightly, raising and lowering his hips.

"Oh," she said, having closed her eyes to concentrate on the sensation.

"Anna told me before Christmas that she believed you would soon discover something about yourself. She was also trying to cool her relationship with Lene".

"What did she mean about my self-discovery?"

"I didn't know at the time, but it's clear to me now that she understood that you had fallen in love with me".

"Oh my god, as early as that?"

He moved again, providing her with several seconds of pleasure.

"Ooh, that's beautiful. So, what happened then?"

"When we arrived home, it struck me that you were dominating my thoughts. I kept admitting to myself that I'd fallen in love with you, then telling myself that I was being ridiculous, and then deciding that I'd loved you for many months".

"Did this affect you with Anna?"

"It did, but not as much as not knowing whether she would continue to have a relationship with Lene. I was trying to come to terms with how Anna felt about Lene and how I felt about you. It was a strange period, really, because Anna and I were, to some extent, still a loving couple, yet I kept yearning for you, as Anna did for Lene".

"That's still a long way from you deciding that you want to leave Anna to live with me in France".

"Yes and no". He made two sudden, forceful thrusts. She gasped. "We came back from Cyprus and Anna's Valentine's card from Lene seemed to clarify things for Anna. Clearly, Anna's reaction to Lene's message provided the impetus I needed to telephone you to tell you how I felt. And, of course, you then told me you loved me too. Despite all that, I'm not sure how everything would have played out if Anna hadn't placed all the cards on the table with the two of us. I think that was very brave of her".

"You still love her, don't you?"

"I suppose I always will. But no longer in the same way".

"Do you regret that?"

"In some ways, I do, because what she and I had was unbelievable. But I'm not going to look back. I see an unbelievable future for me, with you, in France".

He began minimal hip movements. She stiffened as her arousal began its gradual intensity. She wrapped her arms around his back as she climaxed.

Still breathless, she said, "I'll never stop trying to ensure that you don't wish you were still with Anna rather than with me".

"Don't try anything, just be you. It's you who fascinates and challenges me. It's you who I love being with, whether it's like this or in a living room or a car, discussing topics which would bore most of the population".

She was unable to converse further because Charlie hadn't finished providing for her. She moaned when she wasn't chewing on her bottom lip, and she swore when she wasn't moaning. It seemed to last an age, and then it drifted away, her arms and legs dropping away from him. She lay on her back, almost comatose.

Her eyes remained closed until she could summon the strength to look at him. It was as if she had wakened from a long, much needed sleep. She smiled at him and said, "Did you know that fewer than twenty per cent of adult females experience orgasm from penetration alone? I think I nearly had one there, so that was a good effort".

He returned her smile and then moved inside her once more. Her smile changed to a look of panic. "No Charlie, no more, please. Just wait a while and then I'll give you some pleasure".

He ignored her and his minimal movements progressed to grinding into her. Her pleading became grunts of pleasure and she climaxed again, an orgasm so intense that she found herself crying. She held him to her and whispered in his ear, "I've put your world into my veins". He kissed her lips and then licked the dried tears from her cheeks.

"Now," she said, "isn't it about time you came?"

"Yes, unless you'd like just one more first".

"No, Charlie. I'm serious, no".

He laughed. "Make love to me Katya".

"How would you like me to do it?"

"Enough, Katya. I'm done". She laughed in delight. "Oh, so now it all makes sense, does it? A human can take only so much?" As they lay side by side, holding hands, she found herself already desperate by the thought that he would be with Anna, in that bed, that night.

It was then that she decided that it had to be all or nothing: if Charlie and Anna stayed together, she, Katya, would return to Russia to try to make a life for herself there.

Despite climbing onto the train with fully ten minutes to spare, their carriage was already busy. When Anna and Lene located their seats, they noticed that they would be sitting opposite an elderly couple. The standard false smiles were exchanged before Lene and Anna settled down, Lene at the window. As usual, they were being stared at, with both the elderly gentleman and his wife looking from one to the other. The train pulled out of the station and Lene gazed forlornly out of the window. Once away from the metropolis, the train picked up speed.

Anna started to feel irritated by the elderly couple's attention. She turned her head and said, in a low voice, "Lene".

Lene turned to face her. Before she could respond, Anna kissed her on the lips. They parted momentarily, and then Anna kissed her again, more passionately. They separated and Lene smiled at her before turning once again to look out of the window. Anna looked first at the lady and then the gentleman—she had taken the opportunity to fumble in her bag for a magazine to read whereas he, despite being well into the Viagra stage of his life, hadn't drop his gaze. Anna smiled at him, and he matched it with a slight nod of the head. The journey continued.

It was as if the two of them had argued and fallen out with each other. They neither spoke nor looked at each other. Nor did they read or look at their phones. Finally, Lene's right hand sought Anna's left. She surrendered it willingly and fingers were entwined. Shortly after they had passed Three Bridges, Lene spoke her first words. "I'm not sure I have the strength to do this, Anna".

"I think you must. For the good of the girls".

"I shall have to feign it with Greg. I can't face it".

"You can. You still love him. It will come naturally to you once you're back in the routine of home life".

"I want to be with you Anna, not in the routine of home life".

"You know that you can't give up the girls. Even if you could live without Greg, the girls are too important to you".

"How will I cope without you?"

"You won't be without me. We'll continue as we are, for as long as you want".

"But it's not enough for me now. I can't bear the thought of being parted from you".

"Lene, I know it's going to be difficult, for both of us. But once you're back at home and doing the things that you do as wife and mother, you'll manage it. You and I must simply do what we can to arrange time to be together".

"I don't want time together here and there. I want you, Anna. Always. I just cannot contemplate my life without you now".

"Try, Lene. We both have to try. It will be easier than you think, I'm convinced of it".

Lene rested her head on Anna's shoulder and didn't respond. As they approached Chichester station, Anna said, "We're here, Lene". Lene looked up at her and displayed desperation. "It will be OK. It will work out". Anna sounded as if she were talking to somebody who was about to go into the operating theatre. They walked down the aisle, onto the platform and into a taxi. They held hands until they reached Lene's home. Lene then opened the door and exited the taxi. Before she closed the door, she looked at Anna and said, "Thank you, Anna. I've had a wonderful time". She closed the door, took hold of the bag handed to her by the taxi driver and walked up the path of her house without looking back.

Chapter 37

Immediately after Katerina left, Charlie stripped the bed, put the linen in the washing machine, took fresh bedding from the landing cupboard and re-made the bed. He then had a long shower and changed into leisure trousers and a sloppy t-shirt. By the time Anna walked through the door, the washed linen was in the tumble dryer.

They looked at each other and exchanged weak, self-conscious smiles. He went up to her and they kissed. "I'll carry your bag upstairs," he said.

"No, it's OK, I'll need to put some stuff in the washing machine, so I'll go through it first thanks".

"Would you like anything to eat or drink?"

"Would you mind pouring me a small Armagnac? I'll go and have a quick shower then join you in the Snug, shall I?"

"OK".

Ten minutes later they were sitting opposite each other, in front of the log burner, sipping their drinks. Anna broke the silence.

"Do you remember that episode of Frasier when Daphne and Marty's breakfast-time routine was ruined when they broke a bowl?"

"I do. They were totally co-ordinated until a minor incident upset the whole balance, even although it didn't matter in the slightest which bowl was used".

"They banged heads and got in each other's way all of a sudden".

"Yes, it was very clever".

"We've broken our bowl, haven't we? Everything now seems topsy turvy. Can you imagine only a couple of months ago how we would have been if I'd come home after a couple of days away?"

"Yes, we'd be all over each other. You'd be dying to tell me all about your trip and it would simply have been a case of whether you did it before, during or after we made love".

"Are we totally fucked, Charlie? In that episode, without Marty knowing, Daphne picked up Eddie the dog's bowl, which matched the one broken, and used that for Marty's breakfast. Standard procedure was resumed. Could it be that simple for us?"

He couldn't answer immediately, partly because he didn't know what he wanted to say, but also because he was crying.

"Oh Charlie, don't cry. Oh god, what have we done?" and Anna buried her face in her hands. He went to embrace her and, once she had managed to compose herself, said, "How was it left with Lene?"

She stared at him and then responded, "We can't wait to be together again". She began to cry again. He too. "We can't replace the bowl, can we?" she sobbed.

"If we tried, I think we'd still be walking on bits from the broken one with bare feet".

"What are we going to do?"

"I think we should leave it tonight. We're both tired and upset. Do you have any plans for tomorrow morning?"

"No".

"Then let's leave it until then".

Wordlessly, they finished their drinks, prepared themselves for bed and lay side by side, holding hands.

"I love you, Charlie. I will always love you, no matter what".

"I love you too, Anna. Nothing can ever tarnish for me the years we've had together".

Anna was the first to go to sleep, with her tears drying on her face.

The following morning, Charlie thought that it was possible that he had slept more than he thought he had, but he doubted it. He felt, too, that Anna hadn't slept well. He checked his phone and saw that it was still too early for him to get up to make their morning drinks. He therefore lay there, trying to assess his emotions. He was relieved that Anna had addressed the issue almost immediately she had returned home. He had been dreading the two of them sidestepping the implications of Anna spending two days with Lene, and he two days with Katerina. It was less easy for him to determine to what extent he was affected by Anna's admission that she wished to continue her relationship with Lene. Katerina hadn't been discussed but he felt it had become easier for him to arrange to be with her, yet that meant, of course, that his marriage to Anna was over.

Anna stirred, woke and looked at him. Her eyes were bloodshot, perhaps from crying, maybe from lack of sleep but probably from both. "Hello," she said.

"Hello. It's still early, but would you like me to get the drinks?"

"What time is it?"

He checked his phone again. "6.52".

"I doubt that either of us will go back to sleep so, yes please".

Once re-settled, Charlie asked, "How are you feeling?"

"Desperately sad. It was perfect. Our life and our love". She paused before adding, "So sad".

"I guess we both need to say what we want to happen now".

"Yes, I think you're right. I'm sorry, Charlie, but I believe I've reached a situation with Lene whereby my life with you, if we were to try to make it work, would need to include her".

He simply nodded.

"What's your situation with Katya?"

"It's clearer than yours is".

"In what way?"

"Katya's free to do what she wants. Lene is married to Greg and has two daughters".

"Yes," whispered Anna.

"Would she be prepared to leave them, for you?"

"I wouldn't want her to".

"So how do you think the two of you could continue, other than the occasional day or night together?"

"I don't know the answer to that. I only know that I love her too much to give her up altogether".

"You asked Katya what her ideal outcome was and then you told us both that yours would be for you and me to continue our relationship and to be friends with Katya. There was no mention of Lene".

"No".

"So, is it therefore four of us in your best-outcome scenario?"

"I don't think that's possible".

"Nor do I. I'm sorry but it can't be you and me, with you seeing Lene. I can't deal with that any longer".

"Oh god". She began to tremble, the full impact of Charlie's statement sinking in. "You haven't told me how you and Katya now feel about each other".

"I think you know".

"She's been in love with you for months".

"Yes".

"And I would guess even more so, after spending two days with you".

"Yes, I think so".

"And what do you feel for her?"

He remained silent; he just couldn't bring himself to say it. His breathing deepened and tears misted his eyes.

"You need to tell me, Charlie".

He looked distraught. They both did. She was nodding, anticipating his reply.

"I want to be with her," he said.

As she had the previous evening, she placed her face in the palms of her hands and wept. Charlie tried to retain his self-control, yet his tears streamed down his cheeks.

She lowered her hands and stuttered, "I knew that would be your decision, but I still feel the shock is going to destroy me".

"Anna, you know, too, that you've decided you want to be with Lene. It's how it is, and we know how it's happened".

She slumped towards him, and he gathered her in. Her distress was unmistakable, and his was discerned by the thumping of his heart, the gritting of his teeth and the inhaling of breath through his nostrils.

Neither moved for a considerable time but Anna eventually found the will to raise her head from his chest.

"I really haven't wanted this to happen," she said.

"But I'm afraid it has, and it can't now be undone".

She paused to consider. "No, it can't".

"So, we need to make this as painless as possible".

"Yes. I don't want to be in more pain than I have to be, and I don't want you to suffer either".

"We'll find a way, Anna. And I will always love you. I want you to still be part of my life".

"Katya won't".

"I'm sure she will, once everything has settled down".

"Well, I don't know how I'm going to feel, seeing the two of you together. I said to her that I will need her help, should you decide to be with her rather than with me. I don't think I truly thought that it would come to that, even while I was saying it".

"A lot has happened in a short space of time".

"Yes, it has. Can we leave it for now? I can't talk about it anymore at the moment. Let's have breakfast and do something together, and then maybe come back to it this afternoon, or this evening".

"Yes, of course. Would you like breakfast in bed? I'll get you whatever you fancy".

"That would be nice, thank you. Some toast with lemon curd and another coffee please".

"No problem".

"What would you like to do this morning?" asked Charlie.

"The weather's decent so shall we have a long walk? We could maybe have lunch somewhere and then chat some more when we get back. And would you mind if I phone Lene to arrange to see her? I'll need to tell her what's happened since I got home".

"Go ahead".

"And I'm sure you'll want to phone Katya. She'll be beside herself wondering about it all".

"Yes. Thanks Anna".

He left her and went downstairs.

Katerina answered her phone after the first ring.

"Charlie?"

"It's going to be OK, Katya. Anna and I are working things through".

"I knew she'd get what she wanted. I don't blame her. Or you". Katerina's voice communicated dismayed acceptance. "Thanks for letting me know".

"We've agreed that our relationship is over. She knows that I now want to be with you". Silence. "Katya?"

"She knows that you and I are going to be together?"

"Yes".

"In France?"

"No, we haven't got that far yet".

"Is this for real? Please don't get my hopes up if there's still a chance that you two will work things out".

"It's for real, Katya".

"Oh my fucking god". She could hardly contain herself. "You with me, Charlie? Really and truly?"

"Yes, really and truly".

"Oh my god".

"Are you at work?"

"Yes".

"You need to calm down".

"I'm standing in an aisle with a mountain of books on the floor beside me and I feel like I'm going to piss my pants".

"Don't do it over any first editions, whatever you do".

"Nor a classic. I'll aim at the Mills & Boon".

"Look, I'll phone you again as soon as I can, and I'll see you soon. Don't get concerned if it's not for a few days".

"OK. This isn't going to go wrong, is it? Not now".

"No. I've a lot to sort, of course, but it won't go wrong".

"Does she hate me?"

"She doesn't. We'll be OK, Katya. With Anna, I mean. It'll be difficult for a while, but don't worry".

"Oh my god, I just can't believe it".

"I love you Katya".

"I'm going to cry *and* piss myself. I have to go. Bye Charlie. I love you".

"Hi Dani, it's Anna".

"Hi Anna. It's been a while. How are you?"

"I'm fine thanks. Are you? And Molly?"

"We're both great, thanks. Still doing our best to put money aside for a deposit so we can buy our own place. It's very difficult. We keep seeing places we like but we've never got quite enough money".

"Sorted with her parents, then?"

"More or less".

"How much are you short?"

"Well, the apartment we really want works out at ten thousand beyond us, maybe more. That's even if they accept a lowish offer. And there'll be costs, of course".

"Put in the offer. I'll lend you the amount you need".

Dani hesitated. "What do you mean?"

"Make an offer that's acceptable to them. However much you're short, I'll lend you. You can pay me back whenever you can".

"Anna?"

"Look Dani, do two things for me. First, tell me the first available appointment I can get with Lene for a facial, nails and leg wax and then phone the Estate Agent and make the offer".

"I don't know what to say".

"Thank you Anna, and, You'll be the first we'll invite over for housewarming drinks, will be fine".

"Thank you, Anna. And yes, of course, you'll be the first one over the threshold. I'm trembling too much to open the Appointment Book. Bear with me". Twenty seconds later she said, "How about 9am tomorrow? I can easily move the lady she was due to see".

"Are you sure? I don't want to mess anyone up".

"No, it's fine. I'll see you tomorrow".

"Thanks Dani. Now, make that call".

"I will. Thank you so much. I'll let you know how I get on".

"Good luck".

They spoke little during the walk. Sometimes they were hand in hand, occasionally she had her arm through his, but mostly they walked side by side. They stopped at the pub at which Charlie and Katerina had eaten on Sunday.

"How is Lene coping with all of this?" he asked, once they had returned to the cottage.

"She's a little desperate, to tell you the truth".

"She's finding it hard to live the double life?"

"She's finding it hard not being with me".

"How do you think things will work out? With her, I mean".

"I'll have her some of the time. Until it's too difficult for her and she tells me it must stop. And then the girl who had everything will have nothing".

"You won't have nothing Anna. That simply isn't possible".

"Why so sure?"

"Because you're Anna, and you're gorgeous and everybody loves you".

"Thank you".

"I'll do what I can to help you through this".

"Have you and Katya decided what you're going to do?"

"We've talked about it, but I think you and I need to come to an agreement first".

"I'll go with whatever you suggest".

"No, Anna, you need to have your say".

"Just tell me what you have in mind. I'm sure I'll agree it's reasonable".

"OK. How about you have this cottage, I have the villa, you have the Land Rover, me the Alfa and we split the money 50/50?"

"That's fine. Will you sell the villa when you buy something here, or do you intend to keep it? I can't see you being happy for long living in Katya's apartment, especially with Ilya there too".

"We plan to live there".

Tears came to her eyes again. "You plan to move to France? Live in the villa with Katya?"

"Yes, I think so".

She stood and walked around the kitchen, trying to compose herself. "How can you help me from there?"

"I won't go until you are settled. Until you know where you stand with Lene".

"I can't bear the thought of you being that far away from me. I can't bear the thought of you being with her, there".

"We have Stroppy. We'll still share his development and see all his races. I'll fly back often. If you need me, you'll tell me, and I'll come back immediately to be with you".

She sat down. "This is heart-breaking".

"Oh Anna, I'm so sorry". He watched her as she wept, and he felt helpless. "How did you feel when you and Lene parted yesterday?"

"Like a part of me was missing".

"And how did she feel?"

"She said she didn't know how she would cope without me".

"It isn't finished, Anna. You love each other too much. Don't give up hope". He went to her, and they held each other in a loving and tender hug.

"I'm seeing Lene tomorrow," she said. "Is it OK if I tell her what's happened between you and me?"

"Yes, you need to. You can then work together to try to find the best solution for you both".

"What about Katya and Scott? Will she be finishing with him?"

"She already has".

"Really? She didn't waste any time there".

"It happened before all this. She told him on Saturday. It was because he was sulking about her not being with him on Sunday".

She looked past him and said, as if she were on her own, "What a fucking mess".

When Anna arrived at the salon the following morning, Dani was waiting to greet her.

"I didn't phone you or text you because I wanted to tell you in person. They've accepted the offer. Our mortgage was already approved so we can go ahead and buy it".

"I'm so pleased for you, Dani. That's great news".

Dani went to where she and Lene stored their coats and emerged with a huge bouquet of flowers. "Molly and I want you to have these. We just cannot convey how grateful we are".

Anna started to cry. "Oh Anna, no. I'm so sorry. I didn't mean to upset you".

"No, it's me being silly, Dani. That's very thoughtful of you both. They're beautiful".

"Don't start crying again when you see Lene. You'll start her off again. I'm convinced that she'd been crying when she arrived this morning. I hope that everything's OK between her and Greg".

Anna dried her eyes. "We've both reached a certain age, Dani, that's all it is. Make the most of your youth while you have it".

Dani laughed. "I'm not that much younger than you are. You're both so lovely that anything can trigger you off".

"Yes. Maybe Greg did something thoughtful for her this morning, just as you have by giving me these lovely flowers. Make sure to let me know how much you need and when you need it".

"You're so kind".

Anna walked to her and kissed her on the cheek. "Molly is a lucky girl. I'm sure you're both going to be very happy".

Before Dani could respond, Lene appeared. "This is a nice surprise. I was expecting Mrs Doubtfire as my first appointment".

"Mrs Doubtfire?" said Anna, with a questioning look.

"Dani has a name for most of our regular clients".

"Oh dear. I won't ask what mine is".

"Show Anna the Appointment Book, Dani".

Dani took the book out of a drawer and passed it to Anna, who saw 'Mrs D' had been crossed out to be replaced with 'Shaggalicious—F, N, L/W'.

Dani laughed, a little nervously. "Sorry Anna. I named you that the first time you came in after I started working here. Somehow, it stuck".

"No need to apologise. I'm very happy with it". Anna looked at the other names registered for that day's appointments. She saw that Dani's first client was 'Smelly Minge—B/W'. "I hope B/W isn't short for bikini wax, Dani".

Dani shuddered. "I'm afraid so".

"Oh dear".

"To balance things out a bit, maybe Lene will agree to me doing your next 'Brazilian'".

"Hands off," said Lene, "she's mine. Come on through, Anna, before Dani starts getting fruity. Dani, can you remind me how long I've got until the next appointment?"

"You're clear until 10.15".

"Thanks". They walked into the room together and Lene closed the door. They faced each other and, almost immediately, embraced. They kissed, fervently, with Anna's tongue exploring Lene's mouth. "Thank god you're here," said Lene. "It's been far, far too long".

Anna laughed. "Approximately thirty-six hours, Lene".

"That's just what I mean: far, far too long. Do you really want a facial, leg wax and to have your nails done, or was that just an excuse?"

"An excuse. But maybe you could do my nails while we chat. If we've time, I'm due a leg wax too".

"OK. Sit down and I'll make a start".

"Everything OK with Greg when you arrived home? Did you manage to act naturally?"

"Yes, he was his normal self, interested to hear how the two days had gone, whether we'd enjoyed ourselves and if you'd looked after me in the Big City".

"And you were fine with him?"

"Yes. I managed to pull myself together before I put the key in the lock. Greg wanted us to make love before we went to sleep, and I think he would have felt that he had nothing to complain about".

"Well done. It must have been a reassurance to you that you could skip from one role to the other".

"Yes, I suppose so. It obviously keeps things ticking over at home and I still don't want Greg to be hurt in any way".

"Do you still think you can manage to live the double life?"

"I shall have to. I'm not giving you up. No way will I do that. I love you too much and my desire for you is off the scale. I shall have to keep finding ways for us to be together while happily fulfilling my role with Greg and the girls. How about you with Charlie? Does he still feel the same way, that you and I can have our relationship as long as the marriages are not put at risk?"

"We're splitting up".

Lene froze mid-action, the brush remaining on Anna's nail. She looked up at Anna. "What?"

Tears began to roll down Anna's cheeks. She simply nodded.

"You're splitting up? You can't do that, Anna. Not you and Charlie".

"It's happening, Lene. No way back".

"Why did you come away with me if things were fragile with Charlie? I would have understood, you know I would".

"It's simple, yet complicated. It's not just about you and me. Charlie and I have managed to get ourselves into a place which is alien to us. We can't get from that place to where we were before. We can't undo things, we can't backtrack, and we can't stifle our emotions".

"Is he emotional about someone? Is there another girl?"

"Yes, but that's not the cause of it either. It's simply a contributing factor, like me with you. This isn't down to Charlie having an affair, or you and me falling in love with each other".

"Who is it? Do you know her?"

"It's Katerina".

Lene sat back, open mouthed. "What, Chrissy's Katerina?"

"Yes".

"But she's, what, nineteen, twenty?"

"She's eighteen".

"Bloody hell, Anna. Is that wise? Aren't you furious?"

"She's an unbelievable girl. She's perfect for him, and he is perfect for her, too. I've got to know her extremely well over the past few months, since last summer, and, believe me, she's a total one-off. I should have seen it coming".

"Does Chrissy know?"

"No".

"How will she react, when she finds out?"

"If you sense a mini nuclear explosion coming from the direction of her home, you'll know she's found out. She's going to be absolutely fucking livid".

For some reason, Lene saw the funny side of this, and giggled. That set off Anna.

"You're going to have to finish the nails, Lene. I can't have them half-done".

Lene carried on where she had left off. "What are you going to do?"

"Live in the cottage for a while. I'll just have to see what happens".

"What, between Charlie and Katerina? Do you think it may not work out?"

"No, not between Charlie and Katya, that will work out fine. No, I mean between you and Greg. You and me".

Lene stopped again. "Christ, Anna".

"I know. Don't worry, I have no expectations. I'm not asking you to mess up your marriage. I'm mindful of the girls and how wonderful you all are together. I'll simply live my life for a while, maybe pick up a toy boy to play with and be available for you if ever, and whenever, you want us to be together".

"Anna, this is massive".

Anna laughed. "Er, let's think. I'm separating from my perfect husband after twelve years of unadulterated love and mind-blowing sex, and he is going to live, instead, with an eighteen-year-old girl, who has been a ward of my sister. I have to accept it because I know that they love each other and are perfectly suited. Although I'm not bisexual, I'm deeply in love with someone I've known half my life who happens to be female. She happens to be deeply in love with me too, even though she isn't bi either. Oh, and she's happily married with two children yet yearns to be with me whenever she can and now knows I'm free and available twenty-four hours a day. Is that what you mean by massive?"

Lene laughed too. "I haven't a clue what either of us find funny in any of that".

"Nor have I. A final bit of info which I didn't mention: Charlie and Katya are moving to France. They're going to live in the villa".

Lene pondered this. "Maybe that's a good thing. From your point of view, I mean".

"Yes, maybe it is. We'll see".

"I'm going to have to think about things, Anna".

"Don't do anything rash".

"I won't. Are you OK? You've been through so much".

"Do we have time for you to relax me with your fingers?"

"Yes, I'm sure we do, if I concentrate on just one area rather than your whole body".

"Thank you," said Anna, whilst removing her jeans and knickers. "I need this".

"Lie back and let me look after you". Lene used two fingers of her left hand to moisten Anna. She then inserted them while stimulating Anna's clitoris with the index finger of her right hand.

"Don't leave me too, Lene. Not yet. I couldn't bear to lose you too".

"I'm not leaving you, Anna. Relax. Concentrate on my fingers".

"I'll keep the noise down, if I can. We don't want Dani to hear".

"Don't worry about Dani. She and I are watertight. Also, she'll be as jealous as hell".

Anna's giggle turned into a whimper, which progressed to a moan before she couldn't hold back and thrashed around on the couch, oblivious to her distress and her surroundings.

Dani knocked on the door and immediately entered, exclaiming, "Is everything OK?!" She stopped short on seeing what Lene was doing to cause Anna to make the sounds which had alarmed Dani.

"It's OK Dani. Anna was very tense and needed some personal attention".

"Oh, sorry Lene. Sorry". She closed the door, quickly, but silently.

Once Anna had dressed, she said, "Did I hear Dani during that?"

"You did, but it isn't a problem. Are you going to be all right, Anna?"

"Yes, I am. Don't worry about me".

"It goes without saying I'll be worrying about you. But at least it will take my mind off worrying about me".

"As I've said many times before, you must do what's right for you. Don't let any of this affect that".

"No, I won't. Can you see yourself out? I need a bit of time to compose myself before my next client".

Anna kissed her and smiled as best she could. "Speak soon, eh?"

"Yes. Speak soon. Bye Anna".

Anna left the room and closed the door. At reception, Dani was sitting behind the desk. She got up to retrieve Anna's flowers. "Goodbye Anna. I hope to get to see you again soon. And I can't see myself ever wanting to stop saying thank you".

"Bye Dani. No need to thank me again. It's a pleasure. Keep me informed". Anna walked towards the door.

"I will. Oh, and by the way".

Anna stopped and turned to look at Dani.

"The housewarming. We'll have a party, but it would be nice if we could say a special thanks to you. Maybe you'd like to come over as soon as we've moved in. I'm sure the three of us could spend a pleasant evening together. Stay the night too if you like".

"Thank you, Dani. Yes, that sounds good to me. I'll look forward to that".

"Good. So will I".

Katerina behaved as if she'd been administered a life-saving drug. At one point Salty asked her, nearly totally in jest, whether she'd won the Lottery. "No, Salty," replied Katerina, with a laugh.

"Well, whatever the reason is, save a bit for me".

"Sorry Salty, it's not for sharing".

"Intriguing. Must be a boy".

"Something like that. Do you mind if I put in some extra hours over the next few weeks? I'd really like to get this new software system properly integrated. It seems to be working as it should, but there's still some work to be done to get it how you'll want it".

"There's no rush, Katerina".

"I'd like to, if that's OK".

"If that's what you want. You've a key, so you can come and go as you please. Make a note of the hours and I'll settle up with you".

"No, I won't want any extra pay. I'd simply feel more at ease once I know it's all done".

"I'm paying you for extra hours, young lady, like it or not".

"We'll see. I'm off now. Is there anything you'd like me to do before I go? All the new books are sorted and shelved".

"No, that's great, thanks. I'm finishing myself now, too. I'll see you in the morning".

Katerina waved goodbye and walked back to her car. Before starting the engine, she sent a text to Chrissy:

'If Sunday's still OK with you and S it will just be me coming over for lunch. Have kicked Scott into a ditch somewhere off the A27'

She drove home with Radiohead blaring out of the speakers. She checked her phone after parking the car. Chrissy had replied:

'Are you OK about that?'
'Totally fine' she replied.

A text was immediately received:

'A red-letter day for me. Ilya contacted me and he and K both coming for Sunday lunch too. Will be so lovely to be with you all'
'That's great. Will be over Sunday morning'
'Any time. We'll eat 2ish'

Katerina locked the car and walked towards her apartment. If he'd especially arranged to see Chrissy, Ilya must have proposed to Katie, and she must have accepted. Katerina felt delighted and was determined to not spoil Ilya's announcement by asking him about it before Sunday. She knew, with absolute certainty, that Chrissy would welcome Ilya's news considerably more than she was going to welcome hers.

She awoke a little before six and it appeared that she was on her own in the apartment. This wasn't unusual as Ilya often stayed at Katie's house; her father didn't seem to mind in the slightest that Ilya was sharing a bed with his daughter. Katerina had asked Ilya about this, and he had told her that Katie was trusted, that she had a special bond with her father and that he and Katie's dad got on well. She got up, poured herself a grapefruit juice and made a coffee. She opened her laptop and began to work on the bookstore software while she drank them. At six thirty-five she received a text:

> *'Do I still have your 'forever'?'*
> *'Not a day less will do'*
> *'Still sorting. Will see you v soon'*
> *'I understand. Am keeping busy'*
> *'X'*
> *'XX'*

BOOK FOUR: *CRIME & PUNISHMENT*

CHAPTER 38

It was one of those rare evenings when Greg was home early from work and the four of them ate dinner together. The girls made the most of the opportunity, relating events from school: the standard petty arguments and jealousies, the usual criticism of useless teachers and the jousting as to who was likely to bag Deano.

"Who's Deano?"

"Oh Mum, he's so fit".

"He is, Mum, he really is".

"In your class?"

"No. Year above".

"Too old for you, then".

"Mum!!"

"Neither of you have got engaged to him, have you?" asked Greg.

"Dad. Don't be silly".

"Just watch yourselves, that's all. You're both far too good for him".

The girls gave up and changed the subject.

"Good night," said Greg, kissing his daughters in turn.

"I'll be up in a bit. A quick read and then lights out".

"OK Mum. Night Dad".

"They're exhausting," said Greg, once it was just the two of them.

"Good exhausting".

"Yes," he agreed.

They chatted about how work had been for the two of them and then Lene disappeared upstairs to settle the girls. While she was out of the room, Greg remembered that he had promised to send to his mother a photo Lene had taken of his daughters when they had been with their grandmother before Christmas. He saw Lene's phone on the arm of a chair and picked it up. They both knew each other's pass code and he was soon scrolling through Lene's saved photos. As he tried to identify the one that he wanted, he saw something resembling a piece of abstract art.

357

He enlarged it, then studied it. He finally made out what he was looking at, just as Lene entered the room.

"What's this, Lene?" He held the phone towards her so that she could see what he was referring to.

She blushed with embarrassment and concern.

"It's nothing, Greg".

"That's your arm, Lene. You're wearing the Longines watch I bought you for your 30th. And I'm pretty sure I know what else is in the photo".

She stared at him. "Greg," was all she could say.

"Who is it Lene?"

She was unable to speak.

"Is it Dani?"

She remained transfixed, only managing a slight shake of the head.

"Who is it?"

"Anna".

"This photo was taken before Christmas. Have you and Anna been doing things like this all this time?"

She wanted to answer him, to tell the truth, but couldn't articulate the right words in her head, never mind verbalise them.

"I can't believe it, Lene. I just can't believe it".

"I'm sorry Greg".

"Fuck sorry. It's far too late for sorry. God knows what the two of you were getting up to in London. No wonder you were so desperate to go. What's the matter, my cock not enough for you? I had no idea you were like this Lene, no idea at all. Who the fuck *are* you?"

She felt that she had to allow him time to let it all out. Nothing she could say was likely to have any impact.

"Pack a bag and get out of the house. We'll talk about it tomorrow. Go and spend the night with Anna and think about what's at stake here. Go on. I'll sort the girls in the morning. I'll tell them you've gone to look after a sick friend, or something".

"Greg, please".

"I mean it, Lene, go. I'll take the morning off work. Come back after the girls have left and I might have calmed down a bit by then".

"Greg".

"Go!"

She turned, exited the room, and climbed slowly up the stairs. She sat on the edge of their bed and felt in a daze. Why did she leave that photo on her phone? Stupid, stupid, stupid. How was she going to explain what she had been doing with Anna? How would it be possible for him to ever forgive her, ever trust her again? She panicked. She was going to lose Greg, the girls and Anna. She had no future. The four people that she loved, all lost, because she couldn't bring herself to erase the photo Anna had said was the horniest ever.

She began to tremble, as if in the early stages of a fit. 'Breathe. Breathe, I must breathe'. Gradually, she calmed herself. She had to address this. She couldn't lose one of them, let alone four. She gathered herself and, with a resolve which surprised her, she returned to the lounge.

"Sit down, Greg". She hadn't felt like this for many months. In fact, she felt more in control of herself than at any time since she had been a student.

"Lene…"

"Sit down and listen to me".

She watched him comply and then went to a cabinet to pour two glasses of Pinot Noir, a large one for Greg and a smaller one for herself.

"I'll do as you ask. I will pack a bag, drive over to Anna's, and you and I will talk about it in the morning. But you'll not be getting any sleep tonight so you may as well spend the night thinking about what has happened instead of making up all sorts of outlandish betrayals to accuse me of". She passed his glass to him and watched him take a large sip. "It's being going on for about nine months". He started to say something, but she stopped him. "No, hear me out first. It started last summer. It was a kind of experiment, simply re-living a night we spent together while we were at uni. To our surprise, we found that we enjoyed the experience. We enjoyed it immensely. And, before long, we fell in love with each other. I've been in love with Anna for months".

"Lene, come on".

"We're in love with each other, Greg. We've had sex a few times and we've loved it. But think about this, Greg, before you make a final judgement. Tell me, how do you feel things have been between you and me over that time?"

"What do you mean?"

"You know exactly what I mean. Haven't we been extremely close and unusually active, sexually? What was the only period in the past year when you were worried about me? You know when it was, and I'll tell you why it was. It was because I had told myself I would try to wean myself off Anna. And I did try, Greg, and it made me miserable. So miserable that you thought I was ill. That's what she means to me, but, whenever she's tested me about it, and, believe me, she's tested me a lot because she's never wanted to come between you and me, whenever she's tested me, I've answered in the same way. I tell her that something has been added without anything being taken away from how I feel about you. Think about it Greg, during the night when you can't get to sleep. Think about it and be true to yourself. I'd say not only has nothing been taken away, but I believe our relationship has been even better, more loving, more sexual. You know that's true because you've pointed it out yourself, and you've told me how much you've loved it".

She watched him as he processed what she was saying.

"When I come home tomorrow, I know what I'll be telling you. I'll be telling you that I love you, that I want your body, more and more, that I feel we have a perfect family, and that all of that will crumble if I can no longer have a relationship with Anna. It's been to everyone's advantage, Greg, and there's no reason why things have to change, just because you now know about it".

He started to say something, but his words froze on his tongue.

She added, "It wasn't long ago, was it, when you loved the vision of me and Anna together. You told me how much you fancy her and how arousing you found the vision of her joining us in a threesome. Greg, you told me that the thought of her using her tongue to give me an orgasm was horny".

He looked defeated.

"Don't ruin it, Greg. This mustn't be a male pride thing. I simply cannot stop my relationship with Anna, and I desperately want our marriage to continue to be as wonderful as it's been up until you saw that photo. It's possible, that now that this is in the open, we can make our relationship even more pleasurable, more exciting".

She took a swig of her drink and left him alone. Within a few minutes, she had packed an overnight bag and was driving towards Anna's cottage.

Her steely resolve disintegrated en route and, by the time she had reached the cottage, she was a trembling wreck. It was Charlie who opened the door. "Lene! What's the matter?" She broke down and he had to help her in, calling out, "Anna".

Anna tumbled down the stairs. "Lene, what's wrong?"

If Charlie hadn't kept hold of Lene she would have been in a heap on the floor. "Oh Anna," she said, trying to catch her breath, "he saw the photo".

"What photo?"

"Of me. With you. Doing… you know".

"Oh Lene". Anna turned to Charlie. "Charlie, could you help Lene into the Snug and I'll pour her a brandy". They both tended to her until she had calmed sufficiently to communicate coherently. She told them what Greg had said to her and how he had insisted that she leave the house. She explained that he wanted to talk about it the following morning. She then told them, as best she could, although much of it was a blur to her, what she had said to him in return.

"So, he knows about us?"

"Yes. I told him he should admit to himself that everything has been better for him since you and I started seeing each other".

"Did he demand that you finish with me?"

"No, I don't think so. I don't think we got to that stage. And anyway, I told him I couldn't".

"You told him you couldn't finish things with me?" Anna glanced at Charlie as she asked this.

"Yes. I told him that we're in love with each other, and I'm pretty sure that I made it clear that you and I won't stop seeing each other". As she said this, she became conscious that Charlie was standing behind her. She stood and walked around the chair to hug him. "I'm so sorry Charlie. About you and Anna. I'm so, so sorry about the part I've played in it".

Tears came to his eyes. "Lene, don't worry, Anna and I will come out of this".

She held him even more tightly.

"Come on, sit down again and you and Anna can chat it through. Anna, I'll go up. I'll sleep in the spare room and Lene can be in with you. If you need me for anything, let me know".

"I will. Thank you, Charlie".

"Did you bring a bag, Lene?"

"Yes, I left it on the passenger seat".

"Give me your keys and I'll get it. I'll leave it on the bed, and I'll put the keys in it".

"Yes, thank you Charlie. Thanks".

"OK," said Anna as soon as Charlie had left the room, "compose yourself and think hard about what you said to Greg. This is important, Lene. You need to get a grip on how things stand before you see him again tomorrow".

Lene took a long sip of her drink and then a deep breath. She then managed to recount just about all of what she had said to Greg.

Once she had told Anna that she couldn't think of anything to add, Anna said to her, "You were very brave, Lene. I really don't think you could have handled that better".

"You really think so?"

"I do. I think you'll manage to come out of this undamaged".

"What about you? What about us?"

"I think there's a good chance that you've saved us too".

Lene was desperate enough to take Anna's word as gospel. Anna, though, was deadly serious.

"Come on, bed. You're exhausted. Don't think about it anymore tonight. We'll go through it all in the morning so that you'll know exactly how to control things when you see Greg".

"You really think it's going to be all right?"

"I do. I honestly do".

They both got ready for bed and Lene snuggled into Anna. If it had been up to Anna, they would have been intimate. As it was, though, Lene fell asleep almost immediately her head rested on Anna's shoulder. Anna held her until the pins and needles became intolerable, then she manoeuvred Lene onto her side without waking her. She snuggled up behind her and, before long, she, too, was asleep.

In the morning, Charlie waited until he heard the two of them talking before knocking gently on the door and letting himself into the bedroom.

"Tea or coffee Lene? And fruit juice?"

"May I have a black coffee please Charlie. And an orange juice would be lovely".

"Sugar?"

"No thanks".

While they were waiting, Anna asked Lene how she was feeling. "Much better thanks. I must get a text off to Dani to tell her I can't get to work this morning. She'll have to sort it out as best she can".

"Do you know how you're going to handle things when you see Greg?".

"I think so. I've been going over what you were saying to me last night and I believe you're right. I'm proud of myself. I said what I wanted to say, and I hope that Greg will take it all in and not make a stupid decision".

"Good for you".

"Anna, may I ask you something, something which may offend you?"

"There's nothing you could say which would offend me".

"Maybe this will. Do you remember the evening when you encouraged me to get Greg to watch me use the Lelo on myself?"

"Yes".

"Greg and I role played. We imagined that it wasn't the vibrator but a girl licking me".

"Me?"

"No, I asked Greg to tell me who it was doing it to me and the first person he could come up with was Dani. After we'd finished, we talked about it. He admitted that if he hadn't been flustered, it would have been you. He admitted that the thought of a threesome with you turned him on. He said the vision of you licking me was horny. I reminded him of this last night. Held it against him, so to speak".

"And you want to ask me if I'd do it for real?"

"Yes".

"Are you asking me because you think it would improve the chances of Greg agreeing that you and I can continue?"

"In the main, yes. Might be fun too, though".

Anna thought about the request. Finally, she said, "I wouldn't feel comfortable with you offering it. Not in the circumstances. I wouldn't want Greg to begrudgingly accept you and me on the basis that he could have fun with me".

"I can understand that".

"But if he suggests it, if he agrees that the past year has worked out well for him, and he suggests it could work out even better, for the three of us, if I joined you occasionally then, yes, I'd be happy to do that".

At this point, Charlie entered the room and passed over the drinks.

"Are you OK this morning Lene?"

"I am Charlie, thank you. I'm feeling much better. Thank you so much for being so caring and supportive".

"I will always try to help you should you ever feel the need to call on me".

He left the room. Both girls had tears in their eyes.

Lene let herself in and went straight to the kitchen to make herself a cup of tea. Greg joined her. "Did the girls get off all right?" she asked.

"Yes. No dramas".

"Would you like a cup of tea? I'm just making myself one?"

"No thanks, I've just had a coffee".

"Do you want to talk things through straight away? As soon as I've got my tea?"

"Yes please. I'll see you in the lounge".

She went into the room and sat in a chair opposite him. She waited for him to start.

"It's been a difficult night, Lene. It was a shock, that photo".

"Yes. I'm sorry that you had to see that. I should have deleted it".

"It was a shock, too, when you told me that you and Anna love each other".

"It was a shock to us, so I've no idea how it sounded to you".

"I don't want to lose you, Lene. I don't want us to split up. Not for me, and especially not for the girls".

"I can't finish it with Anna, Greg, you have to know that before you carry on".

"Yes, I understood that last night. I'm prepared to see how it goes. As long as it's as it's been until now, with your relationship with Anna not causing you to go off me. If you and I continue as we have, since you started doing what you've been doing with Anna, then I agree with you, that it may well work for all of us without any damage being done".

"And maybe even some benefit? For you as well as us?"

"Yes. I admit that our sex has been better in the past year than it's been since we were first married".

"Good. Thank you, Greg".

"One more thing, though".

"Yes?"

"You know what you were saying, about Anna in our fantasy role play?"

"Yes".

"Do you think she would? Is it something you'd both like to do? With me, if you know what I mean, you know, for real, not just in a role play".

"Yes, I know what you mean. I'll ask her. If she'd like to then I don't see why not. I'd enjoy it too".

"Thanks. Look, as I've taken the morning off, shall we go to bed?"

"That would be nice. Would you like us to behave as if Anna is with us?"

"Shall we?"

"Let's have a go. The real thing will be much better, though, if it happens".

"Do you think it will?"

"I'll see what Anna says".

"What about her husband? Does he know?"

"I shouldn't worry about that. I think he tends to do his own thing and he's been aware of all this for some time".

Greg left for work and Lene, too, got ready to go to the salon. She sent a text to Dani:

'Sorry about that. On my way in'

She then sent one to Anna:

'Can you get to the salon at 5.30?'

By the time she was dressed and picking up her car keys, she had received Anna's reply:

'Yes. See you then. All OK?'
'Yes, all OK'

She drove to work and entered the salon. Dani looked up anxiously. "Is everything OK, Lene?"
"Yes, everything's fine, thanks. Sorry about that. Did you manage to swap things around without upsetting too many people?"
"Yes, all sorted. No clients lost".
"You're brilliant. When's my next appointment?"
"Five minutes. A nice relaxing head massage".
"Who is it?"
"You. You're the client and I'm the beautician. As I said, a nice relaxing head massage. Go on through and I'll be there in a minute. You can decide, too, if you'd also like some personal attention from me, similar to how you helped Anna, when she felt stressed".
Lene didn't argue. Instead, she considered how thankful she was for the wonderful friends she had. She pondered Dani's offer as she walked towards her treatment room.

On the way back from the salon, Anna did something which she had rarely done in her whole adult life: she went into a pub, on her own, and ordered a drink for herself. She sat at a corner table and sipped at the white wine spritzer, taking stock—

Things had worked out badly with Charlie. The worst possible outcome;
Things couldn't have worked out much better with Lene;
She needed to be loved, treasured. She had that from Lene;
She needed to love, treasure. She felt that for Lene;

She needed sex with a man. She couldn't do without what a man provided for her. Lene had made it clear that Greg wanted her to join the two of them, which was fine by her as she'd always quite liked him, and it oiled the wheels. That wouldn't be enough, though. Men had sniffed around her for twenty-five years, and once people found out that she and Charlie were no longer a couple, she felt confident that a number of guys would show their hand. 'There's a guy over there who hasn't stopped staring at me,' she thought. 'If I went over to start to talk to him, he'd either run a mile or we'd be having sex within the hour';

She wanted variety. If there was one thing the past year had taught her, it was that there was fun to be had, in different scenarios. Dani and Molly, or just Dani? Maybe. She quite fancied trying it on with Scott too; a bit of a scumbag, perhaps, but young cock could be a bit of a thrill;

She wasn't a nympho, whatever Chrissy thought of her. She loved what men could do to her. She loved sex. She loved a man's body. And she'd discovered that she loved a woman's body too. 'Mind you,' she thought, 'there could be a hundred opportunities lined up, but without Charlie or Lene being among them, I'd remain lonely and desolate'.

When she arrived home, Charlie was reading a book. "Is everything OK with Lene?"

"Yes".

"And you?"

"Thankfully, yes".

"The two of you?"

"Yes. It's out in the open with Greg, and there's nothing to stop Lene and me loving each other".

"They're staying together too?"

"Yes. He still loves her. Nothing's changed".

"I'm so relieved. That's wonderful news".

"Yes. I've just realised I'm exhausted". She slumped into a chair. "I'm desperate about losing you, Charlie. Absolutely desperate. And I'll never stop regretting trying to improve on perfection. But there you go, what's done is done". Both were silent for a while before Anna added, "When will you go? I guess there's no need to be around to save me now".

"Are you sure?"

"It may be best to just get it over and done with".

"I'll speak to Katya. I won't, of course, make any final plans before speaking to you".

"OK".

"We've Stroppy's first race coming up".

"I'd forgotten about that. That'll be tough, the three of us together. Do you think the Trainer could get a fourth pass for the owners' enclosure? It would be easier for me if Lene was there too".

"I'll phone him tomorrow".

"OK. What's the date of the race again?"

"21st".

She closed her eyes and tried to visualise the direction in which her life was heading.

BOOK FOUR: *CRIME & PUNISHMENT*

CHAPTER 39

He phoned her when she was on the way to work, and she pulled the car over to speak to him.

"What have you in your diary over the next few days and weeks?"

"Er, well I'm at Chrissy's on Sunday for that Sunday lunch she's been trying to arrange with me. Ilya and Katie are going too. I'm working hard to get the software system finalised so that I don't leave Salty in the lurch. Kempton on the 21st. A couple of French lessons. That's about it, I think. Why?"

"When do you think you'll finish the software installation?"

"I'm aiming for the end of the month".

"How much notice do you have to give?"

"I don't know really. We've never sorted a formal contract".

"What would you think would be reasonable".

"Why, Charlie?"

"Come on, what do you think would be fair to both you and Salty?"

"Two weeks? Maybe four would be fairer to her".

"How about aiming for the last week in April?"

"For what?"

"Packing up. Getting whatever we want shipped, shipped. Getting in the Alfa and driving to France".

"Not for a holiday, you don't mean? For real? Drive to our new life together?"

"Yes. How about aiming for the last week in April?"

"Oh my fucking god".

"That phrase has become habit forming, Katya".

"But there's no better phrase to describe how I'm feeling".

"I suppose you're going to tell me now that you're going to pee your pants".

"I wasn't, but now you've drawn my attention to it, I'm desperate".

"Last week in April, Katya".

"Have you told Anna?"

"Not the specific week as I wanted to speak to you first. But she accepts it, now. She hasn't lost Lene. Her husband knows, and Anna and Lene can be lovers, openly".

"Oh, I'm so pleased for Anna. And I'm relieved for Lene too, after hearing how vulnerable she's been".

"She was right on the edge but, remarkably, it was she who had the strength to find the way forward".

"As Anna would say, I like a girl with spunk in her".

He laughed. "You don't forget much, do you?"

"Anna said the same thing to me, and I pointed out that I remember everything".

"They really do love each other".

"Will I meet Lene, do you think?"

"If I can arrange it, she'll be with us at Kempton. I hope you don't mind".

"That's brilliant".

"Still need that pee?"

"I've done it. The driver's seat is soaking".

"If I were there now, with you, what would we do? Would we make love, would you toss me off, would I finger you, would you take me in your mouth, would you allow me to come over your breasts, would I lick you? What would we do?"

"Well, let me take a moment to look around. Yes, that's right, I'm in a lay-by on the A27. Traffic is streaming past. There's a lorry parked behind me and at least three cars in front of me. There's a queue, maybe only a small one, but a queue nevertheless, at Betty's Baps van. Oh, and there's a guy about to disappear into the hedge and his flies are already undone. So, maybe we should put it to the vote. I'll hand out ballot papers".

"OK, not this morning, then. Have you a day off next week? We could check into a hotel as Mr & Mrs Smith".

"I'll take Monday morning off to see you, but I will want to get back to this work project. Rather than a hotel, think of somewhere public, but private, text me the details and I'll meet you there at nine in the morning. I'll ease your tensions with my mouth, how does that sound? I'll leave you to decide if you'd also like to put your hand up my skirt".

"Sounds good to me. You'll be wearing a skirt then?"

"If you're aiming to put your hand up it, then yes".

"I'll text you the details once I've thought of somewhere. Are you turned on as much as I am?"

"I don't know, how much are you turned on?"

"Well, I'm erect, for a start".

"Yes, I'm certainly the female equivalent of that. Any more of this talk and I'll be inviting over that lorry driver who's just got out of his cab to make his selection at Betty's Baps. I'm hopeful that he'd prefer mine".

"I'm sure he would. Why don't you flash them at him?"

"It's a pity you didn't give me a bit of notice. Maybe I could have sold a few tickets; generated a bit of an audience".

"The reviews would have been great. See you Monday. I hope the Sunday lunch goes well".

"It may be the last time she talks to me. When will you tell her?"

"I was thinking of writing it on a postcard once we get to France".

"Yes, I'm sure she'd welcome adding 'coward' to the list of names she'll have in store for you".

"It'll be next week, I should think".

"Just as well we've got that blowjob booked, then. May not be much left to suck after she's finished with you".

"I'm pleased you're finding this entertaining".

"If I wasn't confident about your fighting credentials, I wouldn't be joking about it".

"I'll see you on Monday, Katya".

"Yes, see you Monday".

He climbed into the Alfa and drove to the Amberley Castle Hotel, where he arranged a superior double room for himself. He asked for it to be available to him until the end of April and the receptionist readily agreed that he could finalise his departure date nearer the time.

He drove from there back to the cottage. Anna was out, and he guessed that she was riding Garibaldi. He calmly packed two cases of essential clothing, some books plus his toiletries, placed the bags in his car, made himself a coffee and picked up a book.

Anna returned and joined him in the kitchen. "Hi". She looked and sounded exhausted.

"I've booked a room at the Amberley Castle. I think we need to start the withdrawal process".

Her head dropped. "Yes, you're right, of course". She tried to liven herself up. "Amberley Castle? Good choice".

"I'll be close, should you need me".

"Aren't we supposed to be starting the withdrawal process?"

"Yes, we must try to be disciplined. But if you need me, I'll be here as quickly as I can manage it".

"Thanks. So, you're leaving today?"

"Yes. I've packed a couple of bags".

She started to cry; she couldn't help herself. "Sorry Charlie. I'll be OK in a minute. It'll take a bit of getting used to, that's all".

"Do you want me to hold you?"

"Better not, eh? Does Katya know you're moving out?"

"No, I haven't told her yet".

"Well, she'll be very relieved".

"Anna, I'm aiming to leave for France before the end of April".

She slumped onto a chair. "Oh, so soon? Well, I suppose there's little point in hanging around. You'll be there for May. Our favourite month".

He couldn't speak. She, too, needed time to gather herself. "You know, of course, that you can come and go as you please. You'll need to decide what you want to take with you and whether anything can be dumped or taken to a charity shop".

"Thank you. I've plenty of time to sort it all out. You'll need to let me know if you will want me to send back any of what you have in the villa".

"Yes, I hadn't thought about that. I'll let you know".

"You'll be flying over to see us, won't you? You may want to keep some clothes there".

"Katya won't want that. I'm sure I wouldn't if I were her. No, I'll let you know if there's anything I'd particularly like back here".

"You'll want the white tennis dress, for sure".

She smiled. "Yes, I need to keep that. I'm not sure I'll be able to wear it again though, not with all the stains, you messy boy".

He smiled back. "I'll email a list of it all and you can let me know, once you've decided".

"Yes. That's fine, thanks".

"Well, I'd better go. I'll see you soon Anna".

"Yes, see you soon Charlie".

As she heard him drive away, she collapsed onto the floor and curled her body up into a ball, desperately trying to keep her entire insides from spilling out of her.

Charlie found it difficult to navigate. The tears of a man, shed shamefully, whatever the circumstances and however justified.

He reached the hotel car park and phoned Katerina.

"Charlie? All OK?"

"I'm sorry to disturb you at work, Katya. I thought I'd let you know that I'll be staying in a hotel until we leave. And I've told Anna that we'll be gone before the end of April".

She intuited his sadness. "Thank you for letting me know. If you need company, tell me. You may want to be on your own for a while, but if you want me there, just say".

"Thank you, I will. I'll see you on Monday".

"Shall I come to the hotel, rather than us meet at some lorry park or whatever you had in mind?"

"Yes, that's a nice idea. Do you know the Amberley Castle?"

"Yes".

"Come there on Monday. Whatever time you like".

"Shall I get there early; we could have breakfast together?"

"Yes, I'd like that".

"OK, See you on Monday. Don't hesitate to phone or text or whatever, should you want to talk".

"Yes. Thanks". He closed off the call before his tears flowed once again.

Katerina arrived at Chrissy's house shortly before eleven on Sunday morning. Ilya and Katie had already arrived. Despite Katerina and Ilya owning, and living in, an apartment, it had been a while since they had seen each other, for one reason or another. She waited until it was just the two of them before asking, "Well?"

"Well what?"

"Well, are you going to be a total fucking moron or are you going to answer my, "well?"?"

"She said yes".

Katerina jumped on him. He tried to cling onto her but lost his balance and toppled back onto a chair. She smothered him in kisses. "You lucky, lucky bastard," she teased. "Oh Ilya, I'm so happy for you".

Ilya was laughing whilst trying to prise her off him. "You need to keep yourself under control, Katerina. We haven't told Chrissy yet".

"Does Katie's Dad know?"

"Yes, we told him yesterday and she showed him her ring".

"She's got a ring already? How brilliant! What did he say? Was it, "Not over my dead body, young lady," or, "You'll be disinherited the minute you wed this Cossack wastrel"? Something like that?"

"No. George said he was delighted".

"Well done you. And on first name terms already. I thought he would be insisting on 'Sir' until the big day, then moving onto 'Father-in-Law'".

"Your support humbles me".

"Why hasn't Chrissy spotted the ring? Bit warm for gloves, isn't it?"

"Katie's taken it off. She'll reveal it after we've eaten".

"Do I already know or am I to jump all over you again the second you make the announcement?"

"Spare me that. I've told you first, so you can already know. I've known you longer".

"And like me more?"

"When you're not taking the piss out of me, yes".

"I have some news for you, too".

"What is it?"

"No, you do your great reveal first. Suck up the favourite child behaviour from Chrissy. You'll need to get used to it".

"What are you talking about?"

"I'll tell you later. You'll need to keep it a secret like I've kept yours, that you were intending to ask Katie".

"Yes, of course".

Steve entered the room. "You two ready for a drink?"

"Driving I'm afraid Steve".

"Me too".

"You don't fancy staying over?"

"I'm afraid I can't," was Katerina's immediate response. "I have to be off early tomorrow, and all my stuff is in the apartment".

"What about you, Ilya?"

"I'll ask Katie".

Katerina whispered in his ear, "And so it begins. No longer in a position to make his own decisions".

He whispered into hers, "Fuck off, Katerina".

They finished their meal and Katerina and Katie got up to clear the table. "No," said Chrissy, "Steve will do it, won't you Steve? I rarely get the chance to chat to this lot and I'm going to make the most of it. Besides, Katie can't put those beautiful nails in washing up water".

"Thank you, Chrissy. They're nice, aren't they? I had them done especially".

"Oh, going somewhere nice?"

"No, it's because I need to show this off properly," and she removed the ring from its box, which she'd kept in her handbag. She slipped it on and displayed her hand to Chrissy, who was at the head of the table.

"Engaged?"

"Yes".

Katerina piped in with, "And we thought things had been going so well with Ilya". He tried to kick her under the table but couldn't quite reach.

"Oh Katie, Ilya, how wonderful". Chrissy started to cry. "Oh, I couldn't be happier. Ilya, I'm so proud of you. You could have become such an arsehole".

Steve, Katerina, and Katie shrieked with laughter, and Ilya tried his best to go along with it.

"Katie, I'm serious. I couldn't be happier. Have you told your dad?"

"Yes".

Katerina chipped in again, "And you're still finding a way to go through with it?"

"Katerina, stop it," admonished Chrissy.

"He's delighted".

"And so he should be," added Ilya.

"No doubt he's always wanted a conceited son-in-law". Katerina spotted Chrissy's look. "OK, OK, finished now".

Steve went to fetch and pour some Champagne, and Ilya, together with Katie, agreed to stay the night.

In the early evening, Katerina stood up and said, "Anyone want a coffee?" There were only three takers, yet she still insisted that Ilya give her a hand.

Once in the kitchen she said, "I'm sorry about this Ilya. I know I shouldn't be doing anything which could spoil your special day, but I'd like you to know something before Chrissy is told and all hell breaks loose".

"What is it?"

"Anna and Charlie are separating. Charlie and I are in love with each other; we're moving to France at the end of April".

"Are you fucking kidding me?"

"Of those statements of fact, which is the one that astounds you most? I bet it's that anyone could contemplate splitting with Anna".

"Katerina, be serious for a moment. Is that all true?"

"Yes. Charlie is staying at a hotel, I'm due to hand in my notice, and Charlie is arranging shipment of things we want to take over to France".

"This doesn't have anything to do with me saying he's perfect for you, does it?"

"Oh, don't be so ridiculous. This hasn't been in the making for only a matter of a few days. Just in case you haven't noticed, none of us have the conjuring powers of god".

"Chrissy will go ballistic".

"She will".

"She'll want to kill Charlie. Literally".

"I hope she doesn't do it before he's signed all his goods and chattels over to me".

"I don't think you'll be as flippant as this after she's told".

"No, I'm trying to make the most of it. So, there you are. You're now the Prodigal Son, I'm one of the Pied Piper kids and Charlie's Jimmy Savile".

He laughed. "Have I committed myself to Katie too early? If Anna's on the market, I mean".

"You're sick. You know that, don't you? Sick," and she slapped him around the head with the nearest Jamie Oliver cooking manual.

In bed, that night, after Katerina had driven home and Ilya and Katie had settled themselves into the spare room, Steve asked, "Happy?"

"They're too young, but he couldn't have found himself anyone nicer".

"They probably won't marry for a few years".

"I'm not so sure. Ilya's quite impatient".

"And you're comfortable with that?"

"Yes, he'll sort it out. Always seems to come up smelling of roses".

"Is he your favourite?"

She looked at him with a shocked look on her face. "What? Of course not. Why on earth would you say that?"

"Because from what I've seen from a distance, Katerina is far more capable than Ilya will ever be. It strikes me that he's a 'skin of the teeth' guy whereas Katerina is an organised planner and sorter. When she's introspective, you automatically seem to think she's got herself pregnant or has become dependent on drugs. You've been worrying about her for ages and see what happens: she decides Scott needs to be dumped and she's her old self again".

"Seriously Steve, do I really come across as if I prefer Ilya?"

"No, not really, but at the same time, I often wonder if you're on the same wavelength as Katerina. Mind you, I wonder if there's anyone on the same wavelength as her. I've said it before, I've never met anyone quite like her. I admire her enormously".

"Admire her?"

"Yes, I mean it. If someone said to me that, in ten years' time, she would have found a cure for cancer, or solved UK's housing problem, or managed England to win the World Cup, I wouldn't be surprised in the slightest. And do you know what I admire about her most, I'd say love about her the most if she were my daughter?"

"What?"

"She's great fun, yet she's deadly earnest. She says what she thinks, but she's also contemplative. In a single conversation she can astonish you with her wit and worry you because of her introspection. She's the most brilliant mixture of wonderfulness".

"You were doing so well with those profound words until you said wonderfulness".

He laughed, and then added, "I said to you, after I'd met her for a sandwich that time, that she definitely had something on her mind, but that she was more than capable of solving the problem, whatever it was. I think it would help you if you accepted that she's pretty special. I'm convinced that, if she was ever really up against it, she'd talk to you about it".

"She'd talk to Anna first".

"I don't know whether that's true or not but, if it is, maybe it's because Anna has been better at giving her space, listening and then helping to get the issue sorted. By the way, don't be hard on yourself about that because Anna's role with Katerina is far easier to handle than yours is".

"Are all builders this philosophically smart or is it only those who have a huge dick?"

"How many philosophical builders have you known?"

"One".

"And how many builders have a huge dick, in your experience?"

"Just one".

"There's your answer then".

Chrissy decided that she would rather go to sleep than try to work that one out.

BOOK FOUR: *CRIME & PUNISHMENT*

CHAPTER 40

Charlie waited until 7am before sending a text to Anna:

'I hope that you've been OK. I shall see Chrissy tomorrow to tell her'

He wasn't expecting a quick response so had a shower and readied himself for Katerina. His room phone rang at 7.35. "Good morning, Mr Knightley, it's Francesca on the Reception Desk. A Doctor Suckov is here to see you. She says she has flown in from St Petersburg for your appointment".

"Thank you, Francesca. Please tell her I'll be down in five minutes".

"Certainly, Mr Knightley".

"Doctor Suckov, thank you so much for flying over to see me. How is life under Putin these days? Did you enjoy your holiday in Siberia?"

"Not really. The weather wasn't great, the accommodation very basic and the leisure facilities physically demanding. I was quite relieved to abandon the pickaxe in order to fulfil my obligation to you. Tell me, would you prefer that I administer the treatment now or after breakfast?"

"Let's breakfast first". He led her into the dining room, and they sat at a table for two, facing each other.

"How have you been, Charlie?"

"I cannot deny that walking out of that door, away from Anna, was the most heart wrenching action I've ever taken".

"How has Anna coped? Do you know?"

"No, I don't. I've felt that I cannot on one hand stress the importance of us distancing ourselves from each other while at the same time constantly checking in on her".

"Would you like me to go round to see her?"

He smiled at her, once again amazed at her calm authority when he needed it most. "Probably best that you don't but thank you for offering.

I've been glum, basically since you and I finished speaking to each other on the phone. And then you turn up here and I feel altogether different. I adore your wit".

"Sorry, did you say tit?"

"No, wit".

"I'm afraid you'll have to speak up. Was that clit?"

"Would you prefer tea or coffee, miss?" She hadn't spotted his approach.

"Oh, er, coffee please".

"And for you, sir?"

"Coffee for me too, please. And would you mind bringing us an orange juice and a grapefruit juice? We're feeling particularly lazy this morning".

"Certainly, sir".

Katerina watched him leave. "You could have warned me".

"I could. But I decided upon the entertainment instead".

"I can always withdraw the blowjob offer, you know".

He looked over her shoulder. "That's very kind, thank you. Grapefruit for the young lady".

She swivelled round in a panic but realised he'd been teasing her.

"Bastard".

He smiled, feeling rather pleased with himself.

After breakfast, they went to his room and, after the promises they'd made to each other had been fulfilled, and Katerina was lying in Charlie's arms, she said, "My world is in your veins and there's nowhere it would rather be".

"How I love you, Katya".

"I simply cannot wait for us to be together".

He smiled at her. "Soon. Very soon".

She left him to drive to work, and he thanked the gods and the lucky stars and everything else he didn't believe in. Thanked them for bringing her to him.

Anna had replied:

'I'm fine. Good luck'.

Her phone rang at 7.30am. She was awake due to Steve preparing to leave for work.

"Hello. Charlie?"

"Yes, it's Charlie. Hi Chrissy. I need to see you. It's important. Are you free this morning?"

"Christ, what is it? Has anything happened to Anna?"

"No, Anna's fine. What time will you be free?"

"As soon as you like".

"Thanks. I'll be there around 8.30". The line went dead.

"Charlie says he needs to see me. He's coming in an hour".

"He didn't say what it's about?"

"No. Oh shit, Steve, there must be something wrong. He said Anna's OK which means it must be Katerina. She must have a serious problem which Anna can't steel herself to tell me. I knew something's been wrong".

"Come on, Chrissy, don't get yourself all worked up. Charlie will be here in an hour, so you'll know soon".

"Of course I'm fucking worked up. Who wouldn't be when they've just had the conversation I have? Shit, there's something really wrong, I know there is".

"Come in Charlie. Come through to the kitchen. Steve's already in there. He agreed to stay here while you give me whatever the bad news is".

As soon as they had joined Steve in the kitchen, Chrissy said, "I'll get drinks in a bit. I need to know first what the problem is".

"I need to tell you that Anna and I are separating, I'm going to be moving to France and Katerina is coming with me. We're going to live together".

She simply stared at him, waiting for him to grin and tell her the real reason for the visit.

"You're not joking, are you?"

"No, Chrissy, I'm not. The decisions have been made and we've begun preparations".

"You're here to tell me that you're leaving my sister and will be living a thousand miles away with my eighteen-year-old step-daughter?"

"Your step-daughter?"

"You know what I mean".

"I'm not leaving Anna, we're separating. Our marriage has run its course".

"Fuck off has your marriage run its course. Anna's marriage to you is the subject of study manuals for marriage guidance counsellors. You haven't the guts to tell me the truth have you, you spineless bastard? It's all about your dick fancying getting inside a young girl".

"I've told you how it is Chrissy".

"You sick paedo fuck. When did it start? In France last summer, I bet, when Katerina was walking around with bikinis and shorts on. That's why she came back with a new fancy hairstyle, sexy clothes, and a cocksure attitude. You had a continuous hard on, didn't you, and you couldn't fucking resist grooming a vulnerable, impressionable, young girl".

"Come on, Chrissy," interjected Steve, "you couldn't call Katerina vulnerable or impressionable".

"You can fuck off too, Steve. Typical fucking man, siding with his mate. I bet you've been as bad, waiting for Katerina to come out of the bathroom, wrapped in a towel with her hair all wet. How many times have you gone back to the bedroom for a quick wank?"

Steve remained silent.

Charlie continued. "Katerina will come to see you soon once things have calmed down a bit. Anna too".

"You men can't help yourselves, can you? If you haven't got a hard on you're looking for the nearest female to give you one. And Anna watched all this happen. You're as bad as each other. Sick fuckers".

"Anna has nothing to do with this. She'll need your help and support".

"Help? I'll tell you who needs help. You, you sick paedo cunt. Now fuck off out of my house and leave me to think about how I can sort this out. Or are you going to remind me that it's not, in fact, my house, that you and Anna kindly bought it for me? Well, don't worry, I won't be living in it longer than I need to. I'll be in rented as soon as I can find somewhere. Go on, fuck off out of my sight before I throw up or throw you out". She stormed out of the kitchen and up the stairs.

After a minute or two, Steve said, "Fucking hell, mate, are you sure you're doing the right thing?"

"Yes, I'm sure Steve".
"Katerina's lovely, of course she is, but Anna…"
"I'll see you soon Steve. Look after Chrissy. She didn't mean what she was saying about you".
"No, of course she didn't. Give me a bell if you need to chat".
"That's good of you Steve, thank you". Charlie walked to the front door, departed, and drove away. 'Well,' he thought to himself, 'not too bad. Went better than I expected'. He stopped and parked a short distance away from Chrissy's house. As arranged, he sent a text to Katerina:

'All done. Not too bad. Phone me during your lunch break x'

He received an immediate response:

'I will. I'll phone C too and arrange to see her after work. Hope you're OK. Must have been tough xx'

He then phoned Anna. "Hi. I've just left Chrissy's, so I guess she'll be phoning you soon".
"Are your balls still intact?"
He laughed. "A bit sore, but still attached".
"Was it awful?"
"She's furious, obviously, and I think she may give you a hammering when she phones you. I stressed that you have not been involved with what has developed between Katya and me, so don't let her lead you into a trap on that one".
"OK, thanks".
"Let me know how it goes, will you?"
"Of course. Speak to you soon".
"Bye Anna".
"Bye Charlie".

Anna's phone rang again within a few seconds.
"What the fuck's going on, Anna?"
"I assume Charlie's told you?"

"Of course. That's why I'm ringing you".

"Then you know what's going on".

"Don't take that shitty attitude. I'm asking you to tell me how this has happened and how we're going to stop it".

"It's too late".

"No, it's not. I'm not having that fucker leave my sister, and we must make sure he doesn't go on to ruin Katerina's life".

"He's not leaving me; we've agreed to separate. Why do you think Katerina's life could be ruined?"

"Er, have you noticed the age difference? What is it, twenty years? Turns out he's not Mr Fucking Perfect but Mr Fucking Paedo".

"Why is the age difference an issue?"

"Are you kidding me? It's bordering on sick. Once he's bored with his young totty it will all come crumbling down. Who's going to pay the price then? It won't be Charlie, that's for sure. It will be Katerina. So, then it will be both you and Katerina that he will have fucked over".

"It's not sick. He's not taken a fancy to young totty. Katerina is not a kid being swept up in the excitement of it all".

"What is it then?"

"Two adults who have fallen in love with each other".

"For fuck's sake Anna, what's wrong with you?"

"Katerina is totally in control of her own thoughts and actions. She knows exactly what she is doing and is completely aware of the consequences, both for herself and for others. Charlie, I truly believe, has tried to work with her to reach a different outcome but it hasn't been possible. They've found themselves where they are, and they don't want to be anywhere different. Neither of them".

"I just don't get you at all. You sound like you're on their side. It's as if you want this to happen".

"I certainly didn't want this to happen, and I'm devastated that it has. But behaving as you are isn't going to solve anything".

"Well, I'm astounded. I tell you something though, I'm not leaving it at that. I'm going to have something to say about it. It's not right, and I can't see things turning out well".

"Speak to Katerina and see what she says. Try to stay calm".

"I am fucking calm. I may not be as calm as you, but then you appear to be totally fucked up. There's another thing that's been bugging me. What happened in France last summer?"

"How do you mean?"

"Everyone says the same thing, that Katerina was totally different after her holiday with you two".

"Different in a better or worse way?"

"Just different".

"No, come on. What was she happier, more outgoing, confident and at ease with herself before or after she came to see us?"

"After. But what did you two do to make her that way?"

"We became her friend. We listened to her problems. We counselled her. We made her feel like an adult because we included her in our outings and conversations. She was given an opportunity to buy feminine clothes which any attractive, teenage girl would feel good in. Whatever we did, Chrissy, it was positive and for her benefit. And I'm very confident that people who know Katerina well would say she was a great girl before she went but an astounding one after she returned".

"I hope you're not implying that I didn't treat her as I should have done when bringing her up".

"Not at all. What you have done for both of them has been remarkable. Look how they've both turned out. Everyone who knows the circumstances admires you greatly".

"Well, here's a thought. Before you go, let's arrange for you to do another presentation for the Book Club. I've got the opening lines for you: "Some of you may recall my previous presentation when I patronised you by sharing my secrets to maintaining the perfect loving relationship, well…." What do you think, Anna, they'll lap it up, won't they? You'll make their day. They'll be able to drive home thinking, 'Well, my husband may not have fucked me for over a year but at least I've not been living with a disgusting cunt'. I'll phone you once I've spoken to Katerina".

Chrissy's phone rang almost immediately.

"I guess you've been on the phone to Anna?"

"Yes".

"May I pop round to see you after work?"
"Yes, I think that would be a good idea".
"I should be there around six thirty".
"Will you want to eat while you're here?"
"We'll see how it goes".
"I'll ask Steve to make himself scarce for the night".

Anna sent a text to Charlie:

> 'Have spoken to C. As you say, she's furious. She'll be speaking to K and will be trying to get her to change her mind'
> 'Thanks for letting me know'

At lunchtime, Katerina telephoned Charlie. "I'm going round to Chrissy's after work".

"She'll work extremely hard to try to get you to see that you're making a very big mistake".

"Yes, I know. But don't worry, I'll be able to handle it. I'm more concerned about trying to get her to accept that I know that I'm letting her down and that she really doesn't deserve that after all she's done for me".

"Good luck".

"Thanks. I'll let you know".

Chrissy opened the door to let her in. "I don't know whether I should hug you or slap you".

"Perhaps you should wait until after we've finished talking about what's happened. You'll know then which you'd rather do".

"At the moment, I'm inclined towards the slap".

"Let's talk, Chrissy, but before we start, may I have a glass of water please".

"Go on through to the lounge and I'll bring it in. I'm sure you won't mind if I have something stronger".

Katerina settled onto the couch in the lounge and Chrissy passed her the glass of water before sitting on the chair opposite. She sipped on her gin and tonic.

"This is all wrong Katerina".

Katerina smiled affectionately. "You persist with Katerina".

"Oh, I suppose that's all wrong too, is it? Something for you to feel aggrieved about".

"No, I don't feel aggrieved about anything. I hope that you'll always call me Katerina".

"Why? Why, if you prefer Katya?"

"Because you and Ilya have called me Katerina since you first knew me, and that's a long time. The three of us have gone through a lot, and I've been Katerina throughout it all".

"None of that means anything now, though, does it? Not now that Charlie is on the scene".

"Charlie being on the scene doesn't affect anything regarding you or Ilya. Not as far as I'm concerned, anyway. You mean so much to me. You've always been there for me, and I hope you always will be. I never knew my father, my mother died a drunk and the man she married when I was a baby left us, never to be seen again. I could have been pretty messed up, but I'm not. And that's mostly due to you. I've never let you know how much that means to me, and I'm very sorry about that".

"It means so much that you've decided to bugger off with my sister's husband".

"Oh Chrissy, please give me a chance to explain this. Don't just dismiss me yet, please".

"Go on then. Start explaining".

"Looking back, it began in France last summer, although I didn't know it at the time".

"I knew it, I bloody knew it".

"Chrissy, please".

"OK, I won't interrupt, but I just knew that it was on your holiday with them last summer that he started to seduce you".

"It's a shame, Chrissy".

"What is?"

"That you've already decided what has happened, even although you don't. I was hoping that you would listen to me, and then decide".

Chrissy stared at Katerina. Her inclination was to tell her to fuck off but, instead, she considered for a few moments before replying, "OK, carry on explaining".

"Anna and Charlie were brilliant hosts, and they made me very welcome. They included me in everything they were doing. And not doing, I suppose, because we spent a lot of time in the garden or on the beach just chilling".

"Did they have clothes on? Anna has told me that they are usually naked when they are in the garden".

"She told me that too, but she also said that they didn't do that when they had guests. I would have thought that she would have said that to you, too".

Chrissy didn't respond.

Katerina continued. "After I'd been there a while, and I was becoming increasingly relaxed and confident in their company, Anna got me to open up about why I had been quiet and moody when I was here, before my holiday. I assume that you had talked to her about me?"

"Yes, I told her that you were like a typical teenager with important exams on their mind".

"Well, Anna gave me the space to tell her that it wasn't that. I wasn't being a typical teenager as such, and the exams weren't particularly worrying me. I found myself telling her that Ilya and his friends, and the boys at school, had been bothering me for a while. That they all made me feel I was just another female for them to deride, and to insult, and to test their crude jokes on. I admitted that I had chosen to dress in unflattering clothes to help me to be invisible to them, so that they focussed their attentions on more attractive and feminine girls".

"Why didn't you tell me this?"

"I think we're all poor at discussing our problems with those closest to us. Also, I'm not really a sharer of my issues, am I? I tend to think that I can resolve them myself".

"So, what was Anna's response to this?"

"Well, that's it, I suppose. Anna and Charlie, together and separately, pulled me out of it".

"How did Charlie pull you out of it?"

"Anna didn't *tell* me to do anything but, somehow, she helped me to want to be more feminine. She didn't need to help me to want to be more confident about myself, I wanted that desperately anyway, but she guided me into a much happier state. I'll be forever grateful to her. I was unhappy, Chrissy, before that holiday. I couldn't see a way out. I hated being ogled at and having sexual suggestions and remarks thrown at me. I thought I'd never have a boyfriend because all the boys I knew represented something I hated".

"And that's where Charlie came in?"

"If I answer that by saying yes, then you'll take it that he did things with his own benefit in mind. But the thing is, Chrissy, that, yes, it is where Charlie came in. But I have never had any doubt that the things he has said and done have been purely motivated by his love for Anna and by the simple fact that he is a very decent person. He knew from Anna that I was in a bit of a state, he saw and heard how she was guiding me through a maze, and he assisted with this, from a male perspective".

"He was in his swimming gear, his hard on clear to you both, and you decided it's great being an attractive female after all".

Katerina didn't feel the need to respond to this; her look told Chrissy that Katerina thought it was she who was being the most immature of the two.

"Carry on".

"For the first time in many years I was in the company of a male who didn't make me feel uncomfortable. Not for a moment did he give me the impression that he was sizing me up, trying to work out if I was game. There was never a hint of suggestiveness or sexual innuendo. They both made me feel good about myself. When Anna and I went shopping, I wanted to buy feminine clothes. I wanted to wear short skirts. They made me feel confident, and valuable, and attractive. And I didn't mind feeling attractive because I didn't feel that anyone was going to get the wrong idea about me, and that includes Charlie. Especially Charlie".

"You don't think you're being a bit naïve, Katerina? He's still a man, with a penis".

"Then even more credit to him. He's a man, with a penis and, it turns out, clearly finds me desirable, yet he never, not once, probed for vulnerabilities or tested my availability".

Chrissy was impassive.

"How long have you known him? Well over ten years? Have you ever known him to be anything other than respectful? To Anna, to you, to anyone else? I doubt that you have because he's a decent guy and he respects people. So, yes, it began last summer in France, but not in the way you seem to have in your head. Not in that way at all".

Chrissy resisted the temptation to speak.

"During the holiday, Charlie and I discovered that we had a great deal in common. Even Anna has acknowledged that Charlie and I share interests and opinions which she doesn't, with him. After I came back here, I had loads going on, but I found myself missing them terribly. In truth, it was Anna, more than it was Charlie. I was so relieved when she phoned me and asked me to go to Sandown races with them. We became very close friends, the three of us. I was rarely alone with Charlie but, when I was, like in his car when he picked me up from work, we had fun and we shared views on things which probably wouldn't interest many people".

"Like music and books?"

"Yes, those especially. But other topics too, and the way we think. That's the way it was, between the three of us, until I joined them again in France, just after Christmas". She paused, trying to formulate what had happened to her at that time.

Chrissy urged her on. "So, what happened in France to change things?"

"On the flight home I discovered that I was in love with him. I felt different. Inside, I felt different to how I had ever felt before. And I thought and thought about it and eventually realised what it was. I was in love with Charlie. I'm not ashamed of it. I'm not suggesting I'm the only person that this has happened to. I haven't worked it back, only to discover that one of us has been engineering it all so that we'd end up in that place. I simply realised that I love him, and there's nothing shameful connected to it at all".

"So, was it pure luck, chance, that he realised it too, that he feels the same way about you?"

"I've thought about this, many times. I've studied couples when I've been in their company, and I've concluded that very few love each other. They're together because it's easy, it beats the alternatives. Love is rare, I believe, and I can't explain why Charlie has loved Anna and now he loves me. I can't explain it, Chrissy, but I trust in its existence".

"Well, lucky you two. You're the chosen ones, aren't you? The special couple".

Katerina didn't immediately respond. She teared up a little, moved by Chrissy's cold and suspicious stance. Finally, she said, so quietly that Chrissy strained to hear her, "I guess that time will tell. I'm not a fool and Charlie is even less of one. We both love Anna and it's been very difficult. But I suppose my answer to your questions is, yes. Yes, I believe that to be the case".

Chrissy remained impassive, thoughtful, before responding with, "If you both love Anna, why is Charlie leaving her for you, and why are you allowing it to happen?"

"Charlie isn't leaving Anna for me".

"Don't be ridiculous. Why else would he be leaving her?"

"You'll need to ask Anna".

"I'm asking you. You're in the middle of it".

"I'm sorry, Chrissy, but I'm not answering for Anna".

"Then tell me why you and Charlie see the need to fly off to France to live. If there's nothing shameful, why can't you deal with living together here?"

"It's preference. As simple as that. Charlie loves it there and says it's where he's happiest. I love it too, but if Charlie wanted to live here, I'd happily do that. I'm not hiding from anything. We're not escaping but have simply decided that we have a choice, and Le Racou is our preference".

"In Charlie and Anna's villa?"

"Yes, at least initially".

"How does Anna feel about that?"

"As I say, I'm not answering for Anna. If you ask her about any of this, I've no doubt that she will be open with you. What she says may contradict what I've been telling you, but I doubt it".

Chrissy took it all in. She considered everything Katerina had been telling her. She assessed her demeanour and her rationale. Finally, she said, "I'm going to miss you, Katya".

"Katya?" She smiled as she said this.

"I'm going to miss you, Katerina. But I'll be here for you. If it goes horribly wrong, which I believe it will, I'll be here. I'm disappointed in you and furious with Charlie. I'm pissed off with Anna, too, but I'll never abandon you".

Katerina stood and sat beside Chrissy so that she could embrace her. "One of the best things to come out of this is my realisation that I love Ilya as if he were my brother and I love you as if you were my mum. I cannot thank you enough for what you've done for me. You are the best thing that's ever happened to me".

Chrissy managed to scoff and cry at the same time. "Surely you think that Charlie is".

"Without you, there would be no Charlie. There wouldn't be the life as I've known it, with a feeling of belonging and comfort and safety. Opportunities and options. Being with you has created all of that for me and you've been selfless throughout the time Ilya and I have been dumped on you".

"You weren't dumped. I was happy to take you on. If I hadn't, though, you would have made it. You would always have made it, Katerina, there is absolutely no doubt about that".

The two were crying together. "I'm so sorry to cause you to be furious and upset and disappointed in me. But I hope that this isn't the end to what you and I have meant to each other".

Chrissy gathered herself. "It won't be". Katerina hugged her so tightly that Chrissy felt difficulty in breathing. "But you're not off the hook. And I still think Charlie's a sick cunt".

Katerina laughed through her tears. "You've always had such a way with words".

"Yeah, well, if he hurts you or abandons you, everyone will hear words they never knew existed. And Charlie's balls will be coming out of his ears".

"I love you, Chrissy".

"I think that's the first time you've said that to me. I love you too, Katerina".

"That's the first time, too".

BOOK FOUR: *CRIME & PUNISHMENT*

Neither of them spoke for a while. Finally, Chrissy collected herself and said to Katerina, "Would you like something to eat? You can stay the night, too".

"That would be lovely. Thank you".

As soon as she got into bed that night, she sent a text to Charlie:

'She thinks you're a sick cunt and will make sure your balls are coming out of your ears if you let me down'

An immediate response, suggesting he had been waiting to hear from her:

'She's mellowed. You've done well'
'She and I are going to be OK. Chrissy and Anna too, I think. Not so sure about you, though'
'You with C is the main thing. I'm very pleased for you'
'I can't wait to be with you Charlie'
'Not long to wait'
'Tell me you love me'
'I love you Katya'
'Tell me you desire me'
'Every inch of my body craves every inch of yours'
'I'll go to sleep with that thought. Good night Charlie'
'Good night Katya. Well done again. You're extraordinary. Catch up tomorrow'
'XX'
'X'

Chapter 41

Katerina got up early and dressed. She didn't bother with anything to eat or drink as she'd decided to have coffee and toast in the café near the bookstore. Before she left, she wrote a note for Chrissy:

Thank you, Chrissy, for listening to me last night.
I'm very sorry that I have disappointed you. I hope you at least understood, from my attempts to convey my feelings, that it hurts me knowing that my actions have upset you.
I hope that I will have the opportunity to tell you many more times that I love you. I will always regret that I haven't made it clear over all the years during which you've been so good to me.
I'll try to earn your favour again. I think that you know now that Charlie will be beside me while I'm trying, even if it makes the outcome I'm seeking, with you, more difficult to attain.
I have thought long and hard about one thing that I said to you last night. I told you that I love you as if you were my mum. That was a half-truth, only now recognised. I don't love you as if you were my mum, you <u>are</u> my Mum. If the one who gave birth to me hadn't died, if she'd remained sober and had brought me up as best she could, I would not have loved her more than I love you, and she would not have created a better person, in me, than you have.
It's an amazing thing that you've done, Chrissy, and I cannot ever thank you enough.
Katerina xx

She phoned Ilya as soon as she had sat down in the café. The call went straight to his answerphone. She didn't leave a message but, instead, phoned Katie.

"Hello Katie, it's Katya. Have you got a minute?"

"Hi Katya. What's up?"

"Two things. Most importantly, I want to let you know how thrilled I am about your engagement to Ilya. I've spent many years explaining to people that he isn't my brother, but now I'm going to claim that he is, just so that you can be my sister-in-law".

"That's a lovely thing to say. Thank you".

"The other thing is that I need to see you both. Together, preferably. Are you planning on being at the apartment tonight?"

"We haven't spoken about it. We tend to wait to see how the day goes, but we can be there, for sure, if you'd like us to be".

"Thanks. I doubt that I'll be able to get there much before seven. Is that too late for you?"

"That's fine. Don't worry about the time, we'll see you when you're able to get there".

"Thanks. See you later".

She then sent a text to Charlie:

> 'May I stay with you at the hotel from now on?
> Until we leave?'

As she had expected, his reply came through without delay.

> 'Of course. I miss you terribly when you're not here'
> 'Thanks. I need to see Ilya this evening so won't get to you before maybe 9.30'
> 'Shall I wait to eat, and we can have room service together?'
> 'No, you go ahead. I'll sort myself out. See you later xx'

She finished her breakfast and then walked to the store. She began to work but found it difficult to concentrate, dreading telling Salty that she was leaving, and why.

"While it's quiet, Salty, may I speak to you about something?"

"Of course".

"I'm afraid that I'm giving you notice. I'm sorry to let you down".

"Oh. Oh dear. Well, yes, of course, I always knew that this is not going to be a long-term challenge for you. A book shop in Arundel! I'll be extremely sorry to see you go but I quite understand, dear girl, I really do".

"No, that's not the reason at all. I love working here. I would love to continue to work here, but I'll be moving to France. I'm going to be living there".

"Goodness, you have surprised me. I had no idea that you had connexions in France. I suppose Chrissy knows?"

"Yes".

"I can imagine she's sad at the thought of you going. I'll have to give her a ring".

"Yes, I'm sure she'd like that".

"Well, enough about how sorry Chrissy and I are. It's exciting news. How wonderful for you. You have somewhere to live lined up, I suppose?"

"Yes. Look, Salty, you need to know that I'm not going there on my own. I'll be going with Charlie. We'll be living together".

"Charlie? I don't think I've heard you talk about a Charlie. You're not rushing into a big decision with a new boyfriend, are you? That's not like you at all".

"It's Anna's Charlie. He and I are together".

"Anna's Charlie?"

"Yes".

"I'm sorry, I don't understand. Are you saying he's going to help you to get down there and settle in?"

"No. Anna and Charlie are separating. Charlie and I are together. We're going to be living as a couple, in France".

Salty looked at her, trying to get to grips with what she had heard. Finally, she said, "Well, it's not for me to pass judgement. I hope it works out for you, dear girl. I hope you don't get hurt". Salty moved away to seek something to do. Katerina cautiously added, "I'll get everything set up for you, Salty. I'll make sure you're happy with it all".

"Yes, of course, of course".

"It will be three or four weeks before I leave. I hope that's all right with you".

"Just tell me nearer the time. I'll leave it to you," and, with that, Salty disappeared into her office in the corner of the store.

During a short lunch break, Katerina bought two large suitcases and crammed them into the Mini. She didn't leave until six thirty, and Salty had managed to go the whole day without allowing Katerina the opportunity to discuss anything further with her. Katerina arrived at the apartment shortly after 7pm and was greeted by a smiling Katie, who gave her a hug as soon as she walked through the door.

Ilya was standing behind her. "I couldn't help it, Katerina. I had to explain to Katie why Chrissy has been on the phone to me and making me defensive about you".

"Oh Katya, I'm so excited for you. I understand why Chrissy's not happy, but my opinion is it's wonderful news. I'm shocked, yet it seems totally reasonable to me. You with Charlie! It will work, I'm convinced it will".

"Thank you, Katie". She paused, and then added, "Thank you. You don't know how much that means to me after the past couple of days".

"You look tired, Katya. Why don't you have a shower and get changed. I've made cannelloni. It will be ready in ten minutes or so".

"Perfect. I'm starving".

"What about a drink?" asked Ilya.

"I'll just have water with my meal, thanks. I'm off again a bit later".

Once they'd finished eating, Katerina raised the main reason why she wanted to see them. "Have you any thoughts on where you'll be living? You seem to spend quite a bit of time at your dad's, Katie".

Ilya replied. "We've been chatting about that. Obviously, it's now affected by your plans. We decided before you arrived that you're probably here to tell us that you'll be letting your part, which is totally understandable, of course".

"No, I've no intention of doing that. I just wanted to know if you'd ideally like to live here if it was all yours".

Katie left Ilya to answer. She felt it needed to be agreed between them.

"Well, yes, we'd love it to be ours. We'd much rather live here, but I'm not sure we could pay you for your half. Not in one go, anyway".

"I want you to have it. It yours to live in. I just wanted to check first that you wouldn't rather live somewhere else".

"How do you mean, it's ours?"

"I'll keep the half ownership, but you two can live here as if you own all of it. I don't want any money".

"We should pay you the equivalent of rent, at least".

"No, as I say, I don't want any money. If you ever want to sell it and buy somewhere else at some point in the future, we'll deal with that then".

"What do you think, Katie?"

"I think your sister is being incredibly generous and thoughtful, and that we should both tell her how happy she's made us".

"Yes, that's how it is. Thank you, Katya".

"I'll be moving out tonight. I've got two suitcases to fill. I'll come back for the rest before I leave for France".

"When will that be?" asked Katie.

"Before the end of April".

"Where will you live in the meantime?"

"Charlie is staying at a hotel. I'm going there from here".

"I'm going to miss you terribly, so I don't know how Ilya and Chrissy must feel".

"You have a ready-made holiday destination. You must come and stay as often as you wish. And Charlie and I will be returning here regularly. We own a racehorse, you see, and we're very excited about it".

"You own a racehorse? Since when?" exclaimed Ilya.

"Last autumn. I own a third, along with Charlie and Anna".

"How will that work out, with Anna, I mean?"

"I believe that Anna will be a great friend of both Charlie and me. The three of us are going to his first race on the 21st".

"You always wanted to live your life as if you were in a Tolstoy novel, didn't you? Fair play to you".

"What about work?" asked Katie. "Have you given notice yet?"

"I did it today, and I feel awful. I hate letting people down when I care about them".

"You've let me down plenty of times," joshed Ilya.

"Maybe, but then I don't care about you, so it doesn't count".

"Nice put down," said Katie.

"Can you drive, Katie?"

"Yes. Dad paid for lessons as soon as I was seventeen. I drive his car occasionally, but I've never owned one myself. One of the things on my list".

"And I've never asked either of you about work. How is it, both at the same place?"

Ilya looked at Katie and then answered for the two of them. "Scott pisses off Katie and we'd both rather one of us worked somewhere else. We keep checking opportunities locally, but nothing's appealed yet".

"Would you like my job, Katie, if Salty is willing?"

"Is Salty your boss? The owner?"

"Yes. She's the one I disappointed today. It was Chrissy yesterday and Salty today".

"Is that why you asked me if I could drive? Because the shop is in Arundel?"

"Yes. You can have my Mini. There's no need to pay me what it's worth. I want to buy one of those funny little Citroen CV's when I get over there. It'll be old and battered, of course, but that's what I want. Just pay me what that costs me. When you can, that is. No rush".

"I really don't know what to say".

"We can do the car thing, if you want to, whether or not you fancy the job. I just thought it may be something which would interest you. Not so much the books but running the computer system I'll finish installing before I go. Salty has no interest in it, and she doesn't want to try to understand it, which is fair enough. But the running of the store needs it, and I know that you'd be capable of making it all work".

"What do you think, Ilya? I'd be working in Arundel so I couldn't walk home with you and have a long evening, as we can now".

"If it's what you want, I'd say go for it".

"I'd love to do it, Katya. Would you be able to ask her for me?"

"Of course. If she agrees to it, I'll get you up and running before I leave".

"I wasn't expecting this when you phoned this morning".

"Well, hopefully, it will work out for everyone. Anyway, I'd better start the packing. Will you be able to carry the cases to the car for me, Ilya, once I've filled them?"

"No problem".

An hour and a half later, Katerina was sitting in the bath, with Charlie perched on the closed toilet seat.

"Tough couple of days?"

"Yes, by my standards, but nothing compared to what you've had to deal with".

"How are you feeling?"

"Exhausted, exhilarated, excited, extremely optimistic, excruciatingly tired yet extra-specially horny".

"Amazing alliteration".

"Cheers, Charlie". She lay back and Charlie watched the suds cling to her baby-pink areola bumps. "It's odd, but the period between your bombshell phone call and now seemed an eternity while I was living it, an endless period of doubt and worry, but actually, it was no time at all, was it? And now, at this moment, in this place, with everything that's happened to us both since the New Year, with all the emotions we've had wash through us, and with all the pain and hurt and disappointment that our actions have caused, here, now, I feel we are at the beginning of the beginning".

He stood and picked up a sponge. He soaked it in the bath water and then liberally smothered it with soap. He gently soaked her neck and her shoulders. Then her breasts. She looked into his eyes waiting to hear his response.

"For me, it's as if everything I've done in my life until now has had one sole purpose: to be with you at the beginning of your beginning so that all of your future experiences will be shared with me".

She closed her eyes and enjoyed the attention her breasts were receiving. "I'm finally starting to relax. Will you help me to behave as an eighteen-year-old girl should? I'm weary of holding it together".

"Willingly".

"I need to tell you something, too. A decision I've made".
"OK. Don't look so worried".
"I fear I may disappoint you".
"Let's see".
"I've said I'll do anything for you, but I need to add that I don't want to share you with anybody. Not Anna, no-one. And I want you, only. Only you. I don't ever want either of us to be shared with anybody else".
"You couldn't have made me happier".

Chapter 42

"Ah, your Burberry skirt. Finally, I get to see you in it".

"I've been saving it for a special occasion".

"Well, it's fantastic. You look stunning".

"Not too short, is it?" She waited for him to tell her he liked the colour.

"The skirt merely accentuates your perfect legs. As I say, you're stunning".

Charlie had arranged for Lene to have an owner's badge too so, after Anna had picked Charlie and Katerina up from the hotel in the Land Rover, she drove to collect Lene, before heading off up the A27 and M3 towards Kempton. At Lene's, Anna, Charlie and Katerina stood outside the car so that Anna and Charlie could properly introduce Lene and Katerina to each other.

Once they'd set off, Katerina said, "Both Charlie and Anna prepared me for meeting someone extraordinarily pretty, Lene. They weren't wrong".

Lene turned round in her seat, and she was blushing heavily. "Thank you. You look great in that skirt. Burberry, isn't it?"

"Thanks. Yes, Anna bought it for me".

Anna couldn't resist, "Katya has had a number of things off me".

There was a period of embarrassed silence before Charlie broke it by saying, "The day wouldn't have been the same without you, Lene. It's perfect that it's the four of us".

"Shall we stop off so we can all have a drink of water?" suggested Anna. "Listening to your opening conversation, I fear the three of you are going to start group sex without me".

Lene squeezed her arm. "Just innocent mutual appreciation. I'm sure we're still way short of the number of compliments you've received over the years".

"Right," said Anna, dismissively, "shall we move onto talking about horses, or at least one in particular? Does anyone know the latest odds?"

"I checked Skybet earlier this morning. There are ten runners declared and Place To Be is fourth favourite at 11/2," replied Charlie.

"Our Trainer thinks he's gone under the radar a bit," Katerina explained to Lene. "He hasn't run at a racecourse yet and the people at the Yard have been trying to keep it under wraps that Stroppy has been keeping up with some decent, experienced horses on the gallops".

"Worth a bet then?" asked Lene.

"I've decided not to, purely for the ridiculous possibility of me jinxing him".

"I've decided the same," admitted Anna.

"So have I," piped in Charlie with a laugh, "but we'd all insist that we're not at all superstitious".

"Would you mind if I bet on him?" asked Lene.

They all assured her that they wouldn't. "Thanks. Would you place twenty pounds to win for me please, Charlie?" She reached into her purse to find a twenty-pound note to pass to him. He clicked through his phone and then confirmed, "He's gone out to 6/1. £20 placed to win £120, Lene. Good luck".

Place To Be was due to run in the fourth race, and they were not meeting the Trainer until the pre-race parade. A table had been booked for them in the main restaurant, and, having selected small dishes, Katerina and Lene finished their meals before Anna and Charlie were halfway through theirs. Charlie suggested they had a look around the course so that they could be the guides once their meal had been completed. As they left the table, Katerina slipped her arm through Lene's. When they were no more than five tables away, Lene whispered something to Katerina, who fell away laughing before taking Lene's once again as they continued towards the exit. Anna had watched this, smiling. "Well, they've hit it off".

"We may have lost each other, Anna, but we've landed on our feet. They're both just about perfect".

"They are. Now, what did you want to talk to me about?"

"How did you know I wanted them to leave so that we could talk?"

She looked at him and cocked her head.

"Yeah, OK. Well, I wanted to ask you what you think about adding Lene to the Partnership so that she'll own Stroppy too".

"Buy in or just give her a share?"

"Oh no, I wouldn't think about taking any money. No, giving her a share. At the moment, it's a third each. We couldn't just give part of Katya's pre-agreed share away so I was thinking that you and I could give Lene a third of our two thirds, if that make sense".

"I think that's a wonderful suggestion and the type of thing that makes you who you are. It will be wonderful for me to have Lene included in this venture".

"Great. And I feel we should verbally agree it before Stroppy's race so that, if he does come in the first three, Lene will be entitled to her share of the prize money".

"How do you want to play it?"

"I'll have to run it past Katya first. Once they're back, find an opportunity to leave me alone with her".

Just before the first race, Anna invited Lene to go with her to the parade ring. Once they had left the table, Charlie said, "Katya, would you mind skipping this race? I'd just like to mention something to you".

"Of course. Nothing wrong is there?"

He chuckled. "Relax Katya, nothing is going to go wrong before we head off. No, it's about the ownership of Stroppy. I would like to add Lene to the Partnership. I've spoken to Anna about it and we'd both like to split our shares with Lene. How would you feel about that?"

"So, are you suggesting I'd still have thirty-three per cent ownership and you three would each have twenty-two per cent?"

"Not including the decimal points".

"Yes, I hadn't forgotten about those, I was just trying to keep it simple. Anyway, I'm sorry to be a bore with this but I'm not happy with your proposal".

"Oh, OK, that's fair enough. No harm done".

"Lene has to have twenty-five per cent. We all do. That's the only fair way".

He smiled and responded with, "Yes, I'm sure you're right".

"And the four of us have to shake hands on it before the race. Stroppy will get placed, I know he will, and Lene has to be an agreed part-owner before the race starts".

"Fair point. I'll mention it to Anna and then we'll get it sorted".

"Great. It will be lovely having Lene in on this. I like her a lot".

"You both seem to be getting on well".

"She made me laugh a bit earlier. She said she likes me so much that maybe you and Anna should stick together, and she and I could then hook up".

"That's not going to happen".

"Spoil sport".

She took some persuading, but eventually the revised ownership split was agreed. Charlie stated that he would arrange the necessary paperwork and clear it with the Trainer.

After the conclusion of the third race, they were positioned in the parade ring awaiting Stroppy's arrival. Eventually, in he came, led by one of the stable lasses. The Trainer had joined them, and then the jockey arrived, wearing their chosen colours of red body, red and blue hooped sleeves, and a white cap.

"You may be better off viewing it from the owners' area in the main stand," suggested the Trainer.

"We know where that is, don't we Lene?" exclaimed Katerina, who could hardly contain herself. "Come on".

Once they were in place, Charlie focussed his binoculars on the bookmakers. "Stroppy has become 7/2 favourite. Word must have got out".

"That won't affect us, will it?" asked Lene.

"No, your bet is still at 6/1, and the race winnings are totally separate".

The two-mile hurdle race started. For the four of them, it didn't reach the expected level of fever pitch excitement, simply because Place To Be led from start to finish and hardly broke sweat. Katerina grabbed onto Anna and Lene's hands as he approached the last hurdle, but, once he flew over it, they were transfixed. They didn't even shout him home.

Charlie was the first to find his voice. "Well, I guess we need to go back to the parade ring and head for the winner's enclosure".

"Yes, quick," shouted Katerina, "we have to watch him come in".

The Trainer was waiting for them. "As I've said, I undersold him. You've got yourself a great prospect. We need to keep him sound, but now that we've seen what he can do, we'll pick out his races carefully. We'll aim to get him into a race at the Festival next March".

"Cheltenham?" asked Anna, shocked.

"That's the plan. I doubt we'll run him again this season, but a route will be mapped out for him from October".

Lene was speechless, Charlie couldn't talk for grinning and all Katerina could say was, "Oh my fucking god".

They stopped off on the way back at an attractive-looking pub off the motorway and shared two bottles of Champagne, which Lene insisted on buying. Charlie told Anna he was happy to drive them all home from there, so limited himself to one glass.

They resumed the journey, with Katerina now in the passenger seat. After a short while, Anna said, "Charlie, would you mind putting some music on and playing it just through the front speakers. I'd like to say something to Lene, and she may be embarrassed if you could hear".

"No problem. What shall we start with Katya?"

"It has to be Nick Drake's Place To Be".

Anna whispered to Lene, "I'm feeling tipsy and a little high".

Lene smiled and whispered back, "Me too. Lovely, isn't it?"

"Has Greg made a move to get me to join the two of you?"

"Surprisingly not. I think he's a bit shy about it".

"How about tonight?"

"Yes, that would be fun. I can't imagine he'd say no".

"Find out. Send him a text".

Lene located her phone and typed:

> 'Had a fab day. Anna's horse won! She was telling me earlier that she feels horny. I was thinking of suggesting the three of us to get together'

Anna read it and tried to contain her giggles.

From Greg:

'Does she know you're sending this?'
'No, she's in the front and I'm in the back'
'How do you suggest we play it?'
'From what she was saying earlier I get the impression she'd enjoy getting it on with you. Am wondering, though, if you'd like to watch the 2 of us together first?'
'Could be fun'
'Only if you want to. No pressure'
'I'll be desperate now if A says no!'
'I'll text her now and ask her. Back in a bit'

Lene leaned towards Anna and whispered, "I'm so wet".

Anna didn't waste any time and slid her hand up Lene's thighs. She whispered back, "You are".

Lene focussed on her phone again:

'A is up for it'
'Bloody hell!'
'Should be there within an hour'

They erupted into fits of giggles, so infectious that before long the four of them were in hysterics. Finally, once they had calmed down, Anna said, "Charlie, would you mind dropping me off at Lene's? You can keep the car and I'll get a taxi home tomorrow. I'll collect this when it suits".

"I can drive you home before work," suggested Lene.

"Why don't I pick you up in the morning, Anna? You can drop me back at the hotel and then drive home from there".

"Perfect. Thanks Charlie".

Chapter 43

Charlie and Katerina's move progressed smoothly. Belongings which they had chosen to take with them to France were packed up and shipped, to be overseen on arrival by Thierry and Camille. Charlie had sent a long email to them explaining what had happened, and preparing them for him living in the villa, full time, with Katerina. He knew that they would be devastated as they had always been extremely fond of Anna. However, he was convinced that they would perform a Gallic shrug, would welcome both he and Katerina and that they would be available to assist either of them should the need arise.

Salty told Katerina that she would be delighted to give Katie a trial run and was clearly relieved that there would be a capable young person in charge of Katerina's new computer system and processes. Ownership of the Mini was transferred to Katie, with Katie promising Katerina that she would transfer funds to her as soon as she knew how much her 'funny little Citroen' was going to cost.

Chrissy, Steve, Ilya, and Katie provided a farewell dinner for Katerina at a local Italian restaurant. Charlie attended too because Katerina had insisted upon it. Chrissy didn't speak to him all evening, but at least she left his balls intact.

Anna's birthday was approaching, and she decided she would decline any invitation she may receive from Chrissy, Lene or any other of her friends. Instead of spending it with anyone who found it uncomfortable sharing her misery, she wanted to escape and have some fun. She telephoned Shore Watersports. "Hello, may I have a quick word with Scott please, if he's not too busy".

"Hello".

"Hello Scott".

"Sorry, I don't recognise the voice".

"You've claimed that you'd like to use your tongue to find out if forbidden fruit tastes sweeter".

A long silence before, "Yes".

"Meet me in the bar at the Chichester Travelodge at eight o'clock tomorrow evening. I'll have a room available for us. You'll be given an hour to find out if it does taste sweeter. If I enjoy the experience, I may decide to meet up with you again another time".

She ended the call.

On the 20th April ("Hitler's birthday," said Katerina. "How apposite"), the Alfa Romeo 4C drove away from West Sussex towards Folkestone, where it was driven onto a train destined for Calais and then onwards to the south of France. ("We'll be going over the Millau Bridge," Charlie had told Katerina with schoolboy enthusiasm. "It's majestic").

Anna picked up her phone, having calculated that Charlie and Katerina would have arrived in Calais and begun their drive to Le Racou, and pressed on Chrissy's saved telephone number. "Hi Chrissy. If you've anything planned for this afternoon, can you please cancel it. I'm going to drive over. You need to know why Charlie hasn't been entirely to blame in all this". She wouldn't be admitting to the events with Katerina in France of course, but felt it was time for Chrissy to learn about her involvement with Lene.

Three stops en route had been arranged so that the journey in the small, uncomfortable car would not be too taxing. The journey took a little longer than necessary as Katerina had insisted that, once they had driven over the Millau Bridge, Charlie turn back at the next exit so that they could drive over it again from the opposite direction.

For the fourth and final leg of the journey, Katerina wore the white, knee length, linen, smock dress which Anna had bought for her in Collioure the previous summer. Because she felt liberated and totally at ease at the thought of arriving at her new home in the south of France, she chose to wear nothing underneath it, despite remembering Anna warn her that it was see-through with the light behind it.

They arrived on the 23rd April ("St George's Day," said Katerina. "How apt") and the weather was perfect ("Cerulean sky," exclaimed Katerina) as they pulled up in front of the villa. Charlie unlocked the front door and allowed Katerina to enter first. She was greeted by a mass of cornflowers, some in vases, others strewn across the furniture and over the floor. He heard her intake of breath, and then, "Oh my god, they're beautiful. It's as if the blues of the sky and the Med have formed themselves into shape and are welcoming us to their domain".

"Check upstairs, too".

In the bedroom, their bedroom, it was blue iris which welcomed her. She turned to him, and her eyes were alive with emotion. "Blue flowers," she whispered, "blue flowers, the symbol for desire and love. And iris, too, the emblem of France. Oh Charlie".

He smiled at her. "I had no doubt that you would immediately recognise the significance. And you know that it's the iris, not the lily. What an extraordinary person you are. Welcome to our home, Katya. We will always keep blue flowers alive and on show in the villa, and they will be a permanent, visual confirmation of my love and desire for you".

Katerina picked up an iris from the bed, smelt it, kissed it, and recognised that the beginning of their beginning had begun. She felt blessed.

They did little during their first few days in France, yet immediately established their own routine and, as a consequence, erased one which had been etched in the lives of Charlie and Anna: Katerina left their bed every morning before Charlie stirred, swam in the Med for at least thirty minutes, collected pastries and bread on the way back to the villa, poured fruit juices and made coffee for the two of them, carried breakfast to the bedroom, and re-joined Charlie in bed. "Good swim?" he asked, on every occasion. "Wonderful," was her reply. "What shall we do today?"

Katerina read The Count of Monte Cristo, in French, and Charlie helped her to source her Citroen. It was a 1988 CV2, in blue with a white roof, and they bought it from a French farmer, who had, apparently, used it to deliver eggs to local villagers.

"Do we keep the Alfa and the BMW?" asked Charlie.

"It's up to you, Charlie. Will you want the BMW to collect visitors from the airport?"

"I guess so".

"I suppose you could always leave it there and drive around in the Alfa".

BOOK FOUR: *CRIME & PUNISHMENT*

"Bit daft though, isn't it, keeping it at the airport car park all year?"

"But you love your Alfa".

"How would visitors react to being collected from the airport in your Citroen, do you think?"

"I *have* cleaned it out. I've become so attached to it that if they don't think, 'How quaint,' they can bugger off back to England".

He chuckled. "Or they could just get a taxi. We'll sell the BMW".

Early May unfolded as if they were on honeymoon, but by the third week of the month, it was clear to Katerina that the idyllic lifestyle enjoyed by Charlie would not be enough for her. An idea struck her while overhearing two Frenchmen conversing in a local bar. During the next few days, she spent at least two hours per day researching on her laptop.

"What are you up to?" asked Charlie, inevitably curious.

"Would you mind if I sorted it out in my head before discussing it all with you?"

"Of course not," he replied, a little anxiously.

His curiosity and concern heightened once he noticed that Katerina was corresponding by emails and always carrying her phone with her.

Then, one morning, while they were sitting under the trees, chatting, her phone rang. "Bonjour. Oui, c'est moi". She listened, then began conversing with the caller in Russian.

She completed the call, stood, and said to Charlie, "Sorry, Charlie, but I've arranged to go and meet someone. I need to have a shower and change. Is it OK if I tell you all about it when I get back?"

"Sure. Driving or walking?"

"I'm going the other side of Perpignan, so I'll drive".

"Take the Alfa, if you like".

"No, the Citroen's fine, thanks".

Thirty-five minutes later, as he was making himself a coffee, she joined him in the kitchen and kissed him on the cheek. "See you in a bit".

"Yep". He looked more closely at her. She appeared to be focussed and business-like, an impression confirmed by her choice of clothes: the knee-length, pleated skirt, and the pinstripe shirt which Anna had bought for her the previous summer. "You look terrific," he said, as she walked towards the front door.

"Thanks," she threw over her shoulder. "Have a lovely morning".

She didn't return until mid-afternoon. He had just finished cutting the grass as she parked in the drive. "Did it go well?" he asked.

"Very. I'm hot and sweaty. Would you mind pouring me a G&T? I'll have a shower and change then join you in the shade. I'll explain what's been going on. Can't wait to tell you".

"Great. See you in a bit".

A quarter of an hour later, he watched her as she walked towards him across the lawn. Her short, dark hair was wet, and she had brushed it back so her entire face was exposed to the sunlight. She was wearing a sheer beach dress, beneath which she wore just knickers rather than swimwear. Charlie studied her and concluded that, for him, she personified perfection. She sat next to him, took a long sip of her drink, sighed with pleasure, and said, "That feels better".

"Good. So, what have you been up to?"

"Sorry I've been distracted and a bit mysterious, but I wanted to get somewhere with it before I troubled you. I'll give you more detail later, but the bottom line is I'll be starting work once we return from the Radiohead concert".

"Work?"

She smiled. "Why does that seem so outrageous to you?"

"You don't need to work, my darling Katya. We've still plenty of money. More than enough".

"You have, Charlie".

"It's ours, Katya, not mine".

"I need to work. I'm eighteen. You must know that I can't spend the rest of my life sunbathing and swimming".

"Yes, of course. What will you do?"

"I didn't know this until recently, but apparently Perpignan is a major centre for the commercial airline industry. Montpellier too. The main players are French, American, and Russian. I'm going to be the go-between to help them to communicate with each other; their translator. The guy I've just met has told me that when I've got to grips with the whole process there will be opportunities to go to Russia with him. America too, maybe. I'm really excited about it. The best of all worlds: all this," she studied the villa and the garden, "shared with you, our love for each other, and now also having an interesting challenge. How lucky am I?"

"Bloody hell, Katya, I had no idea".

"I just didn't want to trouble you with it until I knew whether it would be a possibility. I do need you to help me, though, to set up a business entity as I'll be freelance. I can imagine the French red tape will be more onerous than it needs to be".

"Yes, of course I'll help you. Being selfish though, what am I going to do? I hate the thought of you being away from me".

"I've been thinking about that. I think you should write".

"Write?"

"Yes. You should write a novel, or poetry, or, oh I don't know, anything you like. You don't need the money so there's no need to seek an audience. Just start writing and see where it takes you".

He gave this some thought. "Should I write about my love for you?"

"Our story, from you and Anna being the perfect couple and me floundering and trying to appear invisible?"

"Yes".

"Yeah, I think that may interest a publisher or two. Would it be erotica?"

"I think it would have to be, don't you?"

"I do. Have you enough material?"

"Not nearly enough".

"Oh dear. Would you like a research assistant?"

"Well, you'd be ideal, but you already have a job".

"I'm sure I could fit you in".

"When would you be able to start?"

"Right now?"

Before he could ask whether she preferred to stay in the garden or go indoors, she was laying out a towel.

"Dress on or off?" she asked.

"On".

"OK. We'll need to be somewhat imaginative. You won't want to bore your reader".

Later that evening, Katerina suggested that they should invite Ilya and Katie to join them at the villa for a holiday before she started work. "Good idea," agreed Charlie. "Just them?"

"Who else are you thinking?"

"Chrissy and Steve? Maybe Anna and Lene too?"

Katerina considered. "Yes, I think that's a nice idea. For whatever reason, Chrissy seems to have thawed since we arrived here. She's even asked me how you are. Shall I message her and Ilya, and leave you to contact Anna?"

"Yes, that's probably best. Let's decide on a couple of date options".

Emails were sent before they prepared for bed. Katerina was soon asleep, but Charlie lay on his back, thinking about the ramifications of Katerina's announcement. What man of his age and life-experiences wouldn't wonder if this was the first stage in the process of Katerina venturing on a new path, one which wouldn't include him? How long would he be sharing his life and his love with her? Six months, a year, five? Forever? Charlie tried to erase the thought from his mind.

After some email exchanges, a weekend at the villa was arranged with Chrissy and Steve, and Ilya confirmed that he and Katie would love to stay on for a few days extra. Anna said she couldn't commit herself but would try her best. It was mutually decided that Ilya, Katie, Chrissy and Steve would stay at the villa and that, if Anna and Lene were able to accept the invitation, they would arrange a room at a local hotel.

The Saturday arrived, and it was just the six of them in the garden. Charlie was in the shade of the trees, filling glasses with Cava, and Katerina was by his side, ready to help him to distribute them. Their guests were stretched out on loungers placed around the pool.

Shortly after everyone was settled, glass in hand, a car pulled into the drive and stopped behind Charlie's Alfa Romeo. Anna got out from behind the steering wheel and walked towards them.

"Anna," squealed Katerina, "how brilliant. Is Lene with you?" She ran to Anna and flung her arms around her.

"No, Greg made it difficult for her to come. A friend has joined me instead". They both turned their heads towards the car as the passenger door opened and a man climbed out. Because of the glare from the sun, Katerina couldn't make out who it was. He joined them and Anna said, "Katya, this is Guillem".

Full introductions were completed, and Charlie produced two full glasses, also filling the other six. Before long, relaxed chatter bounced around the poolside and all appeared to be feeling the effects of the wine on an empty stomach.

On impulse, Anna jumped up from her chair, so suddenly that everyone stopped talking, wondering if she'd been stung by a bee.

"We're going skinny dipping in the pool," she exclaimed. She didn't hesitate: her bikini top was removed, then the bottoms, then she was in. Katie shrieked in delight, stripped off her swimming costume and dived in. Guillem, finally relieved that he had been persuaded by Anna to join her on the trip, pulled off his trunks and joined them, shortly followed by Ilya.

From the pool, Anna began the chant, "Exocet, Exocet, Exocet…". The others accompanied her, despite not knowing who the chant was aimed at, or why.

Chrissy looked at Steve. "Don't you dare".

"Fuck that," he replied. Swimming shorts were discarded, down it flopped, thumping onto his thigh, and side to side it swung, like an unattended hose, as he ran towards the pool, encouraged all the way by four naked frolickers.

Chrissy simply shrugged, removed her costume, and joined them. All the while, Charlie and Katerina had remained on their loungers.

"Come on you two," shouted Anna from the pool. "Not like either of you to be prissy".

Katerina looked at Charlie. "Game?" she asked.

"Of course," he replied. "You go while I get some music on".

"Play my favourite," demanded Katerina as she removed her bikini and walked serenely towards the pool steps. She smiled as she heard Anna call out to her, "I wish mine swayed like that". As she entered the water, Karma Police's lyrics engulfed them:

This is what you'll get when you mess with us

www.ingramcontent.com/pod-product-compliance
Lightning Source LLC
Chambersburg PA
CBHW020859080526
44589CB00011B/362